MONDO MACABRO

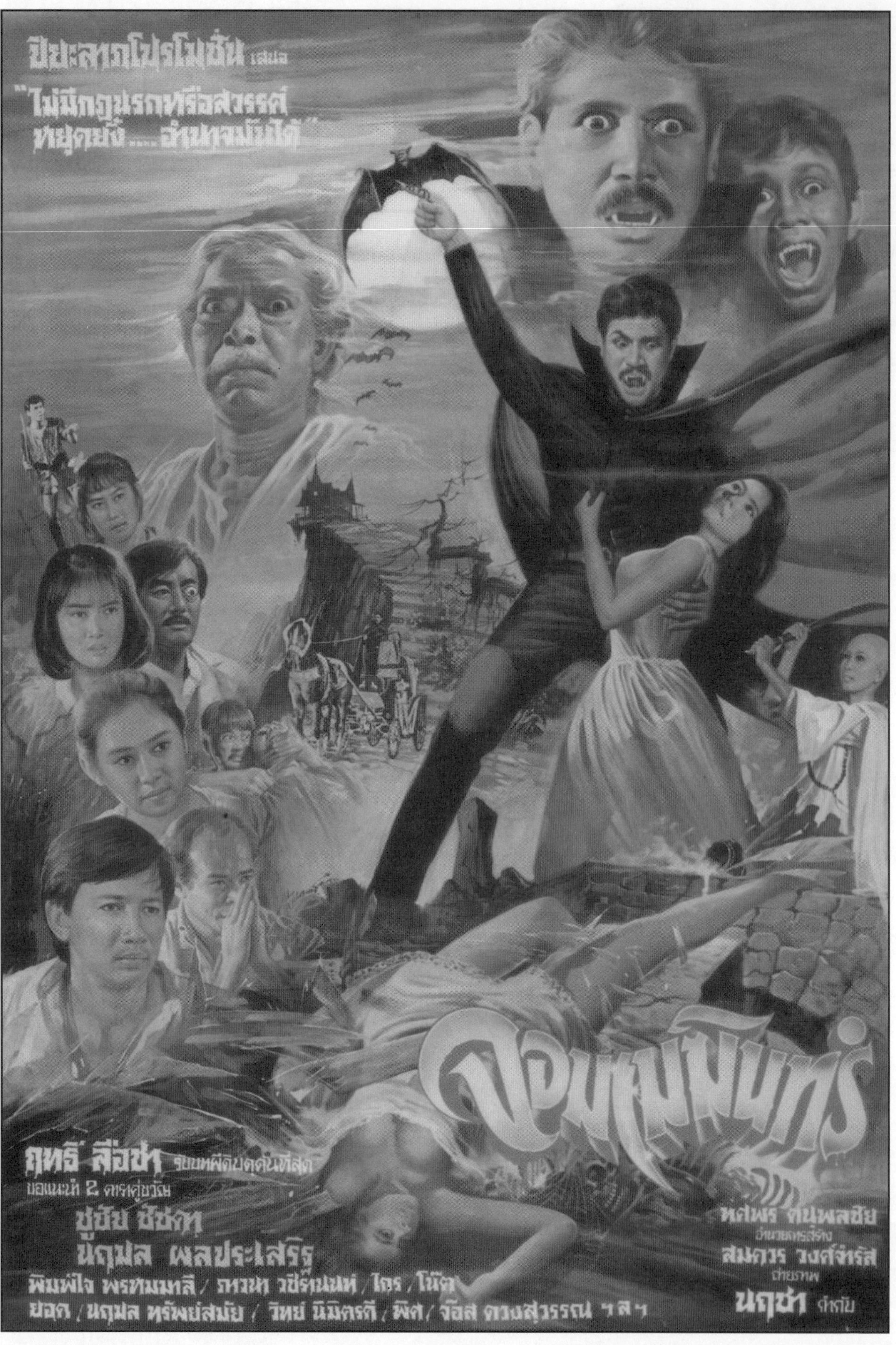
ปิยะลาภโปรโมชั่น เสนอ
"ไม่มีกฎนรกหรือสวรรค์
หยุดยั้ง..... อำนาจมันได้"
จอมเมนินทร์
ฤทธิ์ ลือชา รับบทผีดิบดุดันที่สุด
ขอแนะนำ 2 ดาราคู่ขวัญ
ชูชัย ชัชฎา
นฤมล ผลประเสริฐ
พิมพ์ใจ พรหมมาลี / ภาวนา วชิรานนท์ / ไกร / โน๊ต
ยอด / นฤมล ทรัพย์สมัย / วิทย์ นิมิตรดี / พิศ / จีอีส ดวงสุวรรณ ฯลฯ
หัสพร ศุนพลชัย
อำนวยการสร้าง
สมควร วงศ์จำรัส
ถ่ายภาพ
นฤชา กำกับ

MONDO MACABRO

WEIRD & WONDERFUL CINEMA AROUND THE WORLD

PETE TOMBS

TITAN BOOKS

MONDO MACABRO
ISBN 1 85286 865 1

Published by
Titan Books
42-44 Dolben Street
London SE1 0UP

First edition October 1997
10 9 8 7 6 5 4 3 2 1

Design by Chris Teather and Darren Clark.
Production by Bob Kelly.

British Library Cataloguing-in-Publication Data. A catalogue record for this book is available from the British Library.

'Unless we begin again to tell fairy-tales and ghost stories before going to sleep, and recount our dreams upon waking, nothing more is to be expected of our civilisation' —Jan Svankmajer.

Dedication
This book is for Jean Rollin and his little orphan vampires.

Acknowledgements:
Many people have helped in many different ways to bring this book to completion. In particular I would like to thank Paul Woods for the initial spark; Stephen Cremin (Asian Film Library) for facts, figures and photographs; Bill Bennett for his exceptional generosity; and especially Cathal Tohill, without whose constant help, advice and encouragement the book would not exist.

Thanks are also due to the following: Yilmaz Atadeniz, Lucas Balbo, André Barcinski, Barbara Bennett, Mohan Bhakri, Alvaro Buela, Metin Demirhan, Dragon Art, Gordon van Gelder (St Martin's Press), Julian Grainger, Horacio Higuchi, Jack Hill, Alicia Iglesias, Çetin Inanç, Sergio Sá Leitão, José Mojica Marins, Marc Morris, Francis Moury, Kaya Özkaracala, Michel Parry, Tim Paxton, Lisa Petrucci (Something Weird Video), Tulsi Ramsay, Giovanni Scognamillo, Romain Slocombe, Mick Smee, Adrian Smith, Vinod Talwar, Stephen Thrower, Thomas Weisser (Video Search of Miami), Paul Willemen.

Finally, a big thank you to all the Titan staff who laboured long and hard to make this book what it is. In particular, David Barraclough for being crazy enough to say yes, Adam Newell and Simon Furman for their much needed editing skills and Chris Teather for his swift and elegant solutions to numerous design problems.

Stills and illustrations are from the author's own collection and: BFI Stills Posters and Designs, Bill Bennett, David Wilt, Cathal Tohill, Peter Blumenstock, José Mojica Marins, Marc Morris, Giovanni Scognamillo, Adrian Smith, Diego Curubeto, André Barcinski, Stephen Cremin, Lucas Balbo (Artshiv)

Acknowledgements are due to the following production companies:
Alena Trading Co (Francis Moury), American International, Anıt Film, Argentina Sono Film, Arzu Film, Atadeniz Film, Atlas Films, Azteca Films Inc, Bemisal Films PVT Ltd, Birlik Film, B. Subhash Movie Unit, Bungei, Cinedistri, Cinematografica ABSA, Cinematografica Calderon, Cirio H. Santiago Productions, Daiei, Film Workshop, Filmica Vergara, Films Agrasanchez, Four Associates, Göksal Film, Golden Harvest, Hemisphere Productions, Hokuto/Raizoh, I.C. Apolo, Iberia Filmes, IFD, Kemal Film, Kindai Eiga Kyokai, Lo Wei Motion Picture Corporation, Lynn-Romero Productions, Mapa Filmes, Media Asia, Mier y Brooks SA, MKB Films, Multifilmes, Nepomuceno Films, New World Pictures, Nihon Eiga Shinsha, Nikkatsu Corporation, Ninjin Club, Parkit Films, Pars Film, PC Zé do Caixão, Ramsay Films Combine, Rapi Films, Regal Films, Saner Film, Sceptre Industries, Seasonal Films, Shaw Brothers, Shintoho, Shochiku, Super 8 Produçoes, Supreme Films, Talwar Combine, Toei, Toho, United Artists, Viva, Wakamatsu Productions.
Any omissions will be corrected in future editions.

Front cover photo: *The Boxer's Omen* © Shaw Brothers.
Back cover photos, top to bottom: *Türist Ömer Uzay Yolunda*; *Gate of Flesh*; *Wohi Bhayaanak Raat.*

Author's note
Films are presented with their original release title in italics. If an accepted English language release or export title exists, it follows in brackets in italics. If no accepted English language title could be found, a translation is given in plain script. Any subsequent mention of the film will be with its original release title. Release dates for all films are given in the index. All translations, unless otherwise noted, are by the author

Printed and bound in Great Britain by MPG Books Ltd, Bodmin, Cornwall

Contents

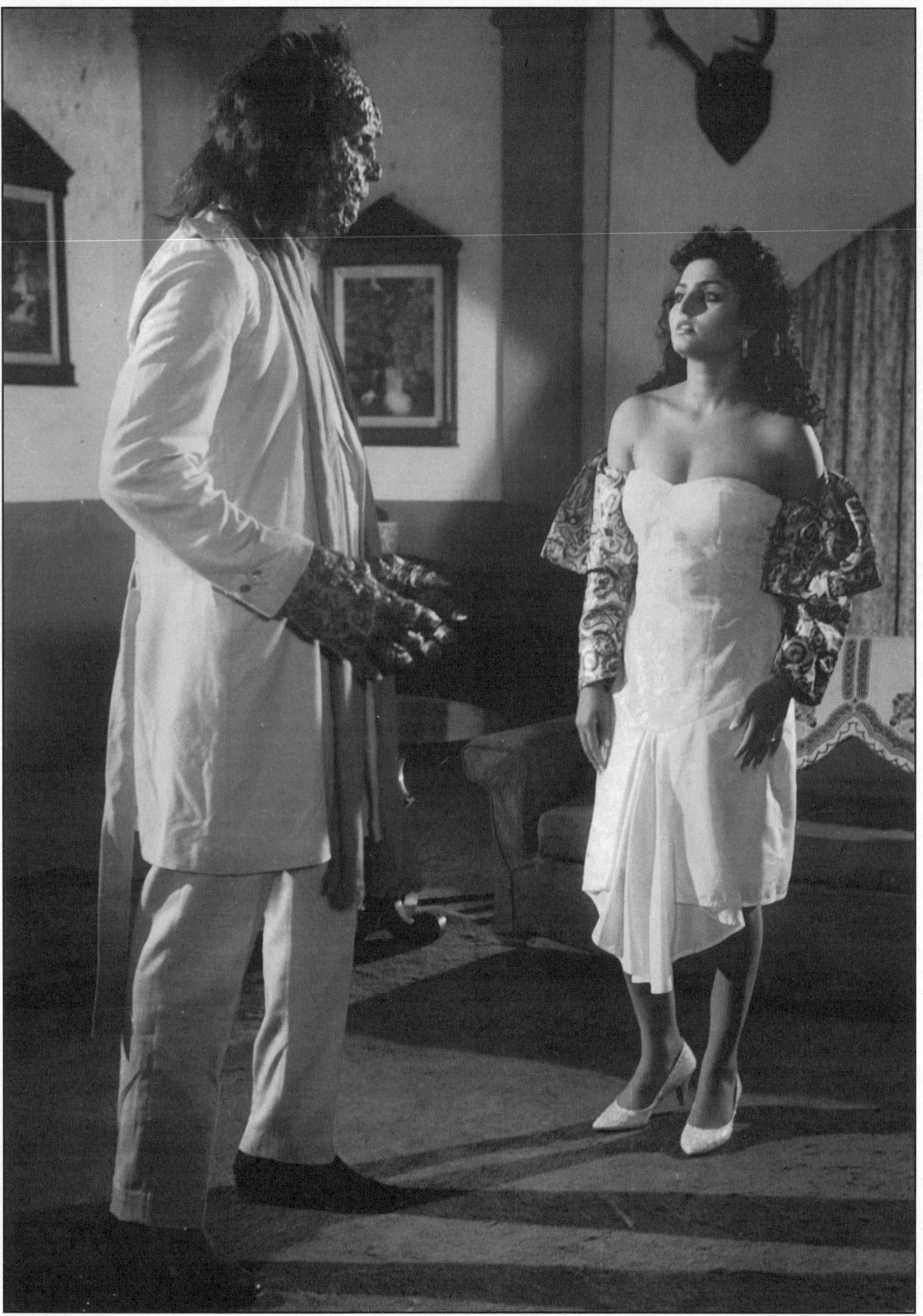

Introduction

Sometimes it feels like there's nothing left to discover. Bookshelves bend under the weight of tomes devoted to all things 'cult', 'B', or obscure. Films you might once have crossed town to see now turn up on new video labels every week. For those who still value the shock of the new, the special kind of thrill that comes from confronting previously unsung greatness, all this might be a little depressing. But don't despair. There are plenty of strange new worlds left to explore. Even if you'll not exactly be "boldly going where no one has gone before." India, Japan, Hong Kong, Mexico; all have a grand tradition of producing movies both weird and wonderful, filled with local colour as well as odd borrowings from the West. These are territories worth more than a passing glance from any fan of fantasy cinema.

Over the last forty or so years, the film industries of many countries seem to have followed a remarkably similar pattern: a 'golden age' in the fifties or sixties, a slide into (s)exploitation in the seventies and a slow decline through the eighties, followed, in the nineties, by video and the inevitable dominance of Hollywood. Great films are still being made of course, all around the world, even if the scale of them is generally smaller. But the amazing energy of the sixties and seventies, the burst of low-budget optimism that produced Mexican masked wrestlers, Turkish superheroes, Japanese monster turtles and Indonesian mystic warriors (to name only a few!) seems to have been filtered away. The odd thing is that Hollywood today is asserting its dominance of the global market by making exactly those sort of costume capers and violent action fantasies that were the mainstay of so many Third World industries twenty-five years ago. The only difference is that Hollywood makes them with a bigger budget and far less imagination.

But we come to praise cinema, not to bury it. And there's plenty here to celebrate. *Mondo Macabro* is a peek into the treasure trove of fifty years of film from around the world. We've sifted through the dross and picked out the dusty jewels. Some of them haven't seen the light of day for far too long. The kind of films we're looking at — action pics, horror films, sex exploiters and monster movies — are usually avoided by heavyweight histories. Which is odd, because in our encounters with Filipino action heroes, Hong Kong horror stars and Japanese bondage queens, we've learned far more about their respective countries than from any number of serious art films. Art cinema, from almost anywhere in the world, tends to follow the same gods of style; the French new wave and the Italian neo-realist still reign supreme. Genre films, on the other hand, always grow out of their country's most deeply ingrained traditions. Like crates of oranges with their brightly coloured labels, these films are always instantly identifiable.

***Opposite:** Beauty and the beast from the Indian film* Wohi Bhayaanak Raat.

***Above:** Turkish cinema has a crazy vitality rarely found in Hollywood movies.*

But acquiring knowledge is only one of the joys of cinema. And probably the least important. There's another route to go. In reading about these films you can simply gawp at the sheer awfulness of some of them while marvelling at the sheer weirdness of others. And that's a valid reaction too. After all, one of the purposes of 'fantastic' cinema is to be fantastic — to show you things you wouldn't otherwise see. If we manage to open your eyes to just a few of the wonders that the world of cinema has to offer, then our job's been a worthwhile one.

The sections that follow aren't intended to be exhaustive. How can you possibly hope to sum up Indian cinema in twenty-six pages, for example? The aim is to give you some of the background, some of the flavour and some of the important names and films that went into making each country's cinema unique. There'll be things left out (and things included) that might surprise some readers. This is my personal view of what's important and fun; others will have a different perspective. I look forward to their books. ■

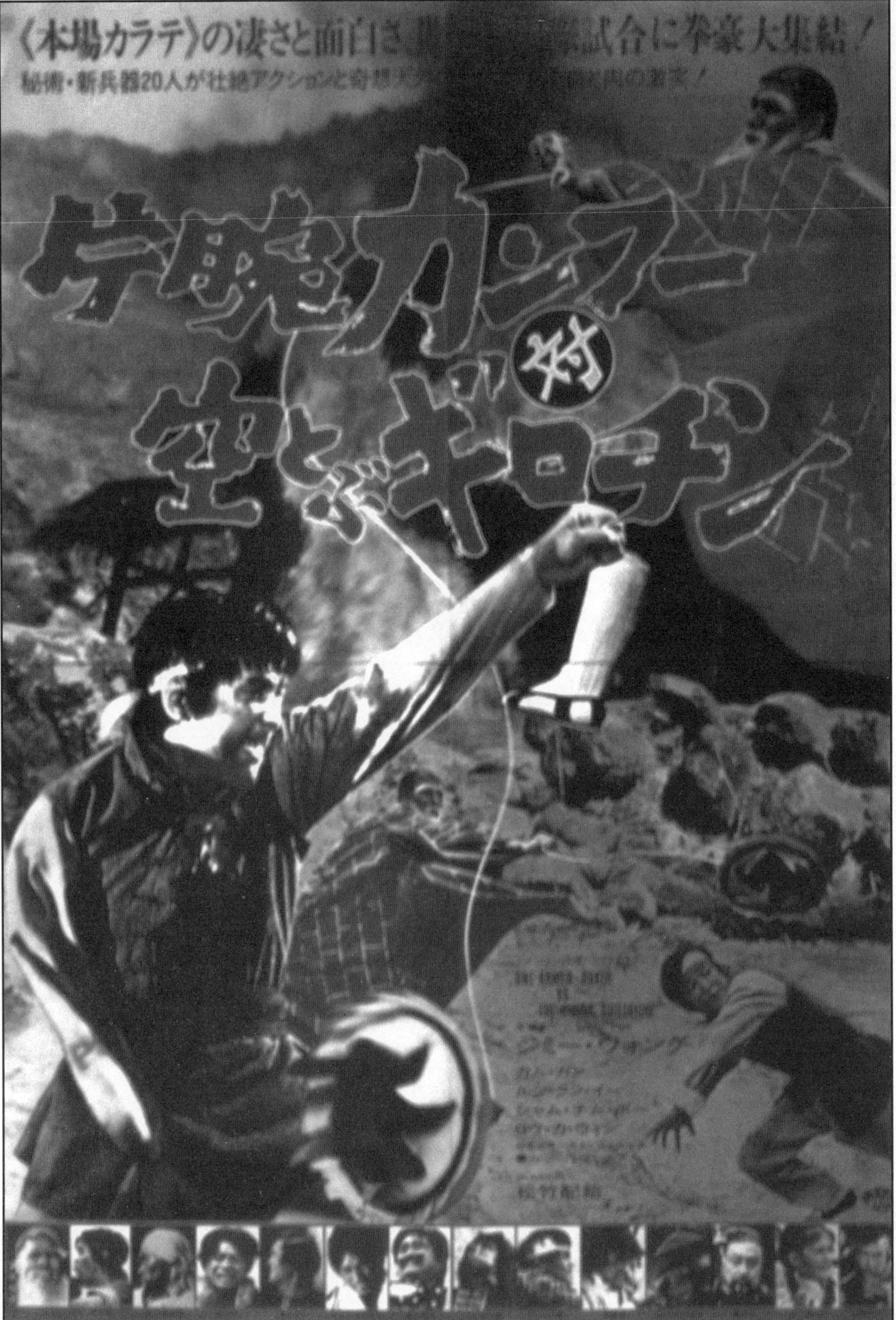

《本場カラテ》の凄さと面白さ
試合に拳豪大集結！
秘術・新兵器20人が壮絶アクションと奇想
片腕カンフー
対
空とぶギロチン
ジミー・ウォング

Crazy Kung Fu!

And in the beginning, there was Bruce...

'The uninitiated might be forgiven for thinking that kung fu was some kind of oriental King Kong,' wrote the British magazine *Continental Film Review* in August 1973. 'Not so, it's a form of Chinese combat which Bruce Lee purveys without stint in the Hong Kong action pictures which are the newest fashion in filmgoing.'

Even before people knew exactly what he did, he was a star.

Of course, martial arts in movies had been around a long time before Bruce Lee arrived on the scene. Their roots lie in techniques developed by the monks of the ancient Shaolin Temple. Built more than 1,500 years ago on the slopes of the Songshan mountain range in the remote plains of central China, the monastery was a centre of Ch'an or Zen Buddhism. This was a form of meditation brought to China by an Indian monk, Tamo. To sharpen their minds and tone their bodies the monks practiced *chi* exercises to control and harness their physical energies. Out of these exercises came many of the techniques that were developed into kung fu.

One of the paradoxes of the Shaolin training is that it is an apparently aggressive art devised as a means of controlling aggression. Anyone who has seen even a few of the classic kung fu movies from the early 1970s will be struck by how formalised and almost balletic many of the moves are; completely unlike a street fight, where punches are thrown merely to inflict damage. As the kung fu adepts say: "Emphasise the inner meaning, not the outer strength."

With the arrival of Bruce Lee, martial arts found a different kind of hero. He had certainly studied the Shaolin techniques and knew their spiritual base. It was circumstance and above all his personal temperament that led Lee in a different direction. Growing up on the streets of Hong Kong in the mid-1950s, he acquired a reputation as a kid who never avoided the chance for a good scrap. What marked him out from traditional martial artists was his hunger to win at all costs.

Lee had been born in San Francisco where his father, a famous Chinese stage star, was working at the time. When things got too hot for young Bruce in Hong Kong, his mother took advantage of his dual nationality to send him back to America to attend college. It was there Lee developed and refined his study of the martial arts, eventually perfecting his own style, which he called jeet kune do, or 'Way of the Intercepting Fist'. It was an aggressive, attacking style that suited him down to the ground. It favoured close physical contact and was perfect for the movies.

Opposite: *Japanese poster for Wang Yu's* Master of the Flying Guillotine.

The Bruce Lee story, in all its mythic ramifications, has been told too many times to go into in detail here. A short version would begin with Lee hired to play the part of the oriental manservant Kato in the 1966 TV series *The Green Hornet*. When the series was shown in Hong Kong in 1970 (retitled *Kato*), Bruce Lee returned to capitalise on his success as a man who'd made it in the West. The first company he approached was Shaw Brothers, one of the biggest players in the whole South East Asian market. The company president, Run Run Shaw, offered him their standard deal — a seven year contract for $2,000 per picture. Highly insulted, Lee signed with former Shaw employee, and now main rival, Raymond Chow. For Chow's Golden Harvest company he began work in 1971 on *The Big Boss* (confusingly known as *Fists of Fury* in America). The film was a big hit and was followed, in the same year, by *Fist of Fury* (which was called *The Chinese Connection* in the States). Then, in 1972, came Lee's first film as director and star, *Way of the Dragon*.

The American company Warner Brothers had enjoyed

WARNER BROS A Warner Communications Company présente
BRUCE LEE JOHN SAXON dans
OPERATION DRAGON
AHNA CAPRI et avec JIM KELLY
PANAVISION • TECHNICOLOR • Produit par FRED WEINTRAUB et PAUL HELLER
Mis en scène par ROBERT CLOUSE • Distribué par WARNER-COLUMBIA FILM

Above: Operation Dragon *is actually Bruce Lee's international hit* Enter the Dragon.
Below right: *In France,* Chinese Hercules *became* The Terror of Bruce Lee!

considerable success distributing a 1972 Shaw Brothers' film called *King Boxer* (aka *Five Fingers of Death*). The deepening crisis in the film business, brought about by the end of the Hollywood studio system, made these low-budget, fast action movies very attractive to profit-hungry executives. Bolstered by the success of Lee's Hong Kong productions, Warner's Fred Weintraub brokered a deal with Raymond Chow to make a modern day, action adventure movie in the style of the James Bond series, but featuring real martial arts. The result, in 1973, was *Enter the Dragon*, directed by the American Robert Clouse. The film was a huge success, and effectively created the world-wide cult for kung fu. Its basic format (good guys versus bad guys, built around a martial arts contest), has been used in innumerable American productions since. As the kung fu craze snowballed, Lee planned his next film.

YANG SZE
LA TERREUR DE
BRUCE LEE
mise en scène de Choy Tak

Then, on 20 July 1973, much to everyone's surprise, Bruce Lee died at the age of thirty-three. His body was found in the apartment of actress Betty Ting Pei. The cause of death still remains cloaked in mystery. Officially he died from a haemorrhage caused by taking aspirin. Other stories say he was experimenting with drugs or bizarre sex. Whatever the reasons, the effect was devastating. It was as if a wedding had been planned, with the guests all assembled... but there was no bridegroom.

Bruce Lee's body was hardly cold in the coffin before the legend began to grow of the hard fighting 'Little Dragon' from the streets of Hong Kong, his rapid rise to the top and his mysterious death in the flat of a sex starlet. Naturally, this was an opportunity too good to be missed. While Lee's death was a tragedy for martial arts fans, it was a godsend for exploitation movie-makers. They had already been profiting from the post-*King Boxer* interest in kung fu movies. Small independent companies had descended on the colony, buying up any film featuring fighting and releasing it to the world with a suitably aggressive title. Now they jumped in to fill the Bruce Lee gap. Strange hybrids began to appear. Real-life events became mixed up with events from Lee's films. The truth became inseparable from the fiction — understandable when nobody really knew the truth in the first place.

The fact that the adult Lee had only starred in four movies during his lifetime was something of a boon. Aware that most audiences wouldn't know this, many companies began to search out lookalike actors and rename them as close as legally possible to the real thing. Soon there was a Bruce Li, a Bruce Le, a Bruce Liang and a Bruce Leung. Slightly more imaginative was Dragon Lee, closely followed by Conan Lee. Even Spanish sleazemeister Jesús Franco joined the fray with Bruce Lin. Martial arts writer Bey Logan calls these the 'Leealikes'.

A popular ploy was to use these imitation Lees in heavily fictionalised biopics. *Dragon Story* is a fairly typical example, starring one of the better Leealikes, Ho Chung Tao, known as Bruce Li. The film begins with Lee working as a newspaper boy in the States. He looks about twenty-seven years old. His supposed martial arts skills are demonstrated by his ability to hit a fat girl's butt with a rolled up newspaper as he cycles past at speed. He comes up against a rival gang of black newspaper boys. This bunch look well into their thirties. "Hey man, we run this place!" they sneer. "Who are you?!" Bruce shows them who he is with a few well placed high kicks.

In Hong Kong, Bruce gets a quick lesson in the economics of the local film business. Demanding US$10,000 per picture he's told that even big stars only get HK$1,000 per month. The balance has to be made up from backhanders and sponsorship deals. The film contains lots of parodies of real people. Mr Lo (*The Big Boss* director Lo Wei) is characterised as a fat, talentless rip-off merchant. "Where shall we set the angle?" asks his assistant director on set. "Ask the cameraman," growls Lo. "What shall we do now?" Lo takes his big cigar out of his mouth just long enough to shout: "Fight! Fight! Fight! Just fight!"

At the film's launch party Lo is besieged by starlets wanting a role in his next flick. "Don't worry," he assures them. "The next picture is about prostitutes. I'll need all of you!"

Soon Bruce is wooing Betty. Hilariously, at this point the schmaltzy soundtrack suddenly becomes a booting sax-led jig, introducing an unmistakable air of Benny Hill to the soft focus love scenes that follow.

The strangest mixture of real-life and fiction came in

the 1975 Shaw Brothers release *Bruce Lee and I.* The film starred Betty Ting Pei, the woman in whose flat Lee had breathed his last. Renamed *The Sex Life of Bruce Lee* in some territories, it purported to tell the truth about their relationship. The story is framed by an encounter with a sympathetic bartender to whom Betty relates the sad saga. The film builds slowly to the long awaited climax. Betty sprays perfume on her giant round bed and strips off while Bruce (as played by Li Hsiu Hsien), popping pills and smoking endless joints, gives her a final workover. If this outrageous blend of fact and fiction was perplexing for the audience, it must have been even stranger for Miss Ting Pei.

Of course, there are only so many variations that can be wrung out of one life, even one as eventful as Lee's. Soon the bandwagon moved on to deal with life after Lee.

Black Dragon's Revenge (or *Black Dragon Revenges the Death of Bruce Lee*) doesn't feature a Leealike. Instead there's a Lee Van Cleef-alike! With one crucial difference — he's black martial artist Ron Van Cliff. A mysterious Chinese businessman gives him $100,000 and an air ticket to Hong Kong to find out who killed Bruce Lee. A local sect of kung fu experts are on the same trail. The film gives plenty of opportunity to rehearse the list of reasons for Lee's death: "People say... he die... of oversex!" one character blurts out. Another maintains that he was killed by drug barons who wanted him to die as a junkie so that kids all over the world would follow his supposed example and buy lots of heroin.

As the kung fu mystic master says at one point in the film: "Stupidity may be great wisdom." Or maybe not.

Probably the wildest of the post-mortem Lee rip-offs was *The Clones of Bruce Lee.* The producer of the film was exploitation legend Dick Randall. In this cheap and cheesy concoction, a scientist takes a syringe of blood from the dead Lee. He uses this to create three 'clones'. It's never quite explained how, but these clones grow to maturity in about three minutes. Their training consists of them breaking piles of roof tiles while uttering Bruce Lee style yelps. Under the aegis of an organisation called SBI, they are sent off to save the free world. Bruce One takes on a crooked film producer who is moonlighting as a gold smuggler. Bruces Two and Three are sent to Thailand to put paid to "a certain Dr Nye". Dr Nye has created an army of bronze men. "Ha ha! Soon I will conquer the whole world!" he cackles, as his metal warriors (actually a bunch of flabby extras covered in gold paint) go into action. Every time someone hits them they go 'clunk'.

Within the low-budget film world, the martial arts formula was like a spark to dry timber. The flames spread quickly. There were martial arts movies from countries as far apart as Turkey (*Tarkan Kolsuz Kahramana Karşı*), India (*Onanondu Kalladali*) and Brazil (*Bruce Lee versus Gay Power*). The most bizarre rip-offs were the ones that were announced but never made. *Ilsa Meets Bruce Lee in the Devil's Triangle* probably takes the prize here. Areas where the Chinese controlled the film business, or had big ex-pat populations, like the Philippines, Singapore and Indonesia, were especially fertile territory.

The world had been starved of real heroes for too long. The martial arts film, particularly the Bruce Lee version of it, with its plucky 'Little Dragon' taking on all-comers and righting wrongs in a burst of screen action, was a godsend. They were cheap to make and returned their investment every time. Even wacky items like *The Human Tornado* found a receptive audience. In this blaxploitation comedy, the overweight, chitlin' circuit comedian Rudy Ray Moore gives the most outrageous display of martial arts ineptitude ever committed to celluloid. The odd thing is that it works a treat.

Unlike the Chinese martial arts films of the 1960s, most of Lee's films had contemporary settings. The imitation Lee movies followed suit. As the time was the early seventies, this meant flared trousers, outrageous afro hairdos and flowery shirts with vicious collars. *Shaft*-style music filled the soundtracks, with wah-wah guitar licks, and there were even psychedelic sequences. Soon, in the immortal words of the Carl Douglas song, "Everybody was kung fu fightin'..."

Had Bruce Lee not died so young, it's more than likely that the *Enter the Dragon* formula would not have taken such a firm grip on the West's view of martial arts. Lee's subse-

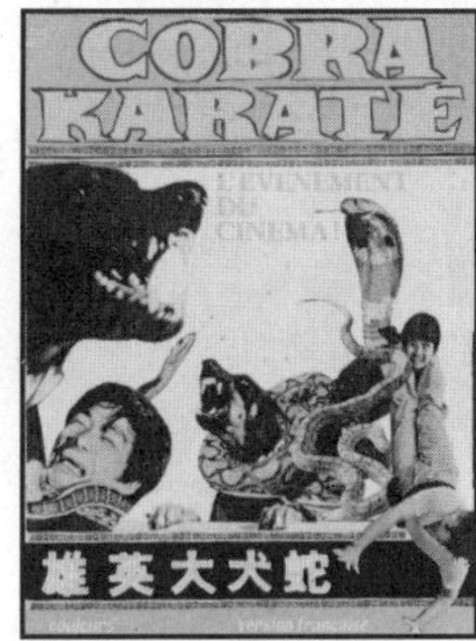

Above: Bruce Lee & I *purported to tell the true story of his last days... and nights!* ***Left:*** *Two of the* Clones of Bruce Lee.

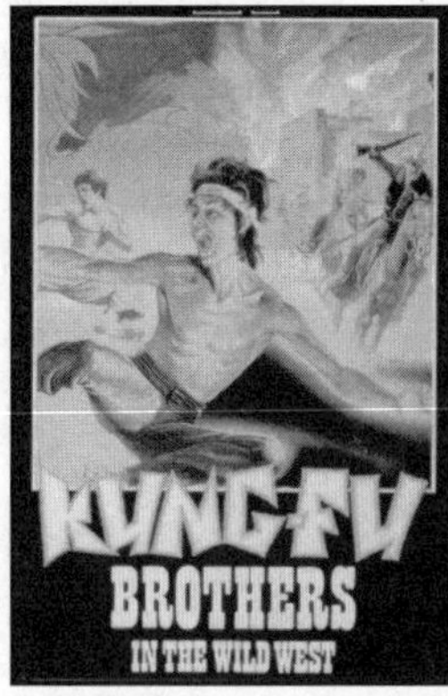

quent movies might well have followed a very different track. More traditional, Shaolin-based stories could have become the norm. However, it's important to bear in mind that by the mid-1970s, when the Bruce Lee cult was still strong in the West, the Chinese martial arts film was already in decline. This was very much a post classic period. The kung fu film had always been a confusing mixture of influences. Tony Rayns singles out 'ancient Chinese drama, pulp fiction, the Italian peplum and the Hollywood fantasy' as some of the more obvious. Now, in a bid to give the genre a boost, all kinds of strange hybrids were being created. In this context the Bruce Lee clones made a weird kind of sense.

By the mid-seventies there had already been Eastern Westerns (*Kung Fu Brothers in the Wild West*), kung fu science fiction (*Three Stooges vs the Wonder Women*), a martial arts/sex comedy from Germany, *Enter the Seven Virgins*, and a Hammer-Shaw co-production, *The Legend of the 7 Golden Vampires* (aka *The Seven Brothers Meet Dracula*). Hong Kong had even taken on Japan (*Zatoichi vs the One Armed Swordsman*). To hedge their bets, the film-makers shot two different endings: in the film shown in Hong Kong, the one-armed Chinaman wins, in the Japanese version, Zatoichi triumphs.

The seventies craze for kung fu meant that all sorts of local productions were being imported to the West. The majority of them would never normally have made it out of the traditional South East Asian circuit for which they were intended. Many of them were highly bizarre. A choice item known as *Snake Girl Drops In* just about takes the biscuit for cheesy weirdness. Three men out for a mini safari in the jungle meet a cheeky forest maiden. She winks seductively at them as she hops from tree to tree wearing a bubbly blonde wig. When they catch her and take off the wig they discover that she's got snakes instead of hair. They take her back with them to 'civilisation', where they attempt to exploit her as a freak. A variety of comic scenes show her eating live frogs and watering her snakes in a gents' toilet as she tries to adjust to her new lifestyle. Eventually, one of the men (the youngest and most handsome of course) takes pity on the snake girl and sets her free. Then, to the sound of wah-wah guitars and Swingle-style background singers, a Keystone Kops chase ensues through bars, cabarets and back streets.

The bad guys hire a transvestite wizard to track down the snake girl. The wizard's number one trick is the ability to free his head from his body. The head then floats off to find the girl. Meanwhile, back in the jungle... The girl's little sister (played by, the credits assure us, 'world known child star Dyna'), who has magic powers, comes to save her, accompanied by hundreds of snakes. At the sight of her, a girl pees her pants. About a gallon of liquid pours down her flared pink trouser-suited leg.

1977's *Shaolin Invincibles* is even wackier. The plot is fairly standard, but it's the incidentals that make this one a standout. A costume drama, set in the Qing dynasty, it begins with two girls who have been trained by Shaolin monks. They've mastered the Lightning Eye Sword and Heaven and Earth techniques. Both skills will stand them in good stead as they set out to take revenge on the evil emperor who slaughtered their family. The emperor has a few tricks up his sleeve, however. Attached to his court are two wizards in tall hats. Alongside their magical powers this pair have three foot long tongues that hang out of their open mouths like thick ribbons while they talk. The wizards have presented the king with two tatty gorillas who have been trained in martial arts.

"Strange. Why have they got those animals here?" asks one of the girls.

"Yeah. And they seem to know kung fu!" the other replies.

The girls discover that the gorillas' only weak spots are the tops of their skulls. Using their Lightning Eye Sword technique they jump on top of the beasts and skewer them in the head. It's like striking oil. Two geysers of blood shoot from the confused gorillas in a great ten foot arc. Despite its trashy visuals, the film does have some literary antecedents. The origin of the kung fu fighting gorillas is probably Jin Yong's novella, *Sword of the Yueh Maiden*, in which a young girl learns kung fu from her 'uncle', a huge white ape.

The idea of fierce fighting females was, of course, pretty exotic in itself for Western audiences. Particularly given the common assumption of oriental women as meek, docile creatures. Angela Mao made quite a name for herself as a high kicking, hard hitting female warrior, but there were plenty more to choose from. In *Matching Escort*, the dainty Pearl Cheong is given huge iron shoes to wear by her father. When she takes them off, she can fly into the air or run at the speed of the wind to evade her enemies. In an earlier film, *Wolfen Ninja*, Pearl plays a girl brought up by wolves. She becomes a mystic warrior who takes on a black magic cult. Because she's eaten the root of the rare white ginseng, her hair turns snow white when she gets angry (or drunk!). The same source material was used for Ronnie Yu's 1992 hit *The Bride With White Hair*. This earlier version, however, is almost totally incoherent. It's like someone has randomly shuffled the pages of the script. Still, there's plenty of crazed action from red-robed ninjas, a green-faced werewolf, zombies with their souls imprisoned in golden needles and even a couple of hopping vampires.

By the end of the 1970s, anything with kung fu in it seemed ripe for exploitation by hungry distributors. Of course they knew little or nothing about the product. Perhaps they bought it sight unseen. That would explain how a film like *Deadly Snail versus Kung Fu Killers* played New York's 42nd Street some time in the early eighties. Despite the title, there's no deadly snail and certainly no kung fu killers. This threadbare theatrical fable is a throwback to antiquated Cantonese fantasy films from the 1950s, like *The Snake Girl and the Flying Monster* or *The Holy Snake and the Flying Tiger*. With the production values of a school play, the film retells an ancient Chinese fable. Three sisters, who are

Below: *Training session for another Bruce Lee clone.*

Left: Chests out girls! Enter the Seven Virgins, *a West German co-production.*
Below: The amazing stilt-fighting scene from Ninja in the Dragon's Den.

really 1,000-year-old sea snails, become involved with a poor farmer. One of the girls assumes human form and marries him. A greedy snake pretends to be a Taoist priest and comes along to exorcise the sea snail. Highly eccentric scenes include the sea snail crucified inside a ring of burning snakes, a stick fighting imp with ginger hair and a plastic mini kilt, and a high camp view of Heaven as a place all fluffy, pink and filled with soap bubbles.

Alongside bizarre martial arts films came bizarre martial arts weapons. The 1977 Taiwanese production *Dynasty* has one of the strangest. This is an enormous chain-mail vest which doubles as a kind of giant, cross-shaped boomerang. The climax of the film is a fight on a hillside where this unique weapon comes into its own. Whirring eccentrically through the sky, it's quite a sight. The same film also features a cast iron umbrella! From a slightly more solid pedigree came the flying guillotine. This deadly killing machine ('a hat box with teeth' according to Ric Meyers) made its first appearance in 1975 in *The Flying Guillotine.* In the same year the film's director Ho Meng-Hua turned in the first of the Shaw Brothers *Black Magic* horror series. His senses must have been finely attuned to the bizarre. The flying guillotine is a tub-shaped object attached to a long chain. Flung into the air it spins like a giant top, then, with a tug of the chain, settles over the head of its victim. Sharp toothed blades inside snap shut, decapitating the poor unfortunate. The following year the device turned up again in Wang Yu's *Master of the Flying Guillotine.* The film features not only the aforementioned killing machine but also an Indian kung fu master with extendable arms.

As though the films weren't strange enough, the marketing of them added another dollop of oddball to the stew. *The Tiger Love,* for instance, is advertised with the wonderful strap line: 'Warning: Some of the scenes in this film actually happened.' The film begins with a pregnant woman hurling herself from the top of a high cliff to escape her captors. She lands in the branches of a tree hundreds of feet below. When she regains consciousness she sees a tiger circling beneath her. Scared witless, she pisses herself. Yes, we actually see a stream of piss pour out of her trouser leg and onto the tiger's head. When she wakes up in the beast's lair she remembers an old proverb: "It is said that if a woman kisses a tiger, the tiger is her slave." The next scene shows the tiger licking the woman's bare behind and progressing to her breasts before the shaky hand of the censor cuts off any further dalliance. Did it really happen...? Or did I just dream it?

Above left: *Ultimate weirdness,* The Tiger Love.
Above right: *Now get out of that!* Buddhist Fist.
Below: *Lo Lieh as a Chinese Superman.*

The indifferent dubbing they were subjected to only increased the already high weirdness quotient of these movies. On-set sound recording was never done in Hong Kong films in any case. Few actors post-synched their own dialogue and local audiences had come to accept the tinny, unreal quality of the dubbing. Most of the people involved in providing the voices for the foreign versions were not professional actors. Many were amateurs or in some cases simply employees of foreign embassies who just happened to be English speakers. For some reason they often affected strange nasal twangs when they spoke and there were the most unnatural pauses between words as the dubbers tried desperately to let the moving lips on screen catch up with the duff dialogue they were overlaying. For example: "The black man... he was... good. In the cat stance... he managed to... hit me... withaMonkeyfistboss!"

"Eeeh! Pretty good kung fu!" (spoken in a whining, mock cockney accent) was a frequent interjection in fight scenes. Or, "So you think you can beat my tiger claw, drunken mantis?" Then would follow a display of esoteric fighting styles drawn from imitations of snakes, mongooses, tigers or birds. The highlight was the drunken kung fu, where the fighter confuses his opponent by pretending to be pissed out of his mind. The wily devil!

The bizarre quality of these films turned many of them into cult items. They became the staple fare of the 'late night' kung fu fans, shown after midnight on a Friday or Saturday when the main feature had finished and the faint-hearted had taken the last bus home. In the mid-seventies such shows became a regular feature of life for filmgoers in the big cities. Such unfiltered exposure to the weird detritus of another culture quickly created a taste for the strange and the striking. Going entirely against the grain of the mainstream films of the time, the martial arts movie opened a lot of eyes to the imaginative and fun possibilities of a cinema without rules. But all too soon it was over. Without the commercial focus provided by a star like Bruce Lee, distributors gave up on the martial arts movie. As video began its inexorable rise in the early 1980s, the flea pit cinemas and drive-ins that showed the movies also disappeared.

Without a crystal ball, or even with one, predicting the future is a dangerous game. Who knows what would have happened to the martial arts film if Bruce Lee had lived. Perhaps it would still have ended up in the straight-to-video ghetto that it inhabits today. With few exceptions, martial arts films don't play on cinema screens outside South East Asia. Their influence on mainstream movies has been minimal. In the last few years only a handful of films, such as John Carpenter's *Big Trouble in Little China* and the Eddie Murphy vehicle *The Golden Child* have touched on Eastern style mysticism. For most people, kung fu still means little guys jumping about and hitting each other.

The only film-maker of influence today who admits to a liking for the old style martial arts movie is Quentin Tarantino. The strong connections between *Reservoir Dogs*

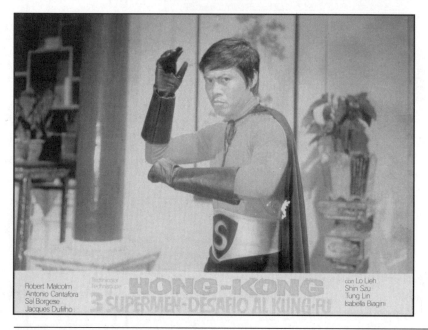

and Ringo Lam's *City on Fire* have been widely reported. Tarantino's script for *True Romance* is full of references to the likes of Sonny Chiba. However the strongest influence on the almost existential mood of the Tarantino universe is from a film-maker whose work had a subliminal, unacknowledged effect on much contemporary action cinema — Chang Cheh. Chang confesses to never being interested in realism. His films inhabit a male fantasy world of violence and sudden death. Without the existence of Chang Cheh films like *Five Element Ninja* and *The Masked Avengers* a certain kind of up-front violence would never have entered the mainstream in the way it has. And yet today's films, for all the controversy they arouse, still have a long way to go to match the inventive and shocking brutality of the best of Chang. Take, for example, the opening scene of *The Crippled Avengers*...

Three men burst through the gates of Tu Tin Tao's mansion. Finding that he's not there they decide to take action.

"Let's cut off his wife's legs and his son's arms!" one of them announces. And so they do.

"I'll get a blacksmith to make you iron hands," the boy's father promises. To make them even more interesting, the hands also shoot deadly poisoned darts.

Over the course of the next ten minutes, Tu's son goes round creating cripples like there's no tomorrow. He blinds one man for simply looking at him. "I have no hands, you have no eyes. Now we're equal."

To stop another man cursing he makes him mute. When he complains, Tu bursts his eardrums to make him deaf. A man has his feet chopped off for accidentally walking into the boy. Another man has an iron band tightened round his skull until it drives him mad.

That's the plot. The rest of the film shows the crippled victims joining forces, training and then taking their revenge. Iron feet meet iron hands in one of the most astonishing battles ever committed to celluloid.

The films of Chang Cheh were about fighting, about stripping away every extraneous element so that the set piece combat scenes were the main focus of the plot. Human relationships were reduced to the struggle to survive. In the films of Chang Cheh women played a very insignificant role. There's no sex in these cruel and brutal fables. In fact, as we'll see in the next section, sex was something that didn't make its mark on Hong Kong movies until well after the departure of Bruce Lee. But when it *did* finally arrive, it was in the most spectacular fashion... ■

Above: *Wang Yu takes on the world in a late night classic from 1973.*

Below left: *No legs? No problem! One of the crippled masters fights a dustbin lid wielding baldy.*

Below right: *French intellectuals redubbed* Crush Karate *and it became* Can Dialectics Break Bricks?

Incredible secrets of Oriental Sex Slavery . . .

Confessions of a Concubine x

starring YUM YUM SHAW

China Blue

Until the 1970s there wasn't a lot of sex in Hong Kong movies. All those spirited swordswomen in films like *Dragon Gate Inn* seemed remarkably prudish when it came to the real bump and grind. The only hint of the lurid occurred in stories about prostitutes. These are as common in Chinese films as they are in films from India and Japan. The convention, however, was to show them as objects of pity — almost of admiration — rather than arousers of lust.

One of the first locally made films to feature nudity was the Australian-American co-production *Sampan*, directed in 1969 by Terry Bourke. Made in black and white and financed by a motley group, including a diamond merchant and Shirley MacLaine's husband, the film featured actresses Dorothy Fu (Fu Yi) and Sabrina Kong ('The Jayne Mansfield of the Orient'). The Thai-Chinese Dorothy starred as a tragic sampan girl torn between her duty towards her elderly husband and her lust for his son. Anyone seen *Desire Under the Elms* lately?

The film failed to make much impact either in Hong Kong or abroad and it was former photographer He Fan who really broke the taboo barrier of nudity with his 1970 production *Lost.* Heavily influenced by Japanese eroductions, the film again featured *Sampan* star Dorothy Fu, by now one of the hottest attractions on local screens due to her willingness to disrobe in front of the camera.

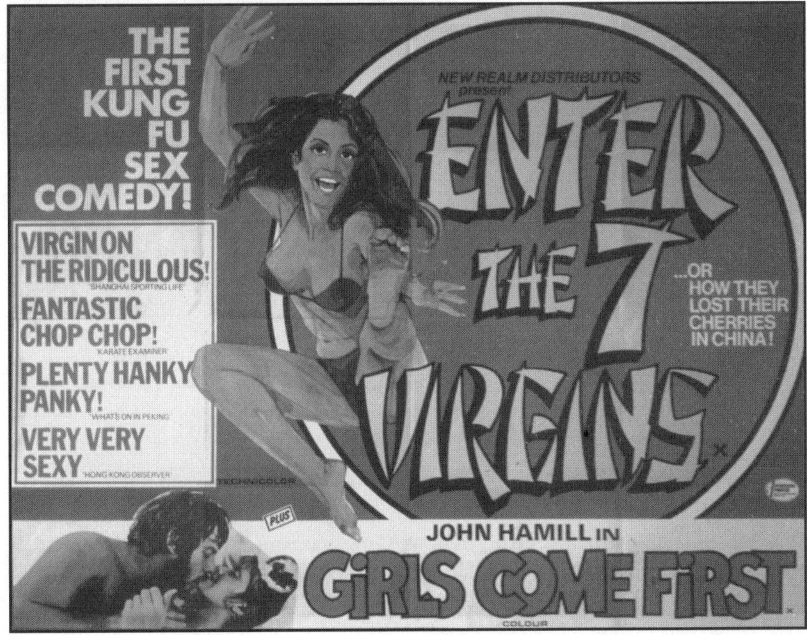

Most of the movies made in Hong Kong during this period were in the Mandarin language. Cantonese cinema was on its last legs by the early seventies. Films like *Magic Feeding* (featuring the ample Tina Ti), *The Sexual World* and *Triangular Round Bed* added a dose of cheeky suggestiveness to tired plots in an effort to draw audiences from the all pervasive power of Mandarin language martial arts movies.

By 1974, following the death of Bruce Lee, economically the kung fu boom was effectively over. The traditional markets for Hong Kong product were becoming restricted. Censorship in Singapore and a quota system for local films in Thailand meant that there was less demand for product from the big Shaw Brothers and Golden Harvest operations. Both companies sought some respite in overseas co-productions. The Shaws turned to Germany for *The Virgin of the Seven Seas* (released in Britain as *Enter the Seven Virgins*) and Italy for *Three Supermen Against the Orient* and *Three Stooges vs the Wonder Women.* Golden Harvest also went to Italy for the amazing *Barbarian Women* and to Australia for the stunt-filled *The Man From Hong Kong,* featuring ex-Bond actor George Lazenby.

In America and Europe the early 1970s was a fertile period for softcore sex movies, culminating in the huge success of *Emmanuelle* in 1974. Inevitably some of these films filtered through to Hong Kong. Censorship in the colony was very confused during the seventies. Whereas local films were subject to severe strictures, this didn't seem to be the case for imported movies. The situation was made even more ridiculous in 1974 when censorship was abolished in the nearby Portuguese colony of Macao. For the price of a short boat trip, Hong Kong residents were able to sample the delights of films like *Last Tango in Paris* completely uncut.

Shaw Brothers were the first major Hong Kong producers to introduce more explicit sex in their films, with items ranging from comedies (*That's Adultery*), through horror (*Killer Snakes*), to women-in-prison films (*Bamboo House of Dolls*). The latter was one of the most extreme. Its mixture of oriental and Western actresses allowed a greater display of skin than would have been possible with a purely Chinese cast, while its anti-Japanese bias provided an acceptable excuse for gruesome scenes of torture and sexual humiliation.

Run Run Shaw put some heavy promotion into selling his new sex-based productions around the world. He set up court in Cannes and also paid a visit to the Sixth Indian International Film Festival in Bombay, where starlets Shirley Yu and Yum Yum Shaw were a big hit with the crowds.

Opposite: *Yum Yum Shaw in a tight spot in* Confessions of a Concubine.

Below: *Women in prison Hong Kong style:* Bamboo House of Dolls.

'Cooing and fluttering and flashing their come-to-bed looks,' gushed an overheated journalist in *India Today.* 'What kind of roles did they play? "Sexy," said Shirley in a throaty, monosyllabic answer which needed no further explanation.'

1973 was the watershed year for the Hong Kong sex film, with titles like *The Sugar Daddies, Sexy Playgirls, Queen Hustlers* and *Sex Maniacs* appearing in rapid fashion. The headline grabbing 'permissive society' was used as a background for films like *Sexy Girls of Denmark* and *Adventure in Denmark.* In the latter, directed by former photographer He Fan, a martial arts expert wins a trip to Copenhagen, where he gets involved with topless Danes and triad gangs.

The prolific Chu Yuan, working for Shaw Brothers, was one of the first prestigious film-makers to venture into the sex arena. His *Intimate Confessions of a Chinese Courtesan,* released in 1972, was an immediate and controversial hit. Not only did it feature scenes of kinky sex and torture that would have been daring even in a Western movie, but it was the first Chinese film to show a lesbian relationship. Obviously indebted to contemporaneous Japanese eroductions, the film also reflects Chu Yuan's detailed knowledge of Chinese culture and literature. Together with his regular art director Chen Chingsen he created a believably baroque world of erotic excess that Tony Rayns compared favourably with Von Sternberg's *The Scarlet Empress.*

Intimate Confessions tells the story of Ai Nu, captured by bandits and sold into slavery at the Four Seasons brothel. She becomes a favourite of the lesbian madam, Chin-i, and uses her privileged position to get access to all the top clients. One by one Ai Nu murders them, arousing the suspicion of a local law officer who also falls under her spell. Ai Nu and the policeman set a trap for her bandit captors, in the course of which Ai Nu's lesbian lover is fatally wounded. Drawing Ai Nu to her, she kisses her with poisoned lips and they expire in each other's arms.

Chu Yuan had made his directorial début in 1959, at the age of twenty-four, and went on to direct well over 100 more films. Following *Intimate Confessions* he began a series of adaptations of the popular martial arts novels of Gu Long. Although set in the distant past, his adaptations have a distinctly contemporary flavour. In 1984 he returned to the theme of his earlier film with *Lust for Love of a Chinese Courtesan.*

Shaw Brothers' rival Golden Harvest entered the domain of period erotica with their 1975 production *Confessions of a Concubine* (also released as *The Story of Su-san*), directed by former cameraman Chen Chi-wah. Like Chu Yuan's film, this one is also set in a Ming Dynasty house of pleasure. The film's early scenes detail the many and varied forms of sexual training engaged in by one of the inmates of these houses, the comely Su San (played by popular pin-up Yum Yum Shaw). The training culminates in her 'graduation', where she loses her virginity to her first paying customer. In time honoured fashion she falls in love with the man, a young scholar called Wang. The rest of the film details her attempts to save herself for him, while being relentlessly pursued by the lecherous Emperor Cheng.

The commercial potential of Chinese erotic literature found its most consistent exponent in veteran director Li Hanxiang, who had made his first film in 1952. *That's Adultery* in 1975 was the first of what became dubbed his *fengyue* films. The term refers to their mixture of erudite Eastern erotica with earthy comedy. The closest parallel in the West would be the work of Walerian Borowczyk, whose films follow a similarly sophisticated approach. Like several of Borowczyk's films, Li's movies are also portmanteau collections of stories set both in the past (usually the Republican period after 1911) and occasionally in the present.

That's Adultery was followed by *Love Swindlers,* another four-story compilation featuring cuckolded husbands, quack sex doctors and willing women played by the likes of Shirley Yu, Dana and Yum Yum Shaw. These three were rapidly becoming fixtures in Shaw Brothers sex comedies. The portmanteau films were extremely successful and in 1977 Li was given one of his biggest budgets for an adaptation of the famous novel *Kokeimu* (Dreams of the Red Chamber). The story tells of the erotic adventures of the fifteen-year-old Pao-yu. The book has been filmed several times. In 1961 it was made Chinese opera-style with the amorous hero played by a young girl. The later *Erotic Dreams of the Red Chamber* consists of a series of Benny Hill-type sketches with jokes about buggery, menstruation and dildos. The funniest episode has

Opposite: *Yum Yum Shaw gets another lesson in love in* Confessions of a Concubine.

Above right: *Kung fu hero meets the permissive seventies in* Adventure in Denmark.
Below: *An intimate moment from* Intimate Confessions of a Chinese Courtesan.

a bunch of novice monks being tested by having two naked women dance in front of them. A drum under their robes pings every time one of them gets an erection.

The Shaw Brothers' other leading maker of sex films was former matinée idol James Lu Qi. After a career as an actor in Cantonese comedies during the 1960s he turned to directing in the early 1970s with a series of low-budget sex movies made very quickly and often with the same cast and crew. Actress Ai Ti featured in so many of these Lu Qi soft-core romps that critic Mel Tobias described her as 'a woman forever suffering or taking a shower.'

Like the portmanteau films of Li Hanxiang, Lu Qi's movies also feature multiple storylines but here they are normally woven together into a continuous narrative. Many of them are set in a version of reality drawn from newspaper headlines, featuring tabloid style exposés of the lives of movie stars and call girls. To minimise the damage inflicted by the local censor, the frequent scenes of nudity in Lu's films are often shot like separate additions to the plot. They could then be cut without the film losing whatever narrative coherence it may have had. It was Lu Qi who gave Hong Kong cinema its first flash of female pubic hair in 1977's *Starlets for Sale* (export versions of films like *The Sex Life of Bruce Lee* and *The Magic Curse* had featured full frontal scenes for several years before this). In films like *The Stud and the Nympho* and *Foxy Ladies*, Lu Qi's women are spunky firebrands who fight back and triumph over the men who have done them wrong.

After the comedy strand and the foreign-located actioner, the main story peg for local sex films was this theme of revenge. It's a convenient way of getting sex and violence past the censors. First you set up the scene, with rape, abduction and sexual slavery. Then you show the long suffering heroine fighting her way back to self-respect and freedom (usually with the help of a sympathetic male). The result can then be sold as a moral fable: the triumph of good over adversity.

In Cheung Sum's 1975 film *Bald Headed Betty*, Lam Chin Ming plays the title character, a girl forced into prostitution by unscrupulous gangsters. Her special trade mark is her shaved head, which she disguises with a series of coloured wigs. The exotic appeal of Betty's shiny pate makes her a popular choice for clients looking for something a little bit different. One man slaps a piece of Buddhist prayer paper on her smooth crown, another man tries to match her by whipping off his own wig. Eventually, with the help of a sympathetic client, she gets her revenge.

There were also, inevitably, many imitations of Western hits. The 1977 release *Hong Kong Emmanuelle* was an attempt to adopt the vacuous glossiness of Just Jaeckin's hit movie. It featured TV star and Miss Hong Kong 1973, Deborah Lee, as Fifi and was set in the swinging, showbiz world of fashion photographers and glitzy night-clubs. Although firmly softcore, Mel Tobias reported that a hot version was available for private showing at the parties of Hong Kong bigwigs.

One surprising result of these Eastern softcores was their effect on countries like France and America, where genuine hardcore was legal. Local producers began to turn out hardcore movies featuring Eastern actors and actresses. *Oriental Blue* was a 1974 American production featuring the lithe Peonies Jong as Lady Fang, an oriental madam who dispenses various cunning aphrodisiacs to unsuspecting females. The following year came *Chinese Blue*. This time the film was a softcore effort made in Hong Kong and spiced up with some hardcore inserts featuring American porn stars and 'body doubles' for the Asian girls. The film played successfully in cinemas in New York's Chinatown, but would have been illegal if shown uncut in Hong Kong.

Throughout the 1970s, horror films, particularly those set in exotic far off lands like Borneo or New Guinea, began to feature sex scenes and nudity. *The Magic Curse* and *Bruce Lee in New Guinea* share almost the same plot, with a story of martial arts experts from Hong Kong trapped in the dark jungle and helping a beautiful snake princess to fight an evil wizard. In *Bruce Lee in New Guinea* the princess is a delightful, pouting little poppet with ruby-red, bee-sting lips and pert little breasts. The film's dashing hero is bitten by a snake and begins to suffer from chills. "We have to keep him warm," the princess's lady-in-waiting tells her. The innocent girl knows only one way to do this: she strips off her leopard skin bikini and matching thigh length boots and climbs into bed with him.

Sex and violence became big draws in Hong Kong cinemas during the late 1970s. Critic Sek Kai reports that at midnight shows of new films, sex scenes drew yelps of delight from the mostly male audience, while more romantic displays of affection elicited groans and a general rise in the constant hubbub of conversation.

The early 1980s saw the arrival of a 'new wave' of Hong Kong film-makers, many of whom had been trained overseas or in the more experimental atmosphere of television. These included Hong Kong's first female director, Ann Hui. Her 1980 film *The Spooky Bunch* not only featured Xiao Fang Fang as an assertive female lead, but was also a precursor of the later horror boom. The new wave films featured women characters in strong dramatic situations. It became possible to include nudity as part of a role, without the unfortunate actress being branded as a sex star. The mighty Shaw Brothers, at the tail end of their involvement in film production, exploited the new freedoms with their remake of *Intimate Confessions of a Chinese Courtesan.* They also invested in the 1983 independent production *An Amorous Woman of the Tang Dynasty.* Here Patricia Xia plays the title character, Yu Yuen Kai, a famous poetess of the eighth century. Her steamy affair with the *louche* Chui (played by pop star Alex Man) and her sexual emancipation are explored in a resolutely modern fashion. The affair awakens Kai's sexuality and when Chui leaves she turns to her maid, Luk, for comfort, giving the opportunity for some titillating lesbian lovemaking.

One of the effects of the new explicitness was that sex could now be dealt with more directly, as a matter of fact, and not always sweetened with the sugar coating of comedy.

Right and below: *The category III classic* Sex & Zen.
Bottom: *Amy Yip and friends in* Erotic Ghost Story.

The 1980 film *The Happening* was a serious drama about teenage prostitutes, as was *Lonely 15* in 1982. In the same year Patrick Tam's *Nomad* gave a controversial portrait of sexually free-wheeling youth. In the West and in Japan this sort of thing had been a staple since the 1950s, but for Hong Kong it was something new. *Nomad* featured sex scenes in a shopping mall and, most controversially, on a late night tram. Following complaints, the film was withdrawn by its distributors and recut.

Throughout the 1980s, nudity became a fairly common ingredient in Hong Kong movies. The out and out sexploiter had gone, but its replacements, the sexy comedy and the horror movie, made frequent use of more explicit scenes. A new generation of actresses rose to prominence during the decade. Many of them, like Pauline Chan, Maggie Cheung and Anita Yuen, had first come to the attention of the public through beauty contests such as the Miss Asia Pageant. Another route to stardom was via the music industry. Stars like Sally Yeh, Anita Mui and Priscilla Chan were able to use their singing as a springboard to successful movie careers. Many of these glamorous pop idols were not slow to imitate the sexy antics of their Western counterparts, Madonna and Tina Turner.

In 1987, the first Chinese language edition of *Playboy* magazine appeared and was soon followed by *Penthouse.* These magazines featured mostly Chinese girls, including many spreads of local sex stars like Amy Yip. Censorship guidelines changed in the late 1980s. The issue that sparked off the changes was the banning of Taiwanese films that were considered politically sensitive because they were critical of mainland China. A press report questioned the government's right to ban these movies and a new Film Censorship Ordinance was introduced to normalise things. One of the results was the introduction, in 1988, of a film ratings system: Category I for general viewing, Category II for parental guidance and Category III for adults only (over eighteen).

Initially, the idea was to allow the screening of more contentious fare, especially prestigious foreign films like *The Last Temptation of Christ,* which would otherwise have suffered severe cuts. In practice, Category III has come to mean little more than sex and violence. The early effects of this were manifested in the huge success of classy Japanese sex movies like *Daydream.* Local producers tested the water with films that included *Jail House Eros* (starring Amy Yip), *Call Girls 88* (with Maggie Cheung) and *Caged Beauties.* Tsui Hark's 1987 production *A Chinese Ghost Story* capped a vogue for spooky tales using traditional Chinese themes. With the added dash of some Category III nudity this soon became a very popular genre. Sexy ghosts and Taoist priests, virgin scholars in love with snake women, seductive fox demons and naked nymphs were soon everywhere. Some of the films were quite close to the bone. 1990's *Ghostly Vixen,* for example, features Amy Yip as a demoness seeking immortality

through performing 100 blow jobs. The *Erotic Ghost Story* series (also starring Amy Yip) upped the ante by having three lascivious lovelies pursued by a priapic demon from the underworld.

The real breakthrough came with the 1991 production *Sex & Zen*. This classy period sex comedy was picked up by *Penthouse* magazine who featured several sexy colour spreads from the film and produced a limited edition hardcover book with stills and scenes specially 'recreated' for the benefit of one-handed readers.

The film is a version of the famous seventeenth century erotic classic *The Prayer Mat of Flesh*. The story had been filmed before, most recently in 1988 as *Yui Pui Tsuen*. However, the new explicitness of the nineties, along with the ample charms of actress Amy Yip and the sultry sexuality of Carrie Ng, made the 1991 film the definitive version. The original novel had a distinctly didactic purpose in its story of a horny but highly intelligent young guy who turns his back on the priesthood in order to bed as many beauties as his dick will allow. Said member not being up to the task, he visits a fearsome quack who fits him up with a new member composed of a dog's penis. Eventually, after much shagging and general merriment, our hero learns the error of his ways and becomes a monk.

Sex & Zen follows this blueprint pretty closely, its major innovation being the substitution of a horse's dick for the dog's dong of the original. By way of compensation (and probably for viewers who know the original story), a ragged hound appears during the surgery scene and runs off with our hero's severed penis between its jaws...

One of the highlights of the film is a lesbian encounter between two women and a flute, which they share in a most unconventional fashion.

Sex & Zen appeared at an opportune time. Fans worldwide were just waking up to the delights of the new wave Hong Kong action cinema. Echoes had been sounding for some years. Jackie Chan's blend of martial arts excellence and knockabout comedy had developed a healthy life on video in the English-speaking world. Some of his films had even made it to the big screen in Britain. Even so, most filmgoers still labelled anything from Hong Kong as 'kung fu' and resolutely old hat, with comically bad dubbing and, as British writer Rick Baker calls them, "oy, didn't you kill my brother?" plots. Then, in the second half of the 1980s, along came films like *A Better Tomorrow* and *The Killer*. Suddenly, charismatic actor Chow Yun Fat was God, director John Woo was his John the Baptist and now Amy Yip... well, to continue the metaphor, she certainly wasn't the Virgin Mary.

Sex & Zen was just what the growing audience for Hong Kong movies needed. A costume film without fighting, humour that actually made you laugh and, above all, sex — lots of it, and very exotic too. The glamorous Amy soon came to be the most prominent of the new Category III starlets. Prominent in more ways than one. Her 35" bust line (unusual in a country where flat chests are the rule) was the subject of much speculation. Lurid magazine stories, complete with tell-tale photographs, implied that she had undergone a silicone job. *She* magazine reports a 1995 story with the headline 'Taiwan Rumour: Broken Tits' telling of the accidental explosion of Amy's faulty implants. In a previous age it had been the daintiness of a Chinese woman's feet that made her an object of erotic interest. Now it was the size of her mammaries. TV game shows with 'guess the weight of the breast' contests began to appear. If the audience guessed correctly, the unfortunate woman had to strip off. Cosmetic surgeons came up with an operation that satisfied local women's desire for larger bosoms as well as their need to be a little discreet about it. Breast implants were supplied with valves attached. Thus equipped, the woman could gradually add saline solution to the bags, so that her breast size would be gradually enhanced rather than suddenly rocketing overnight.

In the same year as *Sex & Zen*, another seminal Category III movie appeared — the outrageous *Robotrix*. Again Amy Yip stars, this time with Taiwanese actress Hsu Hsiao Dan. This exotic looking beauty, who has more than a little of the great Claudette Colbert about her, is featured in the movie's most daring scene, where she is screwed senseless in a variety of positions by a very human looking android with a giant dick! Her past as a nude model must have stood her in good stead here. Or maybe it was her attempt to run for parliament in her native Taiwan with the slogan, 'Using breasts to fight against fists' that inspired the scene.

Robotrix also featured the Japanese actress Aoyama Chikako and was co-produced by the Tokyo based Shochiku company. Japanese actresses had appeared in several Hong Kong films over the years, at least as far back as 1978's *Shaolin Challenges Ninja*. Yukari Oshima and her fellow countrywoman Michiko Nishiwara were just two of a successful breed of actresses who came to the fore in the more liberal 1980s. Their appeal lay not only in their willingness to show some tit, but even more in their ability to kick some ass.

The film that is generally credited with starting this particular ball rolling was 1985's *Yes, Madam* (released under a

Left: *More* Sex & Zen.
Below: *The sultry Carrie Ng.*
Bottom: *Amy Yip gets it off her chest in* Robotrix.

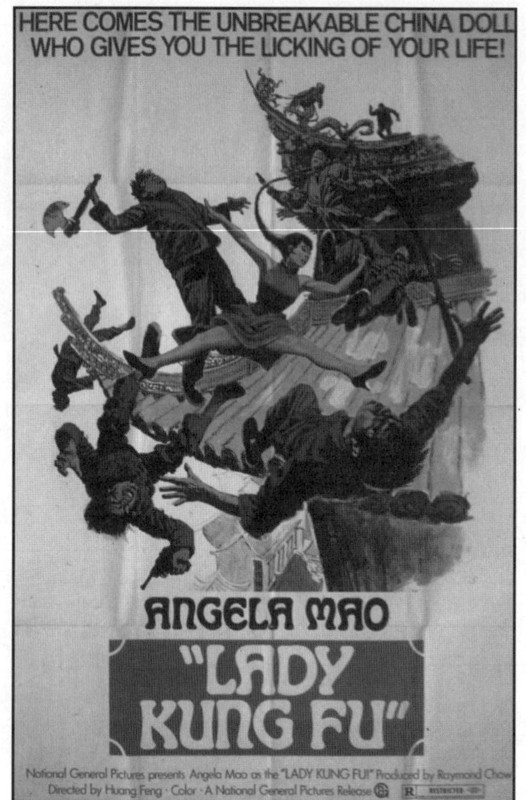

HERE COMES THE UNBREAKABLE CHINA DOLL
WHO GIVES YOU THE LICKING OF YOUR LIFE!
ANGELA MAO
"LADY
KUNG FU"
National General Pictures presents Angela Mao as the "LADY KUNG FU!" Produced by Raymond Chow
Directed by Huang Feng · Color · A National General Pictures Release

***Right:** Angela Mao, pioneer battling babe, kicks ass in* Lady Kung Fu.
***Below left:** Women take the lead in* Gigolo Club.
***Below right:** Chinese girls and guns in a calendar produced by an arms company.*

confusing variety of akas, including *In the Line of Duty*, *Police Assassins 2* and *Super Cops*). In this one, American martial artist Cynthia Rothrock made her film début along with former Miss Malaysia, Michelle Khan. However, the 1979 release *Deadly Angels* is an often overlooked precursor of the battling babes genre. This Shaw Brothers film features a couple of their hottest sex stars, Yum Yum Shaw and Dana, along with German import Evelyne Kraft (also in the *King Kong* rip-off *The Mighty Peking Man*). *Deadly Angels* is a lively romp about four girls recruited to infiltrate a diamond smuggling ring. A delirious training scene at the beginning shows the girls using all the accoutrements of their femininity to deadly effect. High-heeled shoes double as powerful catapults, handbags hide spiked brass balls and pearl earrings become exploding mini bombs.

Hong Kong film-makers have never been shy of adapting Western hits for the home market. Luc Besson's *Nikita* (aka *La Femme Nikita*) featured the feisty Anne Parillaud as an undercover assassin. Hong Kong millionaire Dickson Poon used it as the blueprint for *Black Cat*, starring his girlfriend Jade Leung. During the first twenty minutes of the movie, the lithe Jade is groped by would be rapists, beaten up by lesbian cops, stripped, hosed down, chained up and generally given a very hard time. Then, with the implantation of a micro chip in her brain and a gun that shoots bullets made of ice, she's turned loose to "do good for the Government."

In a line of descent from Western originals like *Charlie's Angels* came a host of movies such as *Angel*, *Beauty Investigator* and *Deadly Dream Woman*. If the sight of a beautiful girl with a gun has always been a turn-on in the West, the sight of a beautiful Chinese girl with a gun seems to have delighted both Eastern and Western audiences. When the mix is flavoured with some Category III spice and martial arts action you have a genre of film-making that the West really hasn't caught up with. Yet.

It's interesting to speculate why. Obviously the legacy of the sixties and seventies, with female action stars like Angela Mao and Cheng Pei Pei, has something to do with it. Hong Kong audiences were used to the idea of lady fighters. It's an odd paradox that in the West, where women are supposedly more emancipated, female roles in films are usually as victims. Of course, the real life of Hong Kong women is very different from the one presented by the movies. Relations between the sexes remain rigidly formalised. The dashing female sword fighters and lusty Miao tribeswomen of the martial arts novels had been attractive fantasy figures for readers of both sexes. In this never-never land men and women could vicariously live out a life of sexual openness and equality without fear of social stigma. In Hong Kong, right into the late eighties, cinema had the same powerful hold on the mass imagination. One of its primary purposes was the creation of wish-fulfilling fantasy worlds. *Deadly Dream Woman*, for example, while far from a classic, is full of insights into how Hong Kong swingers would like to see themselves.

The film begins with Nightingale and Swallow, two daughters of a former Triad boss, leaving their San Francisco home to visit Hong Kong, with dire warnings about the Neanderthal attitudes of the local men. Their first meeting with Jaguar Lui, a cocky gangster, seems to fulfil all their friends' worst fears. Late for a meeting, Lui struts into the room, looking Nightingale up and down. "Sorry I'm late," he growls. "I was just screwing a girl." He apologises for not shaking Nightingale's hand, saying that he didn't have time to wash after having had sex.

Later, when the girls go on a shopping trip, they conclude that "Hong Kong is a good place! Lots to buy here." "Wow!" says Chingmy Yau, staring at a passing car, "a Ferrari!"

For a while the sweet-faced Chingmy Yau became a Category III starlet to rival the delectable Amy Yip. Their differences however are palpable. Whereas Amy is definitely built for action, Chingmy is, if anything, too wholesome looking. However, sometimes her fresh-faced appeal has been used to distinct advantage. Under the tutelage of prolific director/writer/producer Wong Jing, Chingmy starred

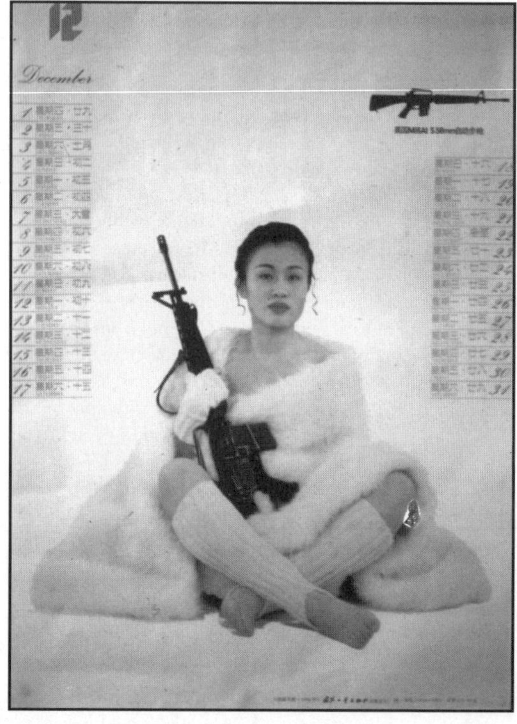

in the first of a series of films that seemed like attempts to revive the mid-seventies costume erotica of *Intimate Confessions of a Chinese Courtesan* and *The Story of Su-san.*

In *Lover of the Last Empress* she plays the notorious Tzu Hsi, the so-called Empress Dowager. This terrifying ex-concubine was the undisputed power behind the throne during one of China's most turbulent periods — the fifty years that ended with the crowning of the boy king, Pu Yi, the Last Emperor of Bertolucci's flaccid epic.

Wong Jing's sleazy history lesson includes all the sex and graphic action that earlier versions of the story had only hinted at. Chingmy Yau begins her rise to the top as a doe-eyed, inexperienced country girl. Her first night with the Emperor is far from a success. A virgin, she is unable to respond to his caresses and displeases him so much that he demands she give back his sperm. This is effected by having her poked in the kidneys with blunt sticks until the emperor's sticky essence pours back out of her (shown in graphic detail splashing down her legs). Returning to her room she finds that the other concubines have boiled her pet cat alive. The emperor's brother, Kung, who takes a fancy to the girl, puts her straight. "The palace is just like a battlefield," he tells her. "If you don't kill, you'll be killed."

Taking his advice to heart she spends a week with two whores, learning the secrets of "pussy power". This includes practising fellatio with a variety of false penises made of ice. In a week she learns what it would normally take three years to acquire. Armed with her new knowledge, she returns to the palace and makes the emperor her love slave. The rest is history. As the commentary informs us: "Those seven days made seventy years of social unrest."

Wong Jing continued the series with *Ancient Chinese Whorehouse* and *A Chinese Torture Chamber Story,* both starring the delightfully named Yung Hung.

The possibilities presented by the Category III label and the success of Western films like *The Silence of the Lambs* and *Basic Instinct* gave rise to a sub genre of cop and psycho

Left: Chingmy Yau, dressed to meet the Naked Killer.
Below left: *A little bit of* Insanity.
Below: *Your concubine awaits:* Profiles of Pleasure.

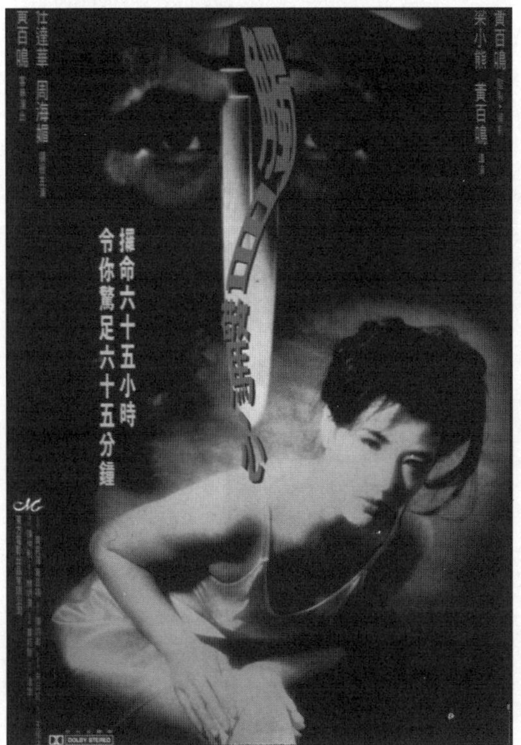

movies like *Midnight Angel, Fatal Love* and *Red to Kill. Naked Killer* is the best of this particular bunch. In fact it's one of the most enjoyable exploitation films of the nineties. The influence here is *Basic Instinct,* with its tale of an obsessed cop and a beautiful bisexual murderess. Chingmy Yau plays Kitty, a slim but feisty fighter for female rights whom we first encounter settling the score with a macho hairdresser. The cruel crimper is about to kick his pregnant girlfriend in the stomach until Kitty stabs him in the head. Later she teams up with the deadly Sister Cindy, a hired assassin who had admired her earlier handiwork. As the two of them murder their way through Hong Kong high society, obsessed cop Simon Yam follows close behind, never quite managing to link the two women to a spate of gruesome murders, which include a series of "castration killings". Things get even hotter for him when Princess, a cold-blooded lesbian killer and former protégée of Cindy turns up. Her orders are to put the older woman out of business, which she does by giving her a passionate good-bye kiss... with poisoned lipstick! The scene strongly echoes a similar one in the seventies classic *Intimate Confessions of a Chinese Courtesan.*

With highlights including an underwater lesbian seduction that turns into a vicious catfight, Chingmy Yau taking on two chained rapists in an underground dungeon and the beautiful Carrie Ng with her female slave, Baby, in tow, we're a long way from the old style heroines of 1960s films like *Dragon Gate Inn* and *Heads For Sale.*

The sex wave had begun in Hong Kong movies in the early seventies at the same time as a new style of horror movie had started to appear. The two genres overlapped and fed off each other. By the beginning of the nineties, with films like *Night Caller, Naked Killer* and *Robotrix,* it was sometimes difficult to see where one ended and the other began. Sex and horror have always been bedfellows in exploitation movies. In the commercial hothouse of Hong Kong, this union has given birth to many memorable and unique films. But first we have to define what we mean by horror... ■

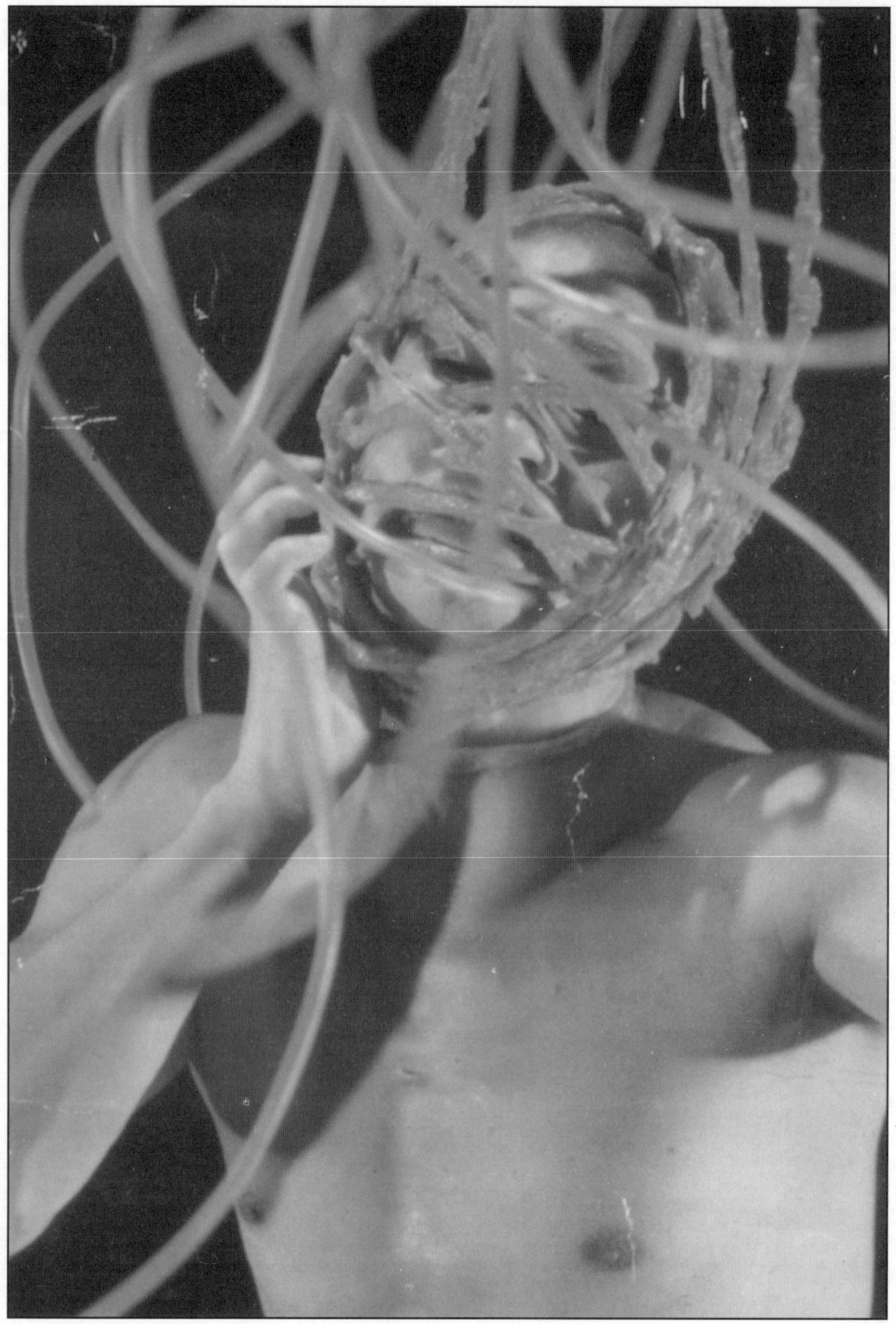

Ghosts Galore

It's a long-standing belief in the West that Easterners like their entertainment gruesome. Partly this stems from familiar colonial fears about 'bloodthirsty foreign devils'. Partly it's based on fact. When it comes to horror, they do seem to prefer things more visceral. Look, for example, at the *penanggalan* — flying head witches — that pop up in films from Indonesia, Thailand, Hong Kong and Malaysia. These are literally what their name suggests: flying heads, zooming through the air with their guts streaming out behind them. Their favourite food is the rotting flesh of corpses or, as a special treat, the blood of newborn babies. Also inspired by the same kinds of folk tales were films like the Shaw Brothers' *Black Magic* duo from the mid-seventies, with their unflinching concentration on bodily deformity, decay and corruption.

This 'horrible' style of Hong Kong horror announces its intentions right from the start. Just as the surrealist classic *Un chien andalou* begins with an eye being sliced with a scalpel, many Hong Kong horror movies also begin with something being cut open. A knife slits a crocodile's belly; pus oozes through cracks in skin; some poor unfortunate vomits up several pints of black bile in unflinching close up; hosts of worms wriggle from open wounds, while boils, ulcers and contusions bubble and fester. The horror here is not fear of the unknown but fear of bodily corruption and death. The difference with Western horror is that whereas we tend only to suggest this, in the East they concentrate on it with loving glee.

This kind of thing first made its mark in Hong Kong films in the 1970s. Before that the supernatural was found in gentle fantasies featuring fox spirits, or wandering scholars who fell in love with ghosts. But even these were a relative rarity. Early Chinese cinema was heavily influenced by Western models. Sword fighting movies were indebted as much to the swashbuckling films of Douglas Fairbanks as to readings of Chinese history. Later influences were Hollywood Westerns and Italian historical spectacles. Inevitably, the first Chinese horror movies also drew on Western hits. The pioneer of the genre is Maxu Weibang, the Chinese James Whale. His 1937 film *Song at Midnight* was a version of the Lon Chaney classic, *The Phantom of the Opera*. Maxu's film was a baroque extravaganza, about a notorious actor/director who falls foul of a rich merchant in Shanghai. He has acid thrown in his face by hired thugs when he attempts to elope with the merchant's already betrothed daughter. Wearing a thick cloak to disguise his scars, the man haunts the shell of his burned out theatre, singing, at midnight, the special song he has composed for his lost love.

The film's success led in 1941 to a sequel, in which the disfigured composer is unfortunate enough to be turned into a sort of living skeleton by a Frankenstein-style mad professor. Something of a horror standard in Chinese cinema, *Song at Midnight* has been remade several times. The most famous version was the 1961 Hong Kong production *Midnightmare*, directed by Yuan Quifeng. Ronnie Yu's 1995 film *The Phantom Lover* was another distant relative of the Maxu Weibang classic. Yu's good-looking film, shot on location in Beijing, is essentially a vehicle for Hong Kong heart-throb Leslie Cheung (who was its producer) and consequently brings to the fore a strain of sentimentality only glimpsed in the original film.

Song at Midnight was not a story of the supernatural. Traditionally, the rationalist Confucian philosophy had rejected any notion of ghosts and spirits as supernatural beings. Their appearance nearly always had a mundane explanation. In the 1952 film *Uproar in Guang Changlong*, based on a popular Cantonese opera, the ghost of a dead prostitute returns to wreak vengeance on those who had done her wrong. It transpires that the 'ghost' is very much alive. The 1957 film *Nightly Cry of the Ghost* has a similar premise, with a girl pretending to be dead to scare off her murderous relatives.

It was through adaptations of classical Chinese literature that supernatural beings and a genuine sense of the

***Opposite:** A sticky moment from* The Boxer's Omen.

Below: Song at Midnight, *a Chinese horror classic from 1937.*

Above: *Horror meets sex in* The Magic Curse.
Right: Revenge of the Corpse.

fantastic began to appear in Hong Kong films. The stories of Pu Songling were a treasure trove for Chinese ghost stories and one that is still being plundered. Pu was a seventeenth century scholar who spent much of his life collecting and adapting traditional tales, as well as composing his own variations on them. The tales are mostly fairly short, sometimes less than a page, but are packed full of little details about contemporary life and manners, as well as some wonderful superstitions and bizarre events. Foxes who turn into beautiful women, demons who suck blood through the soles of people's feet, undersea kingdoms and wandering Taoist priests fill the pages of Pu Songling.

Since the 1950s many films have used his stories as a basis. The 1954 film *Love with a Ghost* and the 1959 production *Enchanting Shadows* are both versions of the same tale, *The Magic Sword.* A nervous young student holes up for the night in an abandoned temple where he meets a seductive female. It turns out she is a ghost, in thrall to an evil demon who uses her to trap new victims. With the help of an eccentric Taoist priest, the student defeats the monster and frees the ghost girl from her curse by burying her bones. If the story sounds familiar, it's because it was also used as the basis for the 1987 hit *A Chinese Ghost Story*, one of the most popular Hong Kong films of the eighties.

Until the 1970s, the tales of Pu Songling were the major source of Chinese fantastique films. The other strand, the gory gross out, was a much more recent innovation. One of the first examples of this tendency to go for the throat was the 1968 production *Leech Girl.* Like many subsequent Hong Kong horrors, the story is set in South East Asia, specifically Thailand. It's a sort of *Jungle Book* fantasy featuring an orphan girl brought up amongst elephants. Things start to turn nasty when a local magician captures the nature girl, Aminah. Egged on by a jealous woman who is in love with Aminah's boyfriend, the magician forces her to eat a load of squirmy leeches. Aminah begins to break out in creepy crawlies. Chained up in the magician's cave, she goes mad. As the creatures bore their way through her skin, she plucks them out and swallows them back down again. Her boyfriend, the son of the local headman, attempts to save her and sets the elephants free to destroy the villagers who are planning to sacrifice Aminah.

Films like *Leech Girl* and the Japanese co-production *The Ghost's Revenge* were one-offs. Horror didn't really take hold in Hong Kong until the mid-1970s. Two events sparked it off. One was the world-wide success of *The Exorcist*, the other was the arrival in the Colony of the British company Hammer.

Looking for a way to breath new life into their long-running, but flagging, Dracula series, Hammer boss Michael Carreras struck a deal with the Shaw Brothers. The idea was to combine Hammer-style horror with the then popular kung fu film. The result, *The Legend of the 7 Golden Vampires*, went into production at the Shaw's Movietown studios in 1974. The film was a real mixed bag. Hammer stalwart Roy Ward Baker directed the horror and dialogue scenes, into which were slotted martial arts sequences choreographed by Chang Cheh's fight specialist, Liu Chia Liang. The result was a Hammer horror with kung fu grafted on. There was no real attempt to use indigenous Eastern elements.

With the arrival of Hammer, interest in horror was at an all-time high in the local film-making community. Before the Shaws could begin to apply the lessons they had learned on *Legend of the 7 Golden Vampires*, the independent Fong Ming company, run by actor Yang Chun, went into production on *Blood Reincarnation*, an omnibus film consisting of three unrelated stories. *Blood Reincarnation*'s three episodes all deal with vengeance from beyond the grave. In the first story, a newborn baby is possessed by the spirit of a dead woman seeking revenge on the child's father. The second episode features a mischievous water spirit and the third tells of an acupuncturist executed for a crime he didn't commit. The blood reincarnation spell brings him back to life for seven days, during which time he settles the score with the man who framed him.

The first of the Shaw Brothers' self-produced horrors following their involvement with Hammer was the 1975 production *Black Magic.* The film's director was the prolific Ho Meng-Hua, who had made his first film in 1957. He was also

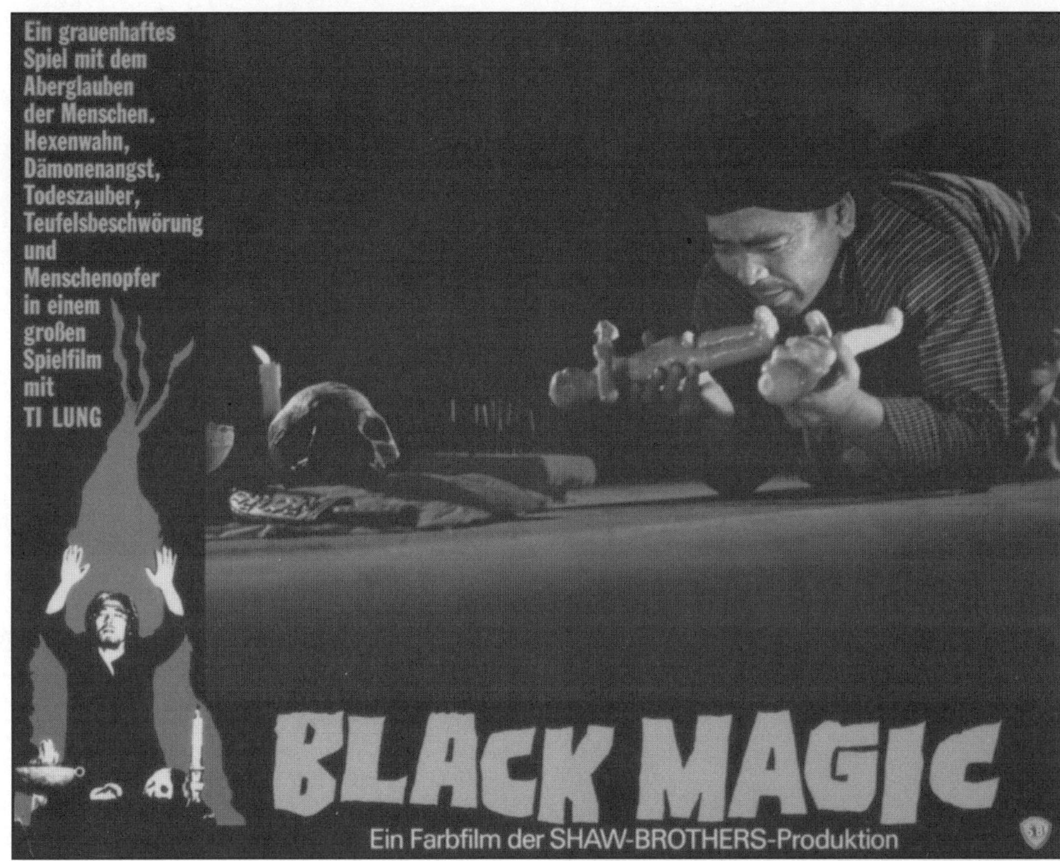

Ein grauenhaftes
Spiel mit dem
Aberglauben
der Menschen.
Hexenwahn,
Dämonenangst,
Todeszauber,
Teufelsbeschwörung
und
Menschenopfer
in einem
großen
Spielfilm
mit
TI LUNG
BLACK MAGIC
Ein Farbfilm der SHAW-BROTHERS-Produktion

Left: Black Magic: *a 'horrible horror' classic from Shaw Brothers.*
Below left: *Not all Shaw Brothers films featured martial arts. Here's their* King Kong *copy* The Mighty Peking Man *from 1977.*

responsible for the wacky *Flying Guillotine* in 1975, the monster movie *Oily Maniac* in 1976 and the Shaw's *King Kong* rip-off *The Mighty Peking Man* in 1977. Eschewing both the gentle atmospherics of Pu Songling and the Western bloodsuckers of Hammer, Ho Meng-Hua's film is a rip-roaring old-fashioned gore fest. A sort of Grand Guignol 'penny dreadful' with little plot but plenty of gruesome visuals.

Sexy widow Mrs Chow (or Miss Lo, as she insists on being called) has got the hots for a young engineer, Wei Tsu-lo. Unfortunately, he's happily engaged and doesn't want to know. Meanwhile playboy Romeo (Lo Lieh) is getting all worked up over Miss Lo. The little vixen spurns his advances and even smashes up his car when she gets really mad (a good performance here from the pouting Lily Li). Romeo takes the advice of an old friend and goes up into the hills to consult with a black magician, Fang. The magician puts a hex on Miss Lo and pretty soon she and Romeo are at it hammer and tongs. Of course, being a suspicious sort the magician assumed that he was not going to get paid for his services and so made a spell that would only last for one night.

The next morning, after she's come to her senses and thrown him out of bed, a shamefaced Romeo confesses to Miss Lo. Although at first furious, she soon realises that she could use the magician's powers to snare Wei. Unfortunately, the magician himself develops a crush on the svelte Miss Lo and cooks up his own potion to get at her creamy white body.

In this and subsequent black magic films, nothing is quite what it seems. Singapore, where the film was shot, looks like a fast-moving, Western-style city of banks, department stores and skyscrapers, but beneath that modern façade the old beliefs are still strong. Nobody can be trusted. The black magician is a wily fox, always looking for ways to catch new victims. Just shaking hands with him is enough.

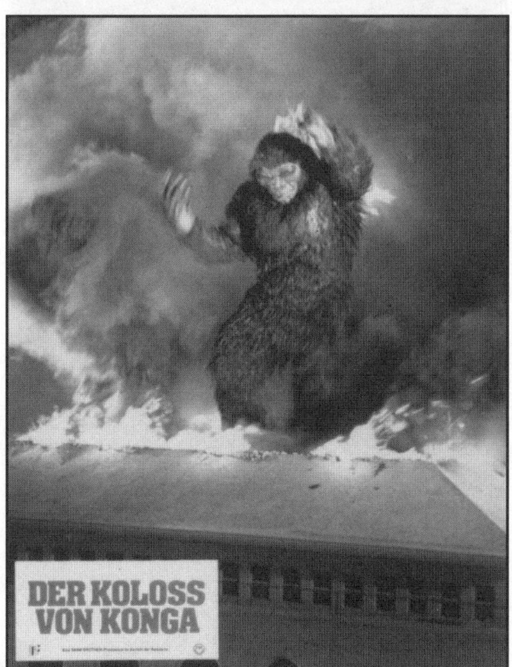

All he needs is a tiny drop of your blood and some of your hair and he can work up a potion to enslave your soul.

The following year came *Black Magic 2* (also released as *Revenge of the Zombies*). The film sets out its bizarre agenda right from the start. In a downtown Singapore night-club a man (a pimp?) leads one of his girls out of the door, shiftily eyeing the men who are eyeing her. He takes her back to his place — a spooky mock Gothic mansion. Once inside, he

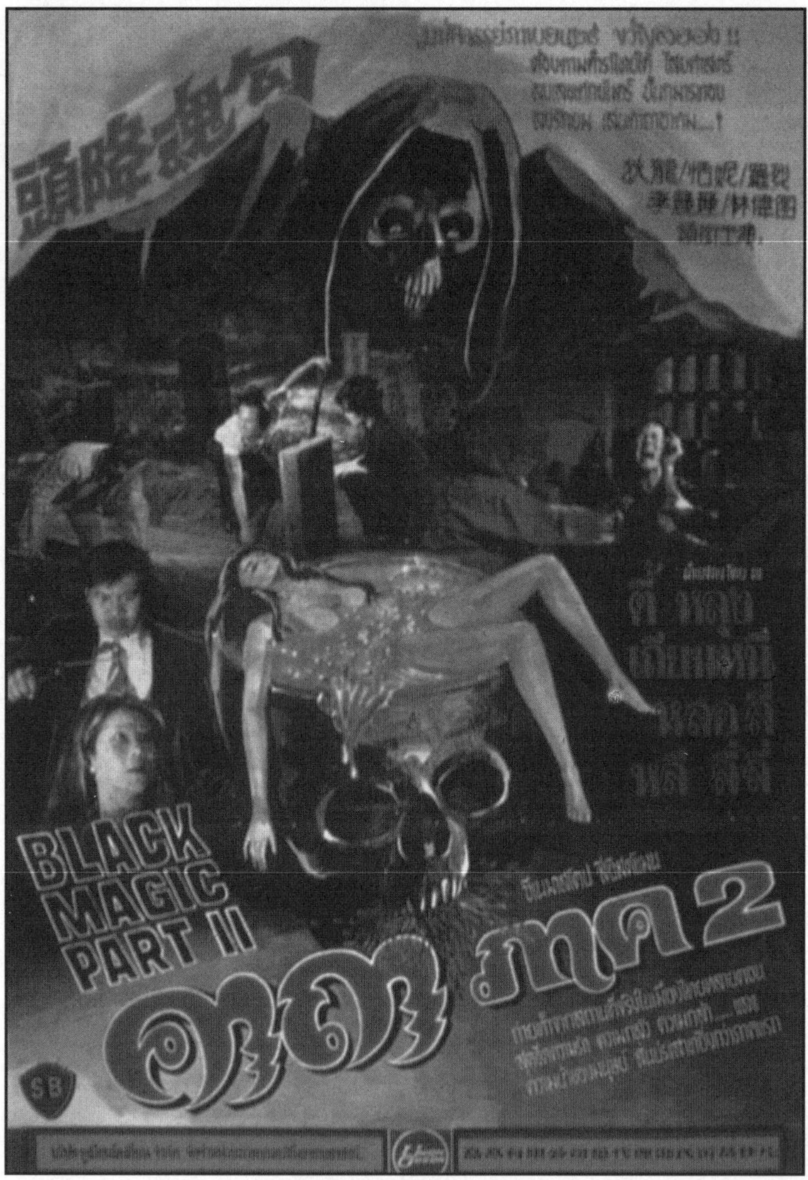

***Above:** Thai poster for the popular* Black Magic 2.

orders her to strip. She obeys as though in a trance. He pulls her head back and parts the hair on top. Then he takes a pair of pliers... and extracts a monster six inch nail from her skull. It's like pulling the plug from a blow-up doll. Almost at once she starts to shrink, her face turning into that of a withered old hag.

The man (Lo Lieh again) is Kang Chang, a black magician. The film details his encounter with a couple of local doctors who are investigating outbreaks of mysterious illnesses in the city. One of the doctors believes these can only be attributed to black magic.

Kang Chang, it transpires, is several centuries old. To keep himself young he needs to drink human milk every day. How he obtains this milk is shown in graphic fashion when he kidnaps Margaret, the wife of one of the doctors. He takes her to his lair where he keeps a team of the blow-up zombies. These are activated, as we saw at the beginning, by hammering a huge nail into the top of their skulls (a device also used in later films like *Return of the Demon* and *Evil Black Magic*). Kang feeds Margaret a potion consisting of, amongst other things, her own pubic hair. When she drinks it, he assures her, she will be able to provide him with lots of milk. Hardly surprising, as the effect of the potion is to make her pregnant almost overnight. Her husband rushes her straight to hospital, where he performs a swift caesarean. From her womb he extracts a horrifying mass of blood, bone and gristle. "A monster!" cries the surgeon, rather unnecessarily, as he holds it aloft.

Black Magic 2 is every bit as gory and gross as the first film. Huge bubbling boils, giant ulcers ("People round here call them human faces," says one of the doctors. "You can see why."), wiggly worms crawling under the skin, people vomiting up snakes — it's all here. Like its predecessor, the film underlines the power of magic by making clear its origins in the country — a place that most city dwellers would like to see as primitive and dangerous.

The obvious commercial inspiration for both films was the enormous success of *The Exorcist.* Its basic format — good magician versus bad magic with lots of gruesome special effects — is repeated pretty much as a pattern in both films. The idea of the curse coming from afar is also something that these films echo. But here the notion of 'afar' is much more localised. The *Black Magic* films had prologues filmed in Thailand, with the bulk of each being shot in Singapore. For Hong Kongers, the vast hinterland of South East Asia — Thailand, Borneo, Malaysia — was every bit as exotic as *The Exorcist*'s Middle East. Furthermore, horror films were extremely popular in those countries. More so than in Hong Kong itself. The Shaws controlled distribution in most of South East Asia and so it made sound economic sense to set the films there for local appeal, with an added frisson of exoticism for the folks who watched them 'back home'.

The most satisfying aspect of the Shaw Brothers' movies is the wealth of physical detail that they contain and the bizarre rituals the participants have to engage in. Both the content and the shooting style of these scenes are reminiscent of deadly serious ethnographic documentaries. In *Black Magic,* Miss Lo wants the magician to cast a love spell that will make the young engineer, Wei, her slave. The magician gives her some human teeth and a severed finger to hide under Wei's bed. When they start to rot, he tells her, the spell will begin to work. Next they visit a strange graveyard where all the plots are covered with umbrellas. The magician digs up one of the fresh corpses — a young girl. He lights a candle and heats up the corpse's chin, collecting the juices that flow. Then he orders Miss Lo to strip off and extracts some of her breast milk (human milk seems to be a powerful ingredient in many Hong Kong spells). The resulting concoction is given to Wei to drink. It makes everyone except Miss Lo look hideously ugly. Naturally, Wei falls in love with her at once.

Worms and squirmy things feature in both these movies. In *Black Magic 2,* to counteract the hex Kang Chang has put on one of the doctors, the medic has to eat a concoction made out of centipedes. These are not the dainty little creatures we get in the West — they're at least four inches long. However, the young doc willingly swallows them down, chopped up in a milky broth.

The ultimate use of these giant crawly beasties comes in the 1981 film *Centipede Horror.* Kay, a young girl from a rich Hong Kong business family, goes on holiday to Singapore. Her brother tries to stop her, reminding Kay that their mother had strictly forbidden them to ever set foot in South East Asia. On a trip in the forest, Kay is bitten by a centipede while taking a pee behind a bush. She falls ill very quickly, her skin begins to crack and fester, and after a few days in hospital she dies, with insects crawling out of the giant boils on her skin. Her brother, Pak, comes to Singapore to sort out the mystery. Together with Chee, a girlfriend from his days as a student in Canada, he tracks down a local magician who tells them that his sister was a victim of the centipede spell: "One of the most powerful spells in South East Asia." Someone, it seems, is using them to exact revenge for a crime committed fifty years before by their grandfather.

Centipede Horror begins, rather intriguingly, like an Asian *Don't Look Now*. Pak is constantly being surprised by the fleeting vision of a red-clad child disappearing round a corner or walking past a window. Pretty soon though, the film dispenses with all subtleties and gets right down to business. There are lots of *Black Magic*-style exorcisms and ritual spell castings. One of the film's many magicians digs up the corpses of dead children, heats up their chins (as in *Black Magic 2*) and uses the resultant oil to animate two invisible dolls that he calls Big Pea and Little Pea. A new trick is the sound spell. To enact this one, all the wily magician has to do is to hide in the dark and call out the name of his intended victim. If the person answers, they are then under the magician's power.

A sound spell is used to trap Chee into seducing Pak. While she drags him back to her flat, the evil magician is amassing thousands of giant centipedes that then invade the lovers' bedroom. That would be a good enough climax to most films, but there's worse to come. Pak manages to defeat the magician and wards off the spell by using a magic amulet that belonged to his grandfather. He tries to arouse Chee, who appears to be unconscious. Suddenly she opens her eyes and begins to retch. Out of her mouth drop at least half a dozen huge, writhing centipedes. These monsters are almost six inches long and are definitely alive. No special effects here. The turd gobbling scene that closes John Waters' *Pink Flamingos* seems mild next to this truly grotesque sight.

Shaw Brothers star Lo Lieh put his experience in horror movies to good effect in *The Black Magic with Buddha* (1983), one of the few films he directed himself. This cheap and cheerful production begins deep in the jungles of Papua New Guinea. Two men open up a stone tomb and steal the brain from an ancient mummy. One of them, Ben, takes the brain back to Bangkok. He plans to use its magic powers to make him a millionaire so he can marry his rich girlfriend. He sets up a little altar around the brain and begins to pray to it. Pretty soon Ben's on his way to accumulating a hefty fortune, as anyone who crosses his path is bumped off. His snooty sister falls to her death through a plate glass window and his girlfriend's brother is attacked in his bath by dozens of bloodthirsty brains, that suck at him like hungry leeches.

The Black Magic with Buddha is a real old-fashioned monster movie cheapie. Its production values (or lack of them) make it more like an Indian film than the usual slick Hong Kong effort. Highlights include a fridge full of pulsating brains and a scene where Ben tries to destroy the beastly lump of grey matter. As he bangs at it with a spade, it slithers down the road away from him like a snail on speed.

Most of the black magic and Asian spell movies of the early eighties were contemporary films. However, Shaw Brothers had invested too much in their period sets and intricate costumes not to put them to use in the horror genre. The ubiquitous Lo Lieh starred in the 1982 production *The Human Skin Lanterns*. This period tale of revenge and cruelty has a lightness of touch and displays such delight in its sadistic set pieces that it's closer to Japanese softcore movies from the 1970s than kung fu films of the eighties.

Two businessmen, Tan and Lung, are rivals in just about everything. Tan is to marry Lung's former fiancée and taunts him with a beautiful lantern, which is sure to win the upcoming lantern contest. Furious, Lung visits a former adversary of his, a swordsman, who is now down on his luck and makes lanterns for a living. The lantern-maker, Chao Chun-fang (played by Lo Lieh), agrees to create an artefact that will beat Tan's in the contest. What he doesn't explain is how he's going to make it. We soon find out. A hideous masked demon covered in orange fur breaks into the bedroom of Tan's fiancée and carries her off to its lair in an old water-mill. The demon turns out to be the lantern-maker in disguise. He ties the woman up and taunts her while she tries to seduce him into setting her free. His response is to take a sharpened knife and peel off her tissue-thin epidermis. This is the material he uses to construct his lanterns.

Next he abducts the woman's sister while she is out hunting with a dainty bow and arrow. He scoops her up in a big black bag and drags her back to the mill. He ties her up and takes great delight in describing how he intends to peel her — by pouring molten silver over her tender skin.

The monster's final victim is Lung's wife. As he prepares to skin her, sharpening his blade on a blood-covered stone, Chao Chun-fang explains that he accepted Lung's challenge as a way of causing trouble between him and Tan. His motive is revenge for the wrong Lung did him years before, when he scarred his face in a fight and cheated him in love. Then, in one mighty motion, he rips the delicate skin from the woman's back.

Now the lanterns are complete and the crazed swordsman gazes admiringly at their beauty. They shimmer eerily, each one seeming to contain a miniature replica of the person whose skin they are constructed from.

Human Skin Lanterns features several nude scenes and at least the suggestion of kinky sex. The arrival of the horror film in Hong Kong in the seventies coincided with a more explicit depiction of sex in locally produced movies. Several films explored the connection between the two in a uniquely Hong Kong fashion. Two of the best examples straddle the decade; one in 1973 and the other in 1979. The first, *Killer Snakes*, was a Shaw Brothers production and one of their darkest ever films. Although inspired by the Hollywood hit *Willard*, *Killer Snakes* entirely lacks the sentimentality of the American film. In its depiction of urban underbelly poverty and sexual frustration leading to violence, *Killer Snakes* is classic 'video nasty' territory, in the same league as Abel Ferrara's notorious *The Driller Killer* or William Lustig's *Maniac*.

The director of *Killer Snakes* was the thirty-seven-year-old Gui Zhihong, who had worked as assistant to the legendary Chang Cheh. He was well suited to the sleazy style of the film, having earlier made the notorious women-in-prison epic *Bamboo House of Dolls*. He would go on to become the Shaws' most experienced makers of visceral horror movies in the 1980s with films like *Hex*, *Bewitched* and *The Boxer's Omen*.

Killer Snakes is a downbeat look at life in the back alleys of Hong Kong. No modern skyscrapers and glistening shopping malls here. The film begins with a flashback. A close-up of a pair of moist lips fills the screen. To the sound of a cracking whip, a woman's strident voice demands to be beaten. "Harder! Hit me again!" she cries. A young boy glances disapprovingly away and reaches into a nearby box from which he takes a snake. Tenderly, he strokes the back of its head.

The boy grows up to be Chi Ho, a nervous, stuttering teenager living in a hovel in one of the poorest parts of Hong Kong. Unable to communicate properly or to understand his own emotions, he's shown as edgy, frustrated and violent. His first reaction when feeling confused is to start smashing things up. The walls of his hovel are covered with

Below: *The bizarre* The Human Skin Lanterns.

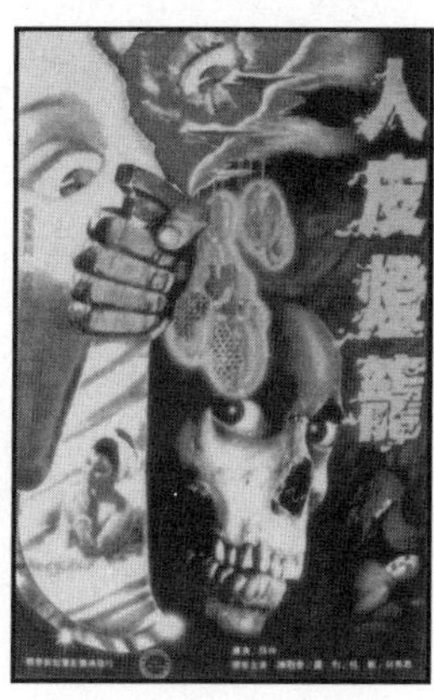

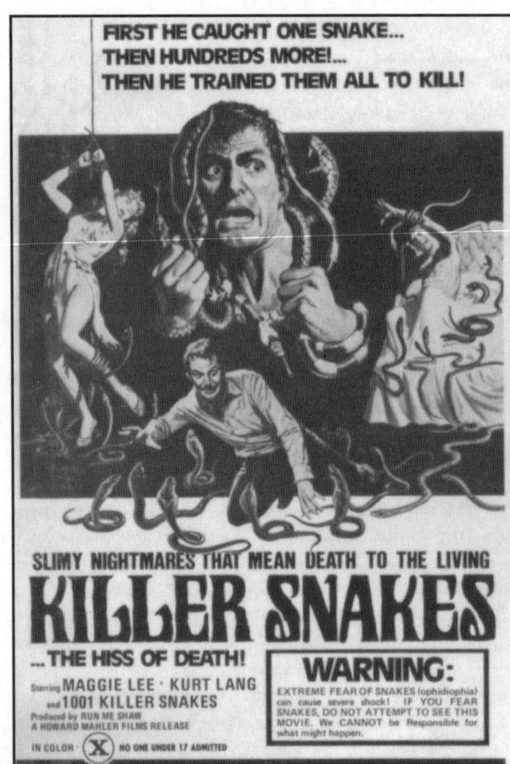

Left and far left: Snakes are a common feature of Hong Kong horror films. Here's Killer Snakes *from 1973 and* Calamity of Snakes *from 1986.*

pictures torn from Japanese bondage magazines; images of torture and submission. The only girl he can communicate with is a local stallholder. One day she comes to his hovel and finds him masturbating, after which he can hardly bear to look at her.

Next door to Chi Ho's hovel is a shop where local toughs go to drink a bizarre concoction made from snakes' gall bladders. Chi Ho rescues the dying snakes, stitches them up and cares for them. They become his only friends.

One day he delivers food to a sordid brothel, where the pimps and girls humiliate and eventually rob him. Frustrated after being stood up on a date with the stallholder, he visits the brothel again as a customer. This time he takes his snake with him. When the pimps try to rob him, he sets the snake on them. They run away terrified, leaving the prostitute behind. Chi Ho drags her back to his hovel and ties her up before letting his pets loose on her. A shot of one of the creatures crawling across the floor and between the girl's thighs leaves very little to the imagination.

"I must get more snakes! Get more snakes! Get more snakes!" the boy cries as he breaks through the wall into the snake shop next door.

The climax to the film comes when Chi Ho's stallholder friend is tricked into prostitution by a local madam. The distraught boy kidnaps the madam and tortures her with his menagerie. To the snakes have now been added some giant salamanders, which march menacingly towards the roped up woman as the boy watches excitedly.

The use of the snake as a penis symbol is a common device in legends and literature. One of the queasiest explorations of this link between slithery reptiles and the male sex organ comes in the 1979 film *Lewd Lizard.*

This joyously trashy piece of nonsense tells the story of David, a young student who returns to Hong Kong to marry his childhood sweetheart, Sun Shun. Unfortunately she has already become hitched to a local gangster, Chan. Oblivious to her claims that she did it to settle a debt her dead father had run up, David vows revenge. A series of bizarre tableaux show his fantasies of strangling and chopping up his ex-girlfriend. Instead, he settles on a much more devious plan of action, one that will put to good use the chemistry studies he had been engaged in at university.

We see him wandering by the sea-shore collecting dozens of tiny lizards. A lurid pin-up on his wall seems to give him inspiration and he marches off to hire a sluttish prostitute. However, sex is the last thing on his mind. All he seems interested in is her used panties, which he sniffs thoughtfully before running off with them. But he needs more, and a series of scenes shows him panty gathering. He steals them through bedroom windows, using a long pole, and snatches them from changing rooms on the beach while their owners are off swimming.

What, we wonder, can he be up to...?

Back in his ersatz lab he extracts both snake and toad venom. This he injects into his little lizards, turning them into raving mini Godzillas. Next he takes his prized panty collection and boils it up into a kind of knicker stew. This also is injected into the lizards. Now we see what he's about. He releases one of the little demons and it races across the table top, burying its head in a well placed pair of panties.

Kitted out with lizards in large test tubes, David now stalks the streets, tracking down the women he believes have wronged him. First stop is the pouting bar girl who set up Sun Shun with the noxious Chan. She thinks she's in for a night of passion with the handsome student and disrobes quickly. Brandishing his giant test tube, David releases the lizards and watches as they race straight to the crotch, hot on the trail of panty odour. The girl writhes, first in ecstasy, then in agony, as the little blighters do their work. Driven over the edge by the sight, David goes on the rampage with his little tubes of "worms", seeking out female victims on whom to revenge his fiancée's two-timing.

Lewd Lizard is one of those films where women always seem to be in the bath or taking a shower — fairly typical for

Hong Kong sex films from the period. Sure enough, when David eventually tracks down Sun Shun she's in the tub. However, it's a trap. The cops are waiting for him and there's a sad showdown on the sea-shore where David finally accepts his guilt — but not before opening his coat to reveal the lizard-filled tubes clipped inside his jacket like a row of fountain pens.

Slithery beasties like lizards and centipedes have featured in a large number of Southern hemisphere horror movies. However, the reptile that gets the very worst press is definitely the snake and it's their sexual connotations that seem to be most resonant. The idea of snakes crawling into orifices is combined with possession and even stranger myths in the 1977 costume drama *Witch with Flying Head*, one of the wildest Hong Kong horrors of the decade.

The film begins peacefully enough, with three dutiful daughters going to pray in a local temple. Suddenly we see a snake slithering over the roof tiles. It turns into a man who eyes the girls lasciviously. A snake pops out of his mouth and crawls into the temple. It wriggles under the skirts of one of the kneeling maidens. As she screams out in horror we see a shot of the snake actually crawling through her innards.

The night watch are patrolling the town. An unbelievable sight hoves into view. The men lift their paper lanterns to get a better look. Suspended in mid air is a woman's head with huge fangs protruding from her lower jaw. Even more bizarre is the fact that her guts are still hanging out of her neck. The men scatter and the head gives chase. It catches up with one of them and sinks its fangs into his neck. Soon we see blood pumping through the creature's suspended entrails.

The head floats off and drifts in through an open window. A headless body is awaiting its return, jumping up and down and flapping its arms impatiently. Like an airship docking, the head positions itself over the open neck and slowly lowers itself down. Now we see that the terrible creature is actually the young girl from the temple, the one possessed by the snake. She wakes up with a start and is horrified to feel the blood still dribbling down her chin. Buddhist priests and a wandering Taoist are powerless to overcome the curse. The magic is too strong for them.

The film's climax is an amazing battle between the flying head and the snake man. There are some genuinely terrifying scenes of the head, its eyes wild with fury, its mouth and cheeks spattered with blood, chasing after the snake man. At one point it spits out a great ball of squirmy centipedes into his face.

During the seventies, horror had been an occasional and exotic deviation from the norm. Its arrival (in 1974) and its gradual fading out (in 1977) spanned a period of change and uncertainty in Hong Kong. The economy was under threat, and wide scale political corruption was being exposed. It wasn't until the mid-1980s that there was a real horror boom in Hong Kong. Again this was against a background of political and cultural flux. Talks between the British government and Peking concerning the handing back of the Colony to mainland control commenced in 1982. The attention of many Hong Kongers was suddenly fixed once again on the past, on what they knew of China, and on an uncertain future. As critic Sek Kei wrote: 'Getting to know China is, at the same time, a pleasurable and frightening experience.'

The early 1980s was also a time of change for the Hong Kong film industry. Many of the film-makers who had helped to create the first boom of martial arts movies in the 1960s had been *émigrés* from mainland China, like most of the ordinary citizens who had settled in the area following the communist take-over. The martial arts films made under the aegis of companies like Shaw Brothers, Cathay and Golden Harvest were mostly set in the past, in a mythical, all purpose China of the mind. Few of these films reflected current social realities. As the children of the 1950s immigrants came of age in the 1970s they began to look around them and wanted entertainment that reflected the world they knew, the Hong Kong they lived and worked in.

Television during this period was enjoying a boom. Broadcast services had only begun in the late 1960s and were still a relatively novelty. Whereas it was difficult for young film-makers to get a foothold in the cinema industry, TV companies were hungry for fresh talent. A generation of young film-makers began to find their feet in this new medium. Among this so-called new wave were several who went on to become important players in the eighties. Among them Ronnie Yu, Ann Hui and, most influential of all, Tsui Hark.

The first to make the move into features was Ann Hui. Her 1979 film *The Secret* was a very low-budget murder mystery with *gialli* trimmings, in some ways reminiscent of Nic Roeg's *Don't Look Now*. The ending was a particular shocker, featuring a caesarean section performed with a meat-cleaver. Hui's next film was something of a change of pace. *The*

***Below:** Thai poster for* Witch with Flying Head.

Spooky Bunch was a comedy about a theatre company stranded on an island where they are haunted by ghosts from China's imperial past. One unexpected source the film drew on was Polanski's *Dance of the Vampires* (aka *The Fearless Vampire Killers*).

In fact, Polanski's film was an influence on several of the new wave film-makers and consequently on the development of horror in Hong Kong cinema of the eighties. Tsui Hark remembers being at a screening of *Dance of the Vampires* in the late seventies where he met Ann Hui. They discovered that they were both working on comedy/horror projects at the time and both were using Polanski's film as a model.

The Polanski connection throws a lot of light on Tsui Hark's early work. Like *Dance of the Vampires,* his films demonstrate an anarchic sense of humour as well as a revisionist attitude to established cinematic myths. The relationship between the wise master and his bumbling student in *Dance of the Vampires* is also a staple of seventies martial arts films, one that was adopted wholesale by the mid-eighties horror comedies. But now we're jumping ahead of ourselves...

Hark was born in Vietnam and studied film in Texas. He returned to Hong Kong in the mid-1970s and soon found work in the burgeoning television industry. Unlike Ann Hui, whose first television successes were with gritty, realistic works, Hark took the other route, into stylised fantasy. *The Gold Dagger Romance,* his first big hit, was a martial arts series based on a work by the popular writer Gu Long.

The programme was a smash and Hark soon found a producer for his first feature. *The Butterfly Murders,* released in 1979, drew on many different sources, including Gu Long's novella *The Vampire Maid.*

The film is structured like a detective story, specifically the *Ten Little Indians* model so dear to Agatha Christie, where a disparate group of characters is drawn together to an old house to hear the reading of a will. Hark's film is set in the distant past of China during a period of conflict amongst warring clans. Two rival groups meet in Shum castle. Their purpose is to uncover the mystery surrounding the apparent death of its inhabitants from killer butterflies. A wandering scribe, by his own admission an outsider with no martial arts skills, eventually discovers the truth. The film reveals its story in a very fractured style, with all the apparent killings occurring in flashbacks or through third-hand reports. Are there really killer butterflies abroad or is something else behind all the death and destruction?

The style of *The Butterfly Murders* marks it out immediately from the mainstream martial arts films of the sixties and seventies. It looks more Japanese than Chinese, with highly stylised widescreen framing and use of unfamiliar camera angles. Its refusal to follow a linear track and a wilful disregard for the conventions of story-telling (there's no real hero, for example) mark it out at once as the work of an iconoclast. Much of this was down to Hark's experience in mid-seventies Hong Kong television which, as Tony Rayns reports, 'included some of the most formally and thematically innovative television in the world.'

Tsui Hark's next film, this time set in the Republican years of the 1910s, was *We Are Going to Eat You.* As its title suggests, it's a film about cannibalism, but told in such a fast, furious and witty way that it entirely avoids the plodding literalism found in Italian gorefests of the *Cannibal Holocaust* variety.

The film begins with a series of caricature sketches of ugly mugs. This sets the tone for the rest of the film, which in many ways is a parade of grotesques. It's filled with twisted faces, bulging eyes, ragged rows of bad teeth and misshapen bodies. Everyone is out for what they can get and, like all of Tsui Hark's films of this period, there are no heroes. In fact, the only hero of *We Are Going to Eat You* is a reformed criminal whose past dooms him to never being taken seriously when he tries to go straight. The setting is a remote island somewhere off Hong Kong — the same sort of location that was used for Ann Hui's *The Spooky Bunch.* The

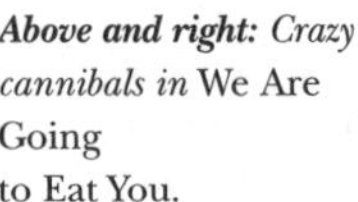
Above and right: *Crazy cannibals in* We Are Going to Eat You.

***Left:** Tsui Hark's* Dangerous Encounters of the First Kind.

inhabitants of the island's only town are a bloodthirsty bunch of cannibals — their motto: "If you don't eat people, they'll eat you." They are presided over by a cynical and vicious chief whose right hand man is the notorious robber, Rolex, famous for the huge tattoo of a fist on his left chest.

Agent number 999 of the Hong Kong secret service comes to the island to apprehend Rolex. There has recently been a shortage of human meat for the islanders to share out and any outsiders are considered fair game. Most of the film concerns the efforts of 999 and his travelling companion, a sort of wandering dropout wearing shades, to avoid becoming the community's next victims. Rolex tries to warn 999 what's going on. But the zealous agent is only interested in capturing another criminal to further his crime-fighting career.

The presiding spirit of the film is Tobe Hooper's *The Texas Chain Saw Massacre.* Consequently, *We Are Going to Eat You* has plenty of masked, meat-cleaver-waving subnormals chasing their victims through the woods. There's lots of gruesome carnage, and many shots of severed limbs and pots of boiling body parts. Conventional morality is turned upside-down. Nobody can be trusted. The only characters who are really honest about their intentions are the cannibals. *We Are Going to Eat You* wasn't a hit, although it's garnered a fair cult reputation since its release. Maybe it was just too dark and off-the-wall to be taken as straight entertainment. The political subtext was also a little premature. The mainland take-over of 1997 probably seemed too remote in 1980 to be the subject of satire.

Hark's other film of that year, *Dangerous Encounters of the First Kind,* suffered an even worse fate than *We Are Going to Eat You.* This modern day story of violence and alienation begins with visions of an urban hell. Mice with pins stuck in their heads race blindly around inside a tiny cage. From this bleak beginning the film moves to a depiction of random youth violence and ends with a shoot-out in an enormous cemetery. The film's lack of any really sympathetic character made it a difficult bet for audience identification. Unlike Hark's other — equally cynical — movies, *Dangerous Encounters of the First Kind* didn't have any comedy or kung fu to sugar the pill. The final nail in the film's coffin was its reference to student terrorism. The authorities, fearing copycat acts, banned the movie. Tsui Hark retrenched, took on acting roles and some hired-hand directing jobs, before making his mark with a very different type of film some years later.

The new wave of Tsui Hark, Ann Hui, Kirk Wong and co had all emerged from the hothouse atmosphere of late-seventies television production. From the opposite side of the spectrum, from deep within the traditional martial arts community, came one of the big hits of 1980, *Encounter of the Spooky Kind.* The film's creative mainspring was Samo Hung. He had been active in the Hong Kong industry for many years, having played his first role in 1961 at the tender age of eleven. Hung was a big guy, but could demonstrate amazing agility in fight scenes. Furthermore, he had an engaging and always comical side, even when he was trading blows with the best of them. This ability was put to good use in the many scenes that he choreographed for local superstar Jackie Chan.

Encounter of the Spooky Kind took one of the clichés of the 1970s kung fu comedy (dim-witted layabout with exceptional martial arts skill) and combined it with traditional Hong Kong spooks to make a new sort of hybrid: the kung fu/ghost/comedy. In fact, the film is little more than a series of set pieces, rather like a Buster Keaton feature. The final effect, however, was far greater than the sum of its parts. It zips along with such zest and style that it was like a breath of fresh air.

The film is set in the Republican 1910s. A local magistrate is having an affair with Samo's wife. Nervous of being found out, the man pays a magician to have Samo bumped off without his involvement being suspected. The magician

Above: Encounter of the Spooky Kind *was one of the first kung fu/horror comedies.*

tricks Samo into spending the night in a local, reputedly haunted, temple. Then the fun really begins.

Centre stage in the temple is a huge wooden coffin. To protect himself from the ghosts, Samo is told to get fifty hen's eggs and a mess of dog's blood. When night falls he perches on top of the coffin. Every time the lid opens he lobs in an egg and it slams shut again. Unfortunately, the egg merchant cheated him and mixed a few duck's eggs in with his purchase — these have absolutely no effect on the ghost. The coffin lid flies open, Samo is hurled to the floor and out pops a very peculiar looking monster: dressed in traditional Qing-style robes, with a flat-topped hat and pigtail, arms held rigidly in front like a sleepwalker, the creature moves with short, rabbit-like hops. The sight is unforgettable: both funny *and* scary. At a stroke, six years after Hammer had tried and failed, Hong Kong cinema had at last found its indigenous vampire.

In fact (or in fiction), the hopping vampire isn't really a vampire at all. It's a corpse given a semblance of life through mysterious Taoist magic. The origins of the hopping corpses are part of Chinese folklore. Apparently the technique of reanimating the dead had been perfected in Hunan province as a way of getting the deceased back to their ancestral burial grounds. A Taoist priest would affix a strip of yellow prayer paper to their foreheads, rope them together, and lead them across country, ringing a bell to warn off the curious. Their unique hopping motion was presumably a result of their feet being tied together. These peculiar creatures had featured in several earlier films, notably in the 1939 Maxu Weibang movie *Moving Corpse in the Old House* and in Wang Tin-lam's 1957 film *The Corpse Drivers of Xiangxi.*

The success of *Encounter of the Spooky Kind* led to numerous imitations and spin-offs featuring comedy and corpses. Two of the most endearing featured up-and-coming star Billy Chong. In *Kung Fu Zombie* he takes on a vampiric martial arts expert. *Kung Fu From Beyond the Grave* is even wilder.

The beginning of the film is loosely borrowed from *Hamlet.* As Billy practises kung fu, the hideous corpse of his father appears, demanding that he take revenge for his murder. Billy travels to a distant village to confront the evil Kan Tai-fu. This wily wizard is conducting a series of rituals which will make him invincible. These involve warm hearts ripped out of the bodies of the recently dead — hence the unusually large number of killings in the area. Chong locates a book of magic spells and begins to practise the black arts. As he chants and incants, a strange device like a television aerial protrudes from a large stone coffin and we hear the dead discussing where the magic is coming from. Emerging from their graves, they hop off to find Chong and offer him their services.

Then it's kung fu zombies versus black magic as Chong and his hopping corpses take on Kan Tai-fu. A couple of long-tongued wizards in tall hats turn up but fail to subdue the army of the dead. In desperation, Kan Tai-fu whips out what looks like a wad of bank notes and calls on Dracula to help him. A shot of the full moon and then suddenly Drac comes swooping down out of the clouds, complete with black cloak and a huge mouthful of fangs.

The film's finale has Kan Tai-fu hounded down by the spirits of those he murdered. A last touch of madness has him battling with the coffins of his victims before they drag him down into the earth with them.

In 1983 Samo Hung returned to spooky comedy with *The Dead and the Deadly,* directed by and starring Shaw Brothers veteran Wu Ma. Here Samo plays his rather dim friend, Fatboy. The farce-like action takes many twists and turns. Wu Ma pretends to be dead, then pretends to be his own ghost, then finally dies for real. His spirit takes over Fatboy's body... then Fatboy dies too! Highlights include Samo transformed into a flea and concealed in his wife's sanitary towel.

The film was a big hit. Seeing the way the wind was blowing, Samo Hung put together a team of experienced cohorts to produce the definitive kung fu/ghost comedy, the 1985 release *Mr Vampire.* The film earned more than HK$20 million at the local box office and led to three direct sequels as well as a host of spin-off vampire comedies. The title character, a yellow-robed Taoist priest, was played by the actor Lam Ching Ying, who had also played a priest in *The Dead and the Deadly.* It was a role he would go on to perfect in a stream of late-eighties horror movies. Lam has a patrician air and a slightly stuffy seriousness that make him the perfect foil for the stupid antics unfolding around him. In *Mr Vampire* he is called in to preside over the burial of a local worthy. His two bumbling assistants allow the corpse to escape and it goes on the rampage (or should that be on the hop), leaving chaos

***Above:** Chinese vampires in Africa:* Crazy Safari.

in its wake. The film's combination of knockabout comedy and straight horror is again reminiscent of Polanski's *Dance of the Vampires*, the film that also coloured Tsui Hark's approach to horror. The relationship between the Mr Vampire character and his bungling assistants in many horror comedies of the eighties also echoes the Polanski film.

The success of *Mr Vampire* spawned a sequel in 1986, this time set in the present day. In *Mr Vampire II*, a whole family of vamps is let loose in the streets of Hong Kong by a careless archaeologist. A descendant of the first film's priest (again played by Lam Ching Ying) is called in to sort things out. Through the character of a child vampire adopted by a bunch of school kids, the film takes a decided turn into juvenilia.

The third instalment of the *Mr Vampire* saga (released in 1987) saw a slight change of mood. The plot concerns a fake exorcist who screws money out of rich people with the help of a couple of friendly ghosts. He comes up against a real exorcist (yes, it's Lam Ching Ying again!) and ends up helping him defeat an evil witch. This time round there are no hopping vampires but, to compensate, there's some rip-roaring magic battles with lots of hocus pocus and weird rituals.

By the time of *Mr Vampire IV* in 1988, Lam Ching Ying was too busy doing his Chinese Van Helsing act in other movies to put in even a token appearance. Shaw Brothers stalwart Wu Ma stood in as the Taoist master with another pair of dumb students in tow. This time their adversary is a rival priest and a gold-clad vampire from China's imperial past.

Unlike some other recent Hong Kong series (*A Chinese Ghost Story, Swordsman*) the *Mr Vampire* films didn't really improve with subsequent episodes. The first one set the mood and the style and from there on it was pretty much downhill. Away from the series, Lam Ching Ying's finest hour was probably the 1990 film *Magic Cop*. Here his slightly stuffy manner is put to perfect use as Uncle Fung, an old fashioned policeman adrift in the modern world of Hong Kong. He seems completely phased by faxes, computers and electronic alarms. However, his knowledge of *feng shui* and Taoist magic is invaluable in tracking down a crime syndicate headed by a deathless witch from Japan. The film's plot allows a seamless integration of two of the most popular Hong Kong genres: police procedural and ghost story. For once the comedy and thrills are mixed with some genuine chills as the witch uses her "ice magic" against Fung and his fellow cops.

The conflict between old traditions and the new world in recent Hong Kong horror films is frequently examined through the generation gap. In *Magic Cop*, Uncle Fung spends a lot of time trying to keep his attractive niece on the straight and narrow: no television, no cinema and certainly no boys — very difficult when they are both forced to share a tiny apartment with a randy young cop.

The generation gap causes more problems in the 1992 film *The Wizard's Curse*, this time with some surprising results. Lam Ching Ying's Taoist priest comes up against a hermaphroditic, brain-eating monster. Its favourite weapon is its own penis — a hideous, barbed, blue-coloured thing as long as a flagpole. Lam has a Westernised daughter whom he's trying to keep pure and unsullied. In one scene he uses his magic to shrink her lover's penis just as they're about to get down to business. Then, to Lam's chagrin, he discovers that the only way to destroy the monster is to persuade his daughter to have sex with a specially selected virgin male...

Just as Godzilla was created with serious intent and ended up becoming a kids' toy and finally a goodie, so too the hopping vampire was turned into a figure of fun. *Crazy Safari* took the concept about as far as it could go, both in terms of plot and geography. This 1990 production was an offshoot of both the *Mr Vampire* series and the 1980 South

***Left:** A surprise guest in* Mr Vampire II.

Above and below: *Hopping vampires from the* Mr Vampire *series.*
Right: *Lam Ching Ying is* The One Eyebrowed Priest.

African comedy *The Gods Must Be Crazy.* The latter must have been a big hit in Hong Kong. Its director/producer Jamie Uys, something of a legend in his homeland, was hired to help make a film in which N!xau, who played the stone age bushman hero of *The Gods Must Be Crazy,* meets a seventeenth century Chinese vampire. The only problem was how to bring the two together. Simple — have a Chinese vampire bought at a Sotheby's auction and then flown back to Hong Kong. On the way the plane crashes in South Africa and vampire meets bushman. Except that South Africa doesn't lie on the route from London to Hong Kong. Oh well, let's have a plane with a faulty compass and a stupid pilot who doesn't know he's several thousand miles off course.

Logic, as you can see, didn't have a big hand in this project. The end result is one of the wackiest cultural collisions for some years. Highlights of the film include Lam Ching Ying riding to battle on the back of a giant ostrich, a contest between the Chinese vampire and a huge, red-haired African zombie, and N!xau being possessed by the spirit of Bruce Lee and engaging in some nifty 'bushman style' kung fu.

Crazy Safari was probably planned as an export item. Much of the action is explained via voice-over narration that would have saved on dubbing expenses. The film begins with a short documentary illustrating the difference between Asian and Western vampires. A confused Chinese vampire has a crucifix and Bible shoved in its face while a becloaked Christopher Lee lookalike recoils in pain. Since Hammer's mid-1970s attempts to bring Western vampires to China, European-style bloodsuckers had played only a minor role in Hong Kong horror movies. *A Bite of Love, Dr*

Vampire and *The Romance of the Vampires* were three rare exceptions. The popularity of the hopping vampire derived from its very Chineseness and its reminders of a past towards which many Hong Kongers felt a distinct ambivalence.

One of the factors that informed the mid-eighties possession and vampire films was the looming spectre of 1997, when control of Hong Kong would pass back to the Communist mainland. In the Hong Kong psyche, the mainland had a fascinating but fearful allure. In *Mr Vampire*, the hopping corpse is an import from China, as is the demon possessed jade vase in the film *Devil Fetus*. Even *Mr Vampire II*'s child vampire is mistaken for a mainland refugee. Although dealt with in a jokey way, this notion of troublesome spirits from China's past was obviously touching a raw nerve somewhere. The previous generation of Hong Kong films had projected a very idealised and partial view of history. There had been almost no mention of the recent past, the Communist take-over in 1949 and the violent Cultural Revolution of the 1960s. One of the first direct references to recent mainland history in eighties horror films comes in the 1986 comedy *Haunted Madam*.

In this lively romp, four rookie policewomen (female cops are called 'madam' in Hong Kong) come up against a fearless assassin. After his death, his spirit possesses the body of one of the madams, in the process turning her into a huge-breasted sex beast who goes on the rampage dressed only in a black leotard. The dead killer is discovered to have been a refugee from the mainland — a former Red Guard who got into drug dealing and crime in Hong Kong. The only thing he really dreads is a picture of Mao's wife, the fearsome Jiang Qing. The other thing that keeps him at bay is the sight of people having sex. To ward off the ghost, a policeman has to make love to one of the 'madams'. It's all in a day's work for Hong Kong's finest...

Some later horror films made more extensive use of

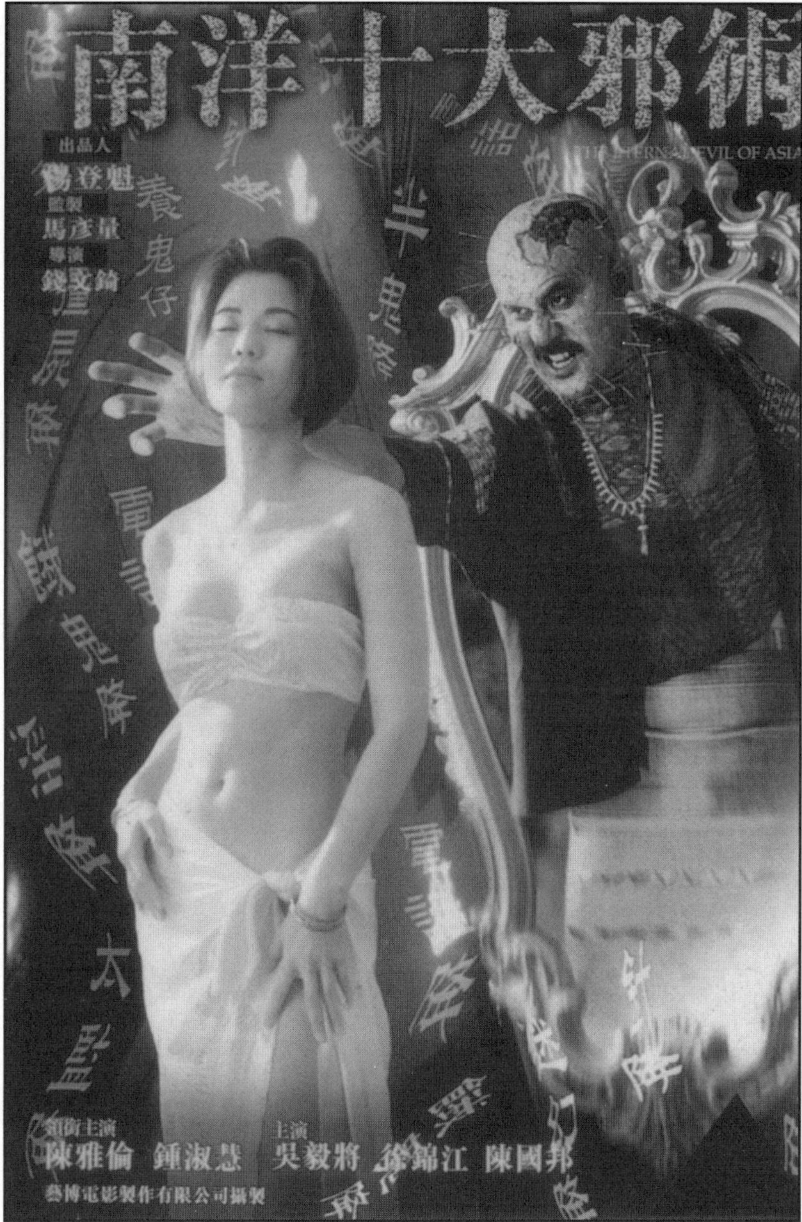

recent history. The 1989 film *Vampire Buster* has a prologue set during the Cultural Revolution of the mid-sixties. An old man tells his Red Guard son that an ancient vase he is about to smash contains the spirit of an evil sorcerer. Twenty years later the vase turns up in Hong Kong and the sorcerer is set free. The 1990 film *Red and Black* is set almost entirely during the Cultural Revolution. The story tells of an evil Japanese demon that possesses the body of a Communist Party leader. Taiwan's unhappy relationship with the mainland led to the cheapskate satire of *Magic Story*, where Communist troops piss their pants at the sight of a hopping vampire. On a slightly different level was the mainland-set psycho killer movie *Bloody Beast*. Mixed in with a series of hideous sex crimes are numerous jibes at the incompetence and dimness of the Communist police authorities. Between the legs of one raped woman two cops find a blood-stained stone. They examine it in detail, they lick it, and eventually they sniff it. "Smells of fish!" one of them finally announces.

As the handover to mainland control came closer, references to it became bleaker. Tsui Hark's 1992 production

Above: The Eternal Evil of Asia.
Left: The Romance of the Vampires *featured a Western-style bloodsucker.*

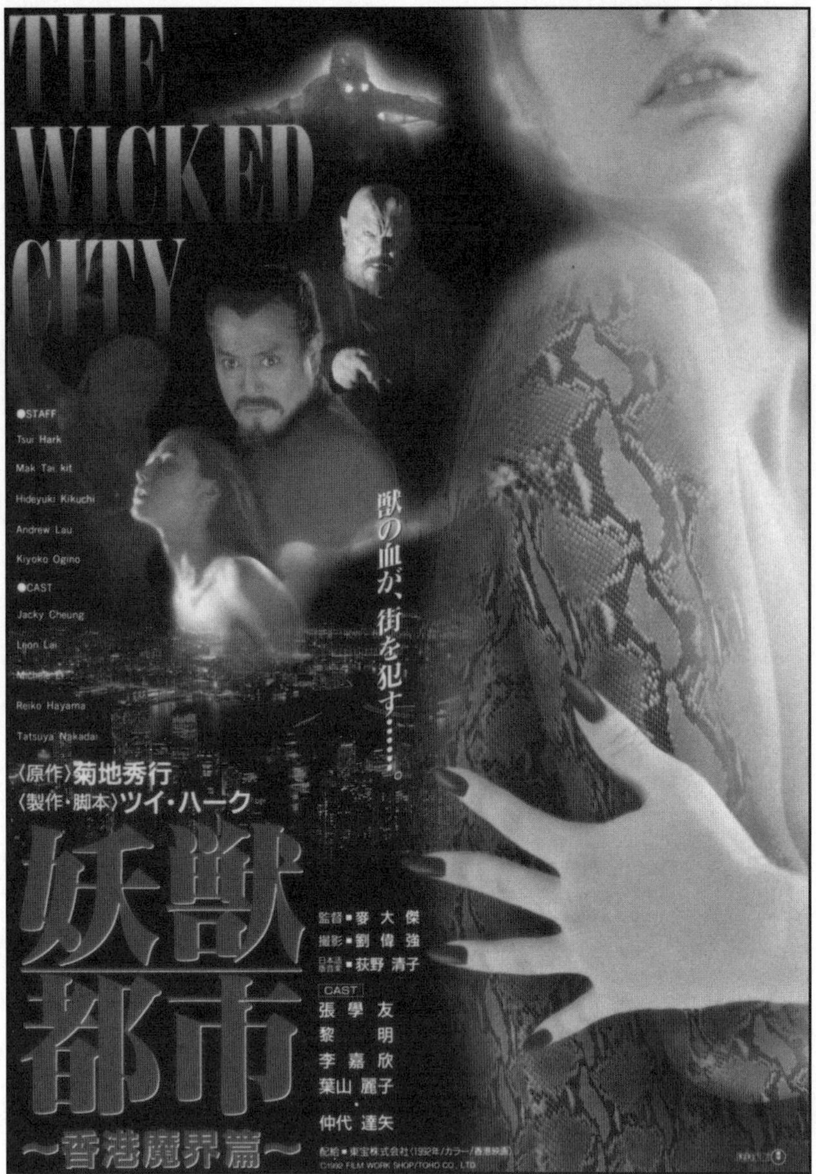

Above: Hong Kong under attack from reptoids in The Wicked City.
Right: Man Behind the Sun*: an orgy of gruesome special effects.*

The Wicked City sees Hong Kong as a beleaguered outpost of freedom and enlightenment about to be invaded by fearsome reptoids. These shapeshifting monstrosities are not really so different from the fox spirits and snake demons of ancient Chinese mythology, except that here they've been incarnated as financiers and drug dealers out to bleed every last drop of life from the tiny island.

Alongside the comedy horrors that flooded the market during the 1980s there was also a smattering of more serious productions. Kirk Wong's 1983 film *Health Warning* was a reworking of the kung fu genre via the sci-fi territory of David Cronenberg and the *Mad Max* series. In the near future, in a society on the brink of chaos, two martial arts schools fight for survival. The Straights Club is run in traditional style, espousing all the old fashioned virtues of training and abstinence. Their rivals, the neo-Nazi Ex Gang are into drugs, weird sex and crime. A later film, 1991's *The Story of Ricky*, treads similar futuristic ground. Based on a popular Japanese comic strip, the film is set in a twenty-first century prison run along militaristic lines. The film offers a uniquely Chinese mixture of slapstick, sentimentality and ultra violence. Maybe it isn't so unique after all. What the film most resembles is a live action *Tom and Jerry* cartoon. Faces are impaled on nails, heads sliced in half by giant choppers, punches go right through people's bodies and eyeballs pop out of their sockets. The highlight of the film is probably the scene where one of Ricky's opponents commits hara-kiri, then pulls his intestines out of his stomach and attempts to strangle Ricky with them. Although made with a highly stylised and 'modern' gloss, many of the more visceral moments of the film are reminiscent of the Chang Cheh kung fu films of the seventies. *Le plus ça change...*

A similar retro note was sounded by the series that began with 1987's *Man Behind the Sun.* This 'based on a true story' film purported to lift the veil of secrecy surrounding experiments conducted by the Japanese in a World War Two prison camp. The echo here was of the 1974 women-in-prison film *Bamboo House of Dolls*, also set in a Japanese prison camp. While such anti-Japanese sentiments had previously been explored in many seventies kung fu films, later Hong Kong movies evinced a grudging respect for their one-time enemy, perhaps as economic links between the two countries became more important. Liu Chia Lang's *Shaolin vs Ninja* has a Chinese martial arts expert married to a Japanese woman. He gradually comes to admire the skill and artistry of her ninjitsu techniques. In later Hong Kong films, Japanese women often played sensuous 'dragon ladies'. Michiko Nishiwaki in *Magic Cop* and Svenwara Madoka in *Naked Killer* are two memorable examples. Japanese actress Yukari Oshima became a star in Hong Kong without ever having worked on screen in her native country.

After all this friendly co-operation, *Man Behind the Sun* set the clock back several decades with its lurid depiction of Nipponese nastiness. The film is based on the activities of Unit 731, a brigade of the Japanese Imperial Army that established a biological warfare unit in North Eastern China in 1936. Many top scientists were involved in the work, which only stopped in 1945 with Japan's defeat in the war. For years the existence of

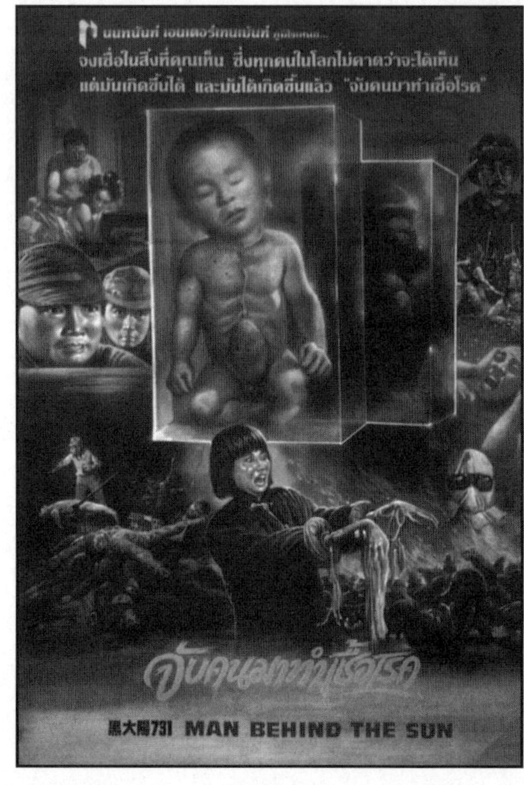

the unit was a closely guarded secret. A 1981 book, *The Devil's Gluttony*, first made public the horrendous story.

Cloaked behind its documentary approach, *Man Behind the Sun* shows a series of truly horrifying experiments. Limbs are frozen to sub-zero temperatures and plunged into baths of hot water to peel off the skin; a man is placed in a decompression chamber where he explodes like a balloon; autopsies are performed on living subjects. If these are special effects, they are extremely authentic-looking ones. To describe these activities as 'entertainment' requires stretching the meaning of the term beyond reason. *Man Behind the Sun* is the kind of film for which the label 'video nasty' was created. Today it's acquired a deserved reputation as probably the ultimate dramatic representation of man's inhumanity to man and should be avoided by all but the most jaded or unshockable viewer.

Similarly visceral entertainment was provided in the early eighties by a number of films that looked back to the exorcisms and worm spewing scenes of the *Black Magic* films of the previous decade. Many of this new wave of gruesome horrors were set in South East Asia. This capitalised both on the popularity of horror movies in those countries as well as the Hong Konger's chauvinistic belief that such countries were full of exotic wonders and dangers.

Shaw Brothers director Gui Zhihong was one of the most prolific makers of these straight horror films. His *Hex*, from 1980, is a tricksy murder mystery with fake ghosts, double crosses and a plot obviously influenced by the smash hit *Les diaboliques*. Much more full-blooded was *Corpse Mania*, a murder thriller based around a brothel. Both of these films were set in the Republican period of the 1910s. Gui Zhihong returned to a contemporary setting with *Bewitched*, released in 1981. The story, largely set in Thailand, tells of a visitor from Hong Kong who falls under the charms of a local girl. Every full moon he is compelled to commit ghastly acts that eventually result in the death of his own daughter. A local police inspector investigating the case also falls under the spell of the witch girl and has to call in an exorcist to combat her evil influence.

Often described as a sequel to *Bewitched*, the 1983 film *The Boxer's Omen* is Gui Zhihong's much more elaborate reworking of the same themes. Here, a boxer from Hong Kong comes to Thailand to settle a score with a rival fighter. He meets a mysterious Taoist priest and discovers that his destiny is to defeat the evil Black Wizard. An amazing series of gruesome scenes, involving demon bats, giant spiders, a huge disembodied brain, crocodile skulls and maggots, ends with the defeat of the Black Wizard. The boxer is then dispatched to Nepal, where he takes on a seductive she-demon created by the wizard's disciples out of a crocodile's stomach.

The Boxer's Omen is almost psychedelic in its excesses. In one scene the boxer regurgitates a two foot long conga eel that leaps around his hotel bathroom before depositing itself in the toilet bowl. Another shot shows a temple erupting into a sea of burning lava. To strengthen his magic powers, the boxer is encased in a pink transparent pot and has Buddhist sutras magically written over his skin. The final conflict takes place in a temple in Kathmandu, where the rising sun, shining on the ashes of a dead priest, frees the boxer from his curse. He pulls two huge needles out of his eyes as ethereal chanting fills the air.

The South East Asian connection is echoed in a wide range of Hong Kong horrors from *Red Spell Spells Red*, through *Brutal Sorcery* and *Curse of the Zombi*, to *Holy Virgin vs the Evil Dead*. Sometimes the story is set in the South East, sometimes (as in *Vampire Buster* or *Ghostly Vixen*) the evil is inadvertently brought back to Hong Kong in the form of a cursed object, a vase containing ashes or secret spells. More subtly, as in *The Boxer's Omen* or *Centipede Horror*, the curse lays dormant in another country until a visitor from Hong

Above left: *The psychedelic excess of* The Boxer's Omen.
Above right: *Hong Kong beauties lost in the jungle in* Stone Age Warriors.
Left: *South East Asian horror in* Holy Virgin vs the Evil Dead.

Above: Devil Fetus *was one of a series of killer foetus films.*

Kong brings it back to life.

The structure of the films is nearly always the same. First, the discovery of the curse, then many scenes detailing its effects, and finally the arrival of a priest or shaman to combat the evil. The 1973 film *The Exorcist* is one obvious model, and *Poltergeist* arrived in the eighties to give new life to the clichés. In homage to the latter, this new wave of possession movies feature countless scenes of people being sucked through windows or into other dimensions.

Possessed and *Possessed 2*, from 1983 and 1984 respectively, are two of the best of this effects-laden bunch. Both are very Western-influenced but both have more than their fair share of spooky Eastern exorcisms and oddball atmospherics. In the first film, two policemen come up against the deathless spirit of a vengeful murderer. In typical Hong Kong fashion, it was the actions of the father of one of the cops that set the evil in motion. The sex-starved spirit rapes the girlfriend of one of the cops and uses a whirring ceiling fan to make mincemeat of his sister. An exorcist is called in to settle the mess. With a nod to *Poltergeist*, she's a short, fat woman with a funny voice. She calls on the power of "the four-faced Buddha" (a deity also featured in *The Black Magic with Buddha*). The evil is defeated but, at the end of the film, as the cop kisses his girlfriend, she turns into a warty-faced fiend. *Possessed 2* is not a direct sequel but has a similar plot. Here the vengeful ghost is Lucy, a dead prostitute from the 1940s. The film features hairy werewolf women with large breasts and a sex scene in a cold meat wagon.

Hong Kong horror films compensate for their debt to Western models and the generic nature of their plots by the detailed exposition of the spells, charms and magic that they feature. The exorcism scene, usually the climax of the story, is always a visual delight, replete with howling winds, swirling mists, sheaves of yellow spell paper, Sanskrit incantations and bodies painted with mystic runes to ward off evil.

The 1982 film *Ghost Nursing* begins with a prostitute, Jackie, fleeing Hong Kong following the murder of her gangster boyfriend. Suspecting there may be a curse on her, she goes to consult a priest, a devotee of the 'God of Gold'. He turns out to be a genuine oddball, painted all over in mystical symbols, who holds a gold pot over his head while he goes into a gibbery trance. He reveals to Jackie that she is suffering bad karma from a former life. The only way out for her is "to nurse a ghost". This consists of her caring for the mummified body of a dead foetus given spiritual life through a bizarre ceremony involving lots of blood and chanting. On the thirteenth day of every month, the priest informs her, she must feed the hideous creature with some of her own blood. Inevitably, one fateful night Jackie overlooks his feeding and things go horribly wrong.

Another fiendish foetus is featured in the 1983 production *Devil Fetus*. The trigger for this particular eighty minutes of weirdness is a green jade vase purchased at an auction. That night, the woman who bought it caresses the vase thoughtfully while lying on her bed. She imagines herself making love with a slimy beastie. In fact we *see* her making love with a slimy beastie. As does her husband when he comes home from work. He smashes the jade and it erupts into smoke which causes the man's face to break out in boils. He rips off the affected skin and underneath are a host of maggots gnawing their way through his bones.

After the woman falls to her death from a staircase, the jade spirit takes possession of the family dog, which is soon summarily dispatched with a samurai sword. The family's young son, under an evil influence, rips open the dog's stomach and gobbles down its guts. The ending of the film has him splitting in half from the navel upwards while a huge slimy fiend emerges from his body. Every time its head is cut off another one sprouts from the neck cavity on a long stalk. The film climaxes with an explosion of grue and the sight of the last monstrous head degenerating before our astonished eyes.

Completing a trilogy of foetus films is the 1983 Shaw Brothers production *Seeding of a Ghost*. Tsu Sui Kung, the suave boyfriend from *Ghost Nursing*, stars again as a married Lothario who has an affair with Irene, a female croupier. Her husband, Chou, works as a taxi driver. Late one night, on the outskirts of Hong Kong, he interrupts a lynch mob thirsting for the blood of a wizard caught indulging in a spot of midnight grave robbing. The wizard thanks Chou for saving him, but warns him that their life lines are now inexorably linked and things might start to turn bad for him.

Sure enough, his errant wife is raped one night on her way back from the casino. Escaping from her assailants, she falls from a rickety fire escape and is impaled on a set of rusty railings. Unable to account for his movements on the night of her death, Chou becomes suspect number one.

Released from police custody, he seeks out the wizard and begs for his help. The pair dig up Irene's remains. Chou is given coconut oil and told to rub the dry skin of his wife's apparently mummified body. As he does so it begins to move and pulse with witchcraft-induced life. The wizard tells him she is now a *plazawa* — "that means 'Venus'," he explains. The implications of this become clearer when the hideous, desiccated cadaver clutches Chou to its wizened bosom and embraces him, lip to lip, sucking the life force from him. In a later, even queasier scene, the *plazawa* draws one of the rapists to the wizard's den. Under the influence of the powerful demon, the youth clambers on top of the now blackened corpse and impregnates it.

The spirit of the *plazawa* hunts down the men who were responsible for Irene's death. Various worm spewing episodes ensue. One of the rapists finds his toilet possessed of a life of its own, as vile muck pours out of the bowl, flooding his flat. The *plazawa* seeks out Irene's former lover and takes over his wife's body. The poor woman becomes mysteriously pregnant and soon after gives birth to a hideous throbbing lump of pus and gristle. As the doctor and his attendants rush from the room, the lump transforms into something between an octopus and a spider. It shoots out huge, rubbery tentacles, lassoes the fleeing medics and draws them toward its slavering maw. In a final burst of outrageous special effects, the now dead Chou's head suddenly juts from between the creature's snapping jaws.

Seeding of a Ghost is perhaps the pinnacle of the 'horrible' horrors that began with the *Black Magic* films of the 1970s. Its simple storyline is fleshed out with just enough sex and incident to keep it on the move, but its trump card is the *plazawa* and the stomach-churning scenes of birth and rebirth. The weird and fascinating lore that underlies Hong Kong horror films — some of it real, much of it invented — is what makes them unique. *Seeding of a Ghost* has some of the best and most unexpected magic of all. While many more horrible horrors have been produced since, none have really matched up to this one (although Ho Meng-Hua's *The Rape After* comes close). Perhaps it was the production power of the Shaw Brothers, at the time very close to shutting up shop, that gave the film the gloss, solid acting skills and excellent special effects that lift it so far above the rut. Subsequent films, particularly after the Category III sex and violence watershed, moved into very different territory. Now the genre has effectively disappeared, so *Seeding of a Ghost* may well stand as the best of its kind for a very long time yet.

The Hong Kong industry is in many ways like Hollywood in its heyday. It's not different styles or genres that are important, let alone individual creative talents, so much as successful films. If a film is a hit it's soon followed by countless imitations. If the hit film is a comedy, the imitations are comedies too; if the hit is a horror film, soon other horrors will follow in its wake. The kung fu comedies and hopping vampire films of the eighties, with their Marx Brothers-inspired, knockabout antics were one strand of hit film. But alongside these came a very different style of comedy, akin to the sophisticated 'white telephone' films of thirties Hollywood.

Esprit d'amour and the similarly titled *Spiritual Love* were altogether gentler, more romantic and more adult horror movies than the hopping vampire films and worm spewing gore fests. Both of them were modern day stories and both explored the time honoured theme of love between a man and a ghost. In these films (as well as in similar productions like *Witch From Nepal* and *Dream Lovers*) the ghost girl is shown as more desirable, more lively and a better match than the protagonist's real-life girlfriend. Both also show the dream girl as ultimately unattainable. The death or self-sacrifice of one of the partners is usually the only resolution to their problems.

This genre of bittersweet, romantic ghost films reached its apogee with the 1987 production *Rouge*. The film was produced by local superstar Jackie Chan and features pop singer and sultry sex goddess Anita Mui. She plays the seductive Fleur, a courtesan in thirties Hong Kong. She falls in love with one of her clients, Chan, played by Leslie Cheung, who specialised in this sort of tragic romantic hero. When he is forbidden by his family from marrying her, Fleur persuades Chan to commit double suicide. This was a common way of escaping the rigid codes of the time. Fifty years later, Fleur's ghost reappears in modern day Hong Kong for a rendezvous with the spirit of her lost love.

Director Stanley Kwan recreates the past with a painter's

Left: Ghosts Galore*!*

Above: Zu: Warriors From the Magic Mountain.
Right: *Lau Siu-Ming in* A Chinese Ghost Story.

eye. This is a world of fragile beauty, of sumptuous banquets and opium dreams. A world where rich men would pay hundreds of dollars just to touch the ear of the beautiful Fleur. Present day Hong Kong seems like a thousand years away from the world she left behind. The theatre where she watched Chan act in Chinese opera has now become a shopping mall, the twisty street where they had their love nest is now a traffic-clogged dual carriageway.

A young journalist and his girlfriend agree to help Fleur find her former lover. They eventually discover that he did not die in the suicide pact. They track him down to a film set where he has become a sad and tragic old man. He squandered his fortune on opium, and now picks up odd jobs as an extra on costume movies. Realising the hopelessness of the dreams that kept her clinging to the past, Fleur exits the world through the backlit doorway of a movie set and fades away into a cloud of dry ice smoke.

By the time pictures like *Rouge* hit the screens, the Hong Kong film industry had changed radically from the 1970s. For a start, the familiar names had mostly gone, replaced by operations like Cinema City and independent producers such as the Wins and D&B. The films' visual style had changed too. The set-bound staginess of the Shaw Brothers classics had been replaced by an equally stylised but somehow more modern look. Stories set in the present day or in the recent past meant that location shooting in the crowded streets of Hong Kong was more common than before. The editing techniques and the shooting style of films had changed. There was now a more fluid use of the camera, and editing was done to a faster rhythm, influenced by advertising films and pop videos. Replacing the athletic, bare-hand fighters of the martial arts films were heroes and heroines who swooped through the air on invisible wires or walked through walls in seamless dissolves.

The prime mover of this new style of Hong Kong cinema was Tsui Hark, one of the new wave gang whose *en masse* defection from television in the late seventies had promised so much. In the end little had been delivered, apart from a radical shift in the surface style of Hong Kong cinema. The reasons for the lack of real change are many. Filmgoing, certainly in the mid-eighties, was still the major form of entertainment in Hong Kong. Audiences wanted action, adventure and romance. Film-makers who tried to do anything different often found their messages failing to connect. As Tony Rayns explained at the time: 'Hong Kong's young film-makers are caught in a vicious circle, hemmed around by a monolithic and ruthless industry, an inflexible and highly restrictive system of censorship and a mass audience with a pronounced taste for the most conservative forms of entertainment.'

Tsui Hark had tried, with his early films, to break through this barrier and produce works that were both entertaining and challenging. The fact that he had failed didn't stop him making films, but it did lead to a very different type of cinema. In many ways the experimentation with content that had gone into something like *Don't Play With Fire* was transformed into an experiment in form. That's not to say that he made avant-garde cinema, but rather that he pushed the available techniques of film-making to their very limits, always looking for something just beyond the edge of what was possible.

His 1982 production, *Zu: Warriors From the Magic Mountain*, took the traditional Chinese martial arts fantasy and reworked it, utilising the most modern and up-to-date special effects techniques available. Technicians were drafted in from Hollywood and Tokyo to help on the film. Tsui Hark's intention was not to make a film that looked like an American production. Far from it. His models were old Cantonese fantasy films and illustrations from printed martial arts serials. His aim was to find a way of making their unreal special effects believable to a modern audience. For example, what in *Star Wars* were laser guns became, in the Tsui Hark fantasy films, magic mirrors that project beams of coloured force. *Zu*'s arsenal of uniquely Eastern wonders includes a Taoist master with extendible eyebrows, magical fights with coloured fire balls, and characters flying though the air on spinning discs.

Hark and his team learned a lot from the Hollywood technicians they worked with on *Zu*. In 1987 his martial arts director Ching Siu Tung applied these lessons to a production that became one of the most influential fantasy films of the decade, *A Chinese Ghost Story*. The generic title is highly appropriate for what is an almost archetypal tale of a love affair between a man and a ghost girl. The script was based on Pu Songling's *The Magic Sword*. As already noted, the story had been filmed several times before, but never as sumptuously as here.

The pre-credits sequence of *A Chinese Ghost Story* is almost a mini version of the entire film. Bathed in a mysterious blue light, leaves blow through a spooky temple. Eerie music plays as the camera crawls through a forest of misty veils. A seductive woman dances. Now we see her making love with a man. She raises her leg and the bells of her anklet tinkle gently, echoed by a row of temple bells. Suddenly something comes rushing at ground level towards the lovers. A stunning steadicam shot takes the audience with it. The man, suddenly alone, grimaces in horror. Some terrible thing has possessed him and is sucking out his life force. Seconds later he falls to the ground, a dry, desiccated husk.

A rather gormless tax collector, Tsai Tsen (played by *Rouge* star Leslie Cheung), is visiting the area. Unable to afford an inn for the night he beds down in the deserted Lan Ro temple. Drawn by the sound of beautiful music he wanders to a house on a nearby lake where he finds the lovely Hsiao Tsing (Joey Wong) playing her lute. The two are attracted to each other but the girl seems reluctant to consummate the relationship. Hiding out in her room the following night Tsai Tsen thinks he has discovered why. She is due to be married in three days time.

The temple's only other inhabitant is a reclusive Taoist and master swordsman, Yen. When he hears the tax collector's story, he tells him that there is no house by the lake, only a graveyard. The beautiful Hsiao Tsing is the ghost of a girl who was murdered nearby a year ago. Her impending marriage is not an earthly union, but to the evil Lord Black, effectively the devil. Lord Black is forcing Hsiao Tsing to seduce passing travellers, who then become his victims. Unless Yen and Tsai Tsen can find the girl's ashes and bury them in sacred ground, her soul will be lost forever and she will never be reborn in the earthly sphere.

The approach of *A Chinese Ghost Story*, as set out in the pre-credits sequence, is a highly effective marriage of Western camera tricks and Eastern mysticism. The racing steadicam and animated corpses of films like *The Evil Dead* meet the mysterious atmospherics and gravity defying leaps of King Hu's *A Touch of Zen*. Palm power magic, Sanskrit sutras and a glowing sword are used to combat the evil demons. The climax of the film is a trip into hell, where Yen and Tsai Tsen must defeat the evil Lord Black. Hsiao Tsing uses the priest's magic sword to pierce the monster's body. This releases the souls of all those he has imprisoned and thousands of screaming faces come rushing out of his chest like a swarm of bees. With the ashes of Hsiao Tsing safely buried in her family plot, Yen and Tsai Tsen ride off into the Eastern dawn: "To a better world!"

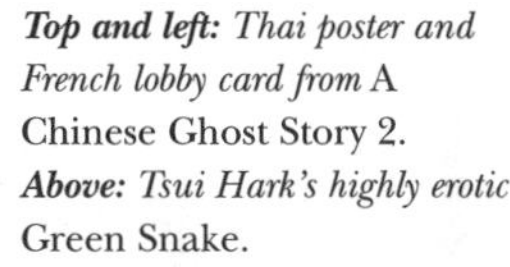

Top and left: *Thai poster and French lobby card from* A Chinese Ghost Story 2.
Above: *Tsui Hark's highly erotic* Green Snake.

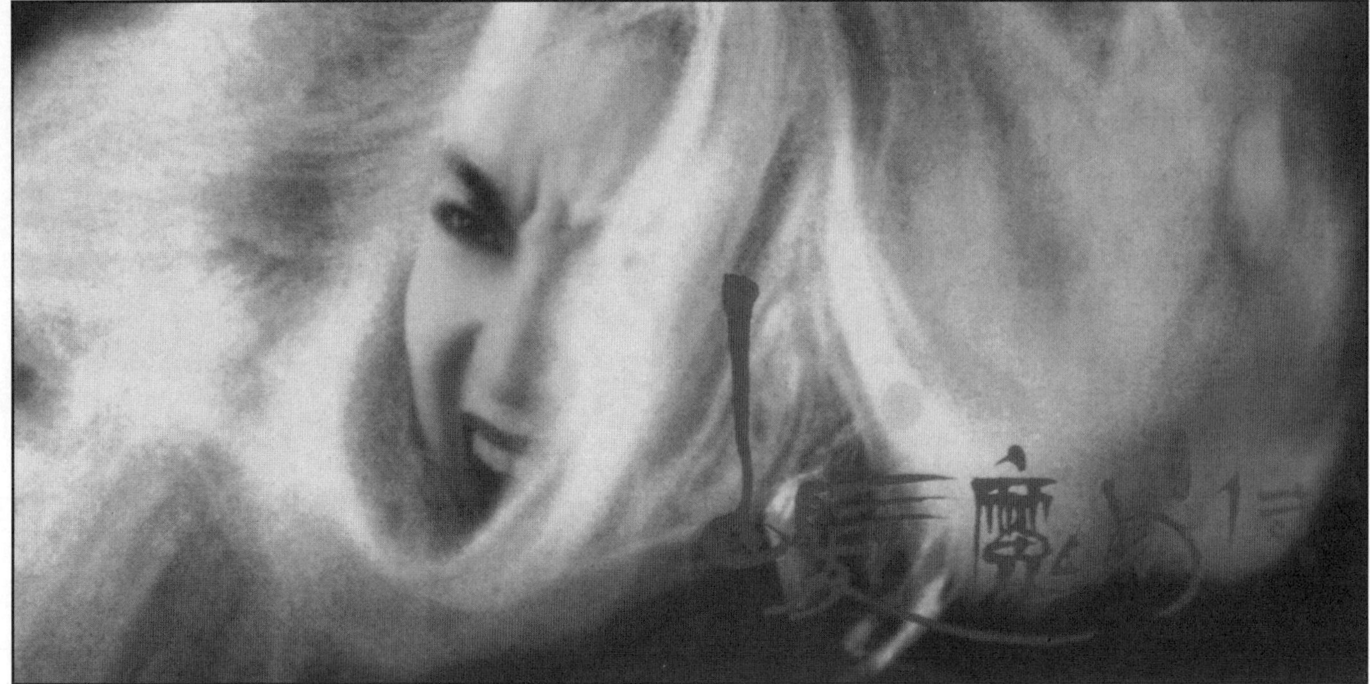

The success of *A Chinese Ghost Story* led to two sequels from the same production team and numerous imitations. The slyest of these was *Portrait of a Nymph*. The film was directed by Wu Ma, who had played the Taoist swordsman in the original film, and starred Joey Wong as the beautiful ghost loved by a wandering scholar. Effectively a remake, but with a story 250 years old who could claim copyright?

The Category III label that had come into force in 1988 allowed a more liberal use of softcore sex in several of the *A Chinese Ghost Story* derivatives. The most successful of these sexed-up spin-offs was 1990's *Erotic Ghost Story*. The film deals with the encounter between three female fox spirits in human form and a priapic god from the netherworld. The foxes have to remain pure for thirty-six days to achieve immortality, but the lustful god Wu Tang, disguised as an innocent scholar, is determined to bed all three of them. *Erotic Ghost Story* had two sequels and, inevitably, several imitations, ranging from the cheap and cheesy *Erotic China Dolls*, to the more passable *Ghost Story of Kam Pin Mui*.

After reviving the martial arts film with his *Once Upon a Time in China* series, Tsui Hark returned to the fantasy genre in 1994 with *Green Snake*. Although it wasn't a great financial success, the film was one of his most beautiful productions and showed his total mastery of the style of cinema he had helped to create. The opening scenes are like something out of *We Are Going to Eat You*, as a Buddhist monk stares aloofly at "humanity", represented by a series of hideous grotesques, fighting, gambling and drinking. The monk comes up against two beautiful snake sisters who have taken on human form. One of them decides to experience human love with a typically unworldly scholar. *Green Snake* is Tsui Hark's sexiest film. The visuals are filled with endless watery scenes of rain or rivers and the two snake sisters seem to be naked in the flow for most of the action. A lesbian-tinged dance scene featuring some Indian beauties and a discretely nude snake girl is more erotic than an hour's worth of Amy Yip's cleavage.

Opposite: *No bedside manners for* Dr Lamb.

Above and right: *The stunning* The Bride With White Hair.

The style forged in these Hong Kong fantasy films by Tsui Hark and Ching Siu Tung was immensely influential. The swooping camerawork, fast cutting and use of wires to facilitate death-defying leaps became ubiquitous. One result of this was to downplay the need for real martial arts skills. This led to actresses like Anita Mui and Brigitte Lin becoming action stars when, by their own admission, they are certainly not trained martial artists.

The enormous skill of Hong Kong's technicians, the undoubted charm of actors like Chow Yun Fat and actresses like Maggie Cheung had helped create a cinema of total escapism. While their films were inevitably moulded by contemporary reality and even made oblique reference to it from time to time, they never engaged with it in any meaningful way. These were sensational films in the true sense of

赤柱監獄內兩個響噹噹人馬
一個係大毒梟——跛豪 另一個就係——佢!!
超 III 級
特別震撼!
連獄卒都唔敢望佢一眼
羔羊醫生
Dr. Lamb
監製/導演 李修賢
執行導演 鄧衍成
李修賢 任達華 鄭則士
劉兆銘 關寶慧 黎海珊 鍾碧穎 汪永芳
李華月 紀家發 林敬剛 瑪莉

the word. They existed to create a series of emotional responses and nothing else. Pure cinema, in many ways.

The emphasis in these late-eighties films on special effects and action, at the expense of character development and real plot, is seen at its most extreme in films like *Saviour of the Soul* and *Heroic Trio*. With their rip-roaring, soaring fight sequences, unreal settings, comic book villains and glamorous heroines they were a triumph of style over content. In that sense they were like opera, and perhaps it's fitting that the film that concluded this particular chapter of Chinese fantasy was the most operatic of them all, Ronnie Yu's 1992 hit, *The Bride With White Hair*.

For all their grandiose staging, films like *A Chinese Ghost Story* were essentially simple love stories played out on a limited canvas. *The Bride With White Hair* marks out its epic territory right from the start. If a true epic is the pinpointing of individual lives against the vast backdrop of history, this is a perfect example of the form. The bulk of the film is set during the last years of the Ming dynasty, a time of warring clans. In a short prologue we are told of a magical, life-giving flower that opens just once every twenty years. The emperor is dying and only the petals of the flower can save him. A team of emissaries voyage to a distant mountain top where they find a lone swordsman guarding the flower. In reply to their request for the bloom he slaughters them all in a spectacular burst of balletic violence.

"But who ranks higher than his majesty?" asks one of the emissaries with his dying breath.

"A woman, in my eyes," announces the swordsman as he settles back for another ten years to wait the blooming.

The woman in question is Lien Ni-chang, a kind of 'nature girl' brought up amongst wild animals. The swordsman, Cho Yi-hang, had a brief encounter with her many years before when he was a young boy, lost in the dark forest, and she saved him from a pack of wolves. He never forgot her. Years later, when he has been trained to take over as head of the famous Wu Tang clan, he discovers that she is a member of their dreaded rivals, the evil Mo cult. In fact she is their slave, held in bondage by black magic. She has been trained in martial arts and can kill dozens of men in a matter of seconds, slicing off their heads with one crack of her deadly whip. Apparently invincible, she appears out of the night like an avenging ghost, wrapped in white.

***Right:** Carrie Ng plays the deadly Miss Tong in* Passion Unbounded.

Cho Yi-hang plans to rescue the girl, escape the destiny that has been mapped out for them, and leave the martial world forever.

The Mo cult are led by a terrifying brother/sister combination who are adepts at black magic. Perhaps the most startling thing about this pair is the fact that they are Siamese twins, joined back to back. The male half of the pair is in love with Lien and desires to take her virginity. When she announces her intention to leave the cult, he demands her body as a forfeit. He tries to make love to her while his sister, fixed on his back, hurls out shrill insults. Unable to consumate his passion, he allows Lien to leave. But first she must strip off her red robes and run the gauntlet of the cult members, who beat her with sticks and strike at her with the blades of their swords.

The evil twins play a trick on Lien. As she travels to meet her lover, they appear at the Wu Tang's castle in disguise. Assuming the form of the wolf girl they slaughter hundreds of Wu Tang members, including their leader. When she arrives at the castle, Lien finds herself surrounded by angry Wu Tang members, demanding her life. When even Cho Yi-hang won't believe her protestations of innocence, Lien goes mad and her hair turns as white as snow. It billows out from her head like an explosion of dust, snaring the surviving Wu Tang and strangling them.

Director Ronnie Yu had begun in the business as one of the foreign-trained technicians who went into television in the late 1970s. His film *The Trail* in 1982 was an early hopping vampire movie. The same year's *The Tenant* was another spooky story with Lo Lieh as a mystic priest. The style that Yu effects for *The Bride With White Hair* is a deliberately unrealistic and stylised one. The colours red and blue predominate, while the panoramic, wide screen camera is often tilted at unnatural angles to induce a sense of disorientation. The whole film has a studio-bound look, even in scenes like the opening one on a snowy mountain top. Here we see the unreal glint of the snow crystals and light refracted through glass-like icicles.

The Bride With White Hair was released just as the boom in costume films was ending. The Hong Kong movie business had enjoyed an incredibly productive ten years. Now, with the spectre of 1997 looming large, many people were leaving the industry. Audience figures had declined more than thirty per cent since 1992. Budgets were being slashed. Video had also taken its toll on the traditional overseas markets for Hong Kong films. It's unlikely that an exotic, big-budget spectacular like *The Bride With White Hair* would be produced today. Against this background there were strong moves to establish links with the mainland. Ronnie Yu shot his 1995 film, *The Phantom Lover*, on location in Beijing. A remake of the 1937 classic *Song at Midnight*, the film has a decidedly anti-authoritarian flavour that must have caught the mainland censors off guard.

One of the effects of the nineties uncertainty and cost cutting was the proliferation of violent crime and slasher films during the decade — films like *Bunman*, *Dr Lamb* and *Don't Stop My Crazy Love For You*. In a sense these were nothing new. Violence and sleazy sex had been a feature of Hong Kong films since the mid-1970s. The Category III label merely allowed local producers more licence to explore the territory. Stylish ultra violence had entered the mainstream through the triad gangland films of the late eighties. Hits like John Woo's *The Killer* had shown an intimate knowledge of not only the likes of Brian De Palma (*The Untouchables, Scarface*) but of arty European fare like the Alain Delon vehicle *Le Samourai*. Combined with the production skills of Tsui Hark and the high-octane acting of Chow Yun Fat this gave the Hong Kong action film a surface gloss and visual sophistication to match the best of world cinema.

Violence wasn't just confined to the screen. The industry itself became increasingly penetrated by triad money. There were many stories of actors and actresses being coerced and bribed into accepting roles in triad-backed movies. As the 1997 deadline approached there was a desperate rush to carve up the territory before it was too late. Several production companies, like the Wins Group and Wang Fat, had alleged triad connections. Wanting a fast return on their investment these producers took an aggressively commercial approach, favouring more exploitative material with sex and violence high on their agendas.

In the wake of the Hollywood hit *The Silence of the Lambs* came several Hong Kong productions that explored similarly dark and devious territory. Producer Danny Lee came up with a couple of 'true life' crime thrillers, *Dr Lamb* and *Bunman*. These are genuinely chilling productions, sparing few details in their depiction of unsettling depravity. *Bunman* deals with the case of a Sweeney Todd-style psychopath who murders a restaurant owner and then serves up his victims in pork buns. Some of this is actually as funny as it sounds. Then the tone becomes darker. The police lock the suspected killer in a cell with the brother of one of his victims, then beat a confession out of him. This includes a flashback showing the meticulous slaughter of an entire family, including young children. Anthony Wong, who plays the killer, brings such dark authority to the role that he was deservedly awarded a best actor prize at the 1993 Hong Kong International Film Festival.

The male bias of these films was balanced by a spate of movies cast in the *Fatal Attraction* mould. As in the Hollywood hit, we are treated to a series of softcore scenes, sexy night-club dances and the titillating spectacle of a bisexual murderess. The 1992 film *Naked Killer* actually has three sexy killers. Carrie Ng, one of the film's stars, reprised a similar role in the 1995 production *Passion Unbounded*. In this amoral piece of exploitation the gorgeous Carrie excels as Miss Tong, the ultimate *femme fatale*. Dressed in figure-hugging dresses, shiny stilettos and dehumanising shades, she haunts the night-spots of Hong Kong looking for victims of both sexes. Eventually she meets an epileptic young man who shares her interests and the pair team up to double their fun. Highlights (?) include a sex scene in a toilet cubicle, which concludes with Miss Tong cracking her lover's skull open with her stiletto heel, a bath tub murder during another sex session and a very downbeat ending that has the evil duo escape to kill again.

Daughter of Darkness is another typically tasteless piece of Hong Kong sleaze. The plot concerns an abused girl who wipes out her entire family. In one of the flashback rape scenes, the girl's beer-swilling father forces her to have sex with him on the kitchen table while he gaily sings "Row, row, row your boat..." The detective called in to investigate the murders is a kind of oversexed Columbo (he's played by *Bunman* star Anthony Wong). He squeezes the breasts of one

Left: *Watch out! There's a* Maniacal Beauty on the Loose.

of the murder victims and sniffs her crotch to see if she'd been raped. "Do all your family have big tits?" he asks the sole surviving relative as he eyes her up while chomping into an apple.

Another suspected female serial killer (in fact she turns out to be innocent) is featured in *Horrible High Heels*. The police are called in to investigate the woman's shoe factory when a successful line of high heel pumps are found to be made out of human skin. In one scene the necrophile killer from whom she obtains the skin makes the woman kiss a corpse's severed head and touch herself up with its dismembered hand. Then, in probably the grossest moment in Hong Kong cinema, the film intercuts the woman's rape with shots that show the rapist apparently having sex with a goose...(!) To cap it all, the sequence ends with him urinating over the woman's body. That's entertainment, Category III style.

Films like these, along with *Red to Kill* (featuring an educationally subnormal rape victim), *Run and Kill* (a little girl is burned to death) and many others have a definite *fin de siècle* feel, like a wild, end-of-term party. The close of the century in Hong Kong is a time of enormous change, when no one really knows what will happen next. The rapid economic growth of mainland Shanghai looks set to return it once again to its former status as "the Paris of the East". Maybe it will also reassert itself as the centre of Chinese film production. Whether or not horror films will be high on the agenda of this new breed of film moguls is impossible to speculate. Whatever the outcome, the legacy of the last twenty or so years is some of the most spectacular, as well as some of the sleaziest horror films the world has ever seen. With directors like Tsui Hark and Ronnie Yu now setting their sights on Hollywood, we can only hope that the enormous style and originality of the films they made in Hong Kong can survive in the very different climate of the West. If so, maybe the best is still to come. ■

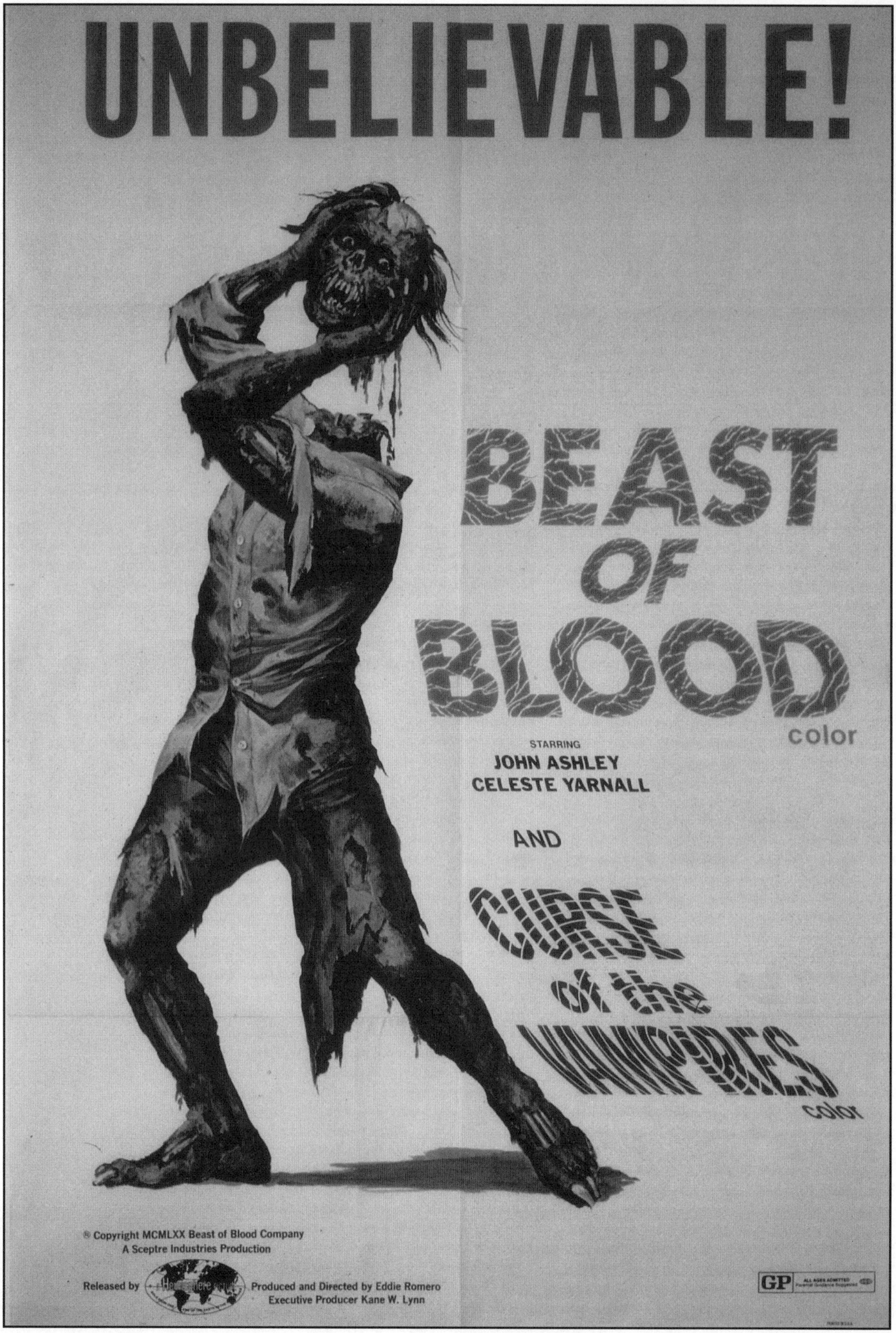

UNBELIEVABLE!
BEAST OF BLOOD
color
STARRING
JOHN ASHLEY
CELESTE YARNALL
AND
CURSE of the VAMPIRES
color
® Copyright MCMLXX Beast of Blood Company
A Sceptre Industries Production
Released by
Produced and Directed by Eddie Romero
Executive Producer Kane W. Lynn
GP

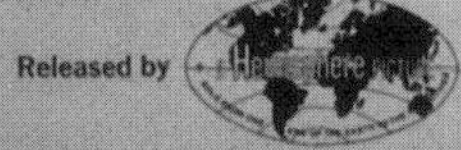

Shoe Queen of Blood Island

The Republic of the Philippines consists of more than 7,000 islands, most of them tiny and uninhabited. Their original settlers, the stone-age Igorots, were later joined by successive waves of immigrants from Indonesia, South China and Vietnam. Beginning in the second century BC, they brought with them a rich and complex system of beliefs and folklore that still survives today. This legacy has influenced many Filipino films. Even American productions shot there have been infused with a spooky magic. The islands abound in tales of ghosts, ghouls and goblins with outlandish names: the *dugong* and the *al-alia*, the *aswang* and the *manananggal*, the *tiyanak* and the *tikbalang*. All have featured in Filipino films from the very earliest days.

It was the Americans who began making movies in the Philippines. Two American-financed films about nationalist hero Dr José Rizal appeared in the same week in 1912. Five years later the country's first film studios were opened by pioneer producer José Nepomuceno. He soon began to capitalise on the Filipino taste for the macabre. His 1926 production, *Tianak* (The Troll), a spooky Gothic melodrama, was a big success and the following year he brought out *Ang Manananggal* (The Witches). This featured primitive special effects, with the actresses portraying the terrifying title characters buried up to their waists around a coffin, making them seem like legless torsos waving their bony arms in the air. *Maria Alimango* was another tale of terror, based on an old legend about an evil spell that turns a woman into a crab. The first Filipino sound film was a horror movie — *Ang Aswang* (The Vampire) — again based on local folklore. The *aswang* is a usually female creature who turns into a fearsome flying fiend at night. It sucks blood through its long hollow tongue and feeds off the flesh of the newborn.

By the mid-1930s there were five major studios operating out of Manila. Their main fare was sentimental weepies, musicals and knockabout comedies, drawing on the acting talent of local vaudeville performers. The Japanese occupation of the islands put film production on hold, but by the late 1940s things were in full swing again, with Hollywood a major influence. Science fiction films like *Ramadal* (about an invisible man) and fantasy-filled romances like *Sohrab at Rustum* (Sohrab and Rustum) and *Prinsipe Tiñoso* (Prince Tinoso) aped contemporary American successes. More unique to the Philippines were 'Satan' films, such as *Satur* and *Kamay ni Satanas* (Hand of Satan). LVN studios became major players. They were run by the formidable Doña Sisang, a remarkable woman of Chinese descent, who had founded the company in 1938 at the age of sixty-one.

A Unique Experience
in motion picture terror!
SO DIFFERENT–
a Bell System Has
Been Installed For
the SQUEAMISH and
FAINT-HEARTED!!!
When the Bell Rings
we suggest you
CLOSE YOUR EYES!
It will ring again
when it's safe to
open them!
The Doctor
The Wife
The Intruder
Terror is a Man
starring FRANCIS LEDERER · GRETA THYSSEN · RICHARD DERR ·
A Lynn-Romero Production · Directed by Gerry de Leon
Screenplay by Harry Paul Harber · A Valiant Films Release

***Opposite:** How to get a head...* Beast of Blood.

***Left:** Behind the lurid ad material for* Terror is a Man *lurked a well-made and sometimes moving film.*
Below: Terror is a Man.

Apparently she had never even seen a film at the time. LVN produced the first full colour Filipino film, *Batalyon 13* (Battalion 13), in 1949. Ten years later, influenced by contemporary Hollywood sci-fi successes, Doña Sisang came up with *Tuko sa Madre Kakaw* (Gekko in a Cacao Tree), detailing an atomic mutation. 1959 also saw the release of another science fiction movie, *Terror is a Man*, that was to have a big influence on the future of Filipino film-making.

The story itself was unremarkable. It was largely based on H. G. Wells' gruesome novella *The Island of Doctor Moreau*, which had been very effectively filmed by Erle C. Kenton in 1932 (as *Island of Lost Souls*). Kenton's film achieved some notoriety by being banned in Britain for twenty-five years. *Terror is a Man* was not so lucky, although it garnered some respectable reviews. The *Monthly Film Bulletin* described it as 'tragically uneven' but 'nevertheless a genuine curiosity.'

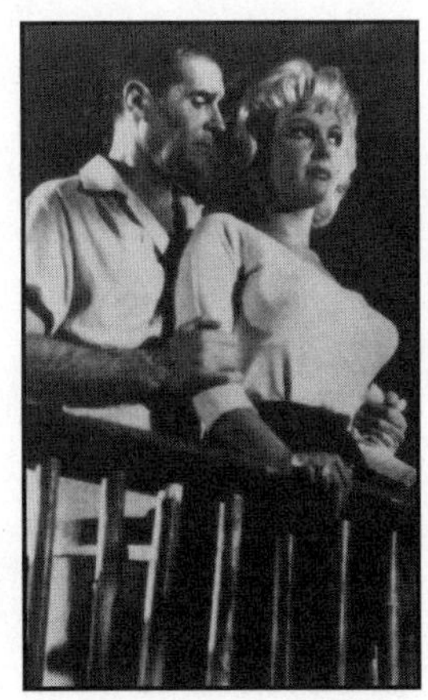

Right: An American Guerrilla in the Philippines.

Far right: Brides of Blood Island.

Below: Filipino horror comic with bloodsucking aswang.

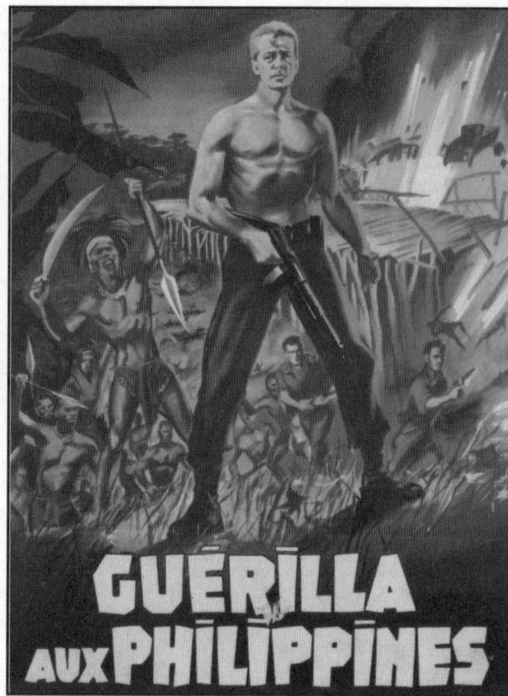

The film was important in that it marked the entry into the global exploitation market of its young co-director Eddie Romero who, over the next twenty or so years, would go on to make some of the most widely exported of all Filipino films.

Born in 1924 on the island of Negros Oriental in South Central Philippines, Romero was something of a child prodigy. He published his first story in the *Philippine Free Press* at the age of twelve. A piece he wrote for *Panorama* magazine in 1941 came to the attention of producer/director Gerardo (Gerry) de Leon. De Leon arranged to meet Romero, unaware of just how young he was. But, as the director later recalled: "he showed not the slightest dismay on discovering that I had been wearing long pants for only a couple of years."

Ang Mæstra (The Teacher), written by Romero and directed by de Leon, was a great success. They collaborated on four more films, with de Leon encouraging the young writer to supervise the shooting of several scenes. Finally in 1947, at the tender age of twenty-two, Romero directed his first solo feature, *Ang Kamay ng Diyos* (The Hand of God). His youth and inexperience were a disadvantage, but an even greater one was the fact that he didn't actually speak the Philippine language, Tagalog, in which the film was made.

Six more films followed, and then in 1949 Romero had the chance to travel to Europe with his family. He took this opportunity to meet some of the greats of world cinema — David Lean, Roberto Rossellini and Vincente Minnelli amongst them — as well as studying at first hand classic movies that had never made it to the Philippines: "I borrowed prints of famous films and went over every shot, sometimes frame by frame."

Returning to the islands a year later he immersed himself in the industry, becoming writer/producer/director of more than fifteen films in four years. The early 1950s was a boom time for Filipino production. More than forty companies were in operation. For the first time, films were being made with an eye to the world market. Manuel Conde's epic *Genghis Khan* was picked up by United Artists. Re-edited by prestigious critic James Agee, it was widely shown in America and Europe. The first Filipino/foreign co-production, *Rodrigo de Villa*, followed in 1952.

The local industry was dominated by four big companies: Doña Sisang's LVN, Sampaguita, Lebran and Premiere. Together they controlled ninety per cent of Philippine production, distribution and exhibition. Their power began to wane during a strike by employees of Premiere. The strike lasted five years and by the time it was over a host of smaller producers had moved in to fill the void. By the end of the decade there were over 100 companies in operation. Lacking the financial resources of the big four, these producers relied on low budgets and quick returns. As veteran filmmaker Lamberto Avellana recalled: "a story is written in two days, shot in eleven and makes money at five days' exhibition, so we make another one just like it."

Eddie Romero despaired of ever getting to make the kinds of films he had dreamed about, the kind that he had seen in Europe. Dragged into an increasing spiral of more work, more financial commitment and ever shorter production schedules, Romero saw only one way out. If he had to make such films, at least he would do them properly, using American money and distribution expertise.

Hooking up with American producer Kane W. Lynn, he began to turn out movies aimed specifically at the American drive-in market. Since the late 1940s, Hollywood films such as *An American Guerrilla in the Philippines* and *Back to Bataan* had used the exotic background of the islands for patriotic war movies. Consequently, many of Romero's early productions were combat films like *The Day of the Trumpet*, *Lost Battalion* and *The Walls of Hell*. This experience led, in the mid-seventies, to second unit work for Coppola's Vietnam epic *Apocalypse Now*. \$3,000,000 of the film's \$20,000,000 budget was spent on location work in the Philippines.

However, it's for his horror movies that Romero is best known and these began with *Terror is a Man*, co-directed with his mentor, Gerry de Leon. The film told the story of Dr Girard, a former Park Avenue surgeon whose experiments have succeeded in turning a panther into a vaguely human creature. The story begins with an American engineer, sole survivor of a shipwreck, washed up on the beach of the remote Isla de Sangre (Blood Island). Gradually he comes to realise the true horror of what Girard has accomplished, creating a thinking, feeling man-beast out of the body of a wild animal. The film's low budget is compensated for by an intelligent script and the excellent playing of Francis Lederer as Girard. The beast is cleverly disguised under swathes of bandages for most of the film. All we see are its terrified eyes, a suggestion of pointed, animal-like ears, and a clawed hand. Skilled direction engenders a real feeling of pity for the poor, trapped creature.

While it may not have broken any new ground in terms of its theme, *Terror is a Man* made very effective use of the geography of the Philippines. Given the many uncharted islands that dot the archipelago, the story's setting was completely believable. This factor, combined with the film's box office success, led to the creation of a new legend specially tailored to capitalise on such remote locations: the saga of Blood Island. The first film in the cycle, *Brides of Blood Island*, was produced in 1965. A few years later it was released to American drive-ins with a great promotional campaign. Free plastic wedding rings were given away to every female viewer — assuring her of her status as a prospective 'bride of the monster'.

The film features all the trappings of late-fifties jungle exotica, including carved stone idols, buxom native girls dancing to pounding drums and a bizarre, vegetable-like monster. By the mid-sixties, when the film was made, much of this must have seemed distinctly old fashioned. A gesture to modernity comes in the figure of a Peace Corps man, Jim Farrell, played by John Ashley. Together with scientist Dr Henderson and his frustrated wife, Carla, played by the improbably named Beverley Hills, he arrives at Blood Island. The trio meet Arcadio, the local big chief, and his granddaughter, Alum. "We have returned to the ways of our ancestors," she informs them. "And we are not too proud of it."

The ways of their ancestors involve live female sacrifices to a hideous creature represented by a gap-toothed carving that looks like a giant Halloween pumpkin.

The new arrivals discover strange mutations and distorted trees that snatch at them as they pass. Could these be the results of atomic tests — or something even worse...? Inevitably, Jim and Alum are attracted to each other. Equally inevitably she is chosen as the next 'bride of the monster'.

Over the following six years, Romero and de Leon continued the saga with another three films. So great was the popularity of the Blood Island series in American drive-ins that a movie entirely shot in Hollywood — Al Adamson's *Brain of Blood* — was promoted as a Filipino production to cash in on the public's taste for exotic gore. Pretty soon the islands became known to film fans as a source of the most unbelievable schlock.

However, not all of Romero's exploitation films are without merit. Given their low budgets ($150,000 on average), they are technically adept and in some cases highly atmospheric. As far back as 1959, the *Monthly Film Bulletin* noted that *Terror is a Man* showed 'a touch of poetry not unlike the great days of *The Hounds of Zaroff* [aka *The Most Dangerous Game*].' As the series progressed, moments like these became rarer. The films Romero made without de Leon are almost entirely lacking any touches of pulp poetry. In contrast, even de Leon's most mendacious products, like the sadistic women's prison film *Women in Cages*, are lit and framed with an artist's eye. John Ashley recalls that on their collaborations it was usually Romero who handled the action and dialogue, while de Leon shot the horror and fantasy scenes for which he had a better feel. De Leon's sympathy with the fantasy genre came to the fore in two films produced by and starring Amalia Fuentes, the Philippines' answer to Elizabeth Taylor.

The Blood Drinkers and its companion piece, *Creatures of Evil*, successfully combine the European vampire film with the corresponding Filipino myths of the *aswang* and the *mandurugo*. The Philippines' unique situation — being the only Catholic country in Asia — makes this fusion work in some surprising ways. In both films the themes of sin, guilt and redemption through suffering and love are every bit as strong as in the classic Italian vampire films of the early

Left: *'Ooh! You wicked beast!'* Brides of Blood Island.

Above right: Mad Doctor of Blood Island.
Right: *The bald-headed Dr Marco claims another victim in* The Blood Drinkers.

1960s. What these films add is a unique hothouse atmosphere, the sense of an enclosed, hemmed-in community. The overripe lushness of green jungle plants frames many of the shots. Strangeness and eroticism threaten from all sides. Yet, in both films the destruction actually comes from within the family itself. In *Creatures of Evil* it is the mother who is the first to be vampirised, and she passes the curse on to her children. In *The Blood Drinkers* the mother's immorality leads her to team up with an evil man who turns out to be a vampire. He then sets his sights on her two daughters. Both movies make the point that these vampires prefer the blood of their own family and loved ones to that of strangers. In the Philippines, blood definitely runs thicker than water.

The Blood Drinkers, like many Filipino films, was based on a *komiks* series. These illustrated novellas, published in weekly parts, are hugely popular and often used as the basis for films. In *The Blood Drinkers,* the original story's lengthy subplots are compressed into an economical eighty-eight minutes, necessitating much voice over narration and leading to some decidedly incoherent moments. Ironically, this incoherence gives the film a mysterious, almost surreal quality that more traditional vampire films, such as the Hammer movies, often lack. The contrast between the pulp story and de Leon's classically framed and lit compositions also helps to make *The Blood Drinkers* one of the most interesting of all Filipino horror movies.

The film's opening scenes are worthy of Mario Bava, as a horsedrawn hearse rolls through misty woods at night, and giant wrought iron gates open onto a gothic mansion. An incongruous note is struck by the sudden appearance of a shiny American car with its rocket fins and polished chrome. Out of the car steps the bald-headed vampire, Dr Marco, and his kinky assistant Tanya. With his retinue of dwarves, hunchbacks and a bat called Basra, Marco has come to the Philippines to find the twin sister of his lover, Christina. She is near death and only her sibling's transplanted heart can save her.

The Blood Drinkers uses an almost avant-garde mixture of colour and tinted film stock. In the middle of dialogue scenes, the screen suddenly becomes awash with violet light, announcing the arrival of the vampire. Cemetery scenes shot in the crisp light of early dawn are shown in a blue tint ed monochrome. In some scenes, characters' faces are picked out in red against an otherwise conventionally coloured background.

Typically for a Filipino film, love, faith and religious ritual save the day and Christina is consigned to a peaceful grave. In contrast with most American and European horror films, the villain, Dr Marco, escapes. After all, as the priest narrator points out, how can you kill the Devil himself?

De Leon's 1970 film *Creatures of Evil* is another story of vampirism within the family. Here, the mother is the first to be infected. After her death the father has her coffin brought to the house and locked up in the cellar. The entrance is then concealed behind a huge portrait of the fearsome matriarch. At night, when she emerges from her coffin, the husband and his hunchbacked servant chain her up, after whipping her to subdue her. Eventually the mother escapes and vampirises her son, Eduardo. In his turn he initiates Christina, daughter of a neighbouring land owner, and takes her for his wife. On their wedding night we see

Christina sitting on the bed waiting expectantly for her husband. As Eduardo enters, her face is suddenly bathed in blue light, making her look like a Tretchikoff painting come to life.

"I, Eduardo, am your lord and master," he announces, before sinking his fangs into her tender neck.

Finally, the villagers, led by their priest, descend on the house to eradicate the evil curse. In one of the most astonishing scenes in the film, we see a moving forest of crosses, effigies and religious carvings surround the house. Doll-faced, wooden Madonnas, huge sprays of flowers and even a proud white cockerel crowd out the lush, dangerous green of the encroaching jungle.

Like *The Blood Drinkers, Creatures of Evil* uses garish, neon tones to heighten the unreality of its horror set pieces. When we see the vampire mother lying in her coffin, sickly greens and yellows highlight her parchment-like skin. As she rises eerily to attack, red light floods the dank cellar. In lesser hands this might have looked cheap or camp, but by this time de Leon was the most technically adept film-maker working in the Philippines. He knew exactly what he wanted and, more importantly, how to achieve it on his limited budget.

As actor Vic Salayan later recalled: "Gerry was a real craftsman. Many of the effects in the film were done in the camera and not in the studio or at the laboratory... Even after he would call a wrap, he continued to think out and do his homework for the following day's work. So he knew all his angles, where he would put his camera, where he wanted his lights... He would walk back and forth, peering through his camera, walk back and forth again until he could finally solve it. It was painstaking."

Other vampire films shot in the Philippines seem anaemic set next to de Leon's two flawed masterpieces. *Tore ng Diyablo* (The Devil's Tower) is another *komiks* derivative, featuring a vampire and a werewolf. *Men of Action Meet Women of Drakula* treads a similar path to Mexican horrors like *Samson vs the Vampire Women*, with high-kicking heroes encountering busty bloodsuckers. Even more ridiculous is Cirio H. Santiago's *The Vampire Hookers*. The title opens vistas of possibility for an enjoyably sleazy slice of trash. Unfortunately, the reality is a sad disappointment. *The Vampire Hookers* is one of those unfortunate films that seems to have been planned as a drama and turned into a comedy in a post-production panic.

De Leon died in 1981, having long since given up the struggle to make serious films in the Philippines. Romero was more sanguine, content just to have fun playing with the conventions of American exploitation movies. He found a willing accomplice in former teen idol John Ashley.

"I always *liked* these movies... I just enjoyed doing them," admitted Ashley, who became quite a star in the Philippines. He made thirteen movies there during a twelve year period and was the only non-Filipino ever to receive an award from the Filipino Academy of Motion Picture Arts and Sciences. As an example of how differently things were done in the Philippines compared to the States, he recalls his final film, *Black Mamba*: "I played a doctor... and we had a scene in which we got a human body, did an examination and then

***Left:** 'Our mother's a vampire!'* Creatures of Evil.
***Below:** Classic Filipino horror:* The Blood Drinkers.

literally took the body apart. We did it with an actual human corpse — we made a deal, arranged to get a dead body from one of the prisons, and exhumed it."

Ashley had got his first Filipino film by chance, but grew to like the country so much that he moved there and in 1970 formed a production company, Four Associates, with Eddie Romero. Roger Corman, a long-time friend of Ashley's, came to visit the set of their first film *Beast of the Yellow Night.* He was impressed with the facilities available and decided to switch production of his New World company's next film from Puerto Rico to the Philippines. The resulting picture — *The Big Doll House,* directed by Jack Hill — was a huge success* and the first in a long series of women-in-prison (WIP) films shot in the islands.

The genesis of the Filipino WIP films was a script by writer Jim White. Jack Hill brought the script to Roger Corman and his then partner Larry Woolner. He knew that both men were looking for a film to capitalise on the huge success of Jess Franco's *99 Women.* Unfortunately, while Jack Hill was working in Europe for Swiss producer Irwin Dietrich, Stephanie Rothman got hold of the script, rewrote it and persuaded Corman that she was now the only person who could direct it. Interestingly, given her 'feminist' reputation, Hill asserts that most of the sadistic torture scenes were put into the script by Rothman. Rothman and Corman had a falling out and Hill regained control of the project. Meanwhile, Rothman took her version of the script to Larry Woolner and made yet another version of the same story as *Terminal Island.*

Below: *The American one-sheet poster for* The Big Doll House *leaves little to the imagination.*

THEY CAGED THEIR BODIES
BUT NOT THEIR DESIRES
Soft young girls behind hard prison bars...
They'd do anything for a man — or to him!
Boiling passions confined behind concrete walls.
Naked lust that builds to a climax of death.
COLOR BY DELUXE
BIG DOLL HOUSE
JUDY BROWN · ROBERTA COLLINS · PAM GRIER
BROOKE MILLS · PAT WOODELL · SID HAIG
JANE SCHAFFER
DON SPENCER
JACK HILL
A NEW WORLD PICTURES RELEASE
COLOR BY DELUXE

The Big Doll House contains most of the clichés of the WIP genre as well as being, occasionally, a genuinely disturbing production. A scene repeated several times throughout the movie has a woman being tortured while a hooded figure, seated on a throne-like white chair, watches through a network of chains. As a kind of revenge for the problems he had experienced in Europe, Jack Hill named the evil wardress of *The Big Doll House* after his former employer, Dietrich.

One of the film's strengths, and of many other American-Filipino co-productions of the period, was the pairing of Pam Grier and Sid Haig. Grier was a statuesque black actress who had begun her career with a small role in Russ Meyer's *Beyond the Valley of the Dolls.* She later became a staple of early-seventies blaxploitation movies such as *Coffy, Friday Foster* and *Foxy Brown.* Unfortunately, she soon became dissatisfied with the whore, junky and 'battling babe' roles she was offered and until recently Hollywood never really found another niche for her.

Sid Haig was a big, gangling, jovial looking actor with a twinkling eye and a huge, toothy grin. Jack Hill had been introduced to him in 1961 by Dorothy Arzner, who had met him at the Pasadena Playhouse where he was a drama student. He had featured in Hill's oddball horror comedy *Spider Baby* in 1964, but truly came into his own in the Philippines. In *The Big Bird Cage* he effortlessly delivers lines such as: "I ain't no bandit! I'm a revolutionary!" as he robs rich clients of their jewels during a raid on a night-club.

The Big Bird Cage, made right after *The Big Doll House,* parodies all the conventions of the genre that the first film had helped establish. Watching the shaking hut in which Grier and Haig are making love after the night-club raid, their bandido comrades comment: "What a woman that Blossom. If only we had more like her. What a revolution we could have."

They decide to "steal some women for the revolution" and plan a raid on the Government's work camp, the 'big bird cage' of the title. In contrast to the sometimes ragged acting and limp dialogue of the first movie, the ensemble playing of *Bird Cage*'s large cast is a constant joy.

Following the success of the Jack Hill movies, it was inevitable that Eddie Romero should follow suit. His 1972 production *The Woman Hunt* (also released as *Escape*), had the potential to be one of his most disturbing films. Based on a story by Jack Hill, it was one of many versions of Ernest B. Schoedsack's 1932 classic *The Most Dangerous Game,* where the sadistic Count Zaroff plays hunt-the-human on his remote island. In Romero's movie the victims are women and the hunters a bunch of businessmen, all of whom owe

* *Made for less than $150,000, it went on to take over $3,000,000 at the box office, making it one of the most successful low-budget features of all time. Roger Corman recalls how one of his co-investors, seeing the Friday night queues for the film, went to church to give thanks to the Lord. He had never seen anything like it in twenty years in the business.*

their success to the sadistic Spiros (played by Sid Haig), who has forced them to take part in his evil game. Steering clear of the rampant misogyny that the title and subject matter suggest, Romero delivers a film that is actually less controversial than the 1932 movie. Even a delightfully leering performance from the ever reliable Sid Haig can't lift the film.

In any case, the women-in-prison formula was starting to tire. In only a couple of years Corman and company had managed to ring most of the changes out of its limited repertoire. By 1973, New World were passing on projects, such as *Caged Heat,* that would have looked like sure-fire winners a couple of years earlier. The WIP movie shifted back to Europe where Franco took it up again, this time with Swiss producer Irwin C. Dietrich, Jack Hill's former employer. Dietrich/Franco collaborations like *The Women of Cell Block 9* and *Wanda the Wicked Warden* brought to the fore all the gruesome torture and sadism that the Filipino films had only dared suggest.

The success of the New World, Filipino-based films led other American producers to follow them and pretty soon there was a generic 'Asian Pacific' look to American exploitation movies. This was the period when martial arts films from Hong Kong were making a big impact on the world's screens. Cheaply acquired clips from any number of these could be easily combined with Filipino-shot footage to make a real Asian stew of a movie. Throw in a couple of semi-name stars (the late Cameron Mitchell was a popular choice) and you had a film for almost no money.

Soon Philippine producers became aware of the commercial potential in their own back yard. They began to put together their own 'Asian stews', exploiting the public's hunger for action heroes. Cirio H. Santiago and Bobby Suarez were only the most persistent of a long list of aggressively commercial film-makers who pumped 'em out in the seventies and eighties. Martial arts films were popular with the crowds. Actor Leo Fong recalls arriving in Manila to make his first picture, *Murder in the Orient,* in 1973. Because he had appeared on a magazine cover with Bruce Lee, all the kung fu fans came out to greet him — and take him on. He had hardly stepped off the plane before he was challenged to two fights by local martial arts experts. Fong, probably the least charismatic of all action stars, made a long series of movies in the Philippines. *Enforcer From Death Row,* like many Filipino movies, deals with redemption and resurrection. Fong plays a convicted killer rescued from the gas chamber by a mysterious organisation called WOP (World Organisation for Peace). They revive him and send him off to save the Philippines from destruction by biological weapons.

Above: *Pam Grier and Margaret Markov are* Black Mama, White Mama.
Left: *The corpulent Vic Diaz was a fixture in Filipino exploitation movies.*

Women are made for men...
TO HUNT!
Set your sights on the Tastiest Game of all!
WOMAN HUNT
Starring JOHN ASHLEY · PAT WOODELL · LAURIE ROSE
CHARLENE JONES · LISA TODD · SID HAIG
Produced by JOHN ASHLEY and EDDIE ROMERO · Directed by EDDIE ROMERO
A FOUR ASSOCIATES, LTD. PRODUCTION · A NEW WORLD PICTURES RELEASE
METROCOLOR
R RESTRICTED

They need a special liquid to stay young.
It is red, thick and warm!!
THE THIRSTY DEAD

In general, few Filipino films made it out of the country. Some were distributed in Indonesia and Thailand but, as the late film director Ishmael Bernal found out: "Our films are not marketable in Asia... It's very strange. We're neighbours but very different from other countries." The films that were exported did little to redeem the reputation of the Filipino industry. Take the notorious *For Your Height Only*.

The star of this sci-fi/martial arts comedy is the two-and-a-half foot high Weng Weng. He was a big draw in the local movie houses, where comedy mixed with action always pulled in the crowds. Weng Weng certainly provides comedy, most of the time while he's trying to provide the action as well. Seeing a two-foot-nine inch guy taking on half a dozen full-grown men is probably funny enough in itself. But when he tumbles between their legs and bites them on the bum as a form of attack, it soon moves into the surreal.

Weng Weng sums up a style of movie star and movie-making that local intellectuals called *bakya*. The term refers to the wooden slippers worn by the poor who inhabit the teeming ghettos of Tondo and Magsaysay. To indicate their approval of anything they saw on screen they would stamp their wooden clogs, a sound that inspired terror in the hearts of serious cinephiles. Although intended as a term of abuse for anything low rent, cheap or vulgar, *bakya* was eventually reclaimed as a badge of honour, rather in the way that black Americans used the word 'nigger' as a term of endearment.

Jokes abound about the supposed ignorance of the *bakya* movie star — usually a dumb female: To a waiter in a crowded, smoke-filled restaurant: "Please open the door. I'm getting sophisticated."...On seeing a black cat pass by: "That's a bad ointment." After singing a song that has met with appreciative applause: "Thanks for the clap."

The only films made in the Philippines that were widely distributed abroad were the American co-productions. Few of these used indigenous myths in any creative way. The drive-in horrors made there during the seventies were a pretty sorry lot. *Daughters of Satan* features a very young Tom Selleck in a plot about witchcraft and reincarnation. Made at the same time and with some of the same cast was *The Thirsty Dead*. Here women are kidnapped to provide life essence for an Aztec-inspired immortality cult. After a boat trip through the sewers of Manila, the film shifts into high camp over-drive when we reach the cult's mountain hide out. It's a cave with flaming torches on the wall, where maidens in pink mini togas dance in front of a head in a glass tank.

Even sadder was *The Deathhead Virgin*. This one actually has some snatches of atmosphere, but manages to blow it all in an uninspired caper plot. Most American-Filipino co-productions use imported myths like vampires and atomic mutations, but *The Deathhead Virgin* dredges up an old legend from the Muslim South of the country about a virgin princess raped by Spanish invaders and chained in a sunken galleon. Aroused from her watery sleep by a scuba-diving treasure hunter, she possesses his soul and sends him off scalping women. Directed by former Orson Welles associate Norman Foster, the film is basically a vanity production for father and son team Ward and Jock Gaynor.

It wasn't only the Americans who came to the Philippines to take advantage of the cheap local facilities. There were strong Chinese connections in the local film business and several Hong Kong co-productions were shot in the islands. One of the most entertaining is *Magic Curse* from 1977. This is a film about snake cults and lost treasure, ostensibly set in Borneo. However, the presence of topless bomba queen Pinky de Leon and actors like Vic Silayan, mark this one out as another Asian stew. The genial Jason Pai Pau stars as a man from Hong Kong searching for his uncle whose plane has crashed in the jungle. He meets the comely snake princess Philona and helps her defeat the evil wizard Abdullah. The film features flying skulls, a green-faced vampire woman who bites off a man's cock and, of course, lots of snakes.

Snakes also feature in the 1970 film *Devil Woman*. This is a Hong Kong/Philippines co-production with a Chinese hero — unusual in locally made movies. The film begins one stormy night with the birth of a baby. We don't see the child, or at least we only see its feet, but it's obvious something is wrong. The midwife runs screaming from the house and is promptly bitten by a large snake. It turns out that the girl, Manda, is a sort of Medusa. "My hair is full of snakes," she soliloquises later via appalling dubbing. "I'm not fit to live with people."

Identifying her as the spawn of the Devil, the local villagers burn her family's hut. But Manda survives to take her revenge. She uses her power over snakes to gain control of a gang of local toughs, who then go round raping and pillaging. A visiting Chinese doctor (and kung fu expert!) crosses their path and several lengthy punch-ups ensue. Eventually Manda falls to her death down a deep ravine.

While the influx of overseas producers continued throughout the seventies, some of the local pioneers began to weary of the game. When Eddie Romero moved on to more serious movies, Cirio H. Santiago stepped into his shoes. Santiago is so prolific that a complete filmography would fill several pages. The 1974 film *TNT Jackson* was one of his early efforts. In the spirit of Jack Hill's *Coffy* and *Foxy Brown*, this is another story of a feisty black woman kicking ass. Former Playboy model Jeanne Bell plays the woman in question, out to find her missing brother in the sleaze pits of Hong Kong. Bell starred again in Santiago's 1976 film *The Muthers*. Here four women are modern day pirates out to settle scores with an assortment of bad guys.

The revenge dramas and WIP movies made in the seventies were a pretty violent and sexy bunch. Given the country's repressive political situation at the time, they might have been expected to encounter problems. In fact, as John Ashley recalls, the Philippines' Government was very supportive: "Particularly in the early days, because the scripts were so generic. Later on, when we started doing *Savage Sisters* and others which involved a military posture within the film, we had some minor problems... several times when we were down there shooting, martial law was in effect and they had curfews."

This was the time of the notorious Ferdinand Marcos, who had come to power in 1966 following his fierce suppression of Muslim rebels in the southern province of Mindanao. During the period of martial law that began in 1972, more than 60,000 of Marcos's opponents were imprisoned. Many never came out alive. In spite of martial law, corruption and oppressive censorship, it was during the Marcos years that cinema boomed in the Philippines. Some of the credit for this has to go to Marcos's wife, the notorious former beauty queen Imelda. She was the sort of first lady for whom the celebrity magazine *Hello* seems to have been invented. With her doll-like but somehow seedy glamour and her tacky wardrobe of kitsch extravagance, Imelda was instantly identifiable, and news wherever she went. She came across as a weird combination of Barbara Cartland, Margaret Thatcher and Zsa Zsa Gabor. Her notoriety derived in large part from her sense of *noblesse oblige*, particularly galling in a country where much of the population lived below the poverty line. Imelda was rumoured to have owned 3,000 pairs of shoes, but maintained that people gave them to her. Too kind to refuse, she kept them so as not to hurt their feelings.

Imelda's most visible contribution to the Philippines' cinema culture was the creation of the Film Centre in Manila, a huge edifice built to host the annual festival and house the newly established archive. In theory an admirable project, but in reality another symbol of the Marcos megalomania. To ensure the building's readiness for the 1982 gala opening, teams of construction workers toiled round the clock. Inevitably, corners were cut and tragedy ensued. Early one morning the roof of the building collapsed, burying 200 workers under a thick carpet of fast drying cement. Desperate to finish the building on time, supervisors

Opposite top: The Woman Hunt*: typical feminist fare from Eddie Romero.*
Opposite bottom: The Thirsty Dead*: dying for a drink.*

Below: Daughters of Satan *featured Tom Selleck in one of his first film roles.*

They're
The Karate Queens!
They're
The Plundering Pirates!
They're
The MUTHERS!
THE
MUTHERS

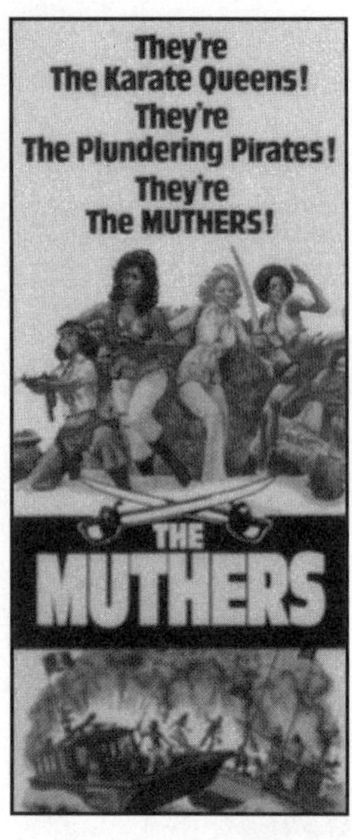

ordered that those caught in the cement were to be left to their fate. Any limbs still projecting when the cement had dried were to be sliced off and the stumps covered over. Weeks later, when the international guests arrived, they found the film centre swarming with flies and the air thick with the smell of rotting flesh. Many years later, in 1996, a service of exorcism was held to lay to rest the angry spirits that were said to be still haunting the building.

The festival was a lavish affair and caught the eye of the International Monetary Fund. Aware of the country's foreign debt burden in excess of seventeen billion dollars, they let it be known that the 'international community' (ie, the World Bank) took a dim view of such junkets. Undaunted, Imelda came up with a novel way of funding the following year's festival. A moratorium on censorship was declared throughout the Metro Manila area. Uncut versions of formerly banned movies would be shown for two weeks in 141 cinemas, with ticket prices at twice their normal level. Sixty-five per cent of the box office would then be ploughed back into the festival. The plan was a resounding success. Audiences flocked to see films like *Lovebirds*, *Virgin People* ('they lived in a world without shame') and *The Victim*.

These violent, sex-soaked melodramas had their roots in the late-sixties craze for what were known as 'bomba' films. These were a close relative of the 'roughies' that had invaded American screens a few years earlier, films like *The Defilers* and *Lorna*. The Philippine variant of the form had been kicked off by Ruben Abalaos's *Uhaw* (Thirst), released in 1968. Soon screens were awash with softcore sex, blood and even a graphic birth scene in 1977's *Nunal sa Tubig* (Mole in the Water). Menstrual blood, abortion and violent rape became a common feature of films that were hypocritically denied the chance to show straight sex scenes and innocent nudity. Working within these restrictions, 'bombas' like *Manila For Flesh*, *The Two Different Worlds of Adam and Eve* and *Nympha* were able to exploit a strange paradox in that the fearsome censorship of the Marcos years was generally directed against films with a political rather than a sexual agenda.

Eventually the 'bomba' became known as 'bold', with sex movies accounting for up to seventy per cent of total production during the 1980s. Imelda's short-lived experiment of allowing uncut movies to be shown during the film festival gave the genre a real boost. Elwood Perez's *Silip* (Peeping) from 1985 included lesbian incest, a beheading, burning at the stake and the inevitable gang rape. Celso Ad Castillo's *Virgin People* was another big hit, with its scenes of teen starlet Pepsi Paloma baring her all. The plot, like several other 'bold' movies, is reminiscent of early Russ Meyer, with a young stud upsetting the rural idyll of three innocent girls. Heaving bosoms fill the screens and pent up desires provide the dramatic tension.

Castillo had been in the business for over fifteen years at this point. He had started as a *komiks* creator and film

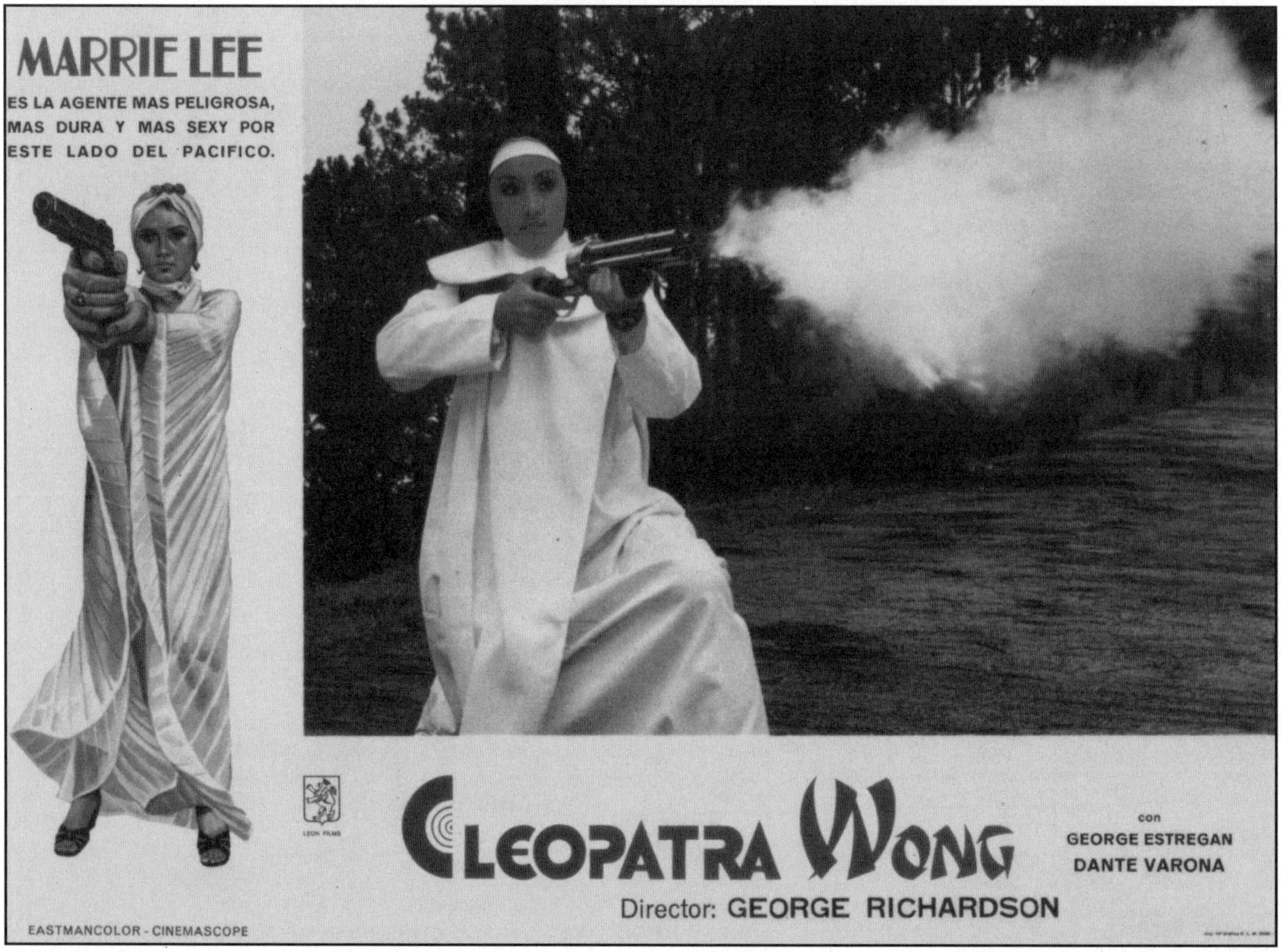

MARRIE LEE
ES LA AGENTE MAS PELIGROSA, MAS DURA Y MAS SEXY POR ESTE LADO DEL PACIFICO.
CLEOPATRA WONG
con
GEORGE ESTREGAN
DANTE VARONA
Director: GEORGE RICHARDSON
EASTMANCOLOR - CINEMASCOPE

scriptwriter before directing *Nympha* in 1970. This highly controversial film combined sex, religion and violence. The ending showed a naked woman bleeding to death after a failed backstreet abortion. One of Castillo's biggest hits was 1973's *Patayin mo sa Sindak si Barbara* (Kill Barbara With Panic), a gory horror film about a woman who commits suicide and returns to haunt her unfaithful husband. All Castillo's early movies had featured sex. With the increased freedoms of the eighties he really went to town. 1983's *Isla* (Island) broke several taboos in terms of language and nudity. The mythic *Snake Sisters* features three delicious 'bomba queens' — Pepsi Paloma, Sarsi Emmanuelle and Coca Nicholas — playing women hatched from snake eggs who turn into real snakes when a man tries to have sex with them.

Peque Gallaga's *Scorpio Nights* was another big hit shown uncut during the MIFF (Manila International Film Festival) celebrations. Originally running 112 minutes, the film was cut on its initial release to a mere seventy-two, but was still acclaimed as 'the most sensual Filipino film ever'. Given the mood of the times and the film's heavy political subtext, *Scorpio Nights* was pretty much a guerrilla production, shot in only thirteen days and in one location. Scenes set outside the studio, in Manila's bustling Chinatown, had to be shot surreptitiously, with the camera hidden inside an old straw bag.

Essentially *Scorpio Nights* is a series of lengthy sex scenes, involving a night-watchman, his wife and a young student who spies on them. In common with many Filipino films, *Scorpio Nights* was based on a true story. Director Gallaga says he was attracted to it because it was "a story of sexual obsession, of perversity and of one-upmanship; there being no rewards except for the sex itself."

The film is set in an overcrowded, run-down mansion in the centre of Manila. The thin partition walls and plywood floors mean that there is little privacy. Danny, a young student, is able to see into the room below. Every morning at 4.00am he watches the man who lives there making love to his bored wife. Danny becomes obsessed with the woman. What begins with masturbation ends with him in the woman's room one night, taking the husband's place in her bed. As the woman seems to be half asleep most of the time, it's hard to tell whether she knows who her lover is. But eventually she begins to respond to the new stimuli. Trapped in a situation where sex is the only thing she has to give and the only front on which she can assert herself, she starts to play off one man against the other. The ending of the film is as bleak as it's inevitable.

Although initially derided by intellectuals, the sex melodramas influenced a new, mostly university educated group of film-makers that rose to prominence in the late 1970s. The group included Mike de Leon, Ishmael Bernal and Elwood Perez. For them the turbulent melodramatic stories of sexual desire and obsession struck a chord with their own feelings, railing against the political and social restrictions of the time. The pioneer of this group, and the only Filipino film-maker to gain any international reputation, was Lino Brocka.

Brocka worked very much inside the industry, turning out the sort of films audiences wanted to see, but giving them a harsh, contemporary feel much closer to the work of American mavericks like Sam Fuller than conventional Filipino melodramas.

"The reason my films are melodramas, film noir, is because I love them, and film noir seems to me to be close to the social reality of the Philippines," Brocka explained. Aware of the aggressively commercial nature of the Filipino film business, he decided to confront the industry on its own terms. "I went to these producers and said, 'How much do you pay your C-directors? What is your budget for these movies?' (I'm talking about the very, very commercial films, the sex movies and all that).

"And I said 'Okay, give it to me. I'll do it. And I'll do it better.' ...That's why in my filmography you have titles like *White Slavery*, *Strangers in Paradise*, *Adultery*... and I will not apologise for those movies or say that I wish they were better forgotten."

However, Brocka certainly appreciated the irony that, as a Third World film-maker, even his exploitation efforts were praised by Western critics. *Angela Markada* is the story of a woman raped by six men who carve their names on her back. As in the similar *I Spit on Your Grave*, she hunts them down and kills them. The film was awarded the Grand Prix at the Nantes Third World Film Festival. "I didn't know whether to play along with them or disappoint them," Brocka confessed. "I tell them, 'My God, you're so impressionable, just because it was written about in *Positif*, *Cahiers du Cinéma*...!'"

The violence and brutality in many Filipino films, even from 'respectable' directors like Brocka, is something that

WHAT POWER SHOULD A MAN POSSESS TO CHALLENGE THE PRINCE OF DARKNESS?
THE KILLING OF
SATAN
CINEX FILMS, INC.
RAMON REVILLA THE KILLING OF SATAN
ELIZABETH OROPESA GEORGE ESTREGAN PAQUITO DIAZ CECILE CASTILLO CHARLIE DAVAO
FRANCISCO C. PUZON, JR. CONRADO C. PUZON PIO C. LEE
JOSE MARI AVELLANA ERNANI CUENCO RICARDO HERRERA EFREN C. PIÑON

Opposite bottom: *Nun with gun has fun in the sun in* Cleopatra Wong.

Above: *Ramon Revilla gives old Nick a kick in* The Killing of Satan.

***Above:** The exotic savagery of* Igorota.

Western critics find hard to handle. Of course poverty itself is a form of violence and to deal with the reality of the Philippines means confronting these issues head on. Popular entertainment of all kinds is much more visceral there than in the West. Cockfighting is a popular spectator sport as is horse fighting, where two lusty stallions fight for possession of a mare on heat. Such spectacles draw huge crowds to the weekly *tabu-an* where the whole community lets its hair down.

This enjoyment of violent conflict underpins one of the most popular genres of Filipino cinema: the action movie. Critic Agustin Sotto traces their basic approach to the *moro moro*, a form of Christian morality play developed during the years of Spanish occupation. In these simplistic narratives, one-dimensional Christian heroes battled with Muslim enemies. The climax of the *moro moro*, as in the films that they influenced, is a long-awaited battle in which good inevitably triumphs. Other influences on the Filipino action movie include martial arts and swordplay films imported from Japan and Hong Kong. Local Filipino forms of martial arts include the *escrima* swordplay and the *arnis*, in which two short sticks are used with deadly precision. Often, as in Chinese kung fu, the martial arts displays have a balletic quality. A popular folk dance in the Philippines involves two lengths of bamboo being slammed together at ground level, narrowly avoiding the ankles of the dancers who daintily hop between them.

The granddaddy of local action heroes was Fernando Poe Jr, usually known simply as FPJ. Joseph Estrada, Ramon Revilla and later Roland Dantes and Ramon Revilla's son, Bong, also joined the ranks of these tough but fair fighters for truth and justice. Like action films from India, Turkey and Hong Kong, Filipino films feature strong men fighting wicked oppressors — often landowners or corrupt politicians.

The idea of redemption through suffering is a feature of many of these movies. Sometimes this is shown by the way the patient hero only fights back after enduring almost endless provocation from the villains. Sometimes the testing of the hero is more ritualised, touching on issues of magic and the supernatural. Often this involves the acquisition of *anting anting* — a sort of talisman that makes its wearer invincible. It's usually bandits and outsiders who use *anting anting*. In *Kapitan Inggo* Ramon Revilla plays an outlaw hero who undergoes a ritual that makes him impregnable to bullets.

The rite of passage of Ben (Roland Dantes) in *The Pacific Connection* is more complex. To fulfil his destiny, whatever it may be, he has to find the mysterious 'old one' his father told him about. The film is set during the Spanish occupation and Ben's route to salvation is littered with reminders of injustice. At the beginning of the film he sees his father killed and his mother raped by the Spaniards. In a gesture as symbolic as it's painful to watch, Ben's mother slices off the rapist's penis. This begins a series of key motifs in which a man's worth is judged by his ability to have sex or to fight with a sword. And the effete Spaniards are useless at both activities. The only 'good' oppressor is an imported Japanese samurai. When Ben defeats him and breaks his sword, the samurai announces that his life is now over and begs to be put out of his misery.

Ben's initiation into manhood involves him climbing a distant volcano and collecting an iron reed that grows there, surrounded by beds of molten lava. From the reed he constructs two unbreakable *arnis* sticks with which he can defeat the Spanish oppressors.

In Efren C. Piñon's 1974 film *The Killing of Satan*, Ramon Revilla undergoes another long and painful endurance test. The film begins with depictions of the mock crucifixions and mystical rituals that take place during Easter Week in the Philippines. In one of these rituals a man is wrapped in coconut matting and a knife is drawn across it. He emerges unscathed. While these pseudo-Christian rituals (also used by the Black Nazarene cults) are nominally derived from the period of Spanish occupation, they are also influenced by ideas remaining from a much earlier age, from ancient Malay magic and folk rituals — a connection that the film soon makes clear.

A tiny island community is terrorised by the red-robed Prince of Magic. Surrounded by his seven black-garbed cohorts, he laughs uproariously at all attempts to defeat him. Old Miguel, the village elder, challenges the Prince to a duel of magic. Effortlessly, the Prince sends Miguel spinning like a top, until he collapses onto the ground, unconscious. Later, lying in his death bed, he names his nephew, Lando, as his successor.

But Lando has problems of his own. Living on another island far from old Miguel, he knows nothing of his call to destiny. He is more concerned with the local tough guy, Ibanez. Lando had killed his brother and served time in prison for it. Ibanez and his henchmen turn up and shoot both Lando and his son. As Lando's wife mourns them, she touches her husband's forehead with her crucifix. Miraculously, the bullet wound disappears and Lando opens his eyes.

"What are you doing to us, Lord?" pleads his confused wife.

Sailing to Miguel's island in a small boat, Lando and family are swept up by a mysterious wind which draws them to the shore where a tousle-haired, pale-skinned boy waits for them. Unable to speak, he leads them to Miguel's village. Lando is astonished to learn that old Miguel died at exactly the moment when he, Lando, rose from death.

"He died from a bullet wound, but nobody round here fired a shot," insists Renzo, Miguel's young assistant.

While Lando and Renzo are away, the Prince of Magic and his cohorts turn up and kidnap Betty, Lando's daughter, and Luisa, Renzo's fiancée. The two men set sail for the island of the Prince of Magic, armed only with faith in the justness of their cause and the hope that old Miguel's powers may have been transferred to Lando.

In his book *God's Dust,* Ian Buruma speaks of the Filipino psyche as being composed of 'Catholic imagery of death and redemption... merged with Malay beliefs in spiritual power or *anting anting.*' Only such a combination could have produced a film like *The Killing of Satan.*

The Prince of Magic's master is, of course, the devil himself. We see him in his traditional form, familiar from medieval church paintings, with horns, a tail and a three-pronged pitchfork. These Christian elements are combined with other images that go right back to the roots of Malay magic. The devil's handmaidens, for example, appear as beautiful women, but when Lando casts his magic on them they turn into snakes, slithering from under their empty clothes.

The notion of a quest and redemption through suffering are ancient ideas found in cultures around the world. Another common folk belief is that of transformation. Folk tales are full of people turning into wolves or foxes, or being gifted with magic powers through possession of a charmed object. The idea of magic transformation is a popular one in the Philippines too. Such stories often have a strong element of wish fulfilment, with the dispossessed and the disadvantaged, cripples or the handicapped, being given sudden magical powers. *Komiks* stories and spin-off films have used magical typewriters, ballpoint pens and amulets to turn poor slum-dwellers into crime-fighting heroes and heroines. In *Super Inday and the Golden Bibi,* a golden goose (the *bibi*) turns a girl into Super Inday, a kind of wonder woman gifted with the power of flight. *Super Islaw and the Flying Kids* is a similar wish-fulfilment fantasy, where a crippled boy becomes a flying superhero. The star of the 1989 film *Supermouse and the Roborats* is a half-human, half-rodent character who transforms into a whiskered, mouse-eared superman to fight a bunch of invaders from outer space. The film, not surprisingly, is mostly played for laughs. A spin-off from a popular Hollywood hit — *Alyas Batman and Robin* (Alias Batman and Robin) — is another gormless farce with a costumed duo of klutzy comedians.

Most of the above were one-offs, cheap attempts to jump onto a passing bandwagon. A much more interesting character is Darna, the Philippines' answer to Wonder Woman. Although derived from an American original, this is one superhero that has been given a distinctly local flavour. The story of the ghetto girl with superpowers was dreamed up by *komiks* artist Mars Ravelo in the 1950s and has been filmed several times since. Rosa del Rosario was the first actress to play the part, with Lisa Moreno, Gina Pareno and Vilma Santos following in her footsteps. In 1991, producer William C. Leary revived the series with the appealing Nanette Medved in the title role.

Narda, a young girl living in the barrios of Manila, is out playing with her little brother. A mysterious voice draws her into a dark cavern where an angel with glowing wings gives her a magic pearl. Every time Narda swallows the pearl and utters the magic word "Darna!", she turns into a flying superwoman in a skimpy red bikini and shiny boots. A shouted "Narda!" ejects the pearl and returns her to normal. In costume, the lithe-bodied Nanette Medved is extremely easy on the eye. As her *alter ego,* Narda, a junior reporter on a local newspaper, she's less impressive. Fortunately, the film features more of Darna than Narda.

The plots of the Darna films are all pretty similar. Her main foe is Valentina, a former photo model 'of a certain

Below: *'Half man, half snake... half Yul Brynner!'* Zuma.

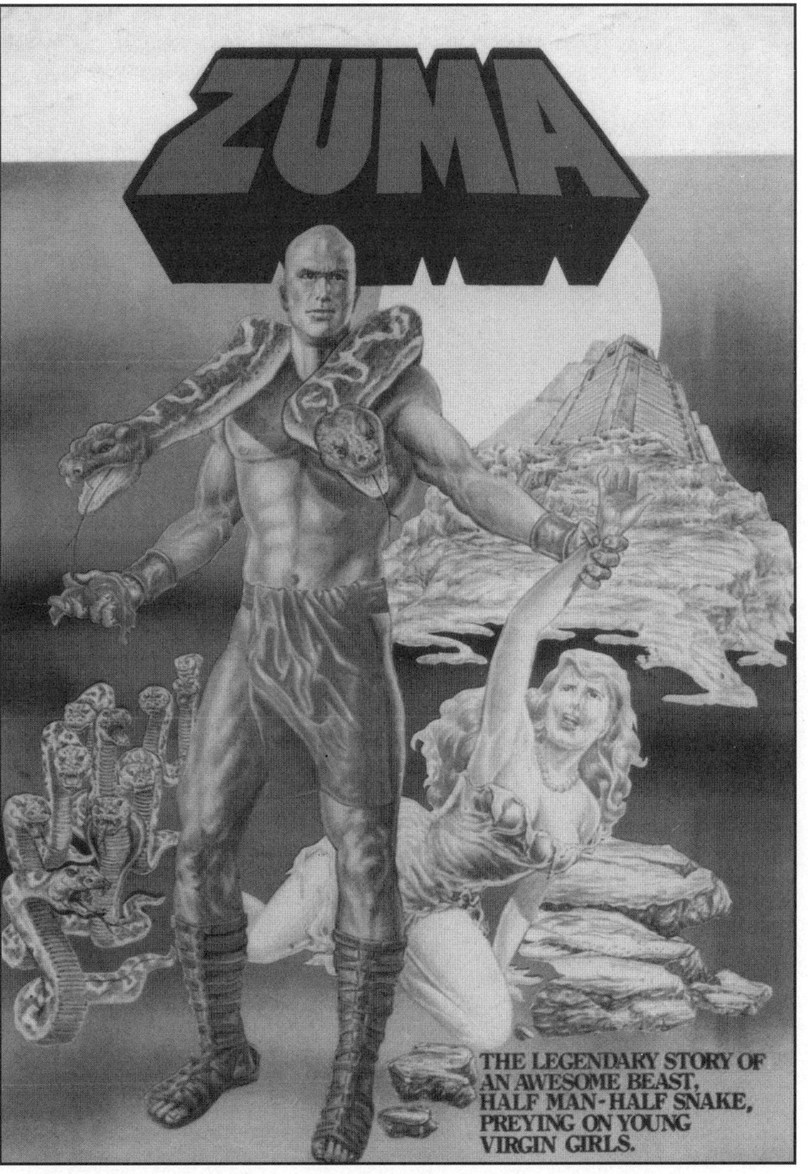
ZUMA
THE LEGENDARY STORY OF
AN AWESOME BEAST,
HALF MAN-HALF SNAKE,
PREYING ON YOUNG
VIRGIN GIRLS.

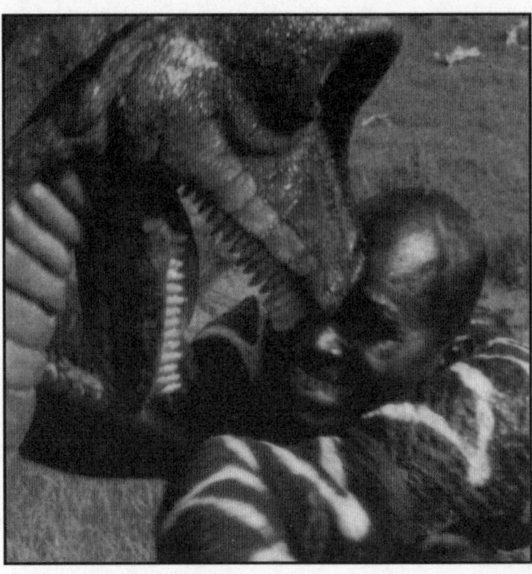

***Right and far right:** Zuma the snake king meets Dino the dinosaur in* Zuma.
***Below:** Teen horror, Filipino style in* Shake, Rattle and Roll V.

age'. This svelte villainess has a bunch of hissing snakes instead of hair, a fact that she conceals cleverly under a range of fashionable headgear. Her constant companion is a sort of talking snake called Vibora that she carries around in her handbag. Vibora keeps popping out at inopportune moments and making sarcastic comments on the action. In the 1991 *Darna*, Valentina joins forces with a demonic industrialist, Dominico Lipollico. Dominico transforms a prim primary school teacher into an *aswang*, a hairy, bat-winged bloodsucker. Together the three of them plan to take over the Philippines (and then, presumably, the world).

Narda, the intrepid reporter, discovers their plan and transforms into Darna to foil them. Her final battle with Dominico is classic *moro moro* territory, as the demonic villain whips out his devil's trident and zaps the tops of nearby apartment blocks, causing them to burst into flame. Darna destroys his power by crunching up his magic medallion. The defeated villain turns into a skeleton before crumbling into dust.

Producer Leary returned to the story in 1994 with *Darna ang Pagbabalik* (Darna – The Return). This time the voluptuous Anjanette Abayari incarnates the intrepid heroine, squeezed into an even skimpier red bikini than the one used for the previous film. Peque Gallaga was in the director's chair for this sequel. His experience in serious and sexy films like *Scorpio Nights* and *Virgin Forest* means that the 1994 *Darna* is an altogether more adult and ambitious affair than its knockabout predecessor.

This time Valentina, the snake-haired villainess, is attempting to take over the Philippines through subliminal religious messages broadcast on television. Narda looses the magic pearl that can transform her into Darna, while her mother becomes swept up in the religious craze. Will Narda find the magic pearl? Will Valentina and her gorgon sisters triumph...? The story is given contemporary relevance by being set against the background of natural disasters rampaging though the Philippines. The eruption of Mount Pinatubo in 1991 had devastated huge areas of the country and was still very fresh in the minds of filmgoers.

Director Gallaga also lent his hand to another successful series, the *Shake, Rattle and Roll* horror anthologies. So far this series has run to five outings, each film consisting of three short stories. A succession of witches, white-haired ghosts, sea monsters and more familiar bloodsuckers plague the mostly teenage casts of these productions. The success of the series inspired *Takbo Talon Tili!* (Run! Jump! Scream!), another portmanteau movie, which included such delights as a dead wizard imprisoned in a clay pot, a ghost in a mirror and toys that come alive at night.

Most of this spate of eighties and nineties Filipino fantasy films are fairly frothy affairs, featuring cheap special effects and even cheaper laughs. A gay superhero turns up in *Bb Tsuperman* and there's even a gay zombie in *Knock! Knock! Who's There?* Equally cheap, but much more serious in the gore department are two films featuring another *komiks* spin-off, Zuma, the Hell Serpent.

Written by Jim Fernandez, the original *Zuma* series ran for more than ten years in Aliwan Komiks. Serialised in twice-weekly parts, the saga featured innumerable twists and turns. The films simplify the story, but still last for nearly two hours each, something of an epic length for Filipino horror yarns. Both films follow more or less the same pattern, with Zuma being captured, escaping and then hunted down for a final climactic battle.

The first film, simply called *Zuma*, shows how an archaeological dig frees the Hell Serpent from his pyramid-like tomb. Zuma is a large, bald-headed green giant. But the most surprising thing about his appearance is the massive, two-headed snake permanently wrapped around his neck. Zuma hides out in the sewers under Manila. He acquires a female slave who brings him fresh victims. This leads to lots of gory scenes with heads being pulled off, hearts being ripped out and Zuma's neck-snakes boring holes through bodies. Eventually the gruesome green giant is captured and imprisoned under a rockfall.

Meanwhile, his assistant has given birth to a baby Zuma, this time a female, who also has two hissing snakes attached to her neck. The baby girl, Galema, is brought up by a kindly archaeologist. Everyone seems too polite to mention the hideous things sticking out of her neck and she grows two extra long braids of hair to cover them. When the girl reaches puberty, Zuma awakens and comes looking for her. The climax of the film is a long battle (natch!) between Zuma and his daughter. Both end up trapped by a rockfall, leaving the way open for a sequel: *Anak ni Zuma — Hell Serpent* (Daughter of Zuma — Hell Serpent).

Zuma was wild enough, but the 1987 follow-up was even more outrageous. Galema is rescued from her underground tomb by her engineer boyfriend and they marry. Soon she is pregnant and gives birth to twins. One of the twins is a normal little boy, but the other is a white snake. The loving couple care equally for both their offspring, pampering the lit-

tle boy and giving the snake a nice, cosy, fur-lined basket to sleep in.

Soon Zuma comes visiting. On the way he rapes a bikini-clad girl he happens to take a fancy to. She becomes pregnant and her stomach swells to monstrous proportions. Like a balloon bursting, it splits and out pops Dino — a half-man, half-crocodile creature. Dino grows to manhood very quickly (it takes about two minutes of screen time) and is soon imitating daddy. He attacks a woman in the woods and has sex with her. A long, slow scene shows Dino pulling her pants down. Then we see his little alligator head bobbing up and down to show that he's on the job.

As in the first Zuma film, the plot, derived from a complex serial story, is very convoluted. It ends with Galema turning on her daddy and tracking him down to his lair in the mountainside. His cave is peopled with a variety of weird monsters, all of whom Galema has to defeat before she can take on Pater. There are horned, gap-toothed monstrosities, straggly-haired, warty witches, and even one horrible creature that has a vagina dentata instead of a face. Eventually Galema destroys her evil father with a flame thrower, but, as return and rebirth feature so strongly in Filipino myths, it seems highly likely that Zuma will be back.

The government of Cory Aquino, swept to office following the display of 'peoples' power' in February 1986, had little interest in cinema. They had other, more pressing concerns. In the 1990s, under President Ramos, Cory's successor, the moral majority and Christian fundamentalists took a strong line on film censorship. There were renewed protests from politicians about the revival of the sexy 'bomba' films of the mid-eighties. Ironically, one of the leading campaigners against the supposed new laxity was former actor Vic Sotto. He railed in particular against the films *Patikim ng Pinya* (Let Me Have a Taste of Pineapple) and *Kara, kaakitakit* (Kara, the Seductress); both resolutely softcore but with copious frontal nudity and 'hot' scenes. There were mutterings about bribery and corruption within the censorship board. Eventually video cameras were smuggled into movie theatres to film the offending flicks. The evidence showed that previously censored scenes had been put back in.

A strict ratings system was imposed. For a film to get an X certificate was a disaster; it effectively meant it would never be screened. Perhaps as a way of undercutting the censor's objections, many films are based on 'true' stories taken from current news events. These peculiar productions feature real-life characters and famous politicians alongside actors impersonating real people. Sometimes the actual character and the actor playing them appear in consecutive scenes — sometimes flagged up on screen: 'This is the real Mr so and so'. Television stars and newspaper journalists are roped in for arbitrary guest appearances.

In 1993, two versions of the same story appeared simultaneously. The gruesome case concerned a Filipino woman murdered and hacked to pieces by her American boyfriend. One of the films, based on her estranged husband's version of events, was called *The Chop Chop Lady*! Even more tasteless was *The Lipa Massacre* (subtitle: *God Save Us From Evil*). The film begins with the badly recorded sound of children talking, overlaid with ominous synthesiser music. The sudden realisation that these are the actual voices of murdered children comes as a jolt. The film tells how the family of a Filipino working in Saudi Arabia was slaughtered by a deranged madman. The climactic scene is particularly offensive. Before the eyes of her terrified children, the man's wife is tormented and abused by the maniac while the soundtrack plays Whitney Houston's schmaltzy hit 'The Greatest Love'. The killer has a knife in each hand. Looking at the woman he is suddenly tormented by sexual desire. A quick flash shows his fantasy of having sex with her. Cutting back to a close-up of the killer, we see him holding the two knives, one on each side of his face, so they look like horns. The ensuing murder scene lasts nearly ten minutes and ends with actual newspaper photographs of the three corpses.

For Western viewers, these films generate a queasy kind of unease in their exploitative mixture of melodrama and naked human suffering. In Britain it would be utterly impossible to mount such a production. The outcry that always follows any plans to film the story of the notorious 'moors murders' that shocked the country in the sixties shows the depth of public feeling over these kinds of issues.

In the face of such gruesome offerings, horror cinema in the Philippines occupies a low status; perhaps lower now than at any time in the past thirty years. Apart from items like the *Shake, Rattle and Roll* series and occasional one-offs like *Impaktita* (She Devil) and *Cobra*, the genre seems to have run out of steam. Besides the actuality films, most production time is devoted to the ever popular action movies and comedies. 1997, the centenary of liberation from Spanish rule, ushered in a wave of historical epics. But there is light on the horizon. The current chairman of the Film Foundation of the Philippines is Cirio H. Santiago. One of his pet projects is to convert the former American military base at Subic Bay into a film production centre: "the Hollywood of Asia". Serious cinephiles might look on his efforts with disdain, but genre fans in the West must feel their hearts beating just a little faster. Yes, it's *that* Cirio H. Santiago. The man who gave the world *TNT Jackson* ("She'll put you in traction!"), *Ebony Ivory and Jade* ("They can lick any man ever made!") and *The Vampire Hookers* ("They kiss and tease but always they please!"). In such hands, the future looks very bright indeed. ■

Above: *Alongside gory horror movies, the Philippines also produced plenty of fantasy films for kids.*

LES PRIMITIFS

INCROYABLE, mais vrai !..

ONGELOOFLIJK, maar waar !..

Un film de - Een film van
SAM GARDNER
avec met
ENNY HARYON
BARRY PRIMAR
JOHN MARDJON
RUKMAN HERMAN

DE PRIMITIEVEN

Mystics From Bali

The first films made in Indonesia were shot by Dutch documentary makers in the 1910s. These mondo-style travelogues, full of the islands' exotic folk culture, were intended for showing in Holland, where it was hoped they might raise the population's awareness of their remote colonial possession. The first full-length Indonesian feature was another European production. *Lutung Kasurung* (The Enchanted Monkey), made in 1926, was an adaptation of a Sundanese folk tale about a princess rescued by a monkey, who turns out to be the son of the King of Heaven. The film was made in Java but, as locals considered movie acting little better than prostitution, it featured a mostly Dutch cast.

Commercial exploitation of films was led by the Chinese, who made and imported films for the large Mandarin and Cantonese speaking communities. The Wong brothers were the pioneers. In 1936, a collaboration between the Wongs and Dutch-Indonesian journalist Albert Balink led to the production of *Pareh* (Rice), the first Indonesian sound film. Unfortunately, it was an expensive flop. Their next film, *Terang Bœlan* (Full Moon), released in 1938, was much more successful. It had two main inspirations. One was popular theatre — at the time the cheapest and most widespread form of entertainment — and the other was Hollywood, specifically the 1936 Dorothy Lamour hit *The Jungle Princess.*

These two influences, theatre and Hollywood, were predominant right up until the late 1960s, when a new form of entertainment, comic books, began to be plundered for plots. The theatre performances that inspired Indonesian film-makers were very different from the kind of drawing room dramas popular in Europe. Indonesian theatre was an epic musical form, often performed outdoors, and full of dances, rituals and mythical plots. Outrageous special effects were employed to have actors flying through the air and gods and devils appearing in a puff of smoke. Horror would collide with humour and romance would always triumph in the end.

The Hollywood influence that had coloured *Terang Bœlan* led to 1940s films like *Srigala Hitam* (The Black Jackal), a version of the Zorro serials, and *Alang Alang* (The Tall Grass), a Tarzan film set in the jungles of Sumatra. Even more exotic were *Tengkorak Hidup* (The Living Skull) and *Kedok Ketawa* (The Laughing Mask), inspired by Universal horror hits such as *Dracula* and *The Phantom of the Opera.* Alongside these were the Chinese-financed Mandarin language films made by the likes of the Brothers Wong and The. To the above-mentioned influences they added Chinese martial arts, in its local version called *silat.* The end result of all this cultural mixing was a form of cinema that was action packed, filled with song and dance and one-dimensional characters, and totally escapist. It certainly had no pretensions to being a serious art form.

In 1949, Indonesia achieved independence. The nation-

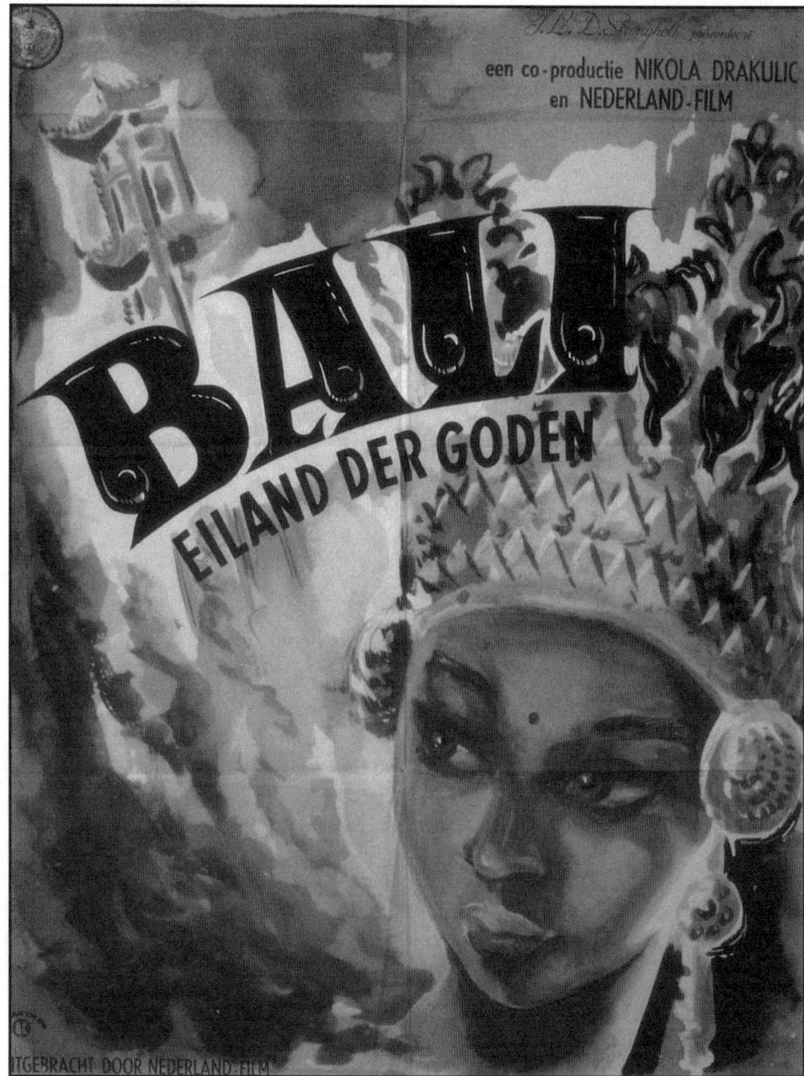

Opposite: Primitiv.

Above: *Bali is the 'Island of the Gods', according to this typical Dutch look at Indonesian life.*

***Above left:** Indonesian horror:* Gondoruwo, The Haunted House.
***Above right:** The Blind Man From Haunted Cave, drawn by Ganes Th., top Indonesian comic artist of the sixties and seventies.*

alist government of Ahmed Sukarno was concerned with higher things than the survival of the local film industry. As one of the most important leaders of the post-war Third World movement, he wanted to establish closer links with China. The decadent influence of Western-style movies was heavily criticised. By the mid-sixties the industry was in a sorry state. Less than forty per cent of the country's cinemas were still open and only a handful of local producers remained. In 1965 a military coup ousted Sukarno. His successor, General Suharto, announced a 'New Order' for Indonesia and things began to change dramatically. The West was now welcomed with open arms. Among the first imports were movies. Desperate to kick start the film business and to earn valuable tax revenue from it, the authorities allowed a loosening of censorship. The result was an influx of sex and violence. In 1970, censorship was relaxed on locally made movies. An exploitation boom was about to begin. During the seventies, nearly as many films were produced as in the previous four decades. The industry grew rapidly on all fronts. In 1969 there had only been 292 cinemas in Indonesia; by 1979 there were nearly 1,500. The top year for production was 1977, with 134 features being completed. This compares with only ten in 1969.

Several factors fuelled the boom. First of all, heavy taxes and tight quotas began to be imposed on imported films. To fill the country's multiplying screens, local producers swung into action. Many of this new breed of commercially minded film-makers were rich businessmen, textile merchants or cinema owners. Generally they produced one or two films a year, hiring equipment and staff as and when they needed them. Local producers also benefited from a government credit scheme of up to $18,000 per film.

Of course, movies from overseas were still popular. In 1973, to lessen their damage, the government initiated a scheme whereby importers were also forced to become producers. For every three films they brought into the country, they were required to produce one film locally. Most of these films were made quickly and cheaply and took full advantage of the relaxed censorship.

The style of the films made during this commercial new wave of Indonesian cinema was a *mélange* of already familiar elements. To the magical fantastical tales derived from folk theatre and legends was added the martial arts of popular Hong Kong and Taiwanese films. A specifically Indonesian ingredient was stories set during the country's colonial past, dealing with the anti-Dutch resistance. Even here, the brave heroes who mobilise the people are frequently gifted with mystical powers, able to fly through the air or resist bullets.

In the late 1960s, a local star system began to develop. In 1968 both W. D. Mochtar (in *Operation X*) and Ratno Timur (in *Jakarta–Hong Kong–Macao*) starred in thrillers that exploited the nation's new internationalism. The following year Mochtar appeared in one of the first big hits of the post New Order cinema. *Si Djampang Mentjari Naga Hitam* (Djampang's Search for Black Tiger) was a martial arts adventure with lots of violent action. On the female front, besides older stars like Rima Melati and Fifi Young, came a new generation of glamorous girls that included Rita Zahara, Itje Dien and Suzzanna.

Suzzanna, one of Indonesia's biggest stars, had started her career as a child actress, winning an award for her role in the 1958 film *Asrama Dara* (Girl's Dormitory). With the increased liberalisation of the early seventies her roles became much more daring. In 1970 she starred in the film *Bernapas Dalam Lumpur* (The Longest Dark), which caused much controversy on account of its numerous bedroom scenes. In the 1980s, in films like *Ratu Ilmu Hitam* (*Queen of Black Magic*), *Nyai Blorong* (*Snake Queen*) and the *Sundelbolong* (*Ghost With Hole*) series, Suzzanna established a reputation as Indonesia's top horror diva.

It was a genre she had helped to define in the groundbreaking 1972 production *Beranak Dalam Kubur* (Birth in the Tomb), generally considered to be the first Western-style horror film produced in Indonesia. The story, set in a remote plantation, tells of two sisters, one evil (played by Mieke Widjaja) and the other innocent (Suzzanna). The evil sister wants to inherit all of the family's wealth, to which end she has killed her mother and crippled her father. She pulls out all the stops to destroy Suzzanna, attempting to drown her and poison her with snakes. Eventually she resorts to the more direct method of throwing acid in the poor girl's face. The body is buried. But things are far from over, for Suzzanna was pregnant. Soon, from far below the earth, the gravediggers hear the cries of a newly born child and take to their heels... Some nights later a white-robed ghost is seen haunting the woods that surround the lonely old plantation house.

Of course, it's not a real ghost but the still living Suzzanna who, together with her child, was rescued from the grave by her father's faithful old retainer. Suzzanna's husband, arriving at the farm, soon uncovers the awful truth and mobilises the estate workers. In a scene found in many Indonesian horror movies (and in films from the Philippines and Thailand), the avenging mob surround the house, carrying flaming torches, to rout the evil woman.

The plot of *Beranak Dalam Kubur* was based on a late-sixties comic strip called *Tangisan di Malam Kabut* (Tears in the Foggy Night). The strip's author, Ganes Th., was one of the most popular of Indonesia's new breed of comic book artists and his stories were the basis of several films during Indonesia's exploitation boom. The first of them was the 1971 release *Si Buta Dari Gua Hantu* (The Blind Man From Haunted Cave), based on a strip published in 1968. This hugely popular hit made a big star out of Ratno Timur, who played Barda Mandrawata, the Blind Warrior.

The Blind Warrior is a man with a mission — to find and destroy a blind killer who is spreading terror throughout the land. To better understand his adversary, Barda gouges out his own eyes with a dagger and practices night and day to perfect his mastery of martial arts. During a fearsome struggle he stumbles into a deep chasm where he finds the cave of a dead mystic. The secrets of the guru's magic are inscribed on rock, which Barda reads like a sort of Braille. Suitably equipped with mystical powers, he defeats his enemy and becomes a champion of the powers of good.

The combination of blindness, martial arts and forest-dwelling mystics runs like a thread through many Indonesian fantasy films. *Misteri di Borobudur* (Mystery at Burobudur), released in 1971, tells the further adventures of the Blind Warrior. The same year saw the screen incarnation of another Ganes Th. character in Liliek Sudjio's big-budget epic *Tuan Tanah Kedawung* (The Master of Kedawung). The following year Ratno Timur was back in *Pendekar Bambu Kuning* (The Warrior With the Cane Sword). Here he plays another mystic warrior, his only weapon a bamboo pole that he wields to deadly effect. His adversaries include a team of devil women, led by Rita Zahara.

The sex and violence in these comic book/martial arts movies took the authorities by surprise. Of course it's nothing new for censors to be several steps behind the public, but the sudden explicitness of Indonesian films came as a shock to many commentators. The magazine *Tempo* opened its first issue in 1971 with a cover story entitled: 'Indonesian Cinema — Say Hello to Sex.' It was also reported that President Suharto had been so shocked watching Suzzanna's sex scenes in *Bernapas Dalam Lumpur* that he had the pro-

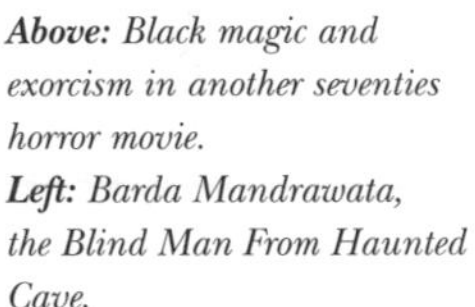
Above: *Black magic and exorcism in another seventies horror movie.*
Left: *Barda Mandrawata, the Blind Man From Haunted Cave.*

***Right:** Many Indonesian horror films were based on Western hits, such as* The Exorcist.

jection stopped and cleared the cinema.

The censors claimed that the film had been shown to them without the controversial scenes and that they had been added later. This was a common ploy, used by several importers and distributors. In 1978 Education Minister Daœd Jusuf condemned films that "incite people to behave more like animals rather than human beings" and there were calls to "reduce, if not completely eradicate, the phenomenon of 'sexploitation' in Indonesian films." However, a consequent reduction in sex scenes led only to a rise in violent and sadistic ones to replace them. Things became even more embarrassing when the Government appointed an official body to market Indonesian films overseas. Doing the rounds of the festivals in 1982, they found that what foreign buyers wanted were the sexy, violent exploiters that were being so strongly criticised back home. While the serious art films that were also part of the package may have been politely received, no one wanted to buy them.

The image of Indonesia seen through its films was something that had troubled the authorities even before the New Order loosening of censorship. The exotic locales of Java and Sumatra had been exploited in several films aimed at the overseas market. Co-productions like the 1962 film *Holiday in Bali* (made with the Sampaguita company from the Philippines) and the Swiss-Italian-Indonesian *The Virgin of Bali* used the islands as little more than exotic backdrops for stories about white adventurers lost amongst the primitive natives. More problematic was another film, *Kutikan Dewata* (The Curse of the Gods), which got its producers into hot water over their depiction of Balinese rites and rituals as cruel and sadistic. The fuss led to a special committee being formed to oversee the image of Bali on film.

The seventies and eighties saw a steady trickle of titles like *Intan Perawan Kubu* (Intan the Kubu Virgin) and *Dia Sang Penakluk* (He is the Conqueror) where anthropologists from the city confront savage jungle tribes. Usually the producers attempted some kind of disclaimer to avoid charges that they were presenting a negative view of the country. The 1979 film *Primitiv*, for example, begins with the statement: 'This is a true story. Filmed on location in the jungle where the events portrayed actually happened...' The story tells of three camera-happy students on a trip up-river to gather first-hand material for their theses. As they go deeper into the jungle, they encounter various savage rites and native dances.

"It's the same as a voodoo dance they have in some parts of Africa," says Rita, the female member of the trio, as they watch some dark-skinned wantons shaking their booty.

"You're right. The rituals of the primitive tribes are the same everywhere," agrees Amri, played by the dashing Barry Prima.

The film seems concerned to make these sort of general points all the time, to separate the story off from any particular geographical location. Partly this was a sop to the Indonesian Government, who were specially thanked in the prologue; partly it was to make the film more exportable — in case Indonesian 'primitives' might be somehow less of a selling point than, for example, Brazilian ones.

Most of the film consists of long, mondo-like sequences of the natives going about their daily business. We see them catching a crocodile, cutting it open and eating its raw flesh. The croc is very obviously alive and snaps at them as they rip out its intestines. A giant snake is seized and put into a kind of compost pot. The tribe then eat the maggoty residue. Other delights show a medicine man sucking the pus from a suppurating wound, bodies caught in man traps and pierced by savage spikes, a woman giving birth in the jungle and eating the afterbirth, treacherous pools of quicksand and so on. There's not a lot of sex. In fact, when one of the primitives tries to get intimate with Rita, the tribal leader drags him off and crushes his balls with a rock.

If the Balinese and jungle movies caused problems with their view of savage natives, even more unsavoury were films that exploited such subjects of eternal interest as prostitution, women in prison and war. A uniquely Indonesian sub-genre combines all three topics into a whole only matched by Hong Kong efforts such as the 1974 film *Bamboo House of Dolls*. In Indonesia, as in much of South East Asia, the 1970s still held bitter memories lingering from the Japanese occupation of 1942-45. Resentment over Japan's burgeoning economic strength in the area added new fuel to an already smouldering fire. The notion of powerless Indonesian

women used as sex slaves by brutal Japs provided an excuse not only for scenes of sadism and torture but for plenty of nudity and titillation as well, all wrapped up with a good patriotic message. A typical example begins with a voice-over reminding us that "war is a barbarian atrocity..." before going on to explain that the film we are about to see will offer us "a brief reminder of the depravity that is the true nature... of war!" Like the investigative reporter who makes his excuses and leaves, these films really want to have it all ways.

The 1983 film *Kamp Tawanan Wanita* (*War Victims*) begins with Armilia, a defiant guerrilla woman, refusing to reveal the location of the rebel forces. Her Japanese tormentors force her to strip naked and parade her round the camp on the back of a donkey. "She could miscarry if they're not careful," one of the other women prisoners comments. No sooner said than we see a trickle of blood flowing down Armilia's leg.

The Japanese soldiers are a strange bunch. They include Takigawa, who has a huge growth plastered onto the side of his face, and Seikeki, known as "the madman", who likes to force naked women against barbed wire fences. One scene shows him caressing his gun barrel lovingly while he listens to two of the women being raped. The Japanese are portrayed as a savage bunch of animals. "Is it possible for a Japanese to have human feelings?" Armilia asks at one point. During an inspection, when one of the women bares her breasts to show she's been tortured, a Japanese soldier calmly shoots her dead.

In Indonesian horror films and jungle movies it's always an outsider, usually someone from the big city, who comes to the bewitched village to save it, or to the jungle to educate the primitive natives. Wisdom and progress are things that the city creates and nurtures. An opposite notion is put forward in *Escape From Hell Hole*, one of several films that deal with the plight of South East Asian girls sold into sex slavery. Here the city is seen as a place of corruption, full of evil men out to exploit the innocence of country women. Their innocence lies not only in their unworldliness but specifically in their being virgins. The dialogue in *Escape From Hell Hole* puts a lot of emphasis on the value of the girls' virginity.

The film begins with a bunch of saronged country women enjoying a dip in the river. The simple primitiveness of the scene is thrown into stark contrast by the sudden arrival of a shiny modern car. From it emerges Kartina, in Western dress, smoking a cigarette and full of the supposed sophistication that the country girls lack. She persuades one of them, her friend Indri, to come back to the city with her to work for her 'uncle' MG.

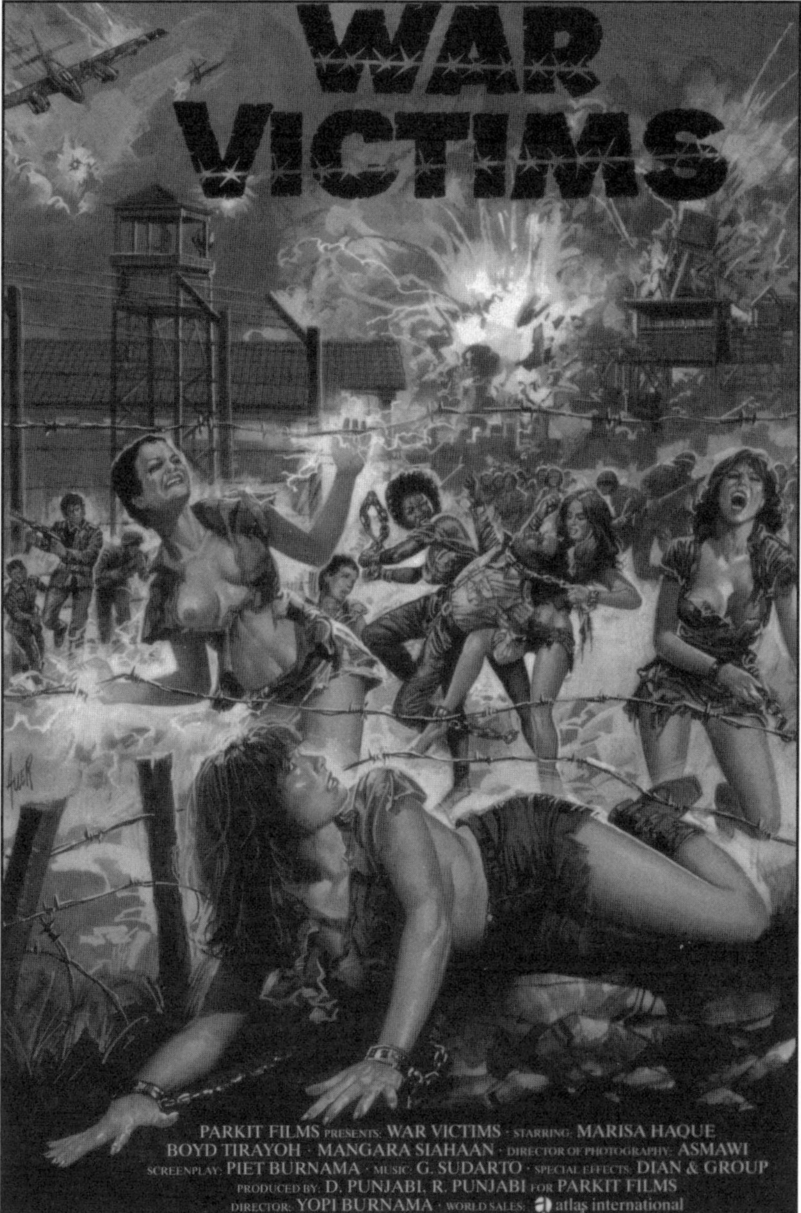

This page and opposite bottom: *Lurid exploitation films like* War Victims *caused the Indonesian authorities lots of problems.*

"Hey, there's no need to bring that old prayer mat," Kartina tells Indri as she waits for her to pack.

We first meet MG (played by Dicky Zulkarnaen at his slimiest) talking to a fellow businessman. "Marketing precious stones is good business," he agrees, handing back the man's rock samples, "but marketing women is better."

MG is like an old style feudal lord. And like them he demands the right to take the virginity of any girl that comes to his walled estate. Indri, despite Kartina's warnings, is determined to resist MG's charms. To punish her and soften her up, Indri is thrown into the Hell Hole, a dank dungeon where the problem girls are kept. The rest of the film consists of numerous scenes of torture and humiliation as Indri refuses to give up her virginity to MG. When she does finally accede to his demands it's only to save another young innocent from rape. As MG embraces her and sticks his tongue down her throat, Indri bites it off and spits the bleeding lump of flesh onto the bedroom floor. Back in the Hell Hole she

P.T. RAPI FILM presents
The WARRIOR against the Blind SWORDSMAN
BARRY PRIMA · ADVENT BANGUN
W. D. MOCHTAR · SRI GUDHY SINTARA · ZURMAINY
H. SJAMSUDIN SJAFEI · TUTY KUSNENDAR · DJAIR WARNIPONAKANDA
VIVI RIO · GRACE SAHARA · MOOSDYK
HANGKY LIKUMAHUA · GINO MAKASUCI
RUKMAN HERMAN
directed by
DASRI JACOB
cameraman
ASMAWI
music
GATOT SUDARTO

Right and opposite: *Barry Prima played the Warrior in a string of eighties hits.*

takes her virginity with a wooden stick. When MG returns from hospital she taunts him, both for his failure to deflower her and for his newly acquired speech impediment.

"Now he won't be able to whisper sweet nothings to his new virgins!" she shouts to the other girls as MG's men strap her to the dungeon's torture wheel. She sticks out her tongue provocatively. Just as MG takes a knife to slice it off, the women break out of their cages and exact their inevitable revenge.

The women-in-prison and war films, along with several Indonesian action films and horror movies, were widely exported. As mentioned earlier, the Government's film promotion body found that these were the only sort of productions that foreign buyers were interested in. At the time, Indonesian companies were making films for less than $100,000. Low production costs and colourful backgrounds made them look much more expensive than they actually were. As overseas rights were available for a few thousand dollars, the films were snapped up.

The Indonesian audience was still mostly a working class one. To satisfy their demands, films had to be imitative of the lower budget American movies and imported Hong Kong and Indian films. In other words, they had to have a bit of sex, lots of action and oodles of violence. A combination that exactly matched the requirements of the international video market. The export potential of these films was helped by having Western-looking, mixed race or 'Indo' actors in the lead roles. The more obviously 'foreign' faces were kept to the background. One of the country's busiest actors was the handsome Eurasian Barry Prima, who had played Amri in *Primitiv*. For the same director, Sisworo Gautama Putra (under the pseudonym of Sam Gardner), Prima starred in another movie that was to have considerable success overseas — the story of nationalist hero Jaka Sembung. The film was exported under the more generic title of *The Warrior*.

The Warrior and its two sequels, *The Warrior and the Blind Swordsman* and *The Warrior and the Ninja*, are typical Asian stews, a mixture of martial arts and mysticism with a sprinkling of sex. More unique is the strong anti-imperialist message that each film carries. In Indonesia, films with nationalist heroes have a long pedigree. These Robin Hood-style figures first appeared towards the end of the nineteenth century in songs and stories. The most famous of them was Si Pitung, who made it to the screen in a 1931 Wong Brothers film of the same name with the strap line 'The Zigomar from Java!' Similar heroes include Pak Sakerah and Jaka Gledek. Unlike Robin Hood or William Tell, their European equivalents, these Indonesian heroes all have mystical powers, usually acquired from a grey-haired guru, and the films are invariably bloodthirsty and gory.

In essence, the approach of the *Warrior* films was similar to lots of Hong Kong movies from the 1970s, particularly Wang Yu films such as *Ten Fingers of Steel* and *Beach of the War Gods*. In the Wang Yu films the enemies are the Japanese and Manchu invaders. Jaka Sembung, The Warrior, is pitted against much more unlikely enemies from Holland. These vicious sadists are a long way from the dope-smoking Dutch that we all know and love today. Van Schramm, a regional governor in 1820s Java, is a particularly nasty piece of work, abusing his own daughter, nailing prisoners to the wall and consorting with evil black magicians to get what he wants. And what he most wants is to get rid of Jaka Sembung, a troublesome local demagogue who is stirring up the people and leading a rent strike in the province. In desperation Van Schramm turns to a local wizard. From a hill of glowing rock the wizard brings forth the headless body of Ki Item, a dead master of the black arts. Once united with his bonce, Ki Item agrees to destroy Sembung. As proof of his superior powers, he turns The Warrior into a black pig that is then chased off into the woods by a pack of dogs.

In a psychedelic sequence where the pig seems to be bathed in multicoloured oils, a forest-dwelling mystic turns the animal back into human form and agrees to teach Sembung magic skills to defeat the evil Ki Item. As Sembung has been blinded by the governor, he has first of all to be given a new pair of eyes. Fortunately, a dead girl is on hand to provide the necessary organs. This is an excuse for some *Eyes Without a Face* surgery scenes and creaky special effects as the disembodied eyes float through the air like two gore-encrusted marbles.

The film ends with an amazing battle between Ki Item and The Warrior. Ki Item seems invincible. Every time one of his limbs is cut off, it bounces back to join the body. Even his severed head seems to have a life of its own, and flies through the air to fasten itself back onto its neck stalk. Eventually Sembung hears the words of his mystic master, telling him that Ki Item's power comes from the earth and that he must not be allowed to touch the ground. He tosses the wizard's body into the air, slices it in two and then skewers each half on a sword before burning them like overdone kebabs.

The mystical, magical elements of this first film came to the fore in its sequel, *The Warrior and the Blind Swordsman*. This marks a return to the screen of Si Buta, 'The Blind Man From Haunted Cave', created in 1968 by comic book artist Ganes Th. and first seen on film in 1971. The mysterious Si Buta is a man with almost superhuman powers. "I can see the souls of men. Even though I am blind," he announces.

A wicked witch called Maki falls in love with the swordsman. She offers him eternal life if he makes love to her. The swordsman rejects her and she swears vengeance. Together with a team of bikini-clad Amazons she takes on both Si Buta and Jaka Sembung, The Warrior.

The film is full of surreal images. A flying chest of gold, a man's decapitated head turning into a goat's head, steaming vats full of skulls, a wizard with a fifteen foot long furry tail...

The erotic elements are stronger in this second film.

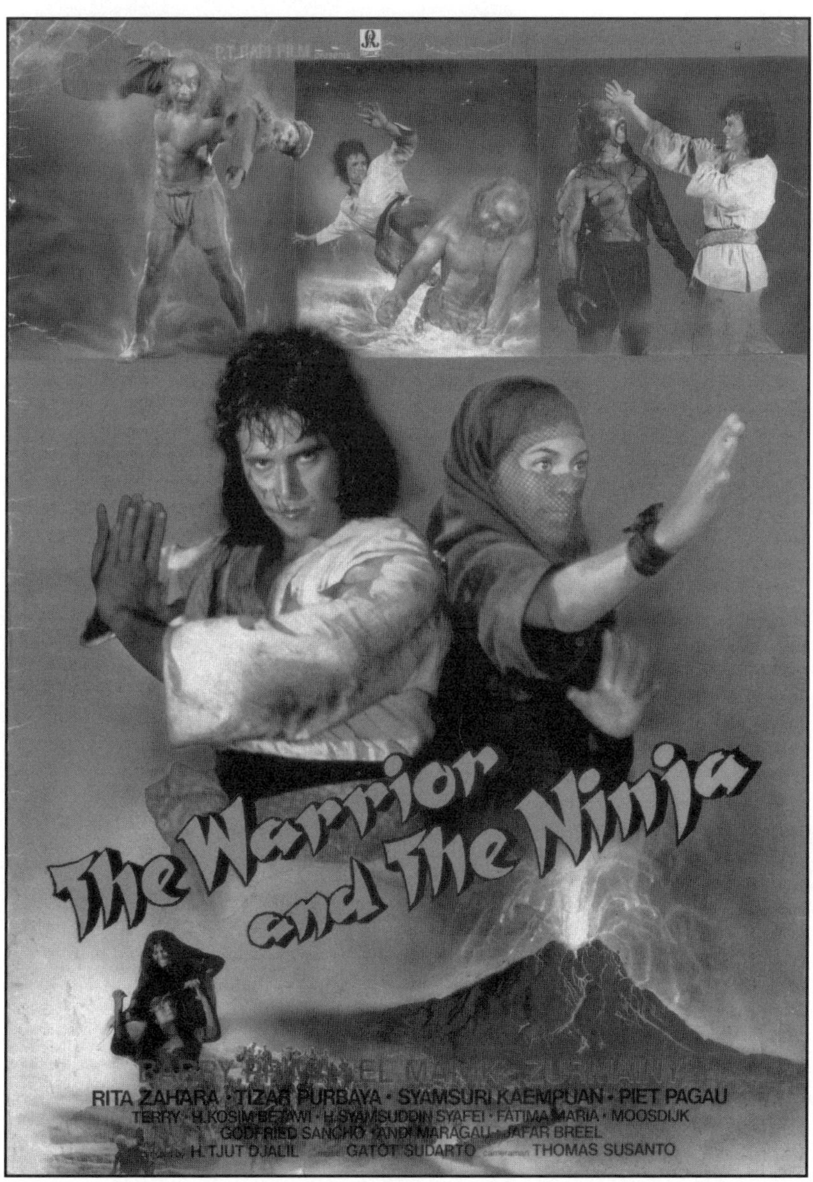

Above: *Sexy Suzzanna at her vengeful best in* Queen of Black Magic.
Below: Satan's Bed *was influenced by the* Nightmare on Elm Street *films.*

Sex is an important ingredient in Maki's magic. Her gift of eternal life always comes with the price of a shag and when, at one point, she's killed, she's revived through intercourse. This element of erotic magic and the notion of a witch as a woman with an insatiable sexual appetite comes to the fore in later films like *The Devil's Sword* (also starring Barry Prima) and the incredible 1988 film *Lady Terminator.*

The third and last episode in the *Warrior* saga, *The Warrior and the Ninja*, has less fantastic elements than the first two films. More than a third of its running time is taken up with lengthy but absorbing bouts of martial arts. The main fighter is a mysterious masked avenger, the Black Squirrel, a sort of female Zorro, who teams up with Jaka Sembung to defeat another evil Dutch colonialist.

The film begins in spectacular style with an erupting volcano. The explosion frees an evil magician who has been imprisoned in the mountain. Over the years his skin has turned to iron. His cohorts are represented by the 'Mistress of Evil' and the bizarre sage Maruta. This crippled magician has spent so long in the Lotus position that he is unable to stand up. One of the highlights of the film is an amazing battle between Jaka Sembung and the cross-legged Maruta, who hops about like a demented frog as he executes dangerous karate kicks and punches. Even more spectacular is the defeat of the iron man. Jaka tricks him into entering a pool of water which weakens his metal skin. The warrior then thumps him on the chest and the iron man shatters like a giant clay pot. The Black Squirrel, meanwhile, has taken on the Mistress of Evil, whom she kills by pulling the skin from her face.

The Warrior and the Ninja was the last Jaka Sembung film, but in the same year, 1985, Barry Prima played a very similar character, called Mandala, in *The Devil's Sword.* The formula is pretty much the same as the previous films, only here there are no Dutch imperialists to conquer. The villains this time around are a bunch of wicked wizards, all seeking the sword of the title. Whoever possesses it, we are told, will rule the world.

Foremost among this evil bunch is Panu Jaggar, a former friend of Mandala. At one time a student of the mystic arts, he is now in thrall to the Crocodile Queen. This busty demoness lives in a well appointed grotto beneath the waters of a huge lake. To do her bidding she has an army of 'crocodile men' (basically a bunch of guys in tatty masks with teeth). The Queen's main, if not only, activity seems to be engaging in group orgies with teams of young men captured from the surrounding villages.

The Devil's Sword was made by the same production company (Rapi Films) and the same creative team as the *Warrior* series: writer Imam Tantowi, producer Gope T. Samtani and art director El. Badrun. This experienced crew had got their act down to a tee by this stage. Consequently, the film rattles along at a terrific pace. An endless procession of weird and wacky scenes parades in front of our disbelieving eyes. Gory fights with heads being severed and numerous disembowellings. A deadly parasol. A man on a flying rock. A cage full of cannibal sex slaves. A stone-headed Cyclops whose single eye is very obviously a car headlamp. And, of course, the sexy Crocodile Queen herself. When she finally gets to bed Mandala, the kitsch high camp of the film goes into overdrive. There's a slow motion nuptial dance and enough glittering spandex on display to have filled a gay night at Manhattan's old Studio 54.

The story of *The Devil's Sword* makes absolutely no sense, the acting is often appalling and the special effects are a no-budget riot. Yet the film works, largely because it draws on local myths and symbols for its effect. Its exoticism and energy more than make up for its cinematic shortcomings. Unfortunately, this wasn't always the case with Indonesian movies. Generally, the more Western they tried to be, the less successful they were.

The horror films that had begun to appear in Indonesia in the early seventies were a hybrid of Western techniques and Eastern ideas. As the Western models changed, so too did the Indonesian versions. *Pengabdi Setan* (*Satan's Slave*), for example, is a version of Don Coscarelli's *Phantasm,* while *Satan's Bed* uses elements from the *A Nightmare on Elm Street* series. Sometimes these borrowings work and the resulting concoction can be a satisfying dish. At other times the mix is a decidedly dodgy one and the cake simply refuses to rise.

A case in point is the 1979 film *Special Silencers.* Barry Prima stars again, as Hendra, and there are plenty of elements familiar from other Indonesian horror movies. The village terrorised by evil, the stranger from the big city who comes to save the day, the power struggle within the family — all these have been used successfully many times before. However, one thing the local industry was never very good at was special effects. The inspiration for *Special Silencers* seems to have been *Alien,* specifically the image of creatures bursting from people's stomachs. The Special Silencers of the title are large red pills, obtained from a forest-dwelling mystic, and allegedly designed to help in meditation. However,

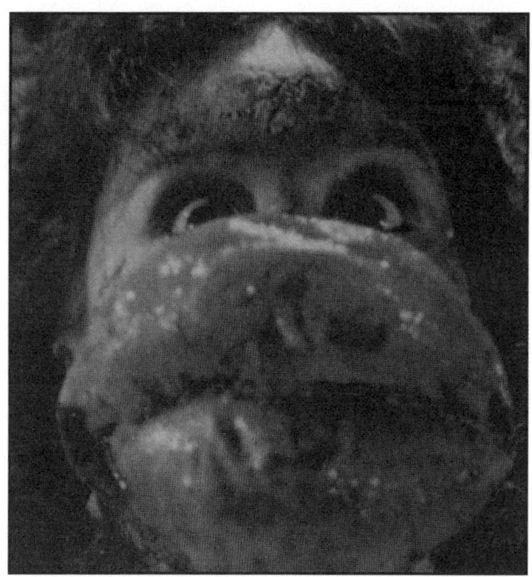

if used by the untrained, they cause a huge tree to grow in the stomach and burst its way out through the skin.

In *Alien*, the stomach-bursting effect is horrifying and shocking. In *Special Silencers*, it's more like a comedy routine. In most of the scenes where the process is shown, it's all too obvious that the head of the victim is poking though a hole cut in the wall or floor, and that the 'body' is a foam and plastic dummy. When the blood-covered twigs are poked through the plastic skin, the result is not so much horrifying as hilarious.

Of course Indonesian producers aren't stupid. They know that audiences laugh at their films, and so they include, in the middle of the horror, plenty of ridiculous, over the top and just plain stupid episodes. The climax of *Special Silencers*, for example, is a scene where Barry Prima's girlfriend is being tortured by the baddies. To show just how unspeakably evil they are, they get a pair of exceptionally smelly shoes and make her sniff them, accompanied by gales of cackling laughter.

"Now clean them out and spread it on her body!" commands the head baddy as the girl recoils in horror.

Other delirious scenes include a killer dwarf with an axe, a gang composed entirely of gay stereotypes, and a man who keeps loosing his wooden leg.

"Bastard! You stole my leg. Give it back immediately!" he cries at one point.

Special Silencers is a notorious example of 'badfilm', much loved by video collectors the world over. However, there are plenty of Indonesian movies that make few concessions to the West and present us with ideas and images that we just won't find anywhere else. The 1981 film *Ratu Ilmu Hitam* (*Queen of Black Magic*) begins, like many classic horror films, with a wedding. To the accompaniment of throbbing *gamelan* music, some evil presence begins to intrude. Heavy clouds gather, threatening rain. Beansprouts in a bowl turn into maggots. The bride sees the groom and his party turn into skeletons as they approach her. Snakes cover her bed. A man suddenly drifts several feet up into the air.

There can only be one explanation. Black magic! And Kohar, the groom, knows who's to blame. It has to be Murni (played by Suzzanna), the girl he rejected to marry Baedah, the daughter of the local headman. The fact that the headman is rich and Murni lives in poverty with her old mother did not, of course, affect his choice.

Leading a gang of villagers with flaming torches, Kohar strides off to Murni's house. They set the shack on fire, killing the girl's mother, and then they catch Murni herself. Ignoring her pleas of innocence, they hurl her from the top of a deep ravine into the green jungle far below...

However, luck seems to be with Murni. A grizzled, grey-haired jungle dweller rescues her and nurses her back to health. What Murni doesn't know is that the man is a *dukun* (a powerful magician) who had been banished from the village. When he hears her story he says she must seek revenge. Overriding Murni's objections, he tells her that it is her duty, she owes it to herself to become what they accused her of being — Queen of Black Magic! And, of course, he will teach her all she needs to know.

With the old man's help Murni soon becomes a mistress of the black arts. She summons a swarm of bees to sting one of her tormentors to death; another's veins swell until they burst, showering him in gallons of gore. A third man turns into a mess of slimy worms. However, the best treatment is saved for the perfidious Kohar, Murni's former lover. She waits for him in the night and casts a giant egg that bursts over his face. He goes crazy, running through the village tearing at his neck. Suddenly, to the horror of the crowd, he pulls off his head and throws it to the ground, his arms flapping wildly as they try to stem the geyser of gore that's gushing from his neck. Then, as the torch-wielding crowd scatters in terror, the head launches itself into the air and chases the village elder. It plunges its teeth into his arm and rips off a great lump of flesh.

Heads being lopped off and limbs flying though the air feature in innumerable Indonesian films. In mystical martial arts movies, dismembered corpses magically piece themselves together, while wizards send parts of their bodies off on solo missions. One of the most unusual forms of decollation is found in the 1981 film *Leák* (better known as *Mystics in Bali*).

The film features an American anthropologist, Cathy Dean, who comes to Bali to study its folklore. She strikes up

Above left: *Cathy gets lippy in* Mystics in Bali.
Left: Satan's Slave *was the export title for* Pengabdi Setan, *a version of* Phantasm.

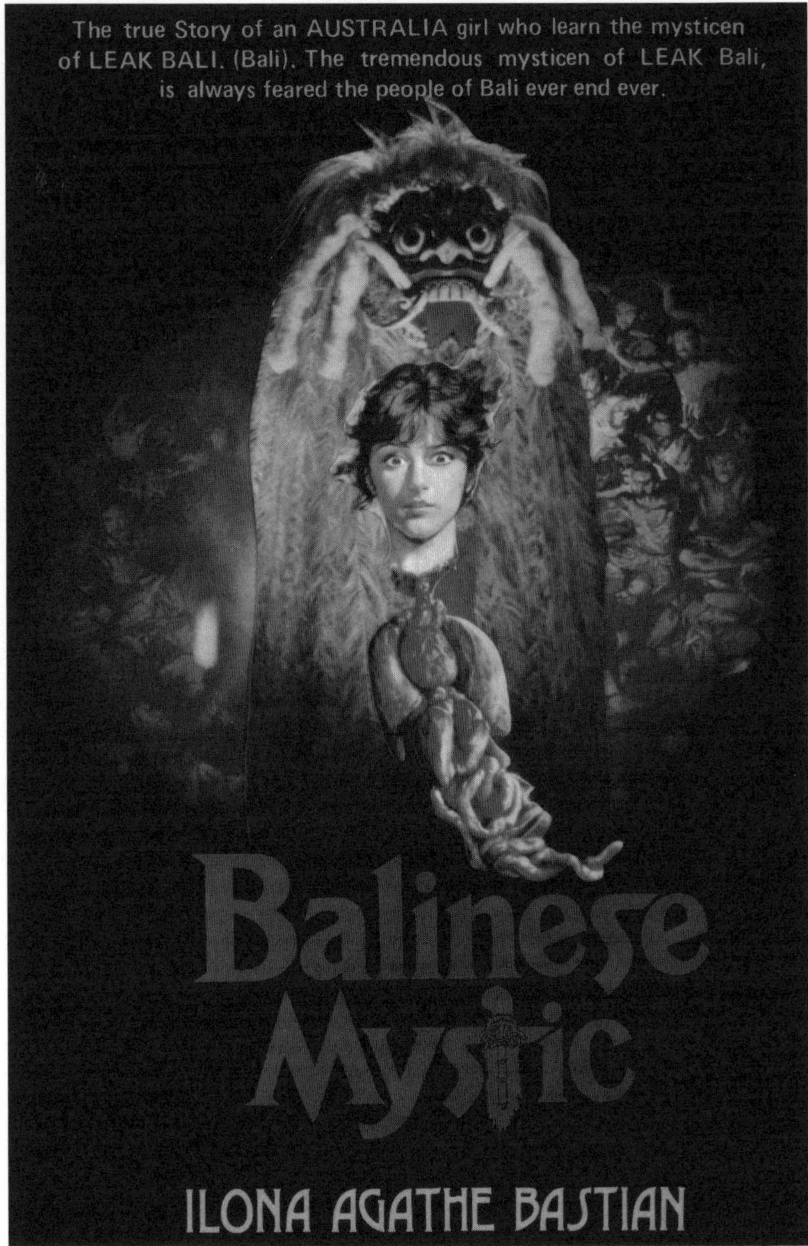

***Above:** An alternative title for* Mystics in Bali.

an acquaintance with a local guy, Mahendra, and persuades him to help her find out more about Leyak, a very powerful and dangerous form of Balinese magic. Mahendra is doubtful at first, but the lingering kiss that Cathy gives him one night helps to change his mind.

A few days later the pair travel to a bleak and isolated spot where, in the middle of the night, they wait for the arrival of the Leyak priestess. The woman makes her presence known with a terrifying cackling laugh — more like a scream, in fact. We hardly see anything of her apart from her hideous hands, their claw-like nails at least a foot in length. She agrees to take Cathy on as a pupil and as they part she insists on shaking hands "as they do in the West."

Gingerly Cathy takes the creature's long-clawed hand. When she glances up again she sees that the woman has gone... leaving her hand behind. Cathy drops it with a cry and it scuttles off along the ground to rejoin its mistress.

Over the next few weeks, Cathy learns mystic dances and mantras and, as she tells Mahendra, she learns "how to think like another life form." But of course, as in all black magic films, the witch has a hidden agenda. When Cathy decides she has learned enough and tries to end the relationship, the witch is having none of it. She needs Cathy, she says. She needs her to get blood. But she doesn't need all of her — just her head.

The witch claps her hands and suddenly Cathy's head begins to pull itself off her body and rises several feet into the air, with her lungs and internal organs still attached. It's a truly grotesque sight. The special effects may be ropey and the dummy head transparently fake, but it's a sight that leaves no spectator unmoved.

The particular type of creature that Cathy has become is well known in South East Asian folklore. In Malaysia they are called *penanggalan*. At night superstitious locals line their windows with thorns so that the creature's entrails will get caught if it tries to fly in. The *penanggalan*'s favourite food is blood, especially that of newborn children. One of the most horrifying scenes in *Mystics in Bali* shows Cathy's flying head attacking a woman in labour. It floats down between her arched thighs and literally sucks the foetus out, gorging itself on the new flesh.

Inevitably, in a small community, such activities don't go unnoticed for long. Mahendra calls in his uncle, an expert in Buddhist spells and mantras, and together they plan to destroy the witch. Unfortunately this will also mean killing Cathy. But, as the witch only needs one more blood meal to achieve her goal of immortality, this seems a small price to pay. In a surprising flash of logic, Mahendra's uncle assures him that of course the Leyak are not omnipotent. If they were, he reasons, they would have taken over the world by now.

To stop the head getting back onto Cathy's body, three sharp needles are inserted into the top of her neck. With the coming of dawn, the body dies and is buried. There then follows three night-long vigils to ensure that head and body are not reunited after death. If this happens, they will never be able to stop the witch. Naturally, the Leyak priestess turns up to settle the score with Mahendra's uncle and a drawn out magic battle ensues.

The film was directed by H. Tjut Jalil, an important name in the world of Indonesian exploitation movies. Born in 1932, he had been a short story writer and theatre director before entering the film world as a scriptwriter. Jalil directed a series of documentaries before *Mystics in Bali*. The film was cheaply and quickly made, yet its awkwardness and shooting style give it a kind of strange authenticity. The camera hardly ever moves; most scenes are filmed in one take, using medium or close shots. In the many night sequences there are no foregrounds. The characters are isolated against the vast, empty backdrop of black space. There's a constant feeling of mystery, of tension, as though almost anything might emerge from the blackness.

In 1988 H. Tjut Jalil (using the name Jalil Jackson) directed one of the most controversial Indonesian horror films of recent years, *Pembalasan Ratu Pantai Selatan* (The Revenge of the South Sea Queen), released in America and elsewhere as *Lady Terminator*. Again, like *Mystics in Bali*, the film was inspired by a famous Indonesian legend.

Ratu Lara Kidul, or the Queen of the South Seas, is a sexually rapacious seductress with magic powers, a Javanese variation on the Indian legend of Kali. She lives in a palace perched precariously by the sea-shore, where she lures men to their doom with promises of great wealth. Occasionally, she rises from the waves to take a human lover. The legend has been the basis of several films, most notably *Nyi Blorong* (*The Snake Queen*). This 1982 hit, directed by the prolific

Sisworo Gautama Putra, starred horror legend Suzzanna as the daughter of the South Sea Queen.

By the late eighties, Indonesian movies were featuring a lot more sex than had previously been the norm. And sex is pretty much the motivating factor for the plot of *Lady Terminator* (it's also known as *Nasty Hunter*). The film begins in 1889, with some spectacular shots of rolling waves crashing against the rocky promontory where the queen has built her black-walled castle. Inside she is being pleasured by her latest lover. The queen sits astride him as he lies back on her satin sheets. As he reaches his climax, blood splatters across his stomach. He screams in agony — his penis has been sliced off inside the queen's vagina.

Her handmaidens carry the body away as the queen ponders aloud: "Is there any man who can satisfy me?"

As if in answer her next lover appears, a macho-looking gent in traditional white robes. He sets to work and pretty soon it's obvious that he's hit the right spot. The queen begins to moan with pleasure. As she achieves her long awaited climax, he reaches down and pulls from between her thighs a wriggling snake. He holds it aloft and it turns into a sort of dagger — a *Kris*, mystic weapon of the Malays.

"You are my wife now," he announces to the furious queen. "I want you to stop the killings!"

"You tricked me!" the queen snarls. "In 100 years I will have revenge on your great-granddaughter!" Having delivered her threat, she walks off into the waves "to consort with the powers of evil."

A century later, in present day Indonesia, Tanya, an attractive American girl, hires a boat to take her to the rocky coast where the legend of the South Sea Queen originated. The boat's surly captain is doubtful about the whole enterprise and tells the "lady" so in no uncertain terms.

"Will you stop calling me lady," snarls Tanya as she strips to her minuscule black bikini. "I'm not a lady, I'm an anthropologist!"

She dives into the water and, moments later, finds herself spread-eagled on the blood-stained satin sheets of the queen's enormous bed. An invisible force pulls her legs apart as a snake materialises from the bed and disappears swiftly up the astonished girl's vagina. Possessed now by the spirit of the South Sea Queen, Tanya rises eerily from the moonlit waves and sets off to get her revenge.

Tanya's ultimate victim is Erika, a rising star on the local pop scene and the great-granddaughter of the queen's last lover. Much of the film consists of an unbelievable orgy of carnage as Tanya offs anybody who gets in her way. Armed with an AK47 and a seemingly limitless supply of bullets, she stalks though the streets, clubs and bars of downtown Jakarta at night, rattling off endless volleys. Sex is never far from her thoughts, however. After letting rip at one guy with a fifteen-second burst of gunfire, she kicks him in the balls just to be sure. An ancient mystic who tries to take her on is also summarily dispatched, his private parts blasted away. To keep up her strength, Tanya also beds a bevy of male lovers. When their bodies begin to turn up, the police are called in.

"It says here all three guys died with their cocks bitten off," announces one of the cops as he reads the coroner's report. "It could be a small animal..." he speculates.

Eventually, Erica's American lover calls up a virtual S.W.A.T. team of former army buddies. A helicopter, tanks, mortar shells and rockets still fail to destroy Tanya. They even try a flame thrower. "Yeah, eat it you bitch!"

She emerges from the fire, horribly burned and blackened, but still alive and even madder than before. Finally, just when all seems lost, Erica remembers a magic dagger she happens to be carrying(!). She stabs Tanya and, accompanied by some cheesy laser effects, the queen evaporates in blue sparks.

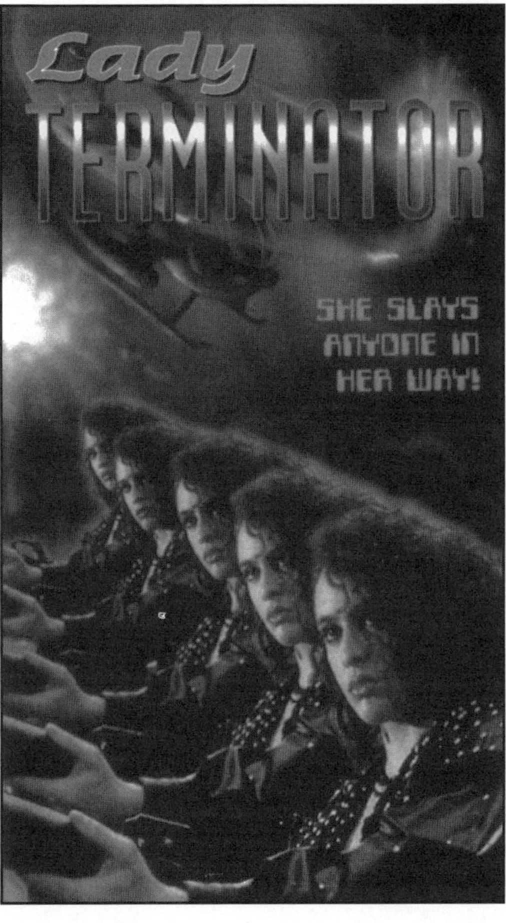

Left and below: *American video cover and Indian ad mat for the controversial* Lady Terminator.

Lady Terminator was released in Jakarta in July 1989 and aroused almost immediate controversy. It was withdrawn from circulation after just nine days, but in that time had been seen by more than 105,000 people. In many ways it marked the end of a particularly rich period for local exploitation movies.

Unlike similar films from the late seventies and early eighties, *Lady Terminator*, although shot and financed in Indonesia, had been edited and finished abroad. This kind of approach seems likely to continue, at least as far as cinema films are concerned. The companies that had most benefited from the exploitation boom, in particular Rapi and Parkit Films, have moved on to a different sort of production. In the 1980s television had become a boom industry in Indonesia. The most popular programmes were so-called *sinetrons* (basically, soap operas). The Punjaabi Brothers (Ram, Dhamoo and Gobind), whose Parkit Films had been behind titles like *Special Silencers*, *War Victims* and *Jungle Virgin Force*, turned their attention entirely to the production of these weekly serials. Their most successful programme, *Bella Vista*, is a sort of Indonesian *Dallas*, attracting over 10,000,000 viewers a week. Parkit also pioneered 3D television broadcasting and are now one of the country's biggest producers of advertising films.

While mystic martial arts, horror films and sexploitation movies are still being made in Indonesia, few of them seem to make it to international distribution. Which is a shame. Given the current predictable state of horror on the world's screens, we need a few flying heads to liven things up. ■

KR KAY AAR FILMS
JUNGLE
QUEEN
CINEMASCOPE
COLOR BY ADLABS.
DIRECTED BY
PRODUCED BY KANTI SHAH-RAMESH K. CHANDRA MUSIC ANAND MILIND
WRITTEN BY MAHENDRA DEHLVI CAMERA NESHA TELANG EDITING I. M. KUNNU

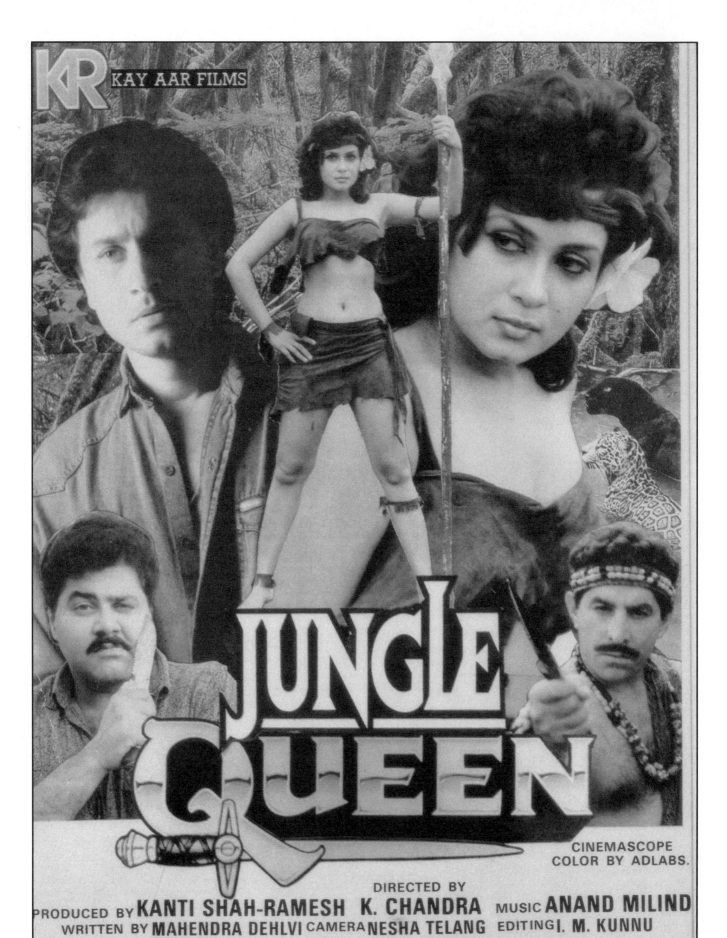

The Bare Facts About Bollywood

Indians are film fanatics. They live and breathe cinema. In a country where many people still don't have enough to eat, they bridge the gap with filmic fantasies from the biggest dream factory the world has ever known. Average production is around 800 films a year, with a daily audience of over 13,000,000. Huge, hand-painted banners advertising the latest blockbusters tower over the teeming streets of Indian cities. Film songs blare from tinny speakers on every corner.

Indian cinema is so successful at satisfying the needs of its own audience that it rarely bothers with the world outside. Few Indian movies are dubbed or subtitled for export. As a result, we've developed some very fixed ideas about them; firstly, that they're full of singing and dancing, and secondly that there's no sex in them. The first point is almost true. As for the second, well, the audience seems obsessed by it, if the content of the magazines they read is any indication. There are nearly 600 publications in India devoted to film. Many of them feature gossip of the most astonishing triviality; much of it is about sex.

A recent issue of *Movie*, in an article entitled 'Future Sex', outlines the way the topic is currently presented on film: 'The zillion rape scenes that are absolutely gross. Or the titillating dances at the villain's harem, not to mention the passionate rain sequences complete with heaving cleavages and pelvic thrusts.'

Actor Rishi Kapoor points out the odd hypocrisy of it all: "We keep insisting 'no sex, please' and we are the country that produces maximum babies."

When Indian film magazines discuss 'exposure', they're invariably talking about the heroine wearing a swimsuit or shorts. Even this is the subject of endless questioning and probing. Current superstar Madhuri Dixit was grilled in the magazine *Stardust* about her role in *Raja*, where she rips open her shirt in one scene and wears a miniskirt in another. "The clothes set the tone for the character," she explained patiently. "The girl... was very bold... outspoken and brash. So she would naturally be wearing a mini." The same issue contained a four page article about an on-set clash between actor Nana Petrakar and starlet Pooja. The cause of their friction seems to have been... that Pooja came on set wearing shorts!

This new breed of female stars are seen as vain, petulant creatures, constantly vying for attention and feuding with each other. Even their names — Silk, Twinkle, Karisma — suggest a breed of pouting super poppets. In a recent fanzine article, entitled 'The Girls Who Are Threatening Madhuri', a galaxy of male film-makers were asked to name their favourite challenger to the superstar throne. The introduction to the article sets the tone: 'A cat pack. Padding along on silent claws. Hissing now and then. Baring a fang every passing moment. A beautiful, sexy, talented cat pack.'

Even after clawing her way to the top, the career of an Indian actress is notoriously short-lived. Marriage to a rich industrialist is the usual full stop. For male stars, it's a different ball game. They have ups and downs but their longevity in this fickle industry is astonishing. When superstar Amitabh Bachchan retired from the movies to enter politics in 1984, he was still the unquestioned king of a box office he had ruled for more than ten years. So great was his fame that when he was hurt in a minor accident in 1982 during the making of *Coolie*, the national television and radio news ran hourly updates on his progress. When the film was released, the screen froze at the point where the accident occurred and a description of the incident flashed up.

***Opposite:** A rumble in the jungle, Bollywood style.*

A Galaxy of Glamour.
***Top:** Sushmita Sen.*
***Above:** Kalpana Iyer*
***Left:** Mamta Kulkarni.*

Right: Hunterwali — *The Woman With a Whip.*

India is a country where tradition holds firm. Traditional roles for men and women and traditional rules for art forms both derive from the sacred texts that are so much a part of every day life. Colourful images of the gods and goddesses of the Hindu pantheon abound in India. Shops, public places, even taxi cabs, all display them proudly. The style of Indian cinema is also derived indirectly from traditional sources. Its immediate ancestor is the ancient Sanskrit theatre, the rules of which were established more than 2,500 years ago. Many of the gestures, steps and movements featured in Indian films mirror paintings and carvings seen on temple walls, hundreds if not thousands of years old.

Sanskrit theatre was intended to elevate the spirits, to create a sense of well-being and harmony in the spectator. It was an absolute that no piece could end with the defeat or death of the hero. In such a context, how can horror films be possible?

One answer is to point to the enormous number of scenes of gore and gruesomeness that fill Indian mythology. In his book *Bare Breasts and Bare Bottoms,* C. K. Razdan lists a whole host of them from the *Mahabharata* and the *Ramayana*: blood drinking, tongues being pulled out, the beheading of children, thumbs and noses being cut off, people being made to lie on beds of arrows, and so on. For Indians, every aspect of the universe has its good and its bad incarnations. Thus the female manifestation of Shiva — Devi — can also become the many-armed Kali, hung about with human skulls and dripping with blood. The infamous Thugees, who practised ritual assassination as a form of worship, were followers of Kali.

The *Mahabharata* includes references to literally hundreds of different types of monsters and demons. Inevitably, versions of these made appearances in films from the very earliest days. There are snake demons, called *nagas,* who take the form of cobras with human shape from the waist up. The female snakes, or *nagins,* are often depicted as beautiful seductresses who lure men to their doom. A whole sub-division of Indian cinema is devoted to these snake films. Directors such as Shantilal Soni specialised in making them, the same way that an American director might become a specialist of Westerns or thrillers. His lengthy filmography includes lots of titles like *Naag Devata* (The Snake God), *Naag Mohini* (The Charming Snake Girl), *Naag Pooja* (Snake Worship) and *Naag Mere Saathi* (My Friend the Snake). The genre was very popular in the sixties and seventies when so-called 'mythological' films were still in vogue. *Nagina* (The Jewel), from 1987, set in motion a belated revival of the snake film, with *Nigahen* (The Eyes), *Shesh Naag* (King Cobra) and *Nagin aur Nagina* (Snake Girl and Jewel) being released in rapid succession to cash in on the renewed interest. Most of these films were romantic tales, with little attempt made to exploit the more obviously macabre aspects of the myth.

The low-budget *Naag Nagin* (Snake and Snake Girl), released in 1989, has some horror elements in its story of a bunch of overweight businessmen who attempt to capture a beautiful *nagin,* played by the sexy Mandakini. They kill her snake lover and she vows revenge. The plot then becomes a version of *The Bride Wore Black* (The Bride Wore Snakeskin?), as the *nagin* bumps them off one by one. Eventually she falls in love with the son of one of the men and they get married. The wedding photographer is the first to notice something wrong. When he develops the prints, he sees the bridegroom embracing a huge cobra! Highlights of the film include a snake driving a bus and a battle between two snake women. In a scene apparently devised to show as much flesh as possible, they are seen crawling through fences, writhing on the grass and slithering up trees, while the eerie wailing of the snake charmer's *been* fills the soundtrack.

So long as we treat them with a reasonable amount of respect, the snakes are generally well disposed towards us. The shapeshifting *rakshasas* are more malicious. Although mostly male, they also have the power to appear as beautiful women, or as animals to lure hunters to their doom. In the

Mahabharata they are sometimes like big hairy gorillas, with pointed ears and glowing, red eyes, feeding on human blood.

Creatures like this pop up all the time in Indian horror films. They may seem comical to us, but to the Indian viewer they are as familiar as Dracula or Frankenstein's monster. *Jaani Dushman* (Beloved Enemy), a pioneering horror film from 1979, features a *rakshasa* in the form of a husband whose unfaithful wife poisoned him in their marriage bed. Now he haunts the nuptial chambers of newly weds, feasting on young, virgin brides. No sooner has he related his story at the beginning of the film than he turns into a huge hairy monster. Arms outstretched, he chases a terrified woman into a vast underground cavern.

Many forms of vampire stalk the woods and lonely places of the Indian countryside. The vampire legend is believed to have originated in the Indus valley more than 3,000 years before the birth of Christ. Through trade and migration it spread eastward, to China and Japan, and westward to Europe. The Victorian scholar Richard Burton, who also brought to the West the erotic classics *The Perfumed Garden* and *The Kama Sutra*, translated a whole set of Indian horror tales in *Vikram and the Vampire, or Tales of Hindu Devilry*.

Burton's vampire was a *vetala*, another shapeshifting creature that often appears as an old hag sucking the blood of the insane. Indian vampire lore also includes the *jigarkwhar*, a female vampire whose speciality is extracting her victim's liver. The *masan* feeds on children, and even its shadow is deadly. The *pisacha*, a sort of ghoul, can also cure illness. Like many other Indian vampires it haunts graveyards and crossroads, and feasts off the flesh of the newly dead.

This huge and colourful body of mythology was a frequent source of material for Indian films, right from the very beginning. The first Indian feature, *King Harischandra*, made in 1913, was a mythological film derived from the *Mahabharata*. Its pioneering director, Dadasaheb Phalke, acted as scriptwriter, cameraman, art director and eventually distributor. He hired an ox cart and carried the cans of film from village to village, setting up makeshift cinemas every time he wanted to put on a show. Using motorised transport, this type of distribution still operates in rural areas of India today.

Phalke's success inspired others to venture into film. Pretty soon an industry began to develop. Just as Biblical and classical subjects were a popular source for early American films, so the rich tradition of Indian mythology was mined extensively. Audiences were familiar with the material, and that made the process of selling the new medium much easier. Moreover — an important consideration for the cost-conscious moneymen — the stories were not copyrighted.

From its inception in the 1930s, the new industry was based predominantly in Bombay. When sound arrived, films were made in the Hindi language, which soon established itself as the voice of 'All India Films'. Using the experience of imported Italian, German and American technicians, Indian film-makers soon began adapting their techniques to reflect local tastes. The result was a spectacular, frothy, escapist type of cinema, full of dashing heroes and glamorous heroines. These films were known as 'stunt' films, taking their cue from the popular swashbuckling antics of Douglas Fairbanks. The prime producers were Wadia Movietone and their biggest star was a woman: Fearless Nadia. Her real name was Mary Evans and she was born in

Left: *A musical fantasy scene with an Indian Superman and Spiderwoman.*

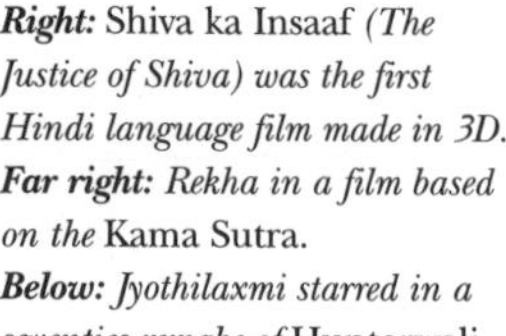

Right: Shiva ka Insaaf *(The Justice of Shiva) was the first Hindi language film made in 3D.*
Far right: *Rekha in a film based on the* Kama Sutra.
Below: *Jyothilaxmi starred in a seventies remake of* Hunterwali.

Australia. Having trained as a dancer and worked in the circus, she had no problems with the stunts. It was the Indian language she couldn't master: "In one film I was held by the gangsters and I had to shout 'Mujhe chhod do!' ('Let me go!'). The way I said it, the entire crew was in stitches. Ultimately, the dialogue-master took me aside and taught me to distinguish between 'chhod' (let go) and 'chot' (fuck)!!"

Nadia's greatest success was in *Hunterwali* (Woman with a Whip), where she's a sort of female Zorro. On horseback, wearing a black mask, a tight black costume and brandishing a huge whip in her hand, she bears down on her enemies with a loud "Hey-y-y-y-y!" Other studios followed suit with titles like *Motorwali* and *Cyclewali.*

The golden age of Indian cinema lasted from the late 1940s, following the country's newly won independence, through to the end of the 1950s. There was a rush to invest in film-making. Many small companies appeared almost overnight. It was no great secret that a lot of this money came from businessmen who had evaded tax during the final years of British rule. They had been able to justify this as a patriotic form of passive resistance. Now they had no such excuse and were keen to launder their cash as quickly as possible. The huge diversity of Indian society, with its enormous range of social agendas, led to a search for a universal dramatic form that would appeal to everyone. Subplots abounded. Comedy collided with tragedy, and songs were sung at the drop of a hat. Music became an amazing amalgam of East and West, where Carmen Miranda-style dance rhythms met Punjabi drumming in a Manhattan night-club.

In 1959 came the first Indian film in Cinemascope, Guru Dutt's *Kaagaz ke Phool* (Paper Flowers). The film was a failure, but the format was not. It was ideally suited to the 'picturisation' (as Indian film-makers call it) of musical numbers. Colour was the next step. Its arrival set Indian screens alight with the kind of kitsch glamour that seems to thrive in bright sun and hot nights. The black and white fifties were over, as were any serious attempts to make meaningful movies. Indian cinema entered the sixties with an aesthetic drawn from Elvis Presley musicals, beach party movies and lurid poster paintings.

If the fifties were a time of creation and the sixties of consolidation, then the seventies became a time of flux and uncertainty. Politically the country seemed to be tearing itself apart. The decade opened with violent student riots and a harsh clampdown from the authorities. War broke out between India and Pakistan. Strikes and regional unrest eventually led to the declaration of a state of emergency in 1975. Opposition leaders were jailed, newspapers banned or censored and the Prime Minister, Indira Ghandi, took steps to lessen the power of the Indian parliament.

The star of the decade was Amitabh Bachchan, and his big hit was 1975's *Sholay,* a violent revenge drama heavily influenced by spaghetti Westerns — in fact the genre it helped to create became known as 'curry Westerns'. Bachchan played the moody anti-hero, Jaidev, but the real star of the film was the villain, Gabbar Singh, played by Amjad Khan. Audiences cheered his every screen appearance and memorised his lines of dialogue by heart.

Following the end of the state of emergency in 1977, there was a strong rush to exploit the new freedoms before they were snatched away again. One of the consequences was a rise in under-the-counter porn. Expensive imports like *Penthouse, Hustler* and *Playboy* gave way to a wide range of home-produced titles. The kings of Indian sleaze were the five Singh brothers, who operated out of a crowded office in Delhi's Connaught Place. Together they produced a raft of more than twenty titles, ranging from *Garam Kahaniyan* ('all that goes on in the sex dens of the world or the privacy of a bedroom') to *Hot Wave* and the true crime magazine *For All. Film Mirror* was a movie magazine that published blurry stills from films like *Deep Throat* mixed in with pictures of local sex stars such as the busty Katy Mirza and Komila Wirk. One of

the Singhs' ploys was to use headlines like 'Raj Kumar arrested in rape case!' Of course, it wasn't the famous actor Raj Kumar, but some poor non-entity with the same name. To make it difficult for purchasers to discover the scam, the pages of the mags were stapled together.

Cinema also began to change in the seventies, with more explicit plotlines and heroines who weren't averse to doing a sexy dance or delivering provocative dialogue. One of the precursors of this movement was the writer/director Babu Ram Ishara. He had come to Bombay as a star-struck kid at the age of sixteen. Starting at the bottom, working in a studio canteen, he eventually rose to become a scriptwriter and assistant director. In 1970, he began his first serious film, *Chetna* (The Awakening). Working with a cast of unknowns, largely drawn from the recently opened cinema school at Pune, he managed to make a film that not only aroused controversy, but actually earned money. The story was certainly strong stuff for Indian cinema. It was about a man marrying a prostitute, who then discovers she is pregnant by one of her clients and commits suicide. The female lead, Rehana Sultan, was a new kind of star, fully prepared to deal with the strong language and nudity that her part called for.

Chetna's most important innovation was not the bare flesh on display or an occasional swear word, rather it was the speed and cheapness with which the film had been made. Previously, only the regional or 'art' film-makers, like Satyajit Ray and Mrinal Sen, had managed to make successful films without stars or big budgets. Like a Hindi version of Roger Corman, Ishara showed the way for a whole generation of Indian producers. As the big studio system collapsed, many fly-by-night companies were set up, often backed by 'black' money gained from dodgy business dealings. In the 1970s, the movie industry began to attract a reputation as a last resort for all sorts of unsavoury characters out for a fast buck. Sex and above all violence began to make their way onto Indian screens.

Cheap 'B' pictures proliferated. From the southern industries based in Madras and Bangalore came quick and colourful spy and thriller films. The buxom Jyothilaxmi starred in dozens of early seventies cheapies like *Lady James Bond* and *Rocket Rani*, mixing sex, thrills and sci-fi into a spicy masala. Her other achievements included a series with a midget secret agent called 'Shorty', *Kulla Agent 000* (Shorty Agent 000), and even a remake of the famous *Hunterwali*.

Sex education films were heavily promoted. The Government could hardly object to these. Compared with their own programme of enforced sterilisation, the message was a gentle one. But there was no getting away from it, films such as *Gupta Gyan* (Secret Knowledge) and *Stree Purush* (Woman Man) owed their success to suggestive advertising campaigns and the fact that, for the first time, at least the results of sex — ie the birth of a baby — could be shown on Indian screens.

The most curious by-product of the Indian sex wave was the rash of caveman movies sparked off by *Adi Manav* (Cave Man), released in 1976. The film didn't have any dialogue, just grunts and groans from its cast of frizzy-haired men in loin cloths and women in bikini pants and fur-covered bras. *Purana Purush* (Prehistoric Man) quickly followed, complete with a huge, fire-snorting dragon. *Adi Yug* (Prehistoric Age) ran into censor troubles when its sex scenes were accompanied by more than usually enthusiastic grunting.

This genre was undoubtedly inspired by Hammer productions like *Slave Girls*, but generally it's questionable how much influence Western films had on the development of this explicit new wave of commercial cinema. Hollywood films are popular in India, but Government restrictions, censorship and high taxation made the country an unattractive proposition for the big companies. Using a system known as the NRI (Non Resident Indian) scheme, Indians living abroad were allowed to import prints of films into the country for limited distribution. As this was a risky business, it was generally the cheaper, lower-budget pictures that were bought. Looking through a list of foreign films available for the Indian market, fans of European and American 'B' pictures will find many familiar names. Schlock directors like Umberto Lenzi, Matt Cimber and Earl Owensby pop up with great regularity.

This diet of garish exploitation had a weird effect on Indian movies. Rather than being influenced by classics, local film-makers had to take their inspiration from the kinds of films that are more or less invisible to Western critics. Low-budget Italian slasher films and their American imitations were a popular source of ideas. The image of the black-gloved, -masked, and -hatted villain, raised knife in hand, occurs so many times in Hindi thrillers that its become a cliché. The climactic murder scenes from films

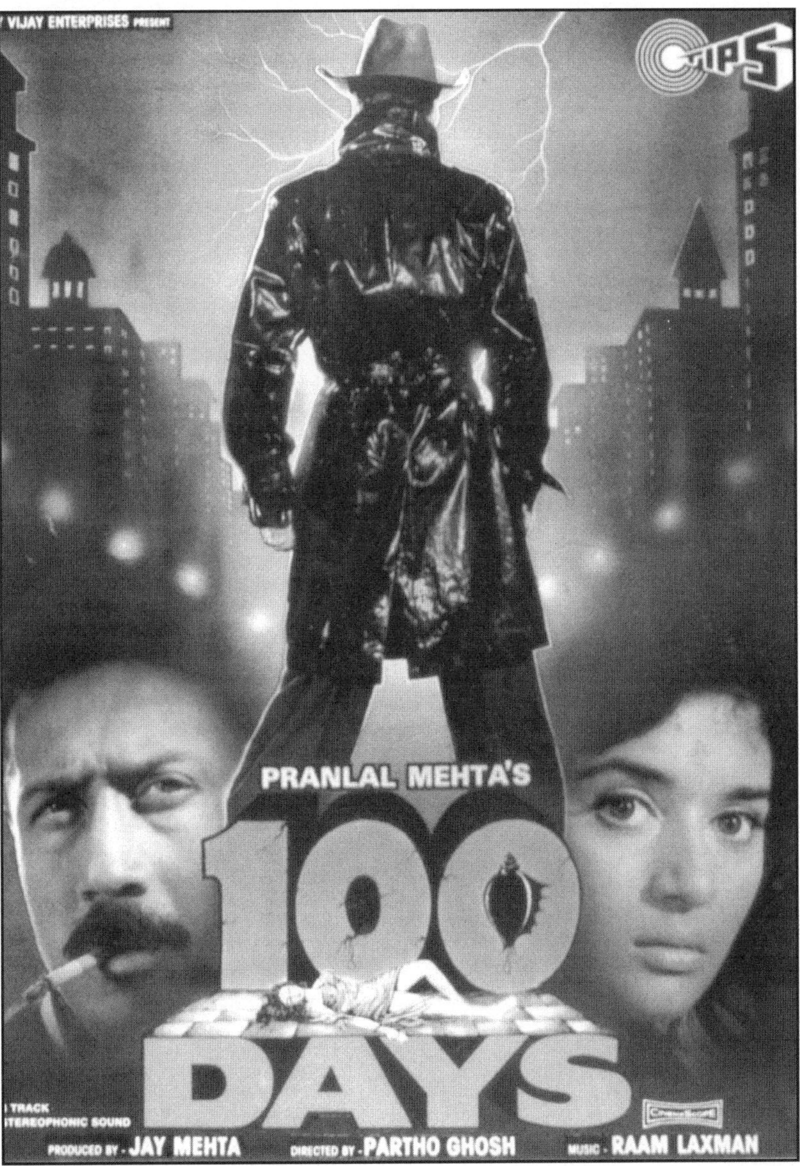

Above: *Many Indian movies are inspired by Western imports. Here's a version of Lucio Fulci's* The Psychic.

YOU'LL BE TALKING ABOUT IT AGAIN & AGAIN
A CINE IMAGES Production
VINOD PANDE'S
SACH
A THOUGHT PROVOKING FILM ABOUT ADULT LOVE
SCREENPLAY & DIRECTION VINOD PANDE
MUSIC JEETU TAPAN

Right: *Sex scenes are still a novelty in Indian movies.*
Below: *South Indian sex queen Silk Smitha.*
Bottom: *Kerala in Southern India was the prime source of lurid sex movies.*

like Mario Bava's *Blood and Black Lace* have been copied blow by blow in several movies and Lucio Fulci's *The Psychic* was virtually remade in Partho Ghosh's *100 Days.*

The influence of Western films on the Indian market remained peripheral, however. Stories, soundtracks and themes may have been copied from foreign films, but the social milieu that created them remained alien to the Indian viewer. The pressures that made Indian cinema open out were internal and economic. Often they were a result of different regional film industries vying for attention with the all-pervasive power of Bombay — or Bollywood as it came to be called.

SILK SMITA
In & As
LEO INTERNATIONAL'S
J.V. RUKMANGADAN
CHELLAPAN

During the 1970s, the southwestern state of Kerala experienced a huge influx of money brought back from the Arabic Gulf states by *émigré* workers. Local business magnates began to join forces with these 'Gulf millionaires' to produce movies. They were also attracted by the Government grants offered to any film shot in the state. By the end of the decade, Malayalam-language productions began to match, and in some cases outnumber, Hindi-language films. A freer and more outspoken attitude to sex was one of the features of this new Keralan cinema. One of the first examples to be dubbed into Hindi for wider distribution was the 1978 production *Avalude Ravukal*, better known under its more racy English title of *Her Nights.* Made by the ostensibly serious — and explicitly political — director, I. V. Sasi, the film caused a furore, largely on account of its title and a salacious advertising campaign.

Keralan cinema, and South Indian films generally, soon became synonymous with sexy cinema for most Indian filmgoers. Starlets like the pouting Silk Smitha and Rathi became the first Indian sex stars. Films with English titles like *Rape on Typist, Sexy Body Killer* and *Sex Flowers* began to proliferate. They were heavily promoted with flesh-filled posters and montages of supposedly 'sexy' scenes. The 'A' rating (the Indian equivalent of the 'X' certificate) was always prominently displayed, usually much larger than the title.

Miss Pamela was a typical Silk vehicle. The title is an obvious reference to the case of Pamella Bordes, a former Miss India who moved to London and became involved in a notorious sex scandal featuring MPs, newspaper editors and state secrets. In the film, Silk plays a star-struck young girl living in a women's hostel who has an affair with a fashion photographer. After seeing him shot dead by a crook, she flees back to her family home, but is raped by three men and sees her father and mother gunned down. The shock drives her insane. She tracks down the three rapists and kills them. One man is squashed to death under a hydraulic ramp, another is castrated during a nude swim and the third is forced into a giant ice crusher. The police watch in horror as the man disappears head first into the machine and the clear stream of ice begins to flow scarlet with his blood. Perfect fare for what the trade papers call 'the front benchers'.

In real life poor Silk didn't fare much better than the unhappy heroines she so often portrayed on film. She decided to give up her wild ways, open a hospital and marry her doctor lover. Unfortunately, he was already married to someone else. Her family astrologer told her that she had to stay away from the man, and from films, for a year. Soon her star was on the wane, and the wonderfully named Disco Shanti was ready to steal her crown as 'South India's Sex Queen'.

Of course, all these films had to pass the scrutiny of the incredibly strict Indian censor. Consequently, their actual sex content was extremely mild by Western standards. Even during the obligatory shower scenes the heroine always wears a towel or swimsuit. Producers began to second guess the censors, putting in strong scenes they knew would be cut in the hope that others might slip through by default. Having flashes of nudity glimpsed through half-open doors or through gaps in curtains became a common ploy. Soon rumours began that unscrupulous theatre owners were cutting hardcore sequences into these soft films to give the audiences some genuine sleaze. This became known as 'interpolation', and audiences sought out these elusive items, hoping for a quick sighting of the forbidden.

The 1980s saw a huge increase in the cost of film-making. A major cause was the rise of 'multi-star' pictures. Whereas before a film might have had a couple of well-known names, it became the trend to have a roster of four or five. As the number of big stars was actually quite limited, the same names were being cast in as many as twenty films at the same time. This resulted in the ridiculous practice of stars hiring themselves out by the hour. They would turn up knowing little if anything about the role they were playing, wander through their part, reading their lines from huge cue cards, and then hightail it off to the next set to do it all over again.

Even with the film in the can, a producer's problems were not over. seventy-five per cent of completed films were failing to find any sort of distribution, particularly if they had a non-star cast. Of the ones that did make it to the screen, only ten per cent broke even and a much smaller number were big hits. One solution was to copy a well-known Hollywood success. Almost every Hollywood hit had a Hindi clone. An Indian *Superman* took to the skies in 1987, with special effects footage 'borrowed' from the Christopher Reeve film. Fresh from his success with *Disco Dancer*, producer/director B. Subhash released *The Adventures of Tarzan* in 1985. He was sued by the estate of Edgar Rice Burroughs for unauthorised use of the Tarzan name. The case was summarily thrown out of court.

In fact, Tarzan films had been made in India since the 1930s. There was even a home-grown version of the Lord of the Jungle, called Zambo (or sometimes Zimbo). In the 1960s, following John Guillermin's 'official' *Tarzan Goes to India* (*Tarzan Meera Saathi*), there was a flood of imitations, including *Tarzan and King Kong*, *Tarzan Comes to Delhi* and *Tarzan and Hercules*. In the mid-eighties, a rash of even lesser product like *Jungle Love* and *Jungle Queen* was rushed into production to capitalise on the continuing fascination with the man in the tiger-skin loincloth.

Sex films proliferated during the 1980s. Imported clunkers like the seventies German sex education movie *Ideal Marriage* broke box office records. Another sex ed movie, *The Body*, was advertised as 'revealing secrets of every organ in intimate details without any shame', and had a packed-out, five-week run at the Liberty in Bombay. Censorship, high state taxes and lack of investment had slowed down the South Indian sex industry, so Bombay producers jumped in to fill the gap. The makers of *Bud Naseeb* (Unlucky) promised 'a homage to the women in love and as a victim of lust. A woman in her pride and in her humiliation. A woman in her tortures and as the instrument of torture.'

Attitudes to women seem contradictory in India. As the description of *Bud Naseeb* shows, the 'whore/Madonna' complex still rules. And yet the popular imagination is captivated by the idea of strong, even murderous, women breaking all social taboos. The various female dacoits of the remote Chambal valley have long been a source of fascination. Phoolan Devi, of *Bandit Queen* fame, is only the latest in a long line that goes back at least to Begum Bashira in the 1940s. As recently as 1978, the armed and vicious Hasina was shot dead with her two lovers and the bodies put on public display. A photo published in *India Today* shows her corpse lying between the two men, minus most of her clothes. Exposure, it seems, is only acceptable in India when the woman is dead.

In the late eighties, inspired by the American film *The Sisterhood*, Avtar Bhogal persuaded fading star Dimple Kapadia to star in his film *Zakhmi Aurat* (Wounded Woman). She plays a policewoman, forming a squad of raped women who go round castrating the men who abused them. The idea caught on, and 1988 saw a host of films featuring women in tight uniforms brandishing guns. 'Latter-day Kalis in black leather', writer Madhu Jain called them. Indian producers rediscovered the notorious *I Spit on Your Grave*, and there were several outright copies like *Yeh Pyar Nahin* (This is not Love), *Vasna ki Aag* (Fire of Passion) and *Khooni Meena* (Deadly Meena). In the latter, sex queen Silk Smitha plays two roles — a black-clad avenger and a policewoman called in to investigate the murders she commits. The same year saw the release of B. R. Ishara's *Woh Phir Aayegi* (She Will Return), where the ghost of a dead woman returns to avenge herself against the middle class men who raped her.

The plots of these films allowed their makers to indulge in all kinds of scenes of violence and prolonged retribution. Given the context, it was possible to use an 'end justifies the means' defence. The censor's guidelines demanded only that 'pointless scenes of violence, cruelty and horror are not shown'. The mood of the times and the continuing commercial success of films oozing with sex and violence encouraged producers to push the definition of 'pointless' to the very limit of its implied meaning.

During the seventies and eighties, the situation for the smaller Indian producers was really no different from that of their European and American counterparts. Unable to afford big stars and advertising budgets, they had to rely on sensational subject matter and notoriety. Sex, or the suggestion of it, was a constant draw for audiences looking for something new. Violence and horror were never far behind. With the industry in crisis in the late eighties, horror films became an increasingly attractive option. In the next section we look at the rise of the Indian horror movie and the men who made it possible. ■

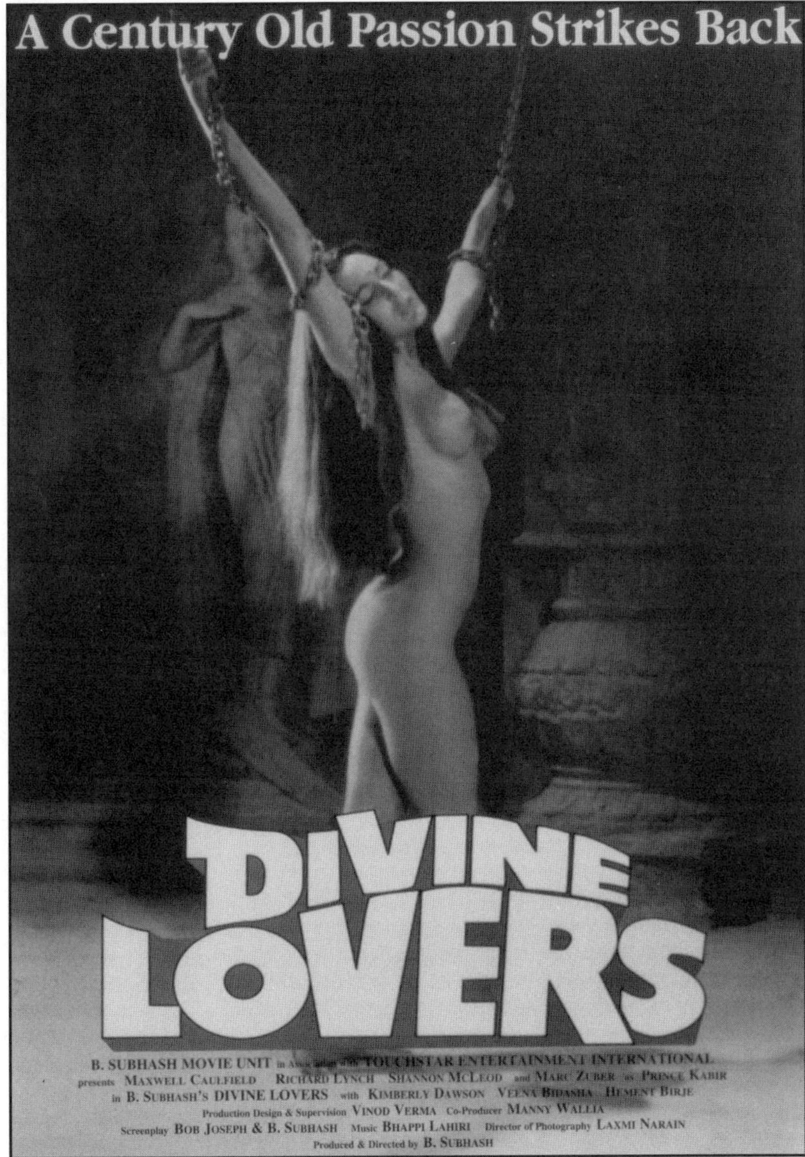

A Century Old Passion Strikes Back
DIVINE LOVERS
B. SUBHASH MOVIE UNIT
TOUCHSTAR ENTERTAINMENT INTERNATIONAL
presents MAXWELL CAULFIELD RICHARD LYNCH SHANNON MCLEOD and MARC ZUBER as PRINCE KABIR
in B. SUBHASH'S DIVINE LOVERS with KIMBERLY DAWSON VEENA BIDASHA HEMENT BIRJE
Production Design & Supervision VINOD VERMA Co-Producer MANNY WALLIA
Screenplay BOB JOSEPH & B. SUBHASH Music BHAPPI LAHIRI Director of Photography LAXMI NARAIN
Produced & Directed by B. SUBHASH

Above: *A 1996 movie set amongst the erotic sculptures of Kajuraho.*

TARZAN
GOES TO INDIA
... FOR HIS MOST SPECTACULAR ADVENTURE OF ALL! ... In CINEMASCOPE and TECHNICOLOR
"TARZAN GOES TO INDIA"

HARSARAN S.B. SINGH NAGI PRESENT

KHOONI
MAHAL

CINEMASCOPE

MUSIC
NADEEM SHRAVAN

PRODUCED • DIRECTED BY MOHAN BHAKRI

PHOTOGRAPHY
ARVIND BHAKRI

From Myths to Monsters

One of the most heartening things about Indian horror is that it remains so disreputable. Asian video shop proprietors will laugh when you tell them that you're looking for horror films. Some will tell you flatly that such things don't exist, or will hastily blurt out that they don't have any, should you be able to name a few titles. Even a sympathetic listener will tell you how bad the films are, and that American or British films are much better.

It's only amongst the young that you'll find anything like a positive response. "Yeah, we love 'em," a video shop worker in east London told me. "Lots of people round here like horror. But not the older people. It's because of the sex. But how can you have horror without a little bit of sex?" he concluded, echoing the question that horror fans around the world are constantly having to pose.

The same horror fan told me astutely that while he recognised the technical superiority of American horror movies, he questioned their real effectiveness. "It's all set in cities and it all looks the same. But in Indian horror films you've got all that beautiful scenery. What's more, such things do happen out there in the country. Or at least it's easier to believe that they could."

Nearly all American and British horror films today are set in cities. Even rural films like *Night of the Living Dead* have a definite townward motion. Geography and budget may have prevented the dead ever reaching their destination, but they were obviously headed for the big city, where the media, the army and the crowds awaited them.

Indian horror films work very much the other way. Essentially, they are still a rural phenomenon. When reviewing the latest horror epic, the trade papers always say snootily, 'Should do well in rural or "B" areas.' The plots of the films reflect this bias. Even when the story begins in a town, the victims always seem to find an excuse to go back to the country to confront the horror. People look to the country to see who they are and where they belong. Cities are places you go to earn a living, but they are false, glittering, shallow. The country is real. Horror can only be defeated out there, where its roots lie.

Just as the myth of the dark wood is so potent for Western film audiences, recalling bedtime stories of Little Red Riding Hood, so it is for Indian moviegoers. Except that they are more likely to relate it to the story of Rama. The future king is banished to the dark jungle for fourteen years by the manipulations of a jealous woman. It's in the jungle that Rama comes across the demons and *rakshasas* that are his undoing. His wife, Sita, is captured by the ten-headed demon Ravana and it's only with the help of Hanuman, the monkey king, that Rama and Sita are reunited.

India, unlike Japan or China, has no literary tradition of horror outside these old folk tales and *puranas*. Consequently the majority of horror films are based on imported models. The most popular being *The Exorcist*, *The Evil Dead* and *The Omen*.

It's useful to define why these three have had such a big effect. Of course, they were all world-wide hits, but something about them resonated with Indian tastes in a way that tells us a lot about the subsequent films they influenced. All three share a clearly defined notion of good and evil, and the opposition between the two. This reflects very much the Indian view of things. The priest from *The Exorcist*, for example, translates very easily into the mystic or guru who pops up in so many Indian horror films as a representative of the powers of light.

Secondly, the notion of possession is one that Indians

Opposite: *One of the big hits of India's horror boom.*

Above: *Kali, the bloodthirsty bride of Shiva.*
Left: *A mythological fantasy from Wada Movietone Studios.*

can relate to strongly. Vampires and werewolves don't really have a place in Indian folklore the way they do in the West. Evil spirits who possess the bodies of the innocent are much more familiar. Even more importantly, both *The Exorcist* and *The Omen* deal with the possession of children. Family values, respect for one's elders and a sense of tradition are much more highly valued in India than they are in the West today. Hence the notion of losing control of your child is a very powerful one.

Possession by demons and a straightforward presentation of the fight between good and evil are also features of *The Evil Dead.* But what made that movie most appealing to Indian film-makers were its mythological aspects and exuberant folk tale elements (the scene with the tree that comes alive has been imitated in numerous Indian horror films). The notion of evil being released through ancient texts is also something that Indian audiences were used to.

On a technical level, the cottage industry approach of *The Evil Dead* was a big attraction for Indian film-makers. Indian horror films are tragically uneven. The make-up and special effects are woefully inadequate. Almost all of them resort to the same simple camera tricks of double exposure or winding the film backwards. The same bits of stock footage are frequently re-used. There's a shot of the night sky rent by flashes of forked lightning that seems to occur in every Indian horror film at climactic moments, usually followed by a wild burst of manic laughter.

The roots of these special effects lie in the mythological fantasies of the fifties and sixties, with films like *Hatimtai* and *Parasmani* (The Jewel). Babubhai Mistry, who became the foremost maker of this kind of movie, was a local master at using back projection, models and mattes to express fantastic scenes. However, to sophisticated Western eyes, his films look extremely crude, the effects transparently obvious in their mechanics. It must have been very reassuring for Indian film-makers to know that *The Evil Dead* had been such a big hit and to see how home-made its effects were. If it's good enough for Hollywood, they reasoned, it has to be good enough for Bollywood, too.

***This page:** Horror themes abound in Indian pulp fiction and comic books.*

So were there really no Indian precedents for the emergent horror films? Apart from the mythologicals with their creaky special effects and the violent revenge sagas of 1970s cinema, the only discernible influence was in the brief vogue for moody mystery movies, usually set around a house, and unmistakably influenced by the likes of Hitchcock's *Rebecca.*

The Indian pioneer here was Kamal Amrohi. His *Mahal* (The Palace), released in 1949, is set in an abandoned mansion with a hidden past. Echoes of this film, with its mysterious portraits, misty atmospherics and romantic, ghostly heroine, abound in later Indian horror films, such as *Ghunghroo ki Awaaz* (The Tinkling of Anklets) and the super hit *Purana Mandir* (The Old Temple).

The directors of both of these films, the Ramsay brothers Tulsi and Shyam, are generally credited with introducing the horror movie to India. They had been involved in film production for several years before their pioneering *Do Gaz Zameen ke Neeche* (Six Foot Under) was released in 1972. There, for the first time, all the disparate elements of Indian fantastic films were combined with a distinctly Western approach to horror.

The seven Ramsay Brothers have since been joined by sons and cousins to make a veritable horror factory. "They call us the Horror Brothers," Tulsi Ramsay announces proudly. The trade papers talk of 'the famous Ramsay touch' and today any horror film made in India has to measure itself up against the Brothers' solid achievement of thirty-two movies in a twenty-five year career.

Their father, F. U. Ramsay, had been a radio manufacturer in Karachi (now in Pakistan). Following partition of the country in 1947, the family moved to Bombay. F. U. Ramsay's first major venture into film production was with the veteran playwright and director, Vishram Bedekar. *Rustom Sohrab,* released in 1963, was based on an ancient

Persian legend, with a script written by Kumar Ramsay. The film was hugely expensive and barely made back its costs. Several medium-budget films followed and then, in 1970, came their next production with Bedekar, *Ek Nanni Munni Ladhki Thi* (Once There Was a Young Girl). Again the script was by Kumar Ramsay, and both Tulsi and Shyam, who had just left college, worked on the film as assistants. It was not a big hit, but the Ramsays noticed something very interesting about audience reaction to the movie's opening sequence.

The setting is a museum in the middle of the night. A startled cat watches as a mysterious shadow emerges from behind a tree and makes its way towards the locked building. A black-robed figure glides through the silent corridors of the museum and smashes open a glass display case, carrying off the jewelled trophy inside. An alarm is triggered, the place is soon swarming with cops. A clawed hand pulls a power switch, plunging everything into darkness. Torches cut through the gloom. A beam of light picks out a hideous, gargoyle-like face. Suddenly it comes to life and a terrifying creature marches down the museum's grand staircase, impervious to the bullets of the police. They scatter in panic at the sight of this apparently deathless monster.

Of course, it's all a scam. The 'monster' is actually a clever thief wearing a mask and a bullet-proof jacket. Unfortunately, the power of these opening moments is such that the film never really recovers. Audiences went crazy for this sequence, but many of them left after the film's interval when it became obvious that the monster was not going to return.

F. U. Ramsay began to work on a plan to recoup the money he had lost on the movie. If audiences were so keen on this kind of thing, he mused, why not give them what they want? Make a film with more such sequences. At least five or six of them. In other words, a real, out-and-out horror film.

At that time, in the early 1970s, there was a steady stream of imported horrors coming into India. Hammer films were at a commercial peak and low-budget shockers from Italy, Spain and the Philippines were being widely distributed. Most of these films were projected at matinée shows, the midday first screening in Indian movie houses. Audiences came back as often as ten times on subsequent days to experience the thrill.

No one had ever made a Western-style horror film in India. To minimise the risk of such a questionable venture, F. U. Ramsay decided to turn his sons into a film-making unit. Kumar would obviously be the writer and Tulsi and Shyam, who had already worked on *Ek Nanni Munni Ladhki Thi*, would be the directors. It was unusual but not unheard of to have dual directors in India. Anyway, F. U. mused, two inexperienced heads are probably better than one in such a situation. Tulsi, the eldest, was made responsible for the technical side of things, the camera placement, framing etc, while Shyam would handle the actors.

Together they concocted a story that placed Hammer-style shocks in an Indian setting. Their influences were both the Western movies they had seen and imported horror comics, of which Tulsi was a keen reader. The film was called *Do Gaz Zameen ke Neeche*, which literally translates as 'Two Yards Under the Ground' — or 'Six Foot Under', a title that gave a solid clue to the horrors to come. The film begins like a pulpy thriller, with a devious woman marrying a rich man and murdering him for his inheritance. Things shift dramatically into new territory when the man's corpse is revived by a chemical compound and he comes back to exact his revenge.

Studio costs would have been prohibitive for such a no-budget production. Fortunately F. U. knew of a perfect location, the Mahabaleshwar hill station about five hours' drive from Bombay. There the team found ruined temples, ancient graveyards, churches, lakes and mountains. As Tulsi Ramsay explained later, there was "everything you need to make a horror film." It was off-season and so there were plenty of hotels eager to house a film crew. The Ramsays found one accommodating owner who would give them a cut-price rate if they mentioned his establishment in the credits. The Ramsay wives and sisters were brought along to make food for the unit and a cast of young unknowns was found who were prepared to work for nothing, with the promise of cash if the film was a success. The budget was so low that the actors even had to supply their own costumes.

Do Gaz Zameen ke Neeche was completed in thirty-five days, and on its release in 1972 was a huge hit. F. U. was pleased that his hunch had proved correct, and there was a market for horror in India. However, no one knew how long it would last and so he quickly greenlighted another film in the same vein, *Andhera* (The Darkness). The Bombay censors had not been happy with *Do Gaz* but had eventually given it a certificate, probably hoping it was a one-off. When they realised that the Ramsays were intent on delivering more horrors, their attitude hardened. *Andhera* was held up in a censorship bottleneck for several years and the family was close to bankruptcy by the time it was released. Undaunted, and convinced that they were on the right track, they came back in 1978 with *Darwaza* (The Door), another horror movie, only this time with a bigger budget, a broader canvas and a sprinkling of humour to sweeten the pill.

Darwaza is a typical Bombay mixed bag. There's an evil landlord, a family curse, sword fights, whipping scenes, secret passages and mysterious portraits, all served up with a bevy of spunky female stars. The story tells of a curse occasioned by the burning of a priest of Kali. Like most seventies Indian horror movies, the shock scenes are few and far between. Here the climax is the on-screen transformation of Trilok Kapoor into a hideous monster. Fur sprouts all over his face and his skin blackens while blood pours from his eyes.

The Ramsays would never again feature such an ambi-

Left: *An early hit from the Ramsay Brothers horror factory.*

MANOHAR AGICHA PRESENTS
पुराना मंदिर
K.R. ENTERPRISES
PURANA MANDIR
DIRECTED BY
TULSI RAMSAY
AND
SHYAM RAMSAY
PRODUCED BY KANTA RAMSAY SCREENPLAY KUMAR RAMSAY MUSIC AJIT SINGH
LYRICS AMIT KHANNA • AUDIOGRAPHY KIRAN RAMSAY • ASSO. DIRECTOR ARJUN RAMSAY • PHOTOGRAPHY GANGU RAMSAY

Above: Purana Mandir.
A smash hit from 1984.

tious 'in camera' effect. Small wonder. The scene took a day and a half to shoot. Kapoor lay on a couch from 7.00am until 3.00am the following day, while Gangu Ramsay set up the stop-motion effects with his big Mitchell camera. The importance given to the scene underlines one of the tenets of Indian horror films: the evil has to be visible on the face of the wrongdoer. To make a 'clean' horror film would be impossible. The audience would be confused. They have literally to see the evil to believe it.

Aur Kaun? (Who Else?), released in 1979, had a female monster, a woman who returns from the dead to continue her affair with a landowner's young son. In 1980 came two films, the comic shocker *Guest House* and the spooky thriller *Saboot* (The Evidence). By 1981 the Ramsays had really got into their stride and for the following decade released at least one horror film a year, sometimes, as in 1989, as many as five. Their films can be divided into three main types. Firstly, the pioneering period of the 1970s, when there were really no models to follow and every film was a leap in the dark. Then the early 1980s, when they experimented with comedy sequences and with thrillers like *Saboot* and *Telephone.* Finally, following the runaway success of *Purana Mandir* in 1985, came the consolidation of that success and the relentless mining of the Ramsay formula. 'When in doubt, bring on the monster' would seem to be the logic of most of these late-eighties movies.

When the Ramsays move away from the formula, or stretch its limits, they can come up with something quite impressive. *Ghunghroo ki Awaaz* and *Hotel,* both released in 1981, show what they can do.

Gunghroo ki Awaaz was a departure for the Ramsays, being a more sombre and serious film than they had previously attempted. It featured famous Hindi actor and director Vijay Anand as Ranjit, heir to a fortune, who falls in love with a girl he sees dancing in the rain. He's drawn to her by the tinkling of her anklet bells — a key scene, found in countless romantic Indian movies. His family refuse to accept her because of her lower caste status. Dancing girls are traditionally seen as little better than prostitutes. Ranjit fights their disapproval but is devastated when another man from the girl's past turns up. Crazed with jealousy, he shoots them both and his father helps him to burn the bodies.

Ranjit is haunted by guilt... and even more by the tinkling anklet bells that he hears in the night.

He goes to Bombay to get away from it all and there he meets the dancing girl's double. The difference is that she's a sophisticated modern girl. She even (heaven forbid) works. Fortunately it's as a nurse. When Ranjit falls ill with nervous exhaustion, she moves in to look after him.

Anyone familiar with Hitchcock's *Vertigo* will recognise the source of the plot. Here it's combined with bits of *Les diaboliques,* as a plan is revealed to drive Ranjit mad and deprive him of his inheritance. The film is much more restrained than the Ramsays' monster movies and the changes of mood and pace are well handled, aided by excellent performances from Anand and sexy South Indian belle, Rekha, who plays both dancing girl and nurse.

This brief holiday from horror must have recharged the Ramsays' batteries. Their next film *Hotel,* shot on location in Mysore, was a rip-roaring horror yarn, complete with gruesome deaths, walking corpses and all the gimmicky excesses they could muster. A bunch of unscrupulous businessmen want to build an hotel on the hilltop site of an old Catholic graveyard. They trick the priest into selling them the land and he dies of a heart attack when he discovers what they really plan to do. Contractors move in, stack the gravestones in an old shed and dump the bodies in a communal pit, marked only by a pile of rocks. The proprietors hold a party to celebrate the opening of the hotel. During a sexy dance number, as the camera leers at the performer in her tight, gold lamé hot pants and thigh boots, a wisp of smoke snakes from the pile of stones. Silent, shrouded corpses are soon stalking the corridors of the hotel. Its owners attempt to flee, but their car breaks down on the mountain road and huge rocks rain from the night sky, cutting them off from the outside world. One by one they meet a gruesome fate. The climax has the surviving baddie making his escape across the hotel's lawn. Crosses spring up in front of him and a forest of hands sprouts from the earth to hold him down. The dead, led by the corpse of the old priest, surround him. The priest raises his spiked crucifix and thrusts it down through the man's chest.

In 1984, the Ramsays began work on *Purana Mandir,* which proved a watershed in the short history of Hindi horror. Its main setting, an ancient palace at Jehangir, about five hours drive from Bombay, was perfect for the story. "Even if you shot a film there at two in the afternoon, you'd get the right atmosphere for horror," Tulsi Ramsay remarked.

The complicated tale takes many twists and turns, with innumerable sub-plots. The pre-credit sequence, set in the distant past and filmed with a delicate blue filter, shows a royal entourage passing through wild countryside. They stop to repair a broken carriage wheel. In a sequence reminiscent of Mario Bava's classic *Black Sunday*, the raja's wife wanders off to a nearby deserted mansion, wreathed in mists. There she is attacked by an evil tantric magician, who kills people by sucking out their eyes. The raja's men capture and behead him, but not before he has had time to lay a curse on them. The magician's head is then put in a box and walled up in the mansion.

Years pass. One of the raja's descendants is a rich businessman with an attractive young daughter. He seems insanely protective of her, refusing to allow her to see boys. Finally, he tells her about the ancient curse. In a flashback we see its results. After giving birth to the girl, her mother turned into a hideous monster. This is the fate for all female members of the raja's line.

Naturally upset, the girl runs away with her current beau, determined to find the source of the curse and put an end to it. Their search leads to the old house. Behind a portrait of the raja, who is the double of her father, they find the chamber with the monster's head. It's not long before the head is reunited with the body and the evil tantric goes on the rampage. The boyfriend eventually saves the day, destroying the monster with a holy trident, symbol of Shiva, the destroyer in the Hindu trinity.

Purana Mandir was released on 19 October 1984, and set an all-time record for first week grosses at several Bombay cinemas. To date it has been the biggest earner of all the Ramsays' films. There are several reasons for its success. For a start, it consolidated all the elements of their previous movies: the theme of the ancient curse carried on into the present day; the journey back to the countryside to confront the evil; the use of atmospheric locations; and the youthful hero and heroine. The fact that here they are a boy and girl forbidden to have sex was a powerful point of identification for the film's young, largely rural, audience. The comedy sequences were also better integrated than in some of the Ramsays' previous films. For the first time an indigenous style of horror film had been forged — influenced by the West, but with an internal logic that made sense only in India.

Distributors clamoured for more of the same and the team swung into overdrive. The demand for product led to more of the brothers venturing into directing. Keshu, whose behind-the-scenes work had added so much to *Purana Mandir*'s success, débuted the following year with *Haveli* (The Mansion). Kiran, formerly in charge of the sound department, followed with *Shaitani Ilaaka* (Devil's Domain).

Purana Mandir made horror much more of a commercial proposition than ever before. Other directors and producers began to look with envy at the film's grosses as reported in the weekly *Trade Guide Information*. The industry was going through one of its worst crises and suddenly horror films, cheaply made and with a sure-fire audience, looked like a safe bet.

For nearly fifteen years the Ramsays had had the field more or less to themselves. Fear of censorship and a general cultural dislike of the area had kept most film-makers away from horror. There had been only a handful of exceptions. *Jadu Tona* (Black Magic) in 1977 and *Jaani Dushman* (Beloved Enemy) in 1979 were both big-budget films produced by mainstream, non-horror specialists, and both suffered from problems with the censor. *Jadu Tona*, directed by action film-maker Raveekant Naigach, was an *Exorcist*-inspired story about the possession of a young girl. In typical Hindi style, the possessor is the spirit of a wronged man, seeking his revenge on the girl's family. The film benefited from Naigach's background as a cinematographer and assistant to special effects master Babubhai Mistry. Its photographic tricks and disorienting use of lenses and perspective made it look much more polished than the lower-budget Ramsay films of the seventies.

Jaani Dushman was directed and produced by Rajkumar Kohli. It had a big star cast (Sunil Dutt, Shatrugan Sinha, Jeetendra) and featured only brief scenes of horror scattered through its multi-layered plot.

In 1978, a good ten years before the horror boom, Madras-based writer/director Baby had experimented with the form in his film *Liza*. This was the story of a young girl, Lakshmi, who lives in a hostel for working women. She becomes possessed by the spirit of Liza, who had committed suicide years before. Liza/Lakshmi then proceeds to take her revenge on the men who seduced her and drove her to her death. Like so many Indian films of the seventies, it's another variation on the three R's — rape, revenge and romance. Ten years later, in 1988, Baby remade the story as *Bhayaanak Mahal* (The House of Horror). This has a haunt-

Below: *Haveli features all the usual Ramsay ingredients: sex, horror, comedy and an old dark house.*

TILAK MOVIES
PVT. LTD.
SANJEEV KUMAR
REKHA
VINOD MEHRA
SULAKSHNA PANDIT
SHATRUGHAN SINHA
AND
AMJAD KHAN
CHEHRE PE CHEHRA

Right: *A Hindi version of the Jekyll and Hyde story.*
Below: *The AUM symbol is a protection from evil in Indian horror films.*

ed mirror, many scenes of possession where objects fly around the room, and a flashback rape scene to explain it all. The film was announced as India's first horror film shot in London. In fact, the London scenes were another flashback, a short trip round the tourist spots that looks very much like home movie footage.

Mirrors and flashbacks feature again in Baby's third and best attempt at horror. *House No 13* was released in 1991 and shows quite a degree of progression from his earlier efforts. The film begins on a stormy night. An artist is working late in his studio, when a young girl seeks shelter from the rain. Both the artist and his assistant are struck by her wild beauty and insist that she pose for him. She sits with her head covered in a shawl while he works, but when the artist moves to look at her we see that the girl's face has turned into a hideous skull mask.

A happy family move into house number thirteen, unaware of its tragic past. However, they soon notice that things are not quite right. Mirrors glow in the night, a young girl's doll comes to life and, behind a door that normally hides a bookcase, is the entrance to a strange parallel world where the tragic history of the house is re-enacted.

Baby's three films demonstrate a feel for atmosphere and a respect for the genre rare in Indian cinema. In contrast, Raj Tilak's *Chehre pe Cherha* (Face to Face), made in 1979, is a real oddity, with no idea at all of what it's trying to do. Basically a version of the Jekyll and Hyde story, it closely follows the 1941 Spencer Tracy vehicle as well as Hammer's cheaper 1960 remake. One of its central conceits is to imitate the nineteenth century setting and costumes of the earlier films. Except that here the Dr Jekyll character recounts his experiences into a tape recorder... and the telephones used in the film are red plastic 1970s models. At one point 'Hyde' makes his escape on a Triumph motorbike, even performing some death-defying, Steve McQueen-style leaps through the air. Like I said, a real oddity. Sanjeev Kumar plays Dr Jekyll/Mr Hyde (here it's Dr Vincent/Mr Blackstone) with make-up effects imported from the Hollywood lab of Mike Westmore. The luscious Rekha plays a showgirl who attracts the attention of the leering Blackstone. Dressed in full nineteenth century tarts' gear (Hollywood version), with low-cut velvet frock, slit to the crotch to show her fishnet stockings and accompanying suspenders, Rekha certainly lives up to her reputation as one of Bollywood's hottest babes. At the beginning of the film, in a dive bar straight out of Hammer, she does a sexy dance in front of the drooling monster, accompanied by two bikini-clad seventies disco dollies. The music for this shamelessly anachronistic dollop of kitsch is a sub-Santana mix of jungle drums and twanging guitars.

Showing a bit more style were *Gehrayee* (Depth), from 1980, and *Pyasa Shaitan* (The Thirsty Devil), released in 1983. The former was another *Exorcist* clone, where the possession of a young girl is dealt with first by psychiatry, including electro-shock therapy, and then by the traditional use of tantric magic. The latter featured Kamal Hassan as 'Puppet Draculla', an evil magician hoping to gain immortality through the sacrifice of seven virgins.

By the beginning of 1985, following the success of *Purana Mandir*, horror, for the first time, was being seen as a distinct genre to put beside action films, love stories and social dramas. The floodgates were starting to open and a host of horror movies were announced or already in production. The Ramsays were eager to reassert their pre-eminence as India's horror pioneers in the face of this rapidly growing band of parvenus. They just needed a direction. A 3D film, *Saamri* (Satan), was an attempt to do something different. Unfortunately, by the time it hit the screen, audiences had already tired of the brief local boom for 'poke 'em in the eye' special effects.

The rise of video in the mid-eighties made Western films more easily available than ever before. This was particularly important in a country like India where films from Europe and America had never been widely distributed. Watching a video cassette of the 1974 British production *Vampyres*, Tulsi Ramsay suddenly had a thought: one aspect of horror that Hindi movies had not really explored was sex. As he studied Joseph Larraz's film more closely, he began to conceive of a way to adapt it to an Indian background. The result was *Veerana* (Loneliness), which went into production in 1985.

This is one of the Ramsays' strongest films, both in concept and execution. When the brothers get an idea, they generally take it as far as it's possible to go. With *Veerana*, sex and vampirism was the theme. Although this had been a familiar combination in Western films since the early seventies, for India it was pretty hot stuff. 'The vengeance of the vampire', ran the pre-release ad campaign. 'The girl was young and virgin, which is why the devil wanted her body!'

The film is especially memorable for a strong performance by Jasmin as the sexually rapacious title character. It also had some strong comedy from Ramsay regular Satish Shah. He had played 'funny fat man' roles in several of their films, including *Purana Mandir*. In *Veerana*, he's a horror film director, obsessed with Hitchcock. He wanders through the movie, framing imaginary shots with his hands, and saying things like: "What a plot!" and "Sound crew! Camera! Action!" At one point, digging up a body, he says, "This is just like that horror film *Do Gaz Zameen ke Neeche*!" Naturally, when events turn nasty he proves to be a total coward.

Jasmin plays the part of a young girl who falls into the

clutches of an evil sect planning to resurrect a dead witch. She becomes possessed by the woman's spirit and begins to talk in strange voices. To satisfy the witch's blood lust, Jasmin is compelled to seduce men and then suck their blood after having sex with them. As in Larraz's *Vampyres*, Jasmin seeks out her victims on the lonely highway, hitching a lift and then taking them back to a deserted mill where she drains their bodily fluids.

The film ends in traditional Hindi horror style. The vampire witch is tracked down by torch-wielding villagers and defeated by the brandishing of a giant AUM symbol. To finish her off, she's sealed up in a coffin and brought before a statue of the blue-skinned Vishnu.

Veerana proved to be something of a millstone for the Ramsays. The film took almost a year and half to make due to the unavailability of some of its featured players and then, when it was finally presented for certification, it was rejected. The sex and horror mixture was not to the liking of the Bombay censor. Of course there had been sex, or sexy scenes, in Hindi movies for years, but Jasmin's lusty portrayal of the ravenous bloodsucker, combined with the gruesome make-up of her transformation into the witch, was pretty unsettling. A re-edited and trimmed version finally made it to the screen in May 1988, nearly three years after the film's *mahurat*.*

The eventual success of the film was heartening for the Ramsays, but they were not out of the woods yet. During the long wait to bring *Veerana* to the screen, they had released the political thriller *Telephone* in 1985 and the horror/adventure hybrid *Tahkhana* (The Dungeon) the following year. Keshu had finished the horror comedy *Khoj* (The Search) and the enjoyable *Dak Bangla* (Rest House). However, in 1988 Tulsi and Shyam found themselves in the middle of another crisis. The film on which they were working, *Om*, suddenly ground to a halt. Their lead actor, former seventies superstar Rajesh Kanna, had been elected an MP. Naturally he was too busy to commit himself to future acting engagements. And perhaps he didn't really consider horror films a suitable calling card for a member of parliament.

Tulsi and Shyam rushed into production on *Purani Haveli* (The Old Mansion) and into pre-production on the film that would more or less be their farewell to the horror film, *Bandh Darwaza* (Closed Door).

Purani Haveli is very much a *masala* movie, with a host of elements thrown into the mix in an attempt to appeal to all sections of the audience. Satish Shah had always been popular, so here he's given two roles, one as a tourist and the other as his double, a bandit leader fond of singing 'Love to Love You, Baby' as he rides about on his horse. The film's pace is relentless, with two murders and a suicide in the first fifteen minutes and numerous subplots. There are several nods to Western horror (including a reference to *A Nightmare on Elm Street*, where a woman is sucked down into a mattress by invisible forces).

The plot of *Purani Haveli* is the familiar Ramsay one of a group of kids stranded in a haunted mansion, menaced by a hairy monster every fifteen minutes or so. Even the film's makers were becoming self-conscious and starting to parody themselves. When the group first arrive at the *haveli*, to a familiar flash of lightning and crash of thunder, Satish Shah looks round and says, "It's like a set from a Ramsay Brothers horror film!"

One of the more interesting aspects of *Purani Haveli* is its use of Christian iconography — graveyards, crucifixes and so on. This occurs in other Hindi horrors and has a strong bearing on many of their plots. Hindu custom dictates that a dead body should be cremated and the ashes spread on the ground. The only way a dead Hindu could manifest himself is as a ghost — something that has been

Below: *Another spooky mansion in a film from 1987.*
Bottom: *Sex and the vampire, Ramsay style.*

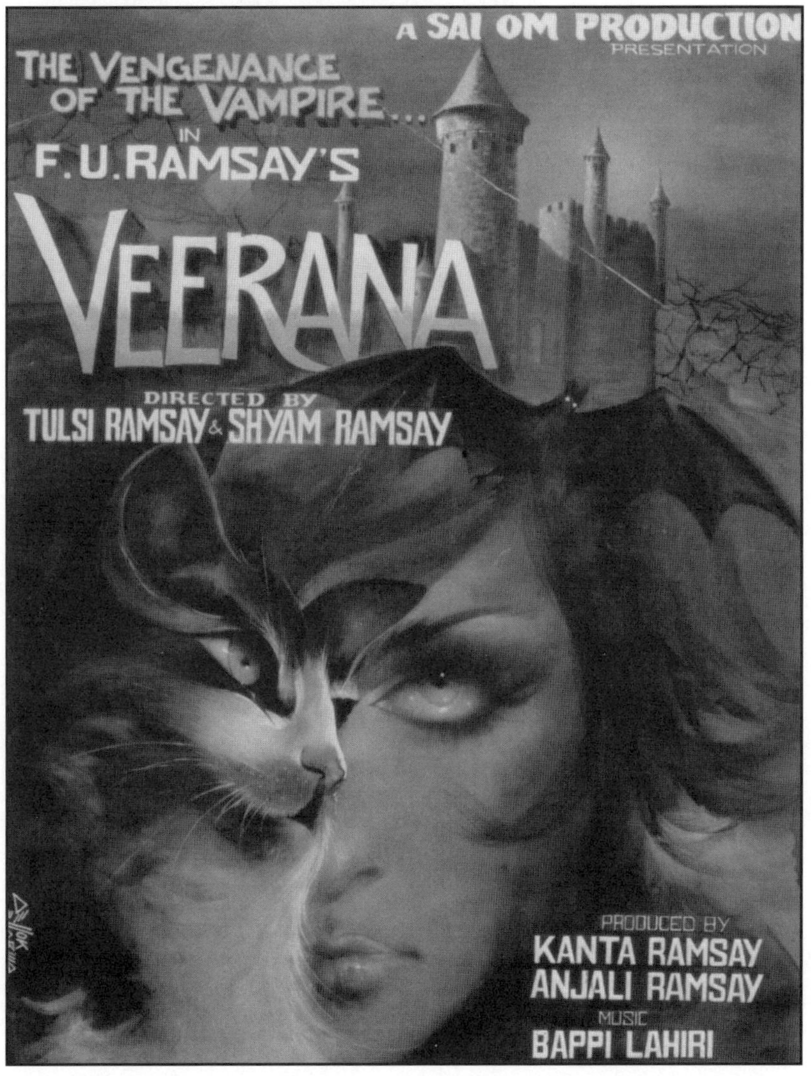

* *This is the traditional opening shot of all Hindi movies. A ceremony is performed, involving the breaking of a coconut and the giving of gifts to all members of the crew. Indians are fairly superstitious and if the* mahurat *is not performed properly it's believed to have a bad effect on the film's chances of success.*

done in countless Indian fantasy films since the 1940s via double exposure and back projection. Real horror, at least as it has developed in the sub continent, demanded a visible monster, usually an animated corpse. One solution is to have the victim bumped off by miscreants and then buried in a shallow grave. The corpse can then emerge, looking suitably gruesome, to exact revenge. The other solution is to make the revenant a non Hindu, usually a Catholic or a Muslim, which provides the film-maker with a rotting corpse ripe for reanimation. The advantage of this latter course is that it justifies the use of spooky graveyards and temple scenes.

In 1990, the Ramsays released three films, only one of which was directed by Tulsi and Shyam. Both of the others, *Aakhri Cheekh* (The Final Scream) and *Shaitani Ilaaka*, were directed by their younger brother, Kiran, who had formerly been in charge of the all-important sound department for most Ramsay movies. As anyone who has ever seen a Hindi horror film will know, the soundtrack is a crucial element in establishing and heightening the climactic scenes of horror. Crashes of thunder, eldritch screams and wild, pulsating

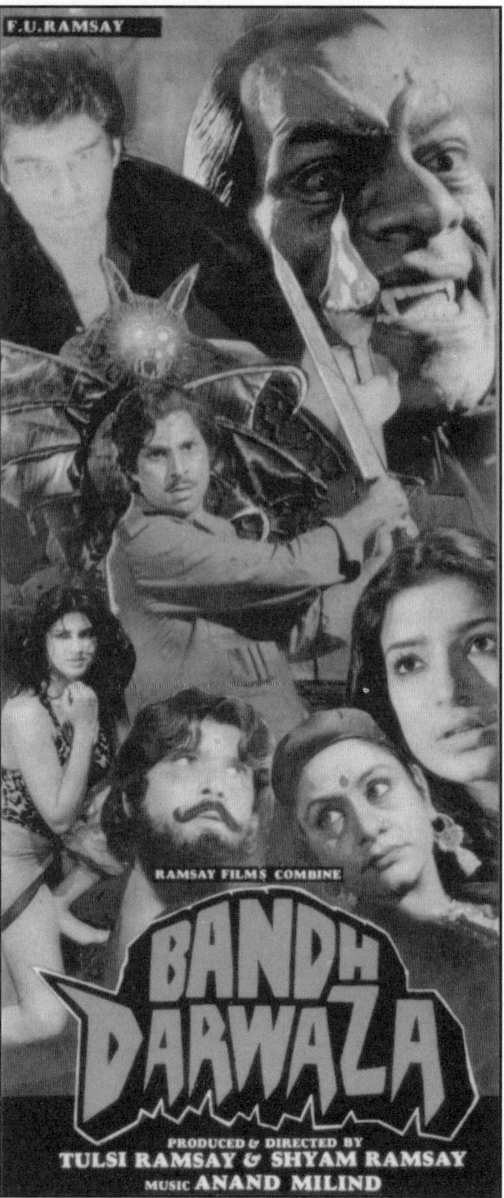

Above: *More horror from the Ramsay Brothers horror factory.* ***Right:*** *Dracula comes to India in the film* Bandh Darwaza.

music are all thrown into the mix, rising to a fearful crescendo as the monster lumbers into view.

Shaitani Ilaaka, like *Veerana*, features another female fiend, a shapeshifting witch who needs human sacrifices to resurrect a terrifying demon. The opening of the film is superb. To the eerie, twisted notes of the theme from *Purana Mandir*, a coach pulled by two white horses thunders along a lonely country road. Clutching the reins and urging the horses on with cracks of her whip is a gorgeous, black-haired woman dressed in a cloak of scarlet satin. The coach comes to a halt and the woman opens the door. Inside is a young girl, apparently drugged or hypnotised. The fiery-eyed witch commands her to follow, and leads her through a misty wood to where a band of masked disciples are worshipping in front of a hideous idol. The girl is doused with a bucket of water and then made ready for the sacrifice. As she lies on the ground, a clawed hand thrusts up through the earth and seizes hold of her. Her screams drown out the chants of the devil worshippers.

The plot soon settles into the recurring Ramsay theme of ancient evil confronted in an old country mansion. However, the film compensates for its familiarity of plot through the terrific energy and inventiveness of its set pieces. In one scene, the witch, Shalaka, is shot, only to shapeshift into a hairy wolf-like creature. She dives into a swimming pool before shapeshifting once again, this time into a hawk, and flying off into the night. This is the kind of scene that would be a climax in a Western horror film. Here it occurs half an hour into the movie!

Tulsi and Shyam's sole film of 1990 was *Bandh Darwaza*, their belated version of the Dracula story. The evil count is played by Anirudh Agarwal, who later had a major role in Shekhar Kapur's controversial *Bandit Queen.* Here some clever lighting makes the most of his cavernous features. He's one of the most effective of all the Brothers' many villains and obviously relishes the chance to show what he can do. In the pre-credits sequence he strides through a typically spooky Ramsay mansion wearing a pair of shiny leather boots, his evil rictus revealing as much of his elaborate dental work as possible.

Although publicity claimed the film was influenced by the 1965 Hammer production *Dracula Prince of Darkness*, there's little evidence of a link. The story tells of two girls, Arpna the good one and Tamia the bad one. They both fancy the same man, Kumar. Through a series of coincidences, Tamia comes into the possession of a book of magic spells. She uses it to ensnare Kumar. But in doing so she becomes a slave of the evil vampire king. The film has many effective moments. The comedy scenes, always a problem for Western audiences, are kept to a minimum and the musical sequences are well integrated into the plot. Many occur in Dracula's spooky dungeon, where white-robed wantons dance in ritual formation round his spread-eagled female sacrifices.

The art direction of *Bandh Darwaza* was by Tulsi Ramsay. The well-appointed rooms, with their rich, red velvet curtains and elaborate carved furniture, are reminiscent of the *mittel Europa* of the Hammer films and indirectly the 1960s Italian gothics of Mario Bava and Riccardo Freda. One of the film's design highlights is the huge, bat-shaped idol with glowing red eyes before which Dracula and company perform their bloody rituals. It's this level of production values that separates the Ramsays' films from many of their rivals. With three decades of film-making under their belt, they have amassed a large selection of props and décors that no newcomer could hope to match. Tulsi guards these treasures jealously and stores them in a secure warehouse in Andheri, from where they are brought out to grace film after film.

By the time *Bandh Darwaza* was released, the Hindi horror boom was at its peak. The film performed well but against stiff competition. Not that there were better films, just that the audience was tiring of the horror genre. The general feeling in India is that all horror films are the same anyway, so one is pretty much as good as another. It's an uphill struggle for any film-maker to find the backing to do something different. It's even more of a struggle to convince audiences to accept innovation. In this context, who can blame producers if they resort to formula time after time?

The Ramsays' final horror film, *Mahakaal* (Time of Death), released in 1993, was a Hindi version of the *A Nightmare on Elm Street* series. It was a surprising choice, as the first *Elm Street* film had recently been released in India (and had been adapted once before in 1989). The film was well made, very atmospheric and took few liberties with the original story. In fact the high school background of Wes Craven's movie, the cop as father and hero and so on, all worked perfectly in an Indian setting. Nevertheless, *Mahakaal* flopped at the box office. By the time it reached the screens, the so-called 'Doom Boom' was over. In fact, no horror film had really performed well since 1991. There were just too many of them. What had formerly been a novelty, and consequently guaranteed to pull a crowd, was now becoming commonplace. It wasn't only the Ramsays who were being affected by this glut of gruesomeness; also feeling the pinch were the other film-makers who had moved into the genre in the late eighties, following the success of *Purana Mandir*.

Bollywood isn't really so different from Hollywood. There may be ten thousand miles between them, but they're remarkably close in spirit. Just like the outer reaches of LA, the hot, dusty, incredibly crowded roads around Juhu, Andheri and Bandra in the Bombay suburbs teem with would-be film-makers. Everyone you meet seems to be an actor, a director or a scriptwriter. Rows of tiny cabins serve as production offices, editing suites and viewing theatres. It's out of this highly competitive background that the Hindi horror boom emerged.

At the low-budget end of the business there are actually quite a small number of active participants. Many of the technicians involved in these 'B' and 'C' productions work on several films at once and there is an almost symbiotic exchange of ideas between them. They discuss each other's jobs, talk about particularly daring scenes and explain novel plot twists. Sometimes a trick from one film will become incorporated in another even while both are still in production. When an idea takes hold, it's difficult to say who originated it (although, of course, there will be many takers). Following the success of *Purana Mandir*, everyone suddenly seemed to be talking about making a horror movie.

One of the first to take up the gauntlet was producer/director Mohan Bhakri. Like many Bombay film men, he had come into the business through family connections. His uncle had been a successful cinematographer in the fifties, working notably with Ravindra Dave, the so-called 'Hitchcock of India'. In films like *Moti Mahal* (The Palace of Pearls), *CID Girl* and *Post Box 999*, Dave had made some of the most successful and influential Indian versions of the 1950s American thriller.

Bhakri started his own company in 1973 and his first production was released the following year. It was a knockabout comedy, in the Punjabi language, called *Morni* (Pea Hen). The film was a big success and Bhakri continued in the same vein for several years, producing and directing a series of low-budget musical comedies, one of which, *Saali Adhi Gharwali* (Sister-in-Law is Almost a Wife), won a government award as best Punjabi film of its year. In the early 1980s, the state was riven by political violence. Thousands of people died in the ensuing struggles, which eventually led to the assassination of the Prime Minister, Indira Gandhi. Naturally, against such a background, the notion of going to the cinema took second place to just staying alive. Receipts for Punjabi films plummeted and Bhakri shifted his attention to making films for the Hindi market.

Above: *'Alright big boy, let's see what you're made of!' The dominant female in Mohan Bhakri's* Cheekh.

Although the potential audience was much bigger, the competition was stronger. Bhakri knew that he couldn't match the big Bombay *masala* movies, with their hit tunes and crowd pulling stars. Like so many low-budget producers before him, he realised that sex and violence were the best bet. His first effort, *Aparadhi Kaun?* (Who is the Criminal?), released in 1982, was a big hit. The film was a low-budget thriller with a dose of sex and violence. Like many Hindi films, it was a loose version of an American hit, in this case Mike Nichols' *The Graduate*, combined with a murder mystery.

Bhakri freely confesses his debt to Western cinema. He has copies of all the latest horror and action movies shipped

in on video long before they are available anywhere else in India. Sometimes he will watch two or three movies a night, scribbling down ideas and replaying scenes that appeal to him. This homework paid dividends in his next Hindi film, *Cheekh* (The Scream), released in 1985. This was another violent thriller with strands drawn from a confusing variety of Western product. The pre-credits sequence shows a young girl watching in horror as her mother is raped and murdered. Twenty years later a black-masked killer is abroad. People are dying in a variety of horrible ways. In one highly effective scene, a man is burned alive at a party, which is intercut with a wild dance where revellers wearing animal masks cavort gaily, unaware of the horror taking place in the next room. Javed Khan, who features in many of Bhakri's films, plays an artist who covers one of the victims in clay. Later, in an extremely bizarre sequence, the clay-covered corpse comes alive, blood seeping from its eyes, and attacks Khan's wife with an axe.

It comes as no great surprise when the knife murderer unmasks to reveal that it's the girl, now grown up, who witnessed the rape twenty years before.

Bhakri was pleased by the reception afforded to *Cheekh* and its follow-up, another sexy thriller, *Padosi ki Biwi* (The Woman Next Door). He decided that his next picture would be a down-the-line horror movie, with a monster, special effects and lots of screaming teens. Together with his regular writer, Anil Pandit, he concocted the script for the 1987 release, *Khooni Mahal* (Deadly Manor), which was his biggest hit yet.

One of the factors in the film's success was its skilful blending of out-and-out horror with knockabout comedy. Bhakri was very familiar with this from his days making films for Punjabi audiences, where comedy is king. The other aspect that drew the crowds was its many sexy scenes.

Oddly, for a man who specialises in such fare, Bhakri is keen to point out that he was never present behind the camera when the scenes were shot: "I had a good relationship with my actors and actresses. They respected me and I didn't want to lose that. So I would explain to my assistants exactly what I wanted and leave them to do the actual filming."

Such was Bhakri's reputation as a man who specialised in skin that even a quite elderly, grey-haired actress, hired for a role in his 1989 film *Sau Saal Baad* (A Thousand Years Later), asked him how much exposure was required of her. He was quite happy to tell her none at all.

One of the reasons Bhakri is able to film such explicit scenes is that he uses the same cast and crew in film after film. They have come to know and trust him. The only problem he ever encountered was with Hemant Birje, whose first starring role had been as Tarzan in B. Subhash's 1985 film. In a scene (in *Sau Saal Baad*) where he was required to massage a swim-suited Sahila Chadha, Birje pleaded to be allowed to keep his shirt on. Eventually he had to come clean and admit that since his muscleman days, he had neglected his daily work outs. He didn't want the audience to see that he had gone to flab.

The success of *Khooni Mahal* meant that Bhakri was besieged with offers from distributors and producers. For the next three years he worked almost exclusively on horror. His most ambitious film of the period, *Kabrastan* (The Graveyard), was something of a *tour de force*, being written, produced and directed by himself. The film was a radical departure for Hindi horror in that it didn't feature a monster — at least, not on screen.

Bhakri explains: "The camera was my monster. It was all done with point of view. Even where the monster is raping a girl, you see the camera go up and down to show he is having sex with her."

This ambitious move was a direct result of his low opinion of the monster make-up he had encountered. "I'm never

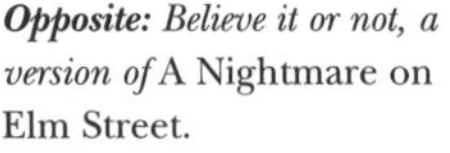

***Opposite:** Believe it or not, a version of* A Nightmare on Elm Street.

***Above:** Mythical horror from Mohan Bhakri.*
***Right:** Surreal scene from* Cheekh.

MKB FILMS COMBINES
KHOONI
MURDAA
Story - Screenplay - Produced & Directed by
MOHAN BHAKRI
Music
BAPPI LAHIRI
Cinematography
ARVIND BHAKRI

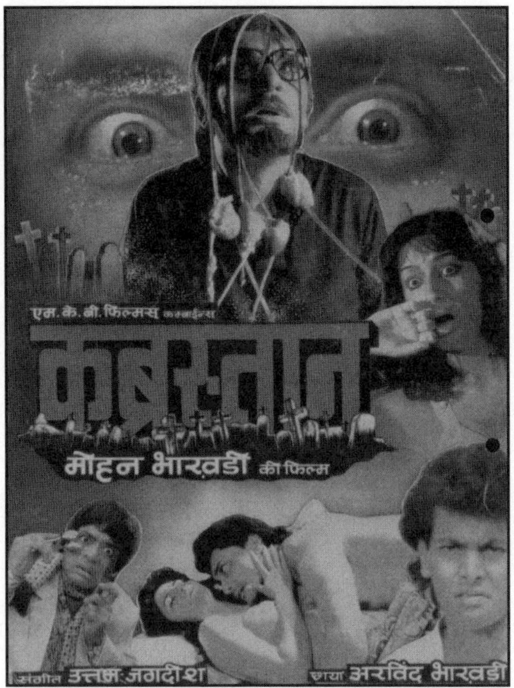

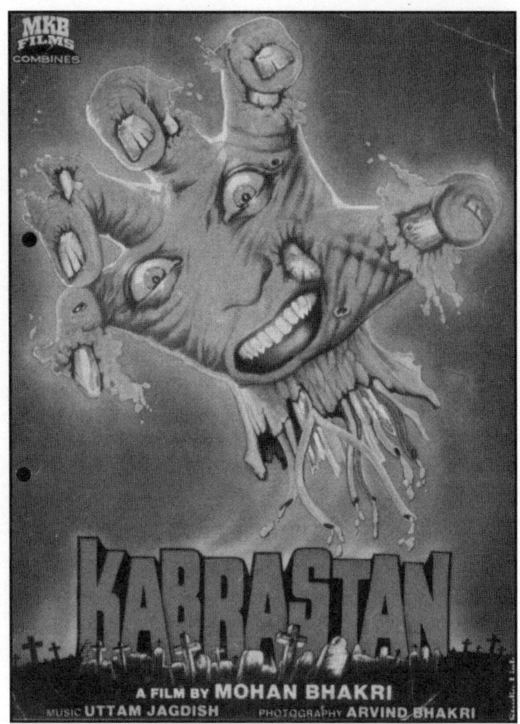

Right: *Indian and English ad material from* Kabrastan *(The Graveyard).*
Below: *Taking a bath is a popular pastime in Indian movies.*

satisfied with the monsters. Not in my films or in any Indian horror films. Whenever you see the monster coming, it's like a comedy scene!"

Kabrastan tells the story of a heart specialist, Dr D'Souza, who steals body parts from graves to conduct his Frankenstein-like experiments. His troubles begin when he murders a man to get a really fresh heart to work with.

The film had a good publicity campaign, one of the most extensive for any horror film so far. In Bombay the distributor paid for a huge forty foot hand-painted banner. 'If you have the guts, see *Kabrastan*!' ran the tag line.

Due to unfortunate industry in-fighting, the film received an extremely poor review in the trade press and did patchy business. In urban centres it did okay, but in the all-important rural areas the audience was confused. As Bhakri puts it: "They want everything on the screen... After seeing the picture they said: 'Where was the monster?'"

Another reason for the film's mixed reception was its setting within a Christian community. As explained earlier, it would have been difficult to place such a story in a Hindi context, as there wouldn't have been any bodies for the good doctor to plunder from. The traditional cremation would have reduced them all to ashes. Although there are sizeable Catholic populations in some large towns, in the country they expected the usual paraphernalia of Indian horror movies — chanting mystics, the *Trishul* (trident) of Shiva and the all important AUM symbol to defeat the evil.

Bhakri's keen plundering of Western sources came to the fore in his next film, *Khooni Murdaa* (Deadly Corpse). Here the model was the *A Nightmare on Elm Street* series. Kiran Kumar stars as Ranjit, a psycho killer fond of giving red roses to girls he is obsessed with. His latest heart-throb, Rekha, goes to the police and they use her to bait a trap for him. The girl celebrates her good fortune with her friends, unaware that Ranjit has escaped and is heading her way. The kids capture Ranjit and murder him. It's a sign of Kiran Kumar's skill as an actor that we actually feel much more sympathy for the mad Ranjit than for the rather annoying good guys, here led by Javed Khan, the Frankie Avalon of Hindi horror.

From this point on it's straight Freddy Krueger, with most of the set pieces of the *Elm Street* films replayed in a cut-price form. So we have the tongue coming out of the phone, the claw-like hand coming up out of the bath, a victim swallowed up by their own bed and a scene where the veins and sinews of a boy's arms are used like the strings of a puppet. In the end, the kids bring on the guru in traditional Hindi horror style, and a long battle between good and evil ensues.

The actor who plays the guru in *Khooni Murdaa*, Rajesh Vivek, had a busy career during the late eighties. Just as Peter Cushing, in the West, came to personify the wise old sage called in to exorcise the demon, so Rajesh Vivek was the all-powerful mystic in numerous Hindi horror movies. He was one of the few actors capable of delivering the complex Sanskrit mantras that such parts called for. He took his roles

Above: Cheekh *(India).*
Left: Wohi Bhayaanak Raat *lobby card (India).*

OA
แหวกนรกดงดิบ!
ชำแหละชีวิตชนเผ่าลึกลับ
หฤโหดขนาดเทวดา
ต้องเบือนหน้าหนี
เรื่องจริงที่ผวากันมาแล้วกว่าค่อนโลก
เทวดายังผวา
PRIMITIV

Opposite page: *Thai one sheet for* Primitiv *(Indonesia), relocates the action to Africa.*

This page:
Far left: Beyond Atlantis *American one sheet (The Philippines).*
Left: 18 Shaolin Bronzemen *German one sheet (Hong Kong).*
Below: Kilink Istanbul'da *lobby card (Turkey).*

Prodüktör: Şahin Koçak
Reji Senaryo: Semih Evin
İNAN ORKUŞ
ATİLLA ERGUN
ERSUN KAZANÇEL
ve
PELİN CEYLAN
ŞAHİN FİLM
SAFİYE YANKI
UÇAN KIZ
Ahmet Karaca
Nermin Dikses
Tevfik Şen
Yusuf Çağatay
Kamera
Muzaffer Turan
Nihat Çifteoğlu
Tek. Direktör Fehmi Tengiz
Bello
OFSET 495043

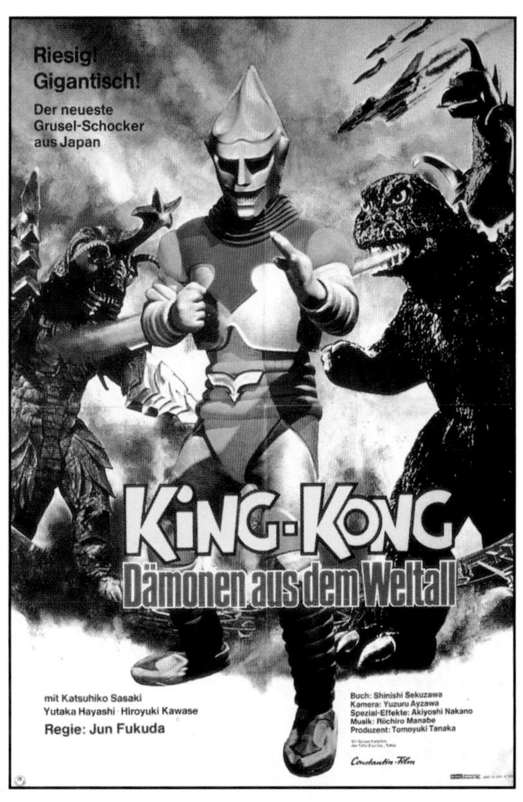

Opposite page: Uçan Kiz *(Turkey).*

This page:
Far left: Exorcismo Negro *press sheet (Brazil).*
Left: *German one sheet for* Gojira tai Megaro *(Japan).*
Below: El Monstruo Resucitado *lobby card (Mexico).*

This page:
Above: La Invasion de los Marcianos *lobby card (Mexico).*
Right: Psexoanálisis *lobby card (Argentina).*

Opposite page: Black Cat in a Massage Parlour *poster (Japan).*

Following page: Aatank *(India).*

怪猫トルコ風呂
かいびょう
ぶろ
カラー作品
成人映画
悩殺とショックの連続! 新人・大原美佐が濡れるとき男たちのうめき声が聞こえる…異色怪奇ポルノの決定版!!
企画/高村賢治
脚本/掛札昌裕 中島信昭
撮影/飯村雅彦
監督 山口和彦
大原美佐(新人)
谷ナオミ
真山知子
女屋実和子
立野弓子
城恵美
二松きぬえ
岬マコ
大泉滉
青山美沙
東てる美
沢リミ子
早川リナ
レズシスターズ・ペギー&リズ
鈴木サミ
藤山浩二
山城新伍
殿山泰司
室田日出男

BF
BEMISAL FILMS PVT. LTD.
आतंक
DESIGNED BY RAVI
AATANK
PRODUCED BY PREM H. LALWANI CO-PRODUCER C.P. SINGH
EXEC. DIRECTOR O.P. KOHLI MUSIC LAXMIKANT PYARELAL LYRICS RANI MALIK, DEV KOHLI

very seriously and practised meditation for several hours a day. In the 1991 film *Khatra* (Danger) he had a rare change of pace, playing a reanimated corpse who turns himself into a hairy monster by biting his own finger and sucking on his contaminated blood.

Khooni Murdaa failed to capture the audience that the similarly titled *Khooni Mahal* had drawn. The film contained all the usual Mohan Bhakri trademarks. It was gory enough (one scene has a human heart being ripped out), had lots of sex and featured the wacky Jagdeep to provide welcome moments of goofy comedy, but was far too slapdash and derivative. The whole enterprise reeked of cynical opportunism.

Bhakri's next film, *Roohani Taaqat* (Spiritual Power), was financed by an outside producer, Deepak Sharma. The film's budget was the lowest Bhakri had encountered since his days making shoestring Punjabi movies. For a horror film, with effects and action scenes, it was really rock bottom.

The size of Indian movie budgets is largely dictated by the way films are marketed there. For the purposes of distribution, India is divided into six territories. A film is presold on the reputation of its stars or subject and usually a producer can hope to recoup his costs several times over before the film has even been shipped. At the peak of their popularity, horror films were fetching advances of between seven to sixteen lakh rupees* per territory. With an average production budget around the thirty-five lakh mark (eighteen to twenty for a low budget), this was good business. When the market became saturated with horror films, distributors started offering less and less. To compensate, producers began to make their films even more cheaply. When the offers fell as low as two lakhs per territory, things got really messy. It was possible, just about, to make a film in India for twelve lakhs (£22,000 at today's rate), but the results were far from special.

Bhakri knew that he would have to tighten his belt on *Roohani Taaqat* and work with some less than top class material. Even so, when he saw one of the film's key elements — the monster — he realised he was in deep trouble. The problem was that the inspiration for *Roohani Taaqat* was the 1989 Stan Winston movie *Pumpkinhead* (aka *Vengeance the Demon*). Winston is one of Hollywood's top make-up artists and the monster in *Pumpkinhead* is one of his triumphs. It probably cost more to build than the total budget of Bhakri's film. To expect an Indian make-up man to match it was definitely asking too much.

To make anything out of the mess he was presented with drew on all of Bhakri's considerable ingenuity. The result is one of his strangest works and certainly one of the craziest Indian horror films. Sometimes, whilst watching low-budget Indian movies, a Western viewer might be reminded of the work of Al Adamson or Jess Franco. With *Roohani Taaqat*, Hindi horror edged closer to the wonderful wackiness of the late, great Ed Wood.

Kiran Kumar stars as Karan, a man whose wife is raped by a gang of city boys. She kills herself and Karan seeks revenge. First stop is a local tantric magician, Bhairavnath. The magician uses some of Karan's blood to revive a hideous monster that then goes on the rampage, killing the rapists but also wiping out innocent villagers. Since the monster is a projection of his own vengeance, only Karan's death can stop the destruction he has unleashed.

The scene in which the monster is reactivated is one of the most bizarre in all of Hindi horror. Karan is commanded by the magician to cross a spooky bridge to a wizened tree under which is buried the creature's skeleton. Using a combination of back projection and double exposure, Bhakri creates a uniquely warped universe, a mixture of Western fairy tales and Eastern mythology. His inspiration came from Hindi horror comics, mythological films and illustrations found in books on special effects techniques.

The next scene, when the monster is given life, is intercut with a couple making love. As they writhe in ecstasy, we see drops of blood fall onto the skeleton. Then a heart appears inside the rib cage. The heart starts to pump and blood courses along the creature's bones which gradually grow flesh. Suddenly it springs to life. A glistening, pointy headed monster with a complexion like burnt porridge, it's about as far as it's possible to get from Stan Winston's high-tech Hollywood creation.

The effects were performed by taping a goat's heart inside the skeleton's rib cage and connecting it to a bicycle pump. As Bhakri's assistant pushed air into it, the organ seemed to start beating. More thin transparent tubes were taped to the skeleton and the same pump was used to drive a red liquid along the bones, to simulate the flow of blood through its veins.

Above: *Kiran Kumar wields a trishul in the film* Roohani Taaqat.

Below: *India's top horror actor Kiran Kumar.*

(1) A lakh is 100,000 rupees. About £1,850 at 1997 exchange rates.

As if all this wasn't enough, the film also features broad, Punjabi-style comedy complete with farting jokes, men with outrageous, bushy moustaches and one actor playing three different roles.

After this, where was there left to go? Well, not very far. *Roohani Taaqat* took two years to make it to the screen, as the market was so depressed. Bhakri's last horror film was another low-budget production, this time for Dalwinder Sohal, *Insaan Bana Shaitan* (Man Into Monster). The film begins promisingly enough with an adulterous couple murdering the woman's husband and burying his body in a lonely wood. He comes back to seek revenge looking suitably gory (one eyeball hanging out of its socket). Predictably, he goes on the rampage, killing everyone involved in his own murder. On the wall behind every crime scene he leaves a single word written in blood: 'Unfaithful'.

From the same Punjabi film-making background as Mohan Bhakri came one of India's youngest horror specialists, Vinod Talwar. He had started his own company in 1983, at the age of twenty-eight, but was having problems getting his second production off the ground. Bhakri suggested that he could recoup his money pretty fast with a horror movie and introduced him to a writer he had worked with who had plenty of ideas. Talwar's first film, *Ishq ni Mana* (Love is Not Forbidden), had been shot in eighteen days on a very low budget. With even less money and a similar schedule, he made *Raat ke Andhere Mein* (In the Dark of the Night), released in 1987 in the middle of the 'Doom Boom'.

Raat Ke Andhere Mein was not really horror. It was a tricksy murder mystery about a girl who avenges the killing of her parents. To disguise herself she uses a monster mask. The development of the story is almost the same as Mohan Bhakri's *Cheekh*. Hardly surprising as the writer of both was the same man, Dharmveer Ram.

The film performed well and distributors were soon asking for more of the same. Talwar decided to try a real, full-blooded shocker. Like most Indian horror makers, he looked to the West for inspiration. He watched the 1985 film *Fright*

Above right: *Director Vinod Talwar frames a shot.*
Below: *Devil in the disco in* Wohi Bhayaanak Raat.

Night and felt that the basic idea could be adapted into an Indian setting. He came up with the story of *Wohi Bhayaanak Raat* (That Same Horrifying Night) in which a young student returns home from college and becomes convinced that a vampire has moved in to the empty mansion opposite. The emotional core of the story concerns the student's growing relationship with a young woman, played by newcomer Neeta Puri. When the boy ventures into the vampire's house for the first time, he is shocked to discover the walls adorned with portraits of a woman who is the exact image of his girlfriend. It turns out that she is the reincarnation of someone the vampire loved and lost many centuries before and for whom he has been searching through time.

As the rebirth theme demonstrates, Talwar was keen to incorporate traditional Indian elements into his horror movies. This is something that marks him out from most of his contemporaries. His inspiration came from the fantasy movies he had enjoyed as a kid, as well as Hindi mythological comics. These highly colourful items feature lively and imaginative retellings of the doings of the ancient gods and goddesses. Cheaply produced and enormously popular, they sell for a few rupees in station kiosks and market stalls. Their religious content allows them to include scenes of incredible violence and gore that would otherwise meet with disapproval.

A key aspect of *Wohi Bhayaanak Raat*'s success was its upfront sex scenes. Kiran Kumar plays a suave vampire who has an irresistible attraction for women. To get fresh victims he visits local discos and puts the hex on miniskirted swingers whom he then entices back to his lair. Once there, he turns into a lumpy-faced fiend and has his wicked way with them. The picture's most shocking scene shows a girl stripped down to her red scanties, dragged by her hair across the floor, tied up and then raped by the vampire. When the film was shown to distributors they went wild. Naturally this sequence was hacked to pieces by the censor. Even so, it remains one of the strongest sex scenes in any Hindi horror movie.

Not surprisingly, the film did well at the box office. Talwar was approached by producer Dalwinder Sohal to make something in the same vein. Together with writer Salim Yousaf he cooked up the scenario for his next film, *Hatyarin*, which was released in 1991. *Wohi Bhayaanak Raat* had been graced by the presence of the beautiful Neeta Puri as the heroine lusted after by the undead vampire. In *Hatyarin*, Talwar was lucky enough to have the services of the spirited Jamuna. She gives a very committed performance as Hatyarin, a woman in thrall to the ghost of an evil tantric magician. He needs the blood of virgin brides to give him life. To satisfy his lust, Hatyarin is forced to hang around wedding parties, luring the untasted spouses back to the magician's forest lair. There they are seized by the branches of a living tree and suspended over the tantric's open grave, while Hatyarin pierces their hearts with a dagger. Their blood flows down into the demon's waiting jaws.

Hatyarin was Vinod Talwar's most accomplished work so far and one that shows he had a real feel for horror, especially for picturising scenes that drew on Hindi mysticism. The ending is a particular stunner. Here again we meet Rajesh Vivek in his familiar role as India's favourite fighter against evil. He summons all kinds of mystic armoury in his battle with the powerful tantric. He mutters mantras and a giant spiked stick appears in his hand. Then a huge silver ball. Finally a silver sword with which he chops off Hatyarin's arms and head. Her eyes begin to pulsate and long red strands of ectoplasm grow from her neck to ensnare the mystic. All of this was done in the camera, with double exposure

Above: *Jamuna as the white-robed vampire in* Hatyarin.

and shooting in reverse.

"If only I had the budget of an American movie," Talwar sighs. "Then I could show you something really special."

His last horror film was the self-produced *Khooni Panja* (Deadly Hand), released in 1992. This is another story of murder and revenge from beyond the grave, with the spirit of a dead woman residing in her severed hand. Said member scuttles across the screen at key moments whenever a killing is about to occur. In a typically Talwarian touch, a mystic imprisons the hand in a clay pot before the final showdown.

Following the success of *Purana Mandir*, dozens of horror films had been released. Some were good, many were very bad indeed, but most were just indifferent. One of the more enjoyable came from the indefatigable Bohra stable. The Bohra family had been involved in low-budget exploitation films for years. In 1977 Shree Ram Bohra had directed *Kaali Raat* (Black Night), a horror-tinged revenge drama. *Naag Nagin* (Snake and Snake Girl) and the Tarzan film *Jungle Love* were more of the family's offerings. In 1990 they signed up the delectable Jamuna for their sleazy horror epic, *Kafan* (The Shroud). The film is energetically directed, with lots of mobile camera work *à la The Evil Dead.* It also benefits from a terrific score — chattering percussion overlaid with

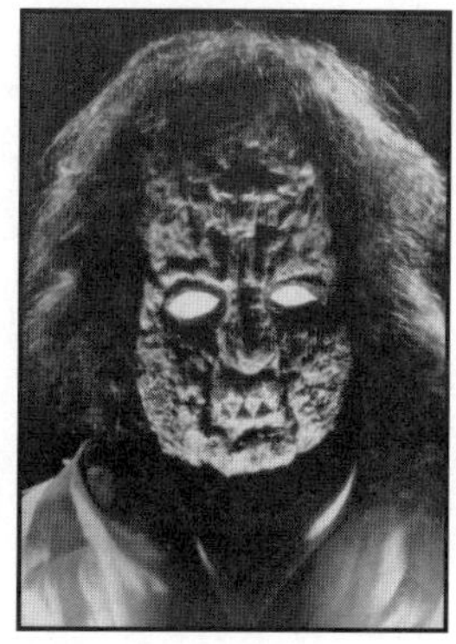

TALWAR
INTERNATIONAL
PRESENTS
VINOD TALWAR'S
KHOONI PANJA
PRODUCED BY
S.K. TALWAR . VINOD TALWAR . ACHAL TALWAR
MUSIC
SURINDER KOHALI
LYRICS
GAUHAR KANPURI
CAMERA
MANISH BHATT

Above: *Beware of the deadly hand!*
Below: *Deadly Lust.*

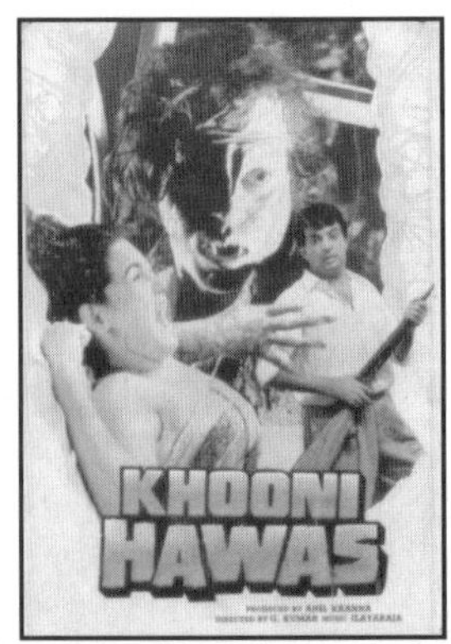

tribal chanting and, in the distance, what sounds like someone doodling on a string synthesiser.

The film begins with the rape and murder of a young servant girl. A particularly lurid scene, with an off-screen fan lifting up her dress as she lies asleep on a bed. Her body is then used in a satanic rite conducted in front of an idol that looks like nothing less than a huge cabbage patch doll with fangs.

Kafan has a terrific climax. Jamuna, possessed by the spirit of the dead girl, turns into a multi-armed, back-lit Kali and zaps a guru with bolts of lightning (scratched right onto the film emulsion). Then, from behind her back come two more female zombies with hideous faces. There's a lot of fast cutting, wild music and heavy storm effects. These scenes rival Brazil's José Mojica Marins for sheer energetic wackiness. Jamuna really gives it her all, which is considerable. She has one of the best cackling laughs going and here it's put to good use.

Another successful one-off was *Khooni Hawas* (Deadly Lust). Directed in Southern India by G. M. Kumar, this is another story of possession, but handled in a more sophisticated way than many Bombay film-makers managed. One of the problems with the studio-bound Bollywood product is that the backgrounds quickly become over familiar. This is a particular problem in horror films, of course, where the novelty of the setting is an important factor in establishing atmosphere. *Khooni Hawas* makes very effective use of some unusual locations, notably an eerie, deserted beach, and there is more than the usual quotient of weird mystical rites and ancient magic.

Of course, these few interesting films were more than cancelled out by the tidal wave of dross that hit screens at the time. Take *Andheri Raat* (Dark Night), for example. This tells the story of a mad scientist who creates a monster — a tall man in tennis shoes called Big John. The doctor works in a lab that's like something out of a 1930s Boris Karloff flick, with bubbling retorts and coloured smoke everywhere... there's even a brace of tatty skeletons hanging on the wall. Naturally Big John goes on the rampage, scattering a bunch of teens who are having fun on the beach. He kills one girl with an umbrella (that'll teach her to shower in a bikini) and has a fight with a bunch of seventies-style pimps, all wearing flares and leather hats. There are even some hilariously bad martial arts sequences. It's surprising that the monster doesn't laugh himself to death.

Even worse, if that's possible, was *Khooni Dracula* (Deadly Dracula). This appalling no-budget rubbish consists of numerous scenes of people talking intercut with shots of girls in shorts, miniskirts and bathing costumes being stalked by a man in a funny hat and bad monster make-up. He grunts lasciviously while the girls shout out "help! help!".

The girls in these horror scenes are remarkably plain. Obvious amateurs, hired only for their willingness to show a bit of leg or cleavage. In one scene, a gruesomely thin and haggard prostitute (she looks tired and desperate enough to be a real one) is shown begging for money which she then spends on drugs. We see her in a back alley stuffing them down like sweets before expiring. Eventually Dracula is killed with a tiny *trishul* that looks more like a toasting fork, while the rest of the cast beat him feebly with strings of garlic.

The film is interesting in spite of itself for what it says about the horror genre in India. When you strip such films of the skill and commitment of the Ramsays, the humour

If there's to be a new 'Doom Boom' it will have to be based on solid cinematic skills. And hopefully this time the stories will use indigenous Indian myths and monsters in a more creative way than before. As actor Kiran Kumar avers: "India is a very mystic country. There are so many subjects here. They haven't begun to realise the potential of the horror market."

By the mid-1990s things were starting to look a lot more promising. Clive Barker's *Hellraiser*, dubbed into Hindi and released in 1996 as *Shaitan ka Beta* (Daughter of Satan), was a big hit in Bombay. The mass audience had their first chance to see what was being done today in the West. A younger generation of horror fans was also starting to emerge. Ramgopal Varma, whose innovative *Raat* had been one of the victims of the earlier horror glut, talked enthusiastically about making another one: "I love horror films... You create an image to play on the fears of the audience. The scope of creativity that you have in a horror film is incredible."

But amidst all this speculation, the older generation shouldn't be forgotten. Given the chance they might still turn out something surprising. Tulsi Ramsay remains above all an out-and-out fan. Flicking through pictures of classic horror movies, he smiled as he recalled the pioneering years of the 1970s: "We enjoyed ourselves a lot then. They were good days. And maybe they can come again." In an industry as volatile and competitive as Bollywood, anything is possible. ■

and inventiveness of Mohan Bhakri and the energy of Vinod Talwar, you end up with a film like this. Proving that there is no real tradition of horror in Indian cinema, nothing for the third-rate film-maker to fall back on. Except sex. Although nothing explicit is shown, pornography is the only genre that *Khooni Dracula* could possibly fit into. The sole reason for its existence is to show half-dressed women in peril, being stalked by the monster, and being raped. Its audience of sex-starved young men, the primary consumers of horror in India, got exactly what they paid for with this one.

The horror boom collapsed as quickly as it had risen. The few big-budget productions that appeared as the tide was turning did little to stop the rot. Mahesh Batt's *Junoon* (Obsession), a 1992 remake of *An American Werewolf in London*, and Ramgopal Varma's *Raat* (Night) both flopped despite their superior technical qualities. Audiences just weren't interested any more. Horror had outstayed its welcome. People were no longer prepared to pay for cheap thrills. Particularly when they could get them for nothing on the small screen.

In 1991, Nittin Keni of Zee TV had the idea of making a horror series. Serials were a big thing then, with the runaway success of programmes like *The Mahabharata*. In pursuing his idea he talked to most of Bombay's horror specialists. Finally he settled with the Ramsays, convinced that their track record and established reputation in the field would carry him over the bad press he feared the series might attract. The format the Ramsays devised was a long story divided up into six twenty-five-minute episodes. What we get, essentially, is a feature film shown in bite-sized chunks. In fact, it is very similar to the old Saturday morning serials that had delighted Western audiences in the forties and fifties. Each episode ends with a cliff-hanger or a shock ending that then leads into the following week's instalment. In this way, the expected five or six peak moments of horror can be paced to greater effect than in a continuous two and a half hour movie.

Zee Horror Show has kept alive the spirit of horror in India. It's also upped the ante for anyone who tries to follow.

STARTS TODAY
YET ANOTHER CHILLING THRILLER FROM THE
HOUSE OF RAMSAYS
TONIGHT AT 9.30 P.M. ON ZEE T.V.
INDIA'S NO. 1 POPULAR HORROR SHOW
TANTRIK
ZEE HORROR SHOW
Produced By :
TULSI RAMSAY – SHYAM RAMSAY
Directed By :
DEEPAK RAMSAY
THE EXCITEMENT CONTINUES !
Courtesy: SREE DEVI SECURITIES LTD.

Far left: *Rock bottom horror in* Khooni Dracula.
Left: *After conquering the big screen, the Ramsays bought horror to Indian television.*
Below and bottom: *Street poster for the Bombay release of Clive Barker's* Hellraiser.

ERDO VATAN · SAFİYE YANKI

RENKLİ
EASTMANCOLOR

YERLİ
FİLM
NO:3

METİN YANKI

SÜPERADAM

"İSTANBULDA"

HAYATİ HAMZAOĞLU · DANYAL TOPATAN

REJİ: YAVUZ YALINKILIÇ KAMERA: DİNCER ÖNAL

Dracula in Istanbul

Turkey came late to the film game. It wasn't until the 1950s that the country had anything worth calling an industry. The local pioneer, Muhsin Ertuğrul, was a man of the theatre. Most of his productions were stagebound, static and decidedly uncinematic. From 1922 until well into the 1940s, Ertuğrul had the field more or less to himself. After the war, Turkish cinema started to expand and new ideas and themes began to appear. In 1952, Turgut Demirağ, a producer who had learned his trade in Hollywood, decided to mount a Turkish version of *Dracula*. Naturally, it was called *Drakula Istanbul'da* (Dracula in Istanbul).

Opposite: *'Take that, you swine!' Superman, Turkish style.*

Left: *Atıf Kaptan as Dracula in* Drakula Istanbul'da.

The script for this ground-breaking production was based on the novel *Kazikli Voyvoda* (The Noble Impaler) by Ali Riza Seyfioğlu, which in turn was a very free adaptation of Bram Stoker's *Dracula*. A major change in the film was the character of Mina. The demure fiancée of Jonathan Harker is here transformed into a shapely dancer. The chubby but charming Austrian Fräulein, Annie Ball, who plays the part, had been discovered working in an Istanbul night-club. This provided the opportunity not only for some exotic belly dancing, but also, as a bonus, a mildly erotic bath scene.

The most interesting aspect of the film, a detail only hinted at in Bram Stoker's novel, is the connection it makes between Dracula and the historical figure of Vlad the Impaler. This fifteenth century Rumanian nobleman acquired his name from his favourite method of execution. During one campaign alone he skewered more than 25,000 men, women and children. A report tells how he ate a hearty breakfast surrounded by a forest of bloody spikes on which his victims writhed, screamed and slowly died. In the title role, Turkish screen veteran Atıf Kaptan gives a very original interpretation of Vlad as a bald, slinky reptile with fangs. According to most film historians, the first post-war vampire film to feature a fanged bloodsucker was Hammer's Technicolor *Dracula* with Christopher Lee. Well, the Turks got there first. *Drakula Istanbul'da* was released five years before the Hammer hit.

In its day, the film was a pioneering venture for the local industry. Special effects were pretty much an unknown quantity and everything had to be improvised on-set. Sometimes with surprising results. As art director Sohban Koloğlu recalled: "All the... effects, even the simplest, caused lots of problems. For example, for the graveyard scene, we needed some fog. We didn't have the necessary equipment. We had to have a backlit cloud of smoke lying on the ground. How did we create this cloud? In a very simple way. The thirty or forty members of the crew, each with three or four cigarettes in their mouths, puffing away relentlessly, lying on the ground just out of shot!"

Drakula Istanbul'da was a considerable success upon release, but it was nearly twenty years before the vampiric Impaler reappeared on Turkish screens. In the late sixties, when historical films were in vogue, he popped up several times as a bald-headed baddie. First came *Malkoçoğlu Krallara Karşı* (Malkoçoğlu vs the Kings), a 1967 episode of the popular swashbuckling series *Malkoçoğlu*, featuring Turkish superstar Çüneyt Arkın. Malkoçoglu was a character from a popular comic strip, a brave warrior in the fifteenth century Ottoman court. In one of his many adventures he comes up against the Impaler.

Vlad played a bigger role in *Kara Murat*, the first episode of another comic-based series. Here the Impaler is involved in a whole series of bloody episodes, most of them taken from fifteenth century tales of the real Dracula. When the

Right: *The Invisible Man comes to Istanbul.*
Below: Ringo Kid, *the first Turkish Western.*

Sultan's ambassadors refuse to remove their turbans in his presence, Vlad has the hats nailed on to their heads. Because she thinks it will please him, Vlad's mistress foolishly pretends to be pregnant. Learning of her deception, Vlad has her disembowelled. Eventually, Kara Murat, the Sultan's brave musketeer, is ordered to put an end to the actions of the tyrant.

Like many Turkish costume adventures from the early seventies, in *Kara Murat* you're never far from a whipping, a fight or a belly dancing scene. Actresses who were prepared to go topless, like the dancer Seher Şeniz, were used to add a bit of extra oomph. This combination of 'boys' own' style adventure, graphic bloodletting and sexploitation indicates the broad range of taste, age and expectation that these films had to appeal to.

Vlad was up to his tricks again in *Kara Boğa* (The Black Bull), directed in 1974 by Yavuz Figenli. This is a return to the territory mapped out by *Drakula Istanbul'da.* In a flashback near the beginning of the film we see the demonic Impaler brought back to life by his hunchbacked servant in a ceremony involving virgin's blood. Later he becomes the leader of a ruthless gang of black-masked villains, who get their kicks in the usual way — looting, pillaging and burning innocent villagers, with a little bit of devil worship on the side. Eventually Vlad gets his just desserts at the hands of another brave hero, staked and beheaded in the traditional way for vampires. Since then the Impaler has stayed dead, at least as far as Turkish cinema is concerned.

Drakula Istanbul'da was one of a number of fantasy films that hit Turkish screens during the 1950s. Vlad the Impaler was not the first mythic figure to wander the banks of the Bosphorus: Tarzan had been there before him with *Tarzan Istanbul'da* (Tarzan in Istanbul) and the Invisible Man soon followed, in *Görünmeyen Adam Istanbul'da* (The Invisible Man in Istanbul). More Eastern influenced was a giant spider in an oriental fairy story, *Balıkçi Güzeli* (The Handsome Fisherman), while a flying carpet was featured in *Uç Baba Torik* (Three Fat Fish). Bringing things more up to date came a UFO, piloted by a crew of cute miniskirted aliens, in *Uçan Daireler Istanbul'da* (Flying Saucers Over Istanbul).

So the pattern was set, and over the next couple of decades Turkish fantasy cinema trod three main paths. Firstly, the costume adventures, Arabian Nights style, with genii, dancing girls and dashing heroes. Secondly there were various imitations of American successes, like Dracula and Tarzan. Finally came the masked superhero/supervillain films. Sometimes all three were combined to produce strange and unique hybrids.

The golden age of Turkish cinema lasted from the early sixties to the late seventies, a period bookended by the new constitution of 1961 and the military take-over in 1980. Greater freedom of expression for artists, increased affluence for the audience and a rampant desire to make money on the part of the producers were the factors that helped to create the Turkish cinema boom and also to destroy it. The rise was so rapid that there was no time, and precious little will, to create a workable infrastructure. It was like an elaborate baroque mansion built on top of a tin hut. Eventually the edifice had to come tumbling down. From a high of 301 films in 1972, the figure had sunk to sixty-eight in 1980. But while it lasted there was fun to be had and, for some at least, a lot of money to be made.

Regional distributors called the shots, dividing the country up into six exclusive territories. Producers would raise their finance from advance sales made to these powerful distributors. The main aim was to turn a quick profit. Stars, stories and subjects were dictated by what had been a proven success at the box office. Comedies, crime films and costume dramas poured from tiny studios perched along the banks of the Bosphorus. Yeşilçam, a small street in Istanbul where many film companies had their offices, became a buzzing hive of activity. The name became synonymous with low-budget, gaudy, made-to-measure productions, just as Tin Pan Alley in New York was known as the home of cheap tunes during the Jazz Age.

Leading stars made more than twenty films a year, often

working on several at the same time. There were stories of actors being practically kidnapped from one set and bundled off to the next to meet a producer's deadline. Writers worked simultaneously on several scripts, moving from one desk to another as they finished each page. Assistant directors would then grab a sheaf of papers and whisk them off to a waiting crew. As director/producer Yılmaz Atadeniz recalls, a film could be written, shot, edited and released in less than two months. Director Semih Evin was noted for his ability to turn out professional-looking films in as little as four days. The record is probably held by the prolific Çetin Inanç, who claims to have shot an entire film in twenty-four hours. Benefiting from the boom, production companies like Seher Film, Saner Film and Erler Film blossomed overnight. Some of these were soon history, others were longer lived. Erler Film, founded by former director Turker Inanoğlu, is still an active force. One of Inanoğlu's innovations was to become involved in co-productions with other countries. First of all, in 1970, with Iran, then Italy, France and even Hong Kong.

In the mid 1960s, during the height of this boom period, came a host of low-budget films that mixed heroes from the comics, the serials and the pulps. The Italians showed the way with their film *Kriminal*, based on a popular comic book. This zappy and colourful production was largely shot in and around Istanbul. Safe from fears of copyright infringement, Turkish producer Mehmet Çaydamar decided to mount a similar version of the more famous Spider-Man. The result, *Örümcek Adam* (Spider Man), was released in 1966. The next year Flash Gordon — in Turkish, Bay Tekin — met Ming and a gang of rock men in *Bay Tekin Fezada Çarpışanlar* (Flash Gordon's Battle in Space). The same year saw an appearance from Batman in *Fantoma Istanbul'da Buluşalım* (Fantômas: Appointment in Istanbul). Here, Batman's adversary was the mysterious Fantoma, a local version of the French anti-hero Fantômas.

One of the most influential of the comics-inspired filmmakers was director/producer Yılmaz Atadeniz. He had

Left: *The female Tarzan.*
Below: *The skull-masked female Killing was a facially disfigured woman who vented her wrath on happy couples.*

Above right: *Hooded Turkish villains show the influence of forties American serials.* **Below right:** *Okan Demir as 'Superman' in* Süper Adam Kadınlar Arasında.

watched the production of *Kriminal* and was aware of the sadistic Italian photo novels featuring a similar character called Killing. In 1967, he formed his own company and in less than three weeks turned out *Killing Istanbul'da* (Killing in Istanbul). The title character, with his skull mask and skeleton suit, was a macabre presence on the streets of Istanbul and the shooting of the film attracted a lot of media attention.

The film was a huge hit. Within a month it had made more than three times the normal profit for a low-budget movie. Rival producers moved fast to cash in. Three more Killing films were released in 1967, including encounters with the Frankenstein monster, in *Killing Frankeştayn'a Karşı* (Killing versus Frankenstein) and Mandrake the Magician in *Mandrake Killing'e Karşı* (Killing versus Mandrake). There was even a 'female Killing' (*Dişi Killing*) and a Western version that combined him with the Franco Nero character Django — *Çango Ölüm Süvarisi* (Django, the Death Rider). Although unknown in the West, Killing's career ran to another seven films in Turkey.

Another Atadeniz masked hero appeared in his 1968 production *Kızıl Maske* (The Red Mask), this time directed by his assistant Çetin Inanç. The purple-suited Phantom had been created in the 1930s by American comics artist Lee Falk. In the same year as Atadeniz's film, a rival producer released another movie with exactly the same title. In 1971, with the addition of some softcore nudity, the Phantom reappeared in *Kızıl Maskenin Intikamı* (The Vengeance of the Red Mask).

The main inspiration for Atadeniz and for the film-makers that followed him were the American serials of the 1940s. Masked heroes such as Zorro and the Lone Ranger were soon joined by local versions, including Demir Pençe (The Steel Claw) and Şimşek Hafiye (The Thunder Detective). Superman, the most famous costumed hero of them all, paid a visit to Turkey in 1969 with *Süpermen Fantomaya Karşı* (Superman versus Fantômas). He returned two years later in *Süper Adam* (Superman) and *Süper Adam Kadınlar Arasında* (Superman and the Women). In 1979, following the success of the Christopher Reeve film, came a Turkish imitation, *Süpermen Dönüyor* (The Return of Superman), starring Tayfun Demir. This film even used some of the John Williams music from the original production and had would-be lookalike actors in the main roles.

Kunt Tulgar, director and producer of the film, was something of a one-man industry. He had begun as an actor in the 1960s before moving into direction and production. His company, Kunt Film, churned out thrillers and crime films as well as a Tarzan movie, *Tarzan Korkusuz Adam* (Tarzan the Mighty Man), and a martial arts feature, *Ejderin Intikamı* (The Dragon's Revenge). The astonishing poverty of *Süpermen Dönüyor* makes one question his sanity. Why attempt to remake one of the most expensive Hollywood productions of its year when you obviously don't even have the budget to hire decent transport? Most of the cast drive around in motors that look like rejects from a stock car race.

The obvious cheapness of these productions is made a virtue of in Yılmaz Atadeniz's *Süper Selami* (Super Salami), a slapstick parody of this whole subgenre. Its nerdish hero is played by comedian Aydemir Akbaş, who specialised in playing horny half-wits — *Astronot Fehmi* (Fehmi the Astronaut), a softcore sex comedy with science fiction trappings, is another of his efforts. In *Süper Selami* he's turned into Superman by a loin-clothed guru in a cave. In one scene his super powers desert him because he leaves his long johns on! The short running time of this film, along with numerous soft core scenes and even the beginnings of a tentative blow-job, suggest that it may well have been cut down from something much harder.

Fortunately, not all Turkish superhero films were so slapdash. The devious and grotesque *Üç Dev Adam* (Three Mighty Men) opens with a scene of astonishing sadism. A young woman is buried up to her neck in sand. The baddies use the propeller of an outboard motor to slice up her face, shown by blood spattering over the bare legs of a female member of the gang. With its one-dimensional characterisations, fast-paced action formula and bizarre plot (Santo, the Mexican masked wrestler, and Captain America meet in Istanbul to fight an evil Spider-Man), *Üç Dev Adam* comes closer than most to being a real 'comic strip on film'.

The simple-minded sadism of *Üç Dev Adam* was a common feature of Turkish popular cinema and not just in the comic strip films. Pretty boy actor Göksal Arsoy produced and starred in three James Bond imitations that were filled with devious cruelty. In 1966's *Altın Çocuk* (The Golden Boy) he comes up against a bald-headed baddie played by Altan Günbay. This sneering black-clad villain likes nothing better than stubbing out cigarettes on naked women and trapping his enemies in spiked chambers. One woman is made to stand on a block of ice with a noose around her neck. The leering Günbay then melts the block with a heater and watches while the noose tightens, strangling her.

A more light-hearted sort of fun came in the shape of *Yılmayan Şeytan* (*The Deathless Devil*), which features another Santo clone. His sidekick is a tubby version of Sherlock Holmes, complete with riding coat, deerstalker hat and meerschaum pipe. Together they battle the evil Dr Şeytan (Dr Satan), a delicious moustachioed villain straight out of Sax Rohmer. His trump card is a giant silver robot, apparently made out of packing cases, that lumbers about flashing coloured lights and emitting showers of sparks.

Yılmayan Seytan had a confusing existence that well illustrates the pitfalls suffered by Turkish producers in a country with no enforceable copyright laws. The film had been produced and directed by Yılmaz Atadeniz. Under the title of *Yılmayan Adam* it was sold without his knowledge to an Italian company. They renamed it *L'invicibile Bedman* (The Invincible Batman). The enterprising Italians then decided to sell it back to Turkey as an American film called *The Deathless Devil*. The credits were Anglicised. The film's director became Robert Gordon and its stars Ruth Taylor and Jack London. Unfortunately, when it came to renaming the top billed Kunt Tulgar, the Italians had a failure of imagination and came up with the name Kunt Brix. This unfortunate handle certainly scuppered the film's chances in the Anglo-Saxon market.

Turkey's cheap production facilities and lack of red tape were a big attraction to Italian movie men. During the 1960s, producer Italo Martinenghi had enjoyed considerable success in his home territory with the Three Supermen series. When money became tighter he began to cast around for a way to cut costs and still stay in business. In 1979, he came to Istanbul to make *Süpermenler* (Supermen) in collaboration with local film mogul Turker Inanoğlu. The result was a knockabout comedy, starring Çüneyt Arkın in a very unbecoming superhero costume. The story tells of a time machine coveted by a bunch of klutzy mafiosi.

A couple of years later, with even less money in the pot, Martinenghi teamed up with the ubiquitous Kunt Tulgar. Together they made the unbelievably creaky *Üç Süpermen Olimpiyatlarda* (Three Supermen at the Olympic Games). Intended as a platform to launch Martinenghi's son, Stefano, on an acting career, this was a film that even Ed Wood might have disowned. Much of its running time consists of huge chunks of unsynched dialogue, laughable special effects (mostly rigged up by Martinenghi and Tulgar),

Above: *This film, starring Kunt Tulgar, was released with several different titles.*
Left: *Santo, Cap'n America and Spider-Man — three mighty men indeed.*
Below: *Turkey's James Bond, the Golden Boy, in Beirut.*

Above left: *Tarkan was Turkey's top film hero.*
Above right: Tarkan Viking Kanı, *with Swedish actress Eva Bender.*

non sequiturs of plot, character and location, great chunks of unrelated stock footage and feeble attempts at comedy. Then, just when you're about to give up, a gang of green-hooded villains, a masked villainess in a skimpy undersize swimming costume and another silver robot pop up to enliven things — in scenes stolen from an obscure 1973 movie called *Üç Süper Adam ve Çılgın Kiz* (Three Supermen and Mad Girl). Like all truly bad films, *Üç Süpermen Olimpiyatlarda* exudes a powerful magic that more prestigious offerings can't hope to match.

These films weren't meant to be taken entirely seriously. Turkish audiences were just as able to appreciate the camp humour of them as Western audiences were of the sixties *Batman* television series. Which is not to deny the ineffable cheesiness of scenes like that in *Supermen Dönüyor* where a galaxy of Christmas tree glass balls against a blue background is shown as a representation of the vastness of space. Hugely enjoyable and endlessly rewatchable, these films deserve a much wider audience than their humble origins consigned them to. As John Baxter wrote in *Science Fiction in the Cinema* about American serials, the obvious inspiration for these Turkish films: 'To anyone who cares about the cinema there is an attraction about [them] that is inescapable.'

More serious was the Tarkan series, starring Kartal Tibet as a hard-fighting warrior from the Dark Ages. Five Tarkan films were made between 1969 and 1972. Their style was close to the Italian *peplums*, Hercules films and 'sword and sandal' epics of the early sixties, with a dash of 'man with no name'/Clint Eastwood stoicism added to the mix. With his ever ready sword in hand and faithful wolf, Kurt, by his side (actually a rather jolly-looking German shepherd dog), Tarkan roams through Central Asia, righting wrongs and defending the weak. On his travels he encounters vicious Vikings, a giant octopus, bloodthirsty Amazons, kung fu killers, evil sorceresses and lots of large-breasted, willing maidens.

Although essentially costume adventures, the Tarkan series includes many delirious fantasy episodes. *Tarkan Altın Madalyon* (Tarkan and the Golden Medallion), the wildest of them all, opens with the abduction of a veiled nun and a topless dancer. An evil magician has them strung up on huge crucifixes and sacrificed. Their blood runs down in channels over a waiting skeleton, resurrecting a seductive vampire woman (played by Swedish ex-strip teaser, Eva Bender), who snares Tarkan in a huge, sticky spider's web. In *Tarkan Viking Kanı* (Tarkan and the Blood of the Vikings), he comes up against a giant, man-eating octopus.

The Tarkan series has the quality of all great fantasy cinema — you never really know what's going to happen next. But whatever it is, it's somehow exactly right. The films have the logic of a favourite, half-remembered dream. With their dance sequences, dollops of gore and bizarre special effects, they are astonishing products to jaded Western eyes. One of their most refreshing aspects is the use of the Turkish landscape as almost a character in itself, giving the films an epic and refreshingly unclichéd appearance from scene to scene. Watching the films in sequence over a short period of time, Tarkan comes to achieve a heroic, almost mystical grandeur that is genuinely impressive.

In *Tarkan Gümüş Eyer* (Tarkan and the Silver Saddle) we see the character's origins. Orphaned, his parents slaughtered by a marauding gang, the baby Tarkan is abandoned in a cave. A family of wolves adopts him and he grows to maturity far from human society. His later experiences amongst his own kind make him prefer the company of wolves, but the pull of his human side is always too strong. His steady, firm but fair demeanour obviously had a deep emotional appeal for Turkish audiences. The hugely popular Çüneyt Arkın had a similar aura. Again, many of his films tell of his character's origins, and the struggle to be a man true to his own vision. The archetype is of someone with great strength, but infinite patience. His past has been tough, full of injustice, giving him more than ample excuse to behave badly. Instead he is controlled, kind to animals and children, and a passionate lover. However, once aroused, his ire is dreadful.

Perhaps this was how the Turks saw their own situation in the sixties and seventies. Isolated from the rest of Europe by their lost empire and bloody past, maintaining a precarious balance between the conflicting demands of a fundamentalist religious right on the one hand and pro-Europe modernisers on the other. They lived under the constant threat of military intervention. When it eventually happened, in 1980, it led to a suppression of trades unions and human rights. Such events must have made the Turks value the patient, waiting strength of their heroes, like Tarkan and Kara Murat, who through thick and thin never lost sight of their true goals or their taste for freedom.

Popular fantasy films like the Tarkan series are often criticised by the Left for the debilitating effect they have on their audiences. The 'opium of the people' factor. Perhaps there's another way of reading them. However, it's no coincidence that the early seventies — a particularly troubled time for Turkish society — saw a sudden rise in the sort of escapist films that serve as a refuge from the harsh realities of life. These were the Arabian Nights-style fantasies and fairy stories. For a couple of years, production of this type of film soared, with numerous sources, both Western and Eastern, being plundered for inspiration.

It began in 1970 with *Adsız Cengâver* (The Nameless Knight), directed by Halit Refiğ. This Iranian co-production benefited from special effects done at the Rank laboratories in London, featuring a giant genie, a magic mirror, a seductive witch and a magic sword. Then came a version of *Snow White and the Seven Dwarfs* (*Pamuk Prenses ve 7 Cüceler*) directed by Ertem Göreç. This live-action film, faithful to the story and spirit of the Disney classic, beat all box office records that year. The time was ripe to flood the market with a host of similar products: in 1971 came *Ali Baba Kırk Haramiler* (Ali Baba and the Forty Thieves), *Aladdin in Lambası* (Aladdin's Lamp), *Binbir Gece Masalları* (The 1001 Nights) and *Altın Prens Devler Ülkesinde* (The Golden Prince in the Land of the Giants). There was even a version of *The Wizard of Oz* (*Ayşecik ve Sihirli Cüceler Rüyalar Ülkesinde*), as well as two versions of *Cinderella*.

This upsurge of fantasy cinema only lasted a couple of years. Pretty soon the screens were swamped with so-called *arabesk* films. This is a genre unique to Turkey. Its roots lie in Arabic-language films imported from Egypt. These were very popular during the forties and fifties. With their melodramatic plots, strongly drawn, almost archetypal characters and cabaret dancing scenes they drew a huge audience. They were particularly popular with the large armies of rural

Above: *Tarkan also starred in his own comic book.*
Below: *Heroic bloodshed in* Bizansi Titreten Yiğit, *based on the* Karaoğlan *comic book series.*

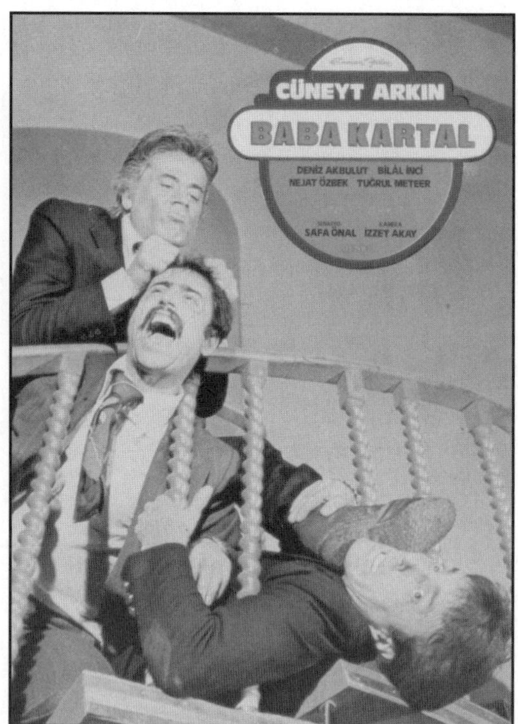

Right: *Çüneyt Arkın (on top!).*
Below: *Çihangir Gaffari in action.*

poor who moved to live and work in the big cities during this period. The Turkish authorities got twitchy about 'Islamic influences' creeping in through these films and began to limit their importation. Local producers picked up the gauntlet and began to make films in the style of the Egyptian movies, using Turkish stars and settings but retaining the operatic excesses of the originals.

Just as drag queens project an overheated, impossibly glamorised view of women, so do the *arabesk* singing stars and the plots of the movies they feature in. Consequently, it should come as no surprise that one of the big 'female' stars of *arabesk*, Bülent Ersoy, is actually a man. In 1980 Ersoy underwent a sex change operation in London. On her return to live performance she was shot and wounded by a right-wing fanatic.

Equally bloody and revenge-filled as the *arabesk* were the many crime movies that also proliferated during the seventies. Imported 'stars' like Richard Harrison and Gordon Mitchell featured in a slew of low-budget thrillers. Some of these, like *Hedef* (*Target*), directed by Guido Zurli, or *Babanın Arkadaşi* (*Revenge of the Godfather*), directed by Farouk Agrama, were decent enough imitations of the Italian models that inspired them. Others, like *Şahit* (Witness) and *Belalı Elmaslar* (*The Diamond Connection*), pushed the boundaries of incompetence until it became almost a virtue. Superman actor Kunt Tulgar, the Ed Wood of Turkish cinema, really came into his own in this genre. His 1983 production *Gizli Kuvvet* (Secret Force) is an astonishing creation. Much of it seems to have been shot through a strange fog filter, as though someone forgot to wipe the lens between takes. This distortion effect adds another weird dimension to an already incomprehensible plot. One of the film's main villains is a black assassin. The dark obscurity of all the scenes in which he appears makes it impossible to discern the poor man's features.

These crime films and action movies were able to capitalise on one of Turkish cinema's greatest assets: its many superb villains and bad guy actors. Heavies like Erol Taş and Altan Günbay played the 'Mr Big's of crime syndicates with the kind of panache that puts them in the Sydney Greenstreet/Erich von Stroheim category of men you love to hate. Their henchmen were played by the likes of Yılmaz Köksal and Behçet Nacar. Whereas the former had the cool meanness of a young Jack Palance, Nacar was the vengeful wildman, with a persona drawn from Richard Widmark's Tommy Udo — film noir's top psycho.

As in American movies of the forties and fifties, the matinée idol 'good guy' of Turkish cinema is of little interest. The real stars of these movies are always darker. Like all classic anti-heroes, they plough their own furrow, often coming up against corrupt authority in the process. The undisputed star of the genre was Çüneyt Arkın. Always ready with a damning sneer, routing gangs of villains with his ready fists, he straddled the low-budget action movie like a colossus. Originally trained as a doctor (and still practising as such), Arkın began his career in the 1960s as a handsome leading man in films like Halit Refiğ's *Gurbet Kuşları* (Birds of Exile) and *Haremde 4 Kadın* (Four Women of the Harem). Over the years he would continue to take on serious roles, such as the political melodrama *Maden* (The Mine) in 1978, but to Turkish audiences he is best known as the hard-fighting, high-kicking star of movies like *Belalı Hayat* (A Life of Trouble) and *Son Vurgun* (The Last Hold-Up). In *Insan Avcısı* (*Heart of a Father*) he plays the crooked brother of a police captain. Arkın's wife dies in childbirth and he is arrested during a bungled robbery. His son is brought up by the police captain to be a good, law abiding citizen. Arkın is released from prison to find that the child has been kidnapped. He has to take on the underworld again, this time fighting on the side of justice.

Together with crime and gangster melodramas, the mid seventies also saw a huge rise in sexy exploitation pictures. Films like *Kocam, Erkek Mi?* (Is My Husband a Man?), *Yudum Yudum Sev* (Make Love Drop by Drop) and *Tornavida* (Screwdriver) were part of a 'new wave' of sex films that soon came to dominate Turkish screens. Even the ubiquitous Emmanuelle put in an appearance in *Kasımpaşalı Emmanuel* (Emmanuelle From Kasımpasa).

Sex and eroticism had been around in Turkish films from the silent days. *Pençe* (The Claw), made as far back as

1917, was condemned for its shocking story line. A couple of years later, *Mürebbiye* (The Governess) told the tale of a wanton Parisian hussy on the loose in Istanbul which roused the ire of the French Ambassador. However, it was only with the popularity of costume dramas in the forties and fifties that Turkish cinema found its first sultry sex sirens. In the more liberal climate of the sixties, Leyla Sayar became the queen of Turkish eroticism in films like *Suçlular Aramızda* (The Guilty Are Among Us) and *Ölüm Perdesi* (The Curtain of Death). In the latter she performs an amazing striptease in a night-club. Her 'partner' is a dinner-jacketed mannequin holding a revolver. The scene concludes with Leyla kneeling down in front of the doll and putting her lips around the barrel of its gun. Pretty steamy stuff for its day and certainly the equal of contemporary European films from Jesús Franco or José Bénazéraf.

The close links between the film-making communities of Rome and Istanbul led to many Italian movies being distributed in Turkey. In the early 1970s this meant exposure to softcore sex comedies starring the likes of Lanzo Buzzanca and Edwige Fenech. Inevitably there were Turkish imitations. *Beş Tavuk Bir Horoz* (Five Chickens, One Cock), released in 1974, is the acknowledged precursor of what soon became an invasion. Osman Seden's 1975 production *Teşekkür Ederim Büyük Anne* (Thanks a Lot, Granny) is fairly typical for its time. This is a frothy, pseudo-sophisticated sex comedy centred around a simple misunderstanding. The confusion begins when a Turkish businessman dispatches his son to the airport to meet a client's *büyükanne* (grandmother). What he in fact encounters is *büyük Anne* (big Anna), played by Italian sex kitten Sonia Viviani. Chaos then ensues as every male over the age of puberty attempts to get into her pants. Eventually she makes a man of the boy in time-honoured fashion. The film ends with the whole family reunited to wave her goodbye as she gets on the plane back to Rome. As demand for this kind of product soared, Turkey rapidly developed its own sex star system, with Arzu Okay, Mine Mutlu and Melek Görgün leading the pack.

1979 was the *annus mirabilis* of this trend. Of the 193 films produced in Turkey, 131 were sex films. This was the year in which Turkey attained the rare distinction of being the first Muslim country to make hardcore porn films. *Öyle Bir Kadın Ki* (A Woman Like That) marked the beginning of this unlikely genre. This 16mm cheapie was directed by Naki Yurter and starred Zerrin Doğan. Together they became Turkey's most prominent makers of sex films. Most of these productions were standard crime melodramas and boy meets

Above: *A Turkish sex comedy, influenced by Italian movies.*
Below left: *Melek Görgün, seventies sex symbol, gives lessons in cigarette smoking and topless dancing.*
Below right: *The leering Yılmaz Köksal and friend.*

girl romances. However, instead of fading discretely out with a chaste kiss, film-makers now had the opportunity to show the love scene that followed in full, hardcore close up. Blow jobs, come-shots and female masturbation were frequently featured, usually in an entirely artless and innocent way.

In Yavuz Figenli's 1980 film *Paylaş ılmayan Kadın* (One Man Woman), a country girl returns from the city, full of sophisticated Western ways. She smokes cigarettes, wears blue eye-shadow and split skirts, and has died her bobbed hair blonde. Whilst out for a walk in the country, she meets a handsome local stud and pretty soon they're at it hammer and tongs. When her boyfriend is framed for a murder he didn't commit, the young hussy uses her charms to fuck a confession out of the real killer. Almost half the film's brief running time consists of three lengthy sex scenes.

Right: *Turkish superstar Çüneyt Arkın was renamed Steve for this British video release.*
Below: *Zerrin Egeliler was one of Turkey's top sex stars in the seventies.*

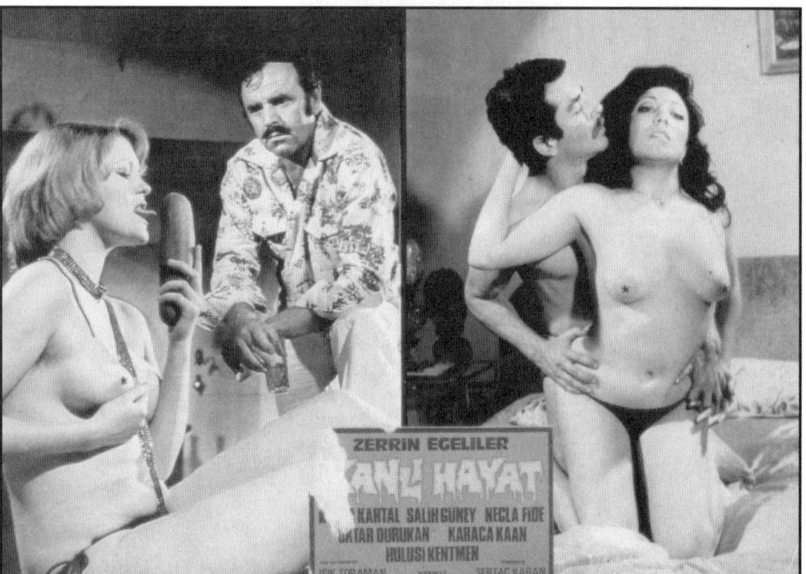

As might be expected, it was not an easy task finding actresses willing to appear in these productions. Zerrin Egeliler was the most popular porno star. This busy lady achieved a world record in 1979 of thirty-one films in one year! Fortunately for the state of her health, if nothing else, the porno trend was soon reversed by the military government that took power in 1980. Censorship increased as civil rights were done away with. Naki Yurter was arrested and told to mend his ways. A heavy press campaign and increasing political violence made going to see sex films in Turkey something of an act of faith. It all ended rather sadly when a couple of cinemas showing softcore films were bombed and the market, not surprisingly, dried up.

Many of the directors/producers behind these films, men like Yavuz Figenli, Mehmet Aslan and Naki Yurter, had been involved with genre production for years, going from costume dramas to comic book films to Westerns as the mood of the market shifted. In this respect, as in many others, the Turkish film business resembled that of Italy. As the cash-starved Italian industry lurched from crisis to crisis, many of its directors, actors and technicians made the trip to Istanbul.

The roots of this relationship go back to the early 1960s, when Italian film-makers came to Turkey looking for exotic, cheap locations for their spy and thriller series. To facilitate matters, they used local producers to arrange the technical side of things. The more astute of these local moguls began to invest in the Italian films in exchange for Turkish distribution rights. Once they got their hands on the footage, it was often extensively recut to make an entirely new product. In the mid-seventies, Turkish film mogul Turker Inanoğlu linked up with the Italian company Filmcenter to market Italian-Turkish co-productions throughout the world. It was through this conduit that continent-hopping actors like William Berger and Klaus Kinski began to appear in so-called 'Turkish' films. Sometimes it worked the other way, too. Çüneyt Arkın starred in several overseas collaborations. Usually his name was changed to Steve or George Arkın to make it sound less exotic. His beefy but energetic style of martial arts even led to a Hong Kong co-production, *Karateciler Istanbul'da* (*Karate on the Bosphorus*).

An Italian influence was particularly strong in the Turkish cowboy films, which closely resembled the spaghetti Westerns of the late sixties and early seventies. These were peculiar hybrids, sort of 'Eastern Westerns', set in a never-never land where turbaned riders of the range clashed with black frock-coated villains and scantily clad 'Indian' maids. Action-packed and every bit as gory as the most Gothic of the spaghettis, this was a borrowed genre that seemed to suit the local industry very well. It started in 1967 with *Ringo Kid* and by 1971, of the 271 films made in Turkey, thirty were Westerns. These films were amongst the few local productions to make it out of the country in dubbed versions, their Turkish origins carefully disguised by the use of Americanised pseudonyms. *Küçük Kovboy* (The Little Cowboy; directed by the Italian Guido Zurli), was partly shot in the Rome studios of Cinecittà with foreign stars like Pascale Petit, added to give it some sales potential in Europe and America.

Television came to Turkey in 1968. Its influence really began to be felt in the early 1970s. The Government-controlled TRT began national broadcasting in 1973 and there

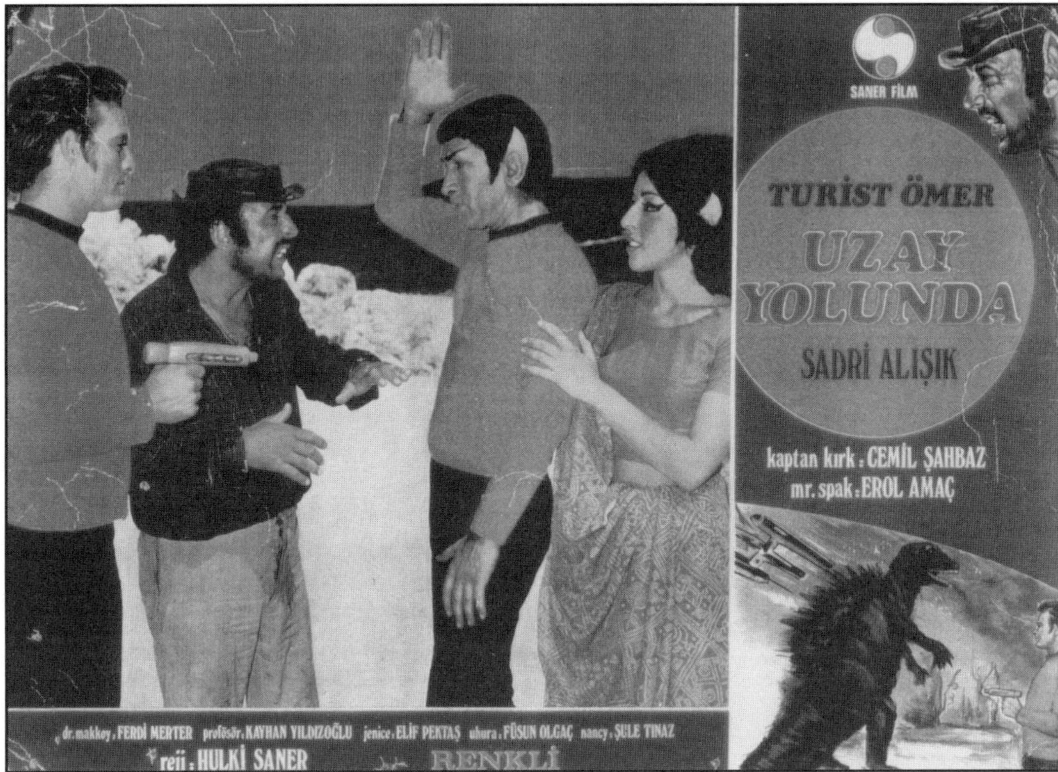

Left: *The Turkish* Star Trek...
Below: *... and the Turkish* Exorcist.

was an almost immediate effect on the cinemas. Audiences began to desert them in droves. From 3,000 cinemas in 1973, the number fell to as low as 334 in 1992: that's one cinema for every 200,000 people.

From the mid-seventies onwards, many examples of fantasy cinema produced in Turkey were heavily influenced by television. The eternally popular *Star Trek* gave rise to the parody *Türist Ömer Uzay Yolunda* (Ömer the Tourist in Star Trek). Ömer was a cheeky and cheerful tramp who featured in a long series of low-budget comedies. Here he's rescued in the nick of time from a shotgun wedding by being transported onto an alien planet. The place is inhabited by a mad scientist, gold-skinned bikini girls and a gang of mechanical muscle men in leopard-skin pants. He teams up with 'Kaptan Kırk' and 'Mr Spak', the latter complete with pointy ears and strange hand signals. In his usual bumbling style, Ömer helps them defeat a monster — a sort of shapeshifting, psychic vampire that leaves its victims covered in what look like lipstick kisses. Teleported back to his heavily pregnant bride and her confused family, Ömer discovers that he has inherited both Spock's pointy ears as well as the Vulcan 'mind grip'.

Another popular American television show, *Bewitched*, inspired the film *Tatli Cadı* (Sweet Sorceress) and its sequel *Tatlı Cadı'nın Maceraları* (The Adventures of the Sweet Sorceress), both from 1975. These were jaunty but fairly pointless exercises in plagiarism, where the special effects mostly consisted of jump cuts and speeding the film up. The husband's job in the fashion industry provided an excuse for featuring girls in skimpy costumes.

Much more inventive and fun was another *Bewitched* imitation, *Minik Cadı* (The Cute Witch). Here it's a six year-old girl with magic powers and a twitchy nose. One bizarre scene has the little girl turn her older sister into a big brown bear while she's grappling with a man under the sheets. Another scene features a topless mermaid. With a little bit of effort the film could have entered similar territory to the famous Jerome Bixby story 'It's a *Good* Life', featured in *The Twilight Zone*, with the tiny sorceress oppressing her indolent family with her sugary superpowers. Unfortunately, the film goes for 'cute' every time and ends up more Disney than devilish.

The male lead from *Minik Cadı*, Bülent Kayabaş, played the heir to the Frankenstein estates in the 1975 film *Sevimli Frankeştayn* (My Friend Frankenstein). This is pretty much a note-for-note replay of Mel Brooks' *Young Frankenstein*. Production values and direction are fairly solid compared with many Turkish fantasy films. However, it adds little to Brooks' original. The only novel element is its setting, with minarets and bright sunshine substituted for the 'Mittel Europa' of the old Universal horror classic that both films needlessly parody. Towards the end, the story shifts gears to include jibes at both the Turkish costume adventure and kung fu movies. But it's pretty much too little and too late to save the film.

Much more interesting was a free adaptation of another successful American movie. *Şeytan* (Satan), directed by Metin Erksan in 1975, was a close copy of Friedkin's *The Exorcist*. In fact, the copy is so close that the result is more or less a scene-by-scene Turkish 'version' of the original, much like the 1931 Spanish version of Tod Browning's *Dracula*. Of course the Spanish *Dracula* was officially sanctioned by Universal. No such clearance was obtained for *Şeytan*. Another important difference is that whereas the Spanish *Dracula* is in many ways superior to the English-language version, *Şeytan* is definitely not an improvement on Friedkin's original. However, in spite of its many deficiencies, the film remains one of the very few genuine Turkish horror films, with shock scenes, monster make-up and of course the inevitable exorcism. Primitive special effects imitate the head turning scene, the spewing up of green bile and the bed that tosses its occupant into the air. Only the bad language is toned down. What's finally most surprising about *Şeytan* is how little evidence it displays of the iconoclastic talents of its director.

Erksan, a former film critic and scriptwriter, was one of

Turkish cinema's most original artists. Like many of the country's film-makers, he worked in a wide variety of genres — comedies, musicals, melodramas — as well as in television. Erksan was one of the first Turkish film-makers to be fêted outside the country. His 1963 film *Susuz Yaz* (A Dry Summer) won the Golden Bear at the Berlin Film Festival. His early films were mostly rural melodramas set in the harsh Anatolian countryside. Then, in 1964, Erksan made the astonishing *Suçlular Aramızda* (The Guilty Are Among Us). With this film, he began to abandon social realism and to examine the internal world of his troubled heroes and heroines. *Sevmek Zamanı* (A Time to Love) is the story of a man who falls in love with the portrait of a woman he has never met. *Sensiz Yaşayamam* (I Can't Live Without You) tells of the strange encounter on a lonely island of a man and a woman. The man is a hired killer and the woman is to be his next victim...

Erksan's sympathy for the tormented hero, as well as his feel for the fantastic, were the creative motors behind his 1976 film *Intikam Melegi: Kadın Hamlet* (The Angel of Vengeance). This is a modern day version of *Hamlet*, but with a female protagonist. Using acid-bright colours, a seventies disco score and helped by a *tour de force* performance from actress Fatma Girik, who is in almost every scene, Erksan turns in a real winner. His female Hamlet plays out her descent into madness in a series of surreal sets. Shot mostly outside the studio, on location, they give the film a unique look, entirely at odds with its claustrophobic story. It all builds to a suitably gory climax, with great splashes of red blood smeared across Fatma Girik's flared white trouser suit.

After this relative triumph, Turkish fantasy films of any sort became increasingly rare birds. The military take-over in 1980 and subsequent increase in censorship didn't help. For some reason, horror always gets up the noses of repressive regimes.

By the dawn of the eighties the distributor-led boom in domestic production had been reduced to a trickle. As the decade progressed, things only became worse. Keen to enter the European market, the new Prime Minister, Turgut Özal, began to implement many World Bank directives over free trade. The tightening up of legal controls within the film industry opened the way for foreign distributors. In 1987, 320 films were imported, compared with a domestic production of only ninety-six films. And that was a good year. New technology also began to have an effect, with made-for-video productions proliferating. Unfortunately, as taped 'quickies' like *Terrörist* and *AIDS* demonstrated, an exploitable subject matter doesn't always make for a good exploitation film. Even worse was *Lanetli Kadınlar* (Cursed Women), an 'erotic horror' film where a bunch of rather ageing ladies stroll about in their underwear while someone bumps them off one by one.

Below: Tatli Cadı *was a mildly kinky version of the TV hit* Bewitched.

The only serious contenders in the field of fantasy cinema were films like Atıf Yılmaz's *Adı Vasfiye* (Her Name is Vasfiye) and *Aaahhh Belinda*. These were gentle parables about loss of identity and a tentative search for meaning. They spoke volumes about the parlous situation for Turkish intellectuals in the politically repressed 1980s. *Ücünçü Göz* (The Third Eye), directed in 1989 by Orhan Oğuz, is genuinely disturbing. Here a film-maker who can't make a film becomes so obsessed by the project that he wills into existence his fictional main character, a young man whom he teaches to speak and act out parts of the film. Then he gives the man a gun. This is the prelude to an extremely gory ending, where the top of the writer's head is blown off and his brains splattered all over the pages of his discarded script.

From the middle of the decade this oneiric, allusive style of film-making contained the only echoes of anything remotely resembling fantasy cinema. The closest parallel would be the post-*nouvelle vague* works of someone like Jacques Rivette or Alain Resnais — arty, self-reflective and occasionally pretentious. Interestingly, one of the founding fathers of this particular French school of moviemaking, Alain Robbe-Grillet, had come to Istanbul in 1963 to make his first film, *L'Immortelle* (The Immortal One). That too was an arty, labyrinthine tale of love, loss and confused identities.

In the 1990s, Irfan Tözüm and Kutluğ Ataman continued this trend, occasionally edging closer to straight horror. In 1994, Tözüm's *Kiz Kulesi Aşklari* (The Lovers of the Tower of Leander) has a writer visit the tower of Leander, where he is haunted by the dead guardian of the place. He meets a mysterious young woman with whom he lives out the loves of the mythical Hera and Leander. In the same year, Ataman's *Karanlık Sular* (*The Serpent's Tale*) managed to mix East-West politics, fundamentalism, vampire mythology and structuralist discourse into a heady brew.

The film begins with a warning. The story we are about to watch is based on fragments of an old manuscript, the words of which have the power to entrance and to kill. A disparate group of individuals are searching for this manuscript, which seems to hold the secret of eternal life. Among the characters involved is a young child, apparently the incarnation of the 800 year-old Empress Theodora of Byzantium — who is now a vampire. Full of in-jokes and dead ends, *Karanlık Sular* plays so fast and loose with genre conventions that at times it comes across as an Argento script directed by Robbe-Grillet. More mythic games were played in *Şahmaran*, a version of the old snake woman legend. This 1994 film featured sixties female superstar Türkân Şoray — in her day, the Brigitte Bardot of the local film scene.

Interesting though these films are, they're a long way in spirit from the glorious days of the seventies-style cheesy epics. For the last blast of that particular trumpet we have to go back to 1982. Written by and starring Çüneyt Arkın, *Dünyayı Kurtaran Adam* (*The Man Who Saves the World*) is nothing less than a Turkish version of *Star Wars*, complete with clips 'borrowed' from the George Lucas classic. The story has two astronauts crash-landing on a distant planet

***Left:** A Turkish version of* Star Wars*, complete with clips 'borrowed' from the George Lucas epic.*

where they encounter an evil Ming-type ruler bent on conquering Earth. The film's director, Çetin Inanç, claims that the story was inspired by the power struggles going on at the time between the Turkish Mafia and the shopkeepers of Beyoğlu in the heart of Istanbul's business district. The use of footage from *Star Wars* was an extension of the metaphor. Just as the best American goods are displayed in the shops of Istiklal Caddesi, he explains, so his film incorporates highlights from the best of American cinema.

In fact, the film looks like an extended episode of *Doctor Who*, but made with a fraction of the budget. The scorpions that attack Arkın in one scene were constructed from large cockroaches with paper tails glued onto them. The mystic sword that our hero wields is obviously a painted plywood prop. Add to this monsters played by men in rubber joke-shop masks and, at one point, wrapped in pink bath mats, and you have a 'bad film' classic.

Dünyayı Kurtaran Adam was the swan-song of low-budget Turkish cinema. The relentless rise of television and the imminent flood of foreign movies meant that audiences would no longer be satisfied with the poverty row productions of their own cash-starved industry. As profits began to dwindle, the producers and distributors who had benefited from the twenty-year boom moved on to pastures new, abandoning film production for good.

Çüneyt Arkın commented that, in its heyday, Turkish cinema was like a family. Its successes were celebrated and its weaknesses were overlooked, the way a family forgives the faults of its own members. Well, to continue his metaphor, by the mid-eighties the family had fallen apart, arguments over the family jewels had replaced cosy dinner table conversation.

The 1980s saw only a handful of Turkish fantasy films, most of them imitations of Western hits. *Badi* (Duckling), from 1983, was a local version of *E.T.* (!), and Remzi Jöntürk's *Altar* was heavily 'influenced' by *Conan the Barbarian*. The film business was in the doldrums. Even the Italians had stopped coming. One of their last visits was for the 1982 film *Yor — The Hunter From the Future*. This low-budget epic melded science fiction, pre-history and unintentional comedy into a uniquely entertaining brew. Originally a three-and-a-half hour television series cut to ninety minutes for cinema release, the film featured several Euro stars, such as Corinne Clery (*Hitch Hike, The Story of O*) and John Steiner (*Caligula, Shock*).

Yor was directed by the Italian fantasy specialist Antonio Margheriti. He still has fond memories of the film: "It was one of the most successful pictures of my life! And I mean, look at it, it's so bad!... It was one of those attempts to combine the Italian and Turkish film industries, and the results are always something very special! I enjoy looking for *Yor* in those movie guides and I always discover a 'bomb' or a 'turkey' rating. It was a fun project, made with almost no budget."

For film fans from the West, where production costs have now escalated to such an extent that $5,000,000 is cheap, that's the greatest discovery of these Turkish fantasy films. Their cardboard sets, stylised acting and outrageous plots give them a charm that's almost totally absent from our screens these days. Critic Alain Petit, in an article in the French fanzine *Fusion Fantasy*, explains:

'I love these films for their weaknesses, but also for their strengths. For they give us the chance to rediscover something, to re-establish contact with a cinema we thought had gone forever. In these films we find again those things that first drew us to this style of movie-making. We call it 'B', but for the Turkish audience it's simply Cinema, with a capital 'C'. A naïve cinema, certainly, poverty-stricken, maybe, but rich in escapism, absolutely enchanting, with its own dream-like quality. And such dreams are getting hard to find these days.' ■

By Pete Tombs and Giovanni Scognamillo

The Strange World of Mr Marins

The career of Brazil's José Mojica Marins has been a strange one indeed. It's a long and twisting road that's taken him from banned film-maker in the 1960s to 'cool ghoul' of the American fandom circuit today. Once upon a time he was a dangerous, wild-eyed madman, staring out of the screen and conjuring evil spells with his long-clawed fingers. Audiences screamed in terror. Now he kisses babies on the streets of São Paulo and their mothers scream with delight. In Brazil they call him Zé do Caixão, in America he's now acquired the more manageable name of Coffin Joe. Looking for a cuddly new king of 'trash cinema', the world-wide cult for kitsch has plonked Marins down onto a throne that he seems only too happy to occupy. Once, though, it was all so different...

Like the work of all true primitives, Marins' early films are full of the subtleties of a soul confronting the essential questions as though for the very first time, without artifice. There is a terrifying energy that bursts from the screen in these films. This raw force reflects Marins' personality and is a product of the uncompromising will that kept him going through the kinds of setbacks that would have sunk most men.

Marins was born in 1936 in São Paulo, where he still lives. His father Antonio had emigrated from Spain, intending to pursue a career as a bullfighter, but eventually ended up running a cinema. Later, in his filmed autobiographical testament *Demônios e Maravilhas* (*Demons and Wonders*), Marins pays tribute to his dying father, telling him that "Your kingdom of fantasy inspired everything I've ever done."

It was from his father that young José received his first 8mm movie camera. The process of filming fascinated him and soon he was showing 16mm shorts in the tents of travelling carnivals. His initial attempts to make a full-length feature were disastrous. In *Sentença de Deus* (The Judgement of God), three different actresses tried their hand at the female lead and all of them met gruesome real-life fates. The first drowned in her swimming pool, the second contracted tuberculosis and the third poor unfortunate lost both legs in an accident. His second project, the appropriately named *O Auge do Desespero* (The Depths of Despair), had to be abandoned when a storm destroyed the sets and equipment, including Marins' precious camera.

In 1959, at the age of twenty-three, Marins embarked on what would be his first completed feature, *A Sina do Aventureiro* (The Adventurer's Fate). The film was a kind of native Western, set in wild and remote terrain. Marins had to leave his pregnant wife behind to go on location. When he returned to São Paulo he discovered that not only had his wife miscarried, but much of the footage he had brought back was out of focus.

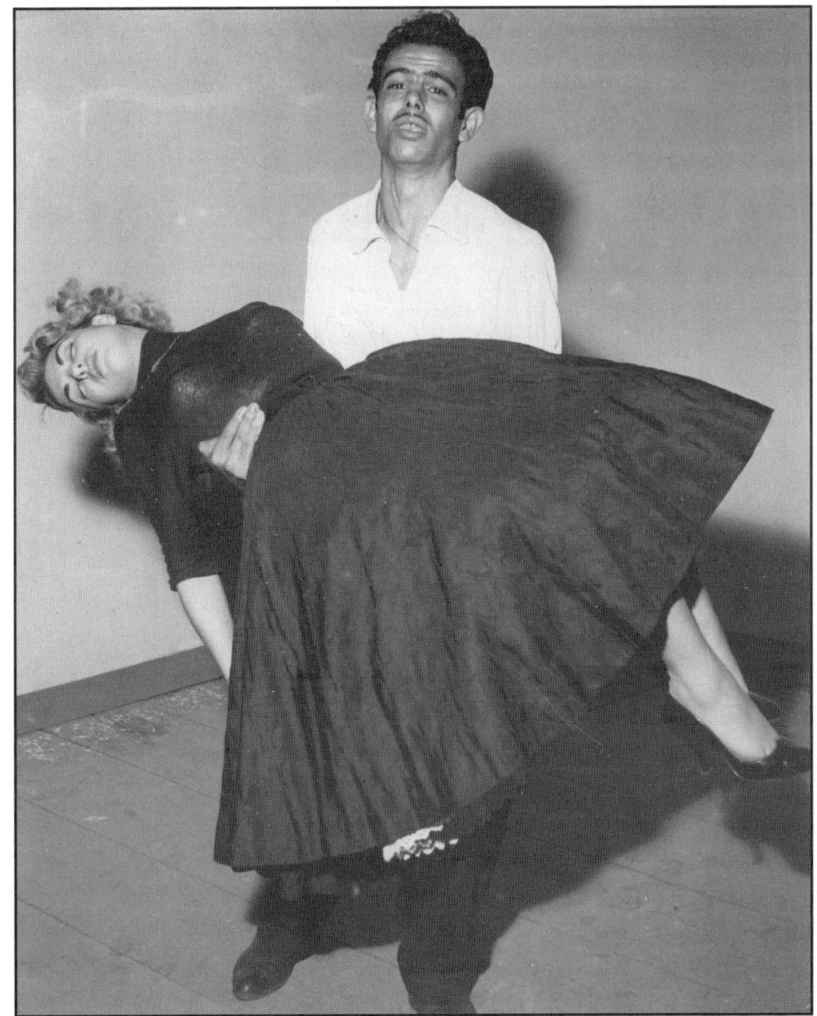

***Opposite:** José Mojica Marins as Zé do Caixão.*

***Above:** The seventeen year-old Marins in* Sentença de Deus.

Given this stormy start to his career it's not surprising that Marins' thoughts eventually turned to horror. What might seem strange is that so few film-makers in Brazil had tried it before him. Brazil is a country imbued with a genuine feeling for magic and mysticism. Its mix of racial and religious groups has produced a rich and complex folklore,

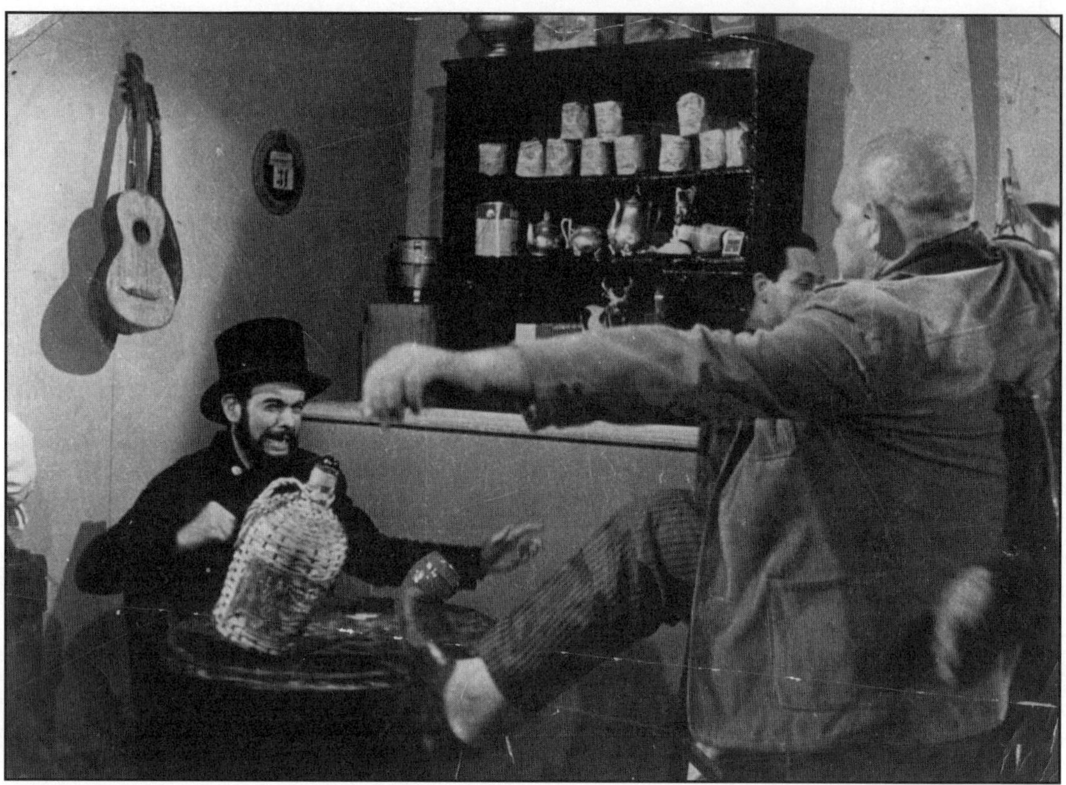

Right: *The sadistic Zé do Caixão provokes a bar-room brawl in* À Meia-noite Levarei sua Alma. *The barman (just visible) was played by Marins' father.*

filled with strange creatures: the *homen-marinho*, the man of the sea, who devours people's fingers and private parts; the *saci-perere*, a one-legged dwarf that lives in the forest; and the *jaracaca*, a type of vampire in the form of a snake that sucked from the breasts of nursing mothers. From Portugal came the *lobishomen*, a kind of werewolf whose bite has a decidedly erotic effect on its mostly female victims. Monsters with their feet turned backwards, headless mules and a whole army of grotesques sprang out of the mystic melting pot of Brazil. This colourful mythology seems to have inspired remarkably few films. From the early thirties through to the late fifties, the most popular form of cinema locally was the *chanchada*. These were musical comedies featuring all sorts of jolly rogues and low-life adventurers.

When, in 1963, he began work on *À Meia-noite Levarei sua Alma* (*At Midnight I'll Take Your Soul Away*) Marins had almost no Brazilian models to draw on. His main inspiration was comic books, particularly 1950s horror comics like the EC *Tales From the Crypt* series. Like them, *À Meia-noite Levarei sua Alma* begins with a warning. A wild-eyed gypsy woman clutching a skull stares into the camera and tells us to leave the cinema. "Don't watch this film... Go home!" Then as the church bells ring midnight she realises that it's too late. We are determined to test ourselves, to see if we can stand the ultimate horror. Very well, she says: "Stick around. Suffer! But be warned," she hisses, bending even closer to the camera, "for at midnight, I'll take your soul away!"

Unlike most classic horror films, *À Meia-noite...* is set in a very real location, a poor town in upstate São Paulo. The local population are terrorised by a godless undertaker called Zé do Caixão (José of the Grave). Dressed all in black, with a cloak and tall stove pipe hat, he swaggers through the small community, insulting men, leering at women and breaking religious taboos. Marins, who plays the part, brings a terrifying authority to the role.

Zé's mistress Lenita is unable to bear the child that he so desperately wants. He has set his sights on another girl, Terezinha. She seems too good for him, remote and pure. Even worse, she's the fiancée of Zé's only real friend, Antonio. But to Zé, who has no conventional morality, things like friendship are little more than a useful convenience. Antonio is just a drinking companion and someone Zé enjoys shocking with his outrageously irreligious views.

Zé kills Lenita in an incredibly sadistic way, taping her mouth so she can't scream and then dropping a huge poisonous spider onto her. He watches with glee as she writhes in horror while the spider crawls over her body. With Lenita out of the way, he then bumps off Antonio. On the evening after Antonio's funeral, Zé visits the distraught Terezinha and rapes her.

He scolds her for her ungratefulness: "After all I did to rid you of that idiot."

Terezinha hangs herself. But not before she has cursed Zé and promised to drag his soul to Hell. A disappointed Zé realises he will have to continue his search for the ideal woman to bear his child. One night he meets a female visitor to the town who seems to match his requirements exactly: pretty, young and with no apparent religious beliefs. It's the Day of the Dead and Zé is the only man brave (or foolish) enough to escort the woman through the cemetery to her aunt's house.

As Zé walks slowly back through the dark graveyard, planning his seduction of the new girl, the atmosphere of the place begins to affect him. He becomes aware of sounds, maybe even voices, and seems to hear footsteps when there's no one there. He stops to light his pipe and a hand appears out of the darkness holding a candle. He sees the horribly disfigured body of his murdered friend, Antonio. Zé stumbles through the cemetery in a state of shock, bumping into gravestones, until suddenly he is confronted with an even more ghastly sight: the mythical 'procession of the dead', marching in spectral line through the cemetery. At the heart of the procession an open coffin is being carried. And the body in the coffin is Zé himself.

À Meia-noite... was unusual in Brazil for lots of reasons, and not just because it was the country's first full-blooded horror film. It was also a film with a determinedly irreligious and provocative approach. Although basically a Western (like *High Noon*, a bad guy taunts the good citizens who are afraid to fight back), the law that Zé is challenging is not the law of man but that of God. In a country where the Catholic church was still a powerful force, this was a dangerous stance to adopt.

"Destroy me, I believe in nothing!" Zé challenges God one drunken night after he has desecrated the graves in the cemetery.

Alongside its sacrilegious attitude, were many scenes of violence, sex and sadism, unprecedented for a film from 1963. What makes these scenes specially disturbing is the luridly upfront way they're presented. Before he rapes Terezinha, Zé beats her savagely, then kisses her bleeding mouth, licking the blood from his lips. The spider that he uses to kill Lenita is very obviously a real one. It's huge and hairy and, were the actress not gagged, her screams would be real too. In another shocking scene, Zé pokes out the eyes of the local doctor with his sharp fingernails. These scenes, and many more like them, are not hinted at or shown in flashes. They're presented in full, glaring close-up, the camera lingering on Lenita's terrified face, for example, or on the doctor's gore-filled eye sockets. The film is full of small but disturbing details. Like the bird that Terezinha holds in her hand, squeezing it to death as Zé rapes her.

The most unsettling aspect of *À Meia-noite...* remains the figure of Zé do Caixão. He's a villain, but a villain you can't simply despise. Although almost entirely evil, Zé is also very honest and direct. He speaks his mind and really believes in what he says and does. He acts without fear and without hypocrisy. He challenges the terrified community to stand up to him and mocks their failure to do so. On the other hand, you feel he would also praise them if they dared to oppose him. One of the rare characters who does disagree with Zé gets two of his fingers chopped off with a broken bottle. And then, having mutilated him, Zé announces: "I like brave men. I'll pay for the treatment."

In many ways, Zé is like Nietzsche's Zarathustra, a man beyond good and evil. Like Zarathustra, Zé believes in action. He's a real existentialist. The purpose of life is to live, is his message. The local townspeople are prisoners of their own superstitions and fears.

"Yes, I am a rebel — against fools like you," announces Zé to his friend Antonio. "You fear what you don't see and become slaves of that which really exists — life."

Another mythic character Zé resembles is that other sharp-clawed movie demon, Freddy Krueger. Like Freddy, Zé always says what he feels, and also like Freddy, he's fond of sick jokes and gallows humour. "I want so much to make you happy," his mistress tells him. "You're going to make me very, very happy," Zé assures her. "I'll have the pleasure of seeing you die before my very own eyes."

Over the course of the films that followed his début, Zé, like Freddy, would move from the real world into the realm of dreams, to become a kind of mythic bogeyman, haunting the edges of people's nightmares and eventually presiding over his own hell.

Like several other characters from the world of horror (Dracula, the Frankenstein monster, Mr Hyde), the demonic Zé do Caixão was the product of a troubled dream. In this case, a dream that came at a crucial time for Marins. After his bad experiences trying to make feature films in the late fifties, he had dabbled in publishing, with a fotonovella series called *A Voz do Cinema* (The Voice of Cinema). Again the experiment failed, and this time Marins ended up flat broke. He was forced to move in with his wife's family. The stress and disappointment made him ill. His family thought

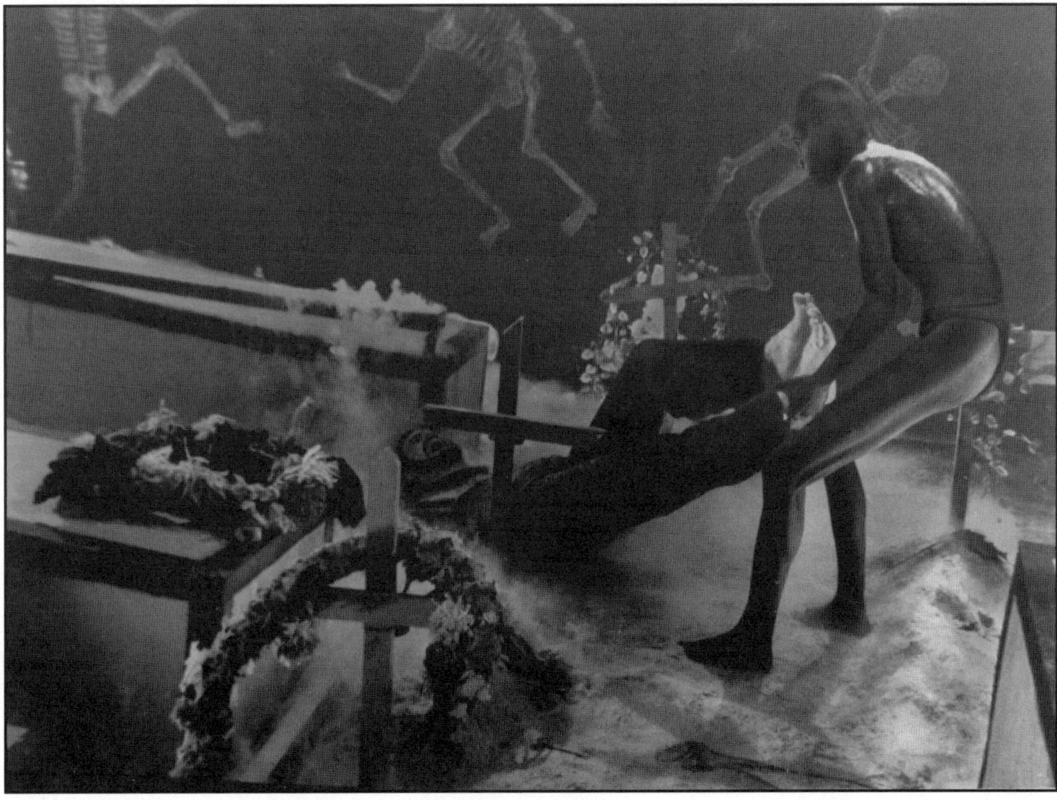

***Left:** Zé do Caixão is dragged off to Hell in* Esta Noite Encarnarei no Teu Cadáver.

he was going mad. Even a Macumba priest was unable to help him. He fell into a deep fever and experienced a powerful vision. He saw a terrifying, wild-eyed man in black. The man grabbed hold of Marins and dragged him off to an overgrown graveyard. He found himself confronting a huge headstone with his own name carved into it. Even worse, he now saw the grinning face of the man in black and realised it was himself.

The very next day, Marins rose from his sick bed, got dressed and went off to see his producers to tell them he had an idea for an astonishing new movie. Even the title had come to him in a flash. The plot and main character of the film were firmly fixed in his head even before a word of the script had been written. In just two weeks, shooting in a converted São Paulo synagogue, the film was in the can.

The story of Zé do Caixão as originally conceived by Marins was to be developed over six films. However, even with the notoriety afforded the first part of the story, there were few backers brave enough to fund a sequel. Moreover, a censorship bottleneck held up the film's release for over a year. To pay off his debts, Marins took on the completion of a film produced by the distributor of *À Meia-noite Levarei sua Alma.* Fortunately the final product was a hit and in 1966 the second part of the Zé do Caixão saga, *Esta Noite Encarnarei no Teu Cadáver* (*Tonight I'll Incarnate in Your Corpse*), was back on the rails.

***Below:** Marins watches as a potential actress is 'tested' for a role in his next film. Here, a slimy toad is being dropped down her cleavage.*

The demonic Zé survives the shock in the cemetery and returns to the poor benighted town. There he continues to search for the perfect woman to bear him a son. This time he has a willing assistant in the form of the hunchbacked Bruno. In a specially constructed torture chamber, Zé subjects a variety of hapless females to a series of tests. In one scene, dozens of live spiders are let loose in the room where the women are sleeping. Those who fail the tests are dumped into a snake pit.

At last Zé finds his perfect woman, Laura, the daughter of a powerful local landowner. However, his joy is marred by the discovery that one of the women he killed in his search was pregnant. In a terrifying vision, Zé is dragged by a spindly demon to a lonely graveyard. Dozens of hands spring out of the ground to pull him head-first into Hell, where he witnesses the torments of the damned and sees himself as Satan, presiding over a litany of horrors.

The scenes in Hell are the highlight of the picture, filmed in colour and shot through with Marins' unique mixture of tackiness and terror. No one really knows where he got his inspiration from, but these scenes are like a combination of Hieronymous Bosch and the ghost train from a travelling carnival. Marins' trump card was making his Hell a place of freezing ice and falling snow rather than the traditional flaming pit. Papier mâché walls were constructed and dozens of extras were glued up inside them, their arms, legs and heads poking through. Demons with pitchforks, chains and evil grins march up and down the corridors of this unique Hell, poking and prodding at the poor unfortunate sinners, while the heavily echoed soundtrack plays a series of cries, moans and whipcracks.

Zé wakes from his nightmare to find that his mistress is pregnant. His joy, however, is short-lived. The mother dies during childbirth and the baby is stillborn. With his spirit broken, Zé is hunted down by the angry townspeople. He falls into a swamp and is dragged to his death by the ghosts of his victims.

In many ways the film is like a demented, drug altered version of *À Meia-noite Levarei sua Alma.* The story is similar but the leering sense of evil is more pronounced, its set pieces more charged with an hallucinatory quality. In the first film, Zé is at his most powerful when entering into scenes. The classic shot is in the local bar. The bar is in a basement with steps leading down to it. Every time Zé appears, the door flies open and there he stands at the top of the steps, grinning. In the second film, with Zé as the King of Hell, he appears at the top of another flight of steps — only these are made out of naked human bodies down which he strides, grinning madly.

The film was a big hit. By now people were starting to appreciate the uniqueness of Marins' vision. Popular magazines were featuring stories about him and the dedicated team who worked in his São Paulo synagogue. He was invited onto television and radio programmes to talk about his work and his ideas. In particular, audiences were fascinated by stories of his auditions where pretty, half-naked actresses were made to caress huge toads and snakes, and have poisonous spiders crawl all over them.

In fact, these auditions were an economic necessity. Marins didn't have the means to create realistic fake spiders. He found a man who bred them as a convenient way of frightening off burglars: they were cheaper than guard dogs and you didn't need to take them for walks. Marins hired

Left: In the snake pit, from Esta Noite Encarnarei no Teu Cadáver.
Below: Marins played the part of a carnival fakir in O Profeta da Fome.

dozens of the brutes for the torture scene in *Esta Noite Encarnarei no Teu Cadáver*, but when they were let loose the actresses panicked and ran off set. To make sure this didn't happen in future, Marins tested all his cast members to see if they were up to it.

Such colourful stories began to contribute to the growing myth of Brazil's king of horror. They also began to confuse the line between Marins the man and his creation Zé do Caixão. As his notoriety grew, so did interest in him from a surprising source: the left-leaning intellectuals and film-makers of the post-*cinema novo* movement.

In the late sixties, Brazilian society and Brazilian cinema were going through changes. The military-controlled government that gained power in 1964 had effectively banned opposition parties and imposed a new, highly repressive, constitution. In São Paulo, where Marins lived and worked, a cinematic underground was being formed. Taking their name from a working class district called Boca do Lixo (Mouth of Garbage), this new movement was named *cinema do lixo* (or 'trash cinema'). Although he predated them by several years, the underground film-makers saw Marins as one of their own. To oppose the increasingly glossy products of *cinema novo*, they envisaged a form of film-making that was cheap, raw and provocative. Exactly the kinds of films that Marins was making.

Marins' connection with the São Paulo underground led to him acting in films like Rogério Sganzerla's *O Abismu, ou Sois Todos de Mu* (The Abyss, or We're All From Mu) and working on a horror project with Ozualdo Candeias, one of the founders of the *cinema do lixo* movement. For former critic Maurício Capovilla he starred in *O Profeta da Fome* (The Prophet of Hunger). Here Marins plays a carnival fakir much given to grandiose gestures — not unlike a down at heel Zé do Caixão, in fact.

The intellectuals loved Marins, and he was happy to make use of the credibility they gave him in what would be his next full-length Zé do Caixão film, *Ritual dos Sadicos* (*Ritual of the Maniacs*). But before going into production on that, Marins worked, in 1968, on a couple of horror anthologies, each featuring three short films. He only directed one episode of *Trilogia de Terror* (*Trilogy of Terror*), but the second anthology movie, *O Estranho Mundo de Zé do Caixão* (*The Strange World of Zé do Caixão*) was all his. The film also marked the beginning an association with another recent Marins fan, the popular Brazilian horror writer R. F. Lucchetti.

All three stories are concerned in various ways with voyeurism and the power of the look. The first, *O Fabricante de Bonecas* (*The Dollmaker*), features a strange old man who makes dolls with human eyes. *Tara* (*Obsession*) was an experiment in making a film without any dialogue. It tells of a poor hunchback who follows a rich society girl through the streets of São Paulo, observing her in bars and restaurants with her rich admirers. On the day of her wedding, the girl

***Right:** Marins, his cast and crew at the opening of* Quando os Deuses Adormecem.

is murdered by a jealous love rival. The hunchback breaks into her crypt to possess her corpse.

The final story, *Ideologia* (*Theory*) is the most shocking. It's also one of Marins' most coherent expositions of the Sadean philosophy of Zé do Caixão. The main protagonist is a man called Professor Oaxiac Odez (Zé do Caixão spelled backwards!). We first meet him on a television show called *Homens Que Fazem a Notícia* (People Who Make the News). He is being interrogated by a panel of pundits about his theories of human behaviour. Instinct, asserts the Professor, will always triumph over reason. Foremost among the dissenters is Alfredo, an urbane journalist. After the programme is over, Odez invites the man and his wife to visit him. Then, he claims, he will present evidence to prove his theory.

In Odez's mist-shrouded mansion, the suave Alfredo and his svelte wife, Vilma, are presented with staged tableaux, featuring a series of horrific and sadistic episodes: a man is tortured upside-down and then eaten alive, a chained woman has acid thrown in her face and a man has huge needles stuck through his skin. As the horrors unfold, Odez keeps reminding Alfredo and his wife that the people performing these hideous acts were normal, civilised people — just like themselves — before Odez "treated" them.

The outraged couple try to leave, but Odez's assistants restrain them. They hold the couple's heads so that they are forced to look at the horrific sight before them. This metaphor for the act of seeing a film goes right back to the gypsy's warning in *À Meia-noite Levarei sua Alma.* If you stay to watch the film, you have to accept the worst it has to offer.

After his "burlesque show" is over, Odez imprisons Alfredo and his wife in two separate cages in his dungeon. There, for the next seven days, he visits them to read various passages from the Bible and to tempt them to give up their altruistic views. Eventually the Professor stabs Alfredo in the neck, and his wife, whom hunger and fear has reduced to an animal level, sucks the blood from the wound.

"Instinct has triumphed!" declares the Professor. The next scene shows Odez and his helpers sitting down to a cannibal feast composed of the bodies of Alfredo and his wife.

The conclusion the film draws is, of course, preposterous. But it remains an almost perfect *conte cruel.* The great cynic Ambrose Bierce would have loved it. The censor, however, was not of the same mind and insisted on a new ending where Odez's house is destroyed in a series of explosions.

By now Marins was at the height of his popularity. He was desperate to start work on a third Zé do Caixão film, but was still unable to find backers for the project. It was certainly an ambitious scenario. Zé takes LSD and imagines himself being flushed down a toilet. He emerges in Purgatory, where a Christ-like figure leads him to the shores of a huge yellow lake. In fact, they are inside the human body. Zé enters the testicles and through intercourse passes to the female womb where he witnesses "the wedding of the King and the Queen — the beginning of life..."

Keen to capitalise on his fame and to keep alive the spirit of Zé, Marins used some of the elements of the story in his next project, *Ritual dos Sadicos.*

The starting point for the film was a television chat show, of the type that Marins had already parodied in the third episode of *O Estranho Mundo de Zé do Caixão.* In 1969, he had been invited to take part in a program called *Quem tem Medo da Verdade?* (Who's Afraid of the Truth?). Here he was subjected to questions by a panel of self-important 'experts' to determine whether or not he was a fake. At the end of the programme they considered their verdict: guilty or not guilty. In *Ritual dos Sadicos,* Marins had the last laugh by creating a fictional television show, *Homens Que Fazem a Notícia,* on which he appeared as a mostly silent guest. The panel was composed of his heavyweight friends from the cinema and art world. They included film-makers Carlos

Reichenbach and Maurício Capovilla and critic Jairo Ferreira. *Cinema do lixo* film pioneer Ozualdo Candeias was also roped in to play a character in the movie.

At the time the film was made, in the late 1960s, Brazil was rather belatedly discovering hippies, drugs and the rock and roll lifestyle. For a man who makes images with the power of screaming tabloid headlines, the hippie movement was a godsend. In fact, Marins would use the idea of drug and sex orgies in several films over the coming years. *Ritual dos Sadicos* begins with a shot of a young girl injecting something into her foot. The act is shown in clinical detail in a long, unwavering close-up. We see the needle going in and the skin puckering up as the liquid passes through it. Then the camera pulls back to show a group of nervous, sweaty men looking on excitedly. They nod towards an object wrapped in newspaper. Beside themselves with expectation, they watch as the girl unwraps a chamber pot. Laughing, she strips and lowers herself onto the pot. As she urinates, a tiny record player blares out a Brazilian protest song:

"War! War! War!
A word I deplore, That drives deep inside;
There's nowhere to hide, When it comes to kill
Until all is still..."

The first half of the film consists of similarly weird and bizarre scenes. They are being described, by a psychologist, to a panel of fellow academics to illustrate the level of degeneracy that drugs can induce. Some of the episodes are not much more than in-jokes for Marins' arty friends: well known stage actress Ítala Nandi, for example, appears in a short sketch with a lecherous and repulsive film producer. Other episodes show Marins' startling originality and put to good use the live-action horror shows he was working on at the time. The most bizarre episode is like something out of an Artaud-inspired Theatre of Cruelty piece.

A girl is taken to a seedy furnished room, where a bunch of wild-eyed hippies are cavorting. One of them lies on his back playing a sentimental song on the guitar. Another man, perched on top of a set of step ladders, beats a drum kit, while a third man hangs upside-down from the wall. They chant, they smoke dope, at one point they all start whistling the Colonel Bogey march from *The Bridge On the River Kwai.* Then the door opens and a robed figure enters carrying a long, gnarled staff and a set of engraved tablets. The girl lies down and, shown only in silhouette, the hippie Moses appears to insert his staff inside the girl's vagina.

Marins' part in the enterprise is explained gradually. The professor is writing a book about his theories of the human mind. He wants to conduct an experiment involving LSD. Four people from different walks of life, all of them drug addicts, have agreed to take part. After exploring various forms of visual stimulant — a theatre show, a hippie rock act etc — the four all concur that Marins' film, *Esta Noite Encarnarei no Teu Cadáver,* was the one that moved them the most. The professor has them take the drug in a bare room dominated by a huge poster of Zé do Caixão. Gradually, all four of them enter his strange world and each has a very different view of it when they finally emerge.

The half hour showing the quartet's visions contains some of the strangest and most powerful images ever put onto celluloid. Far from the high-tech, computer-generated fantasies of Hollywood, these visions are much rawer and more disturbing. Marins makes a positive advantage of his low budget to create effects that few art directors would dare to even dream of. In one scene, a man is menaced by

***Below:** From the hallucination sequence in* O Despertar da Besta.

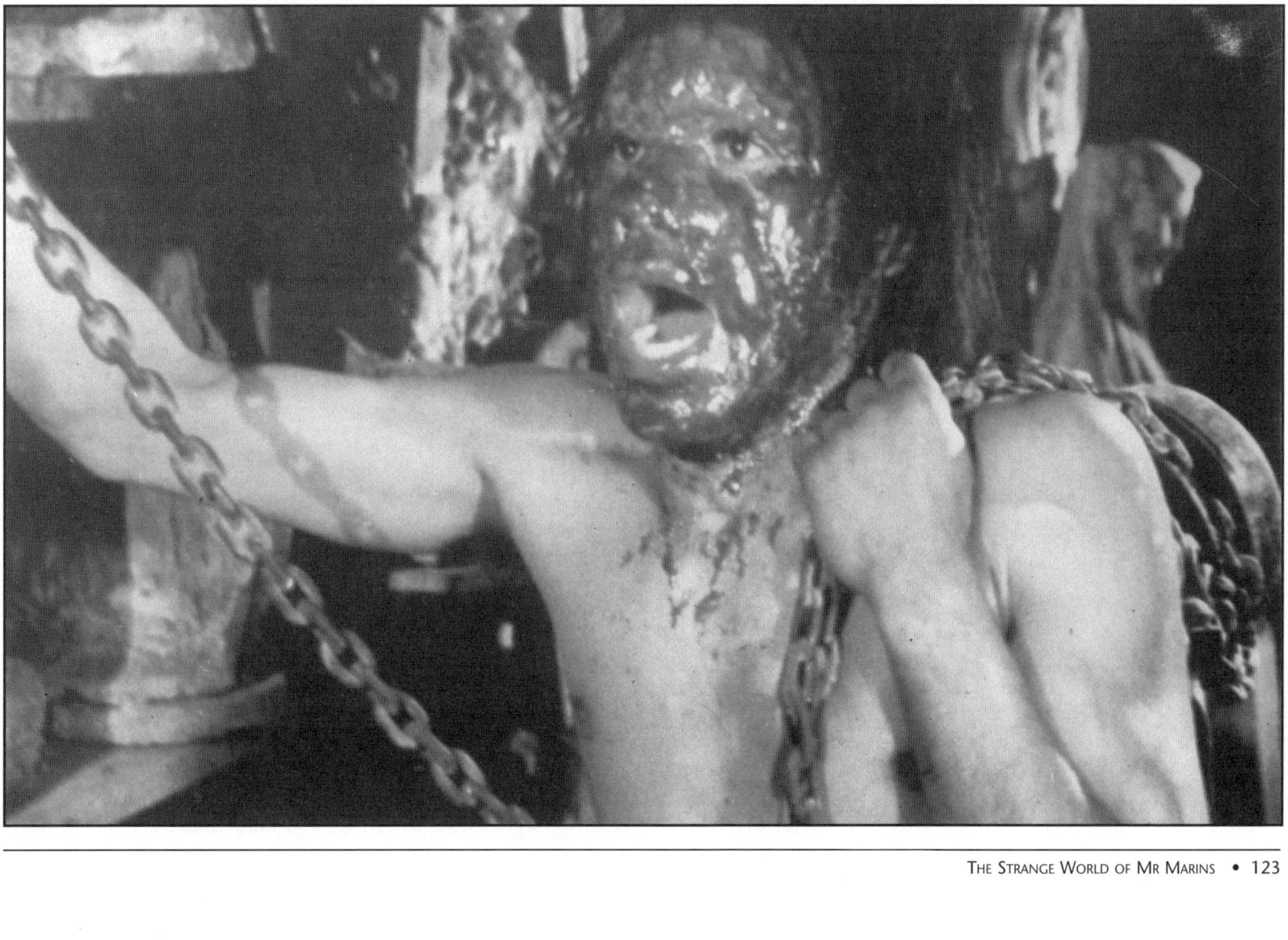

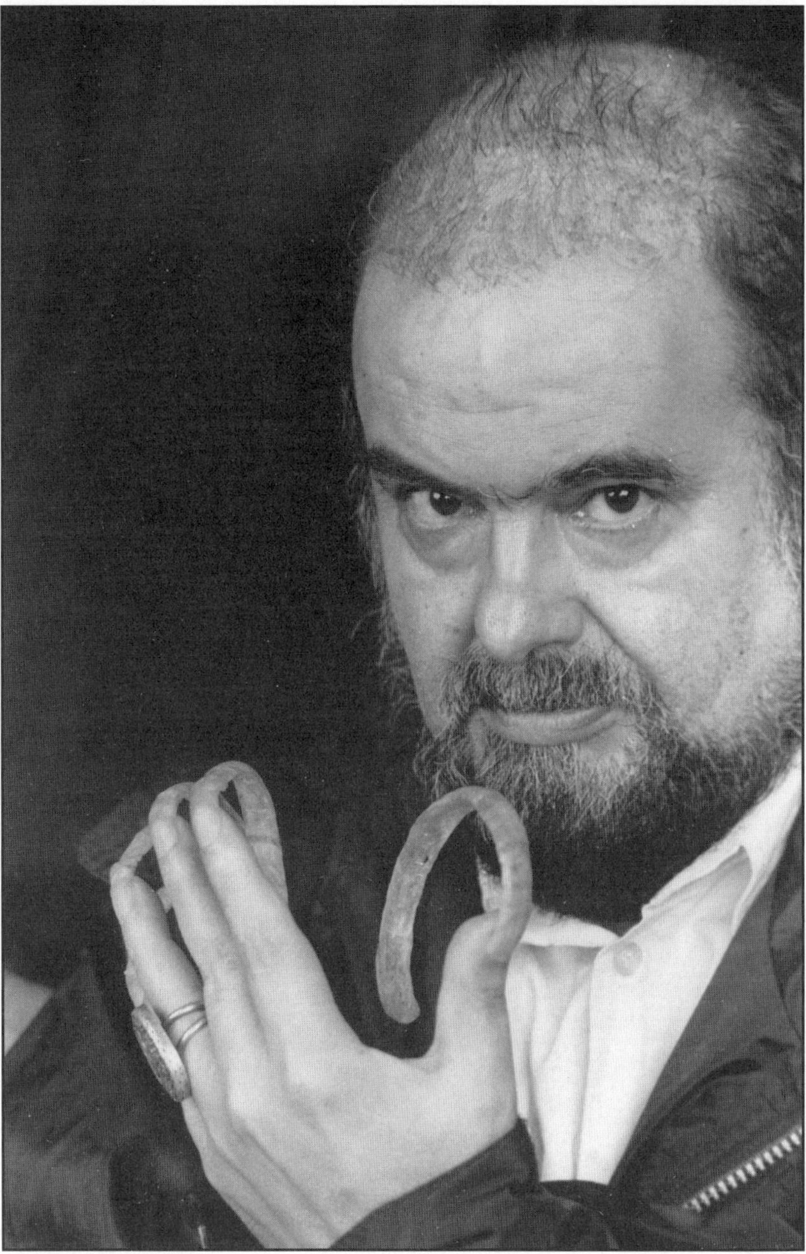

***Above:** Marins in 1997, his trademark fingernails still uncut.*

strange, fleshy faces that appear to be closing in on him. Gradually it becomes obvious that these 'faces' are in fact a row of human arses, with features painted onto them, including moustaches and top hats. The natural reaction would be to laugh, but the hellish context of the scene makes the trick almost unbearably bizarre.

The sense of fear and isolation that these scenes create is quite terrifying. Like a powerful drug, the film can only be taken in small doses and is difficult to watch more than once. *Ritual dos Sadicos* may well be Marins' best film. It's definitely his strangest. The line between good and bad taste is crossed so many times it ceases to have any meaning. It soon becomes impossible to judge the images presented to us; we simply have to experience them. It's certainly the closest thing to a genuine acid trip ever put on film.

The film's final punchline is the revelation that the professor had not, after all, used LSD. What the subjects had been injected with was distilled water. The visions they experienced had been entirely self-induced, under the powerful influence of Zé do Caixão. The film ends with a close up of Marins' smiling face staring benignly into the camera. It's been a good joke, but so much more than just that.

The authorities predictably failed to see the humour. The film was promptly banned. In fact, it wasn't shown on screen in Brazil until 1986.

One of the things that emerges from *Ritual dos Sadicos* is the increasing fame of Marins and his demonic creation. The opening credits are played out over a selection of panels from Zé do Caixão comic books and there are references in the film both to his television shows and to the extensive range of Zé do Caixão products available at the time. These included not only posters featuring the character, but also such bizarre items as Zé do Caixão nail polish and perfume. There was even a carnival song about him, snatches of which are heard on the soundtrack.

Unfortunately, none of this was sufficient to persuade producers to fund the long-awaited third part of the Zé do Caixão saga. They seemed afraid of the notoriety that went with the name. Rather than stand still, Marins began to experiment with different kinds of films. Over the years he has made Westerns, sex comedies and adventure films. In fact, *Esta Noite Encarnarei no Teu Cadáver* marked the last appearance of the 'original' Zé. Subsequent sightings of him have all been in the form of dreams or hallucinations. The real-life Zé, the godless undertaker from the country, is presumably still at the bottom of the swamp.

The notion of Zé and Marins as one and the same thing (or of Zé as a projection of Marins' 'psychopathic' personality) has been proposed by several critics over the years. Disproving this mistaken notion seems to have been Marins' intention when he created the mysterious character of Finis Hominis. This benign, Christ-like figure (his name means 'the end of man') appeared in two little-seen films made in the early 1970s.

Finis Hominis — O Fim do Homem (Finis Hominis — The End of Man), released in 1971, begins with a naked man rising from the sea. To the astonishment of passers-by he parades silently through the streets of a nearby town, righting wrongs and making weighty pronouncements as the soundtrack plays a bouncy, bubblegum version of 'Raindrops Keep Falling on My Head'. "Truth is in every one of us!" he announces grandly. And: "The true miracle is the existence of mankind." The end of the film sees Finis Hominis returning to the insane asylum from where he had escaped. "I told you he always comes back," one of the doctors remarks to a companion.

The first Finis Hominis film was no great commercial success. It only played for a couple of weeks in São Paulo. However, the following year came a second part of the saga. Essentially a repetition of the first film, *Quando os Deuses Adormecem* (*When the Gods Fall Asleep*) begins with Finis Hominis leaving the asylum again and entering a world where God has ceased to have any importance. To the familiar strains of the 'Raindrops Keep Falling on My Head' theme, he sorts out a fight in a *favela*, saves a virgin from being sacrificed and stops two men from killing themselves. On his return to the asylum, it is discovered that the mysterious benefactor whose cheques have kept the place going is in fact Finis Hominis himself.

The two films, while in no way horror movies, are interesting mirror images of the Zé do Caixão films. Here the desire to provoke through evil acts is replaced by the ability to conjure up the positive power that lies dormant in people's hearts. The message all the way through is that the meaning of life is only to be found in action and that we all carry our purpose within us. The one lasting image that survives from the films is Marins, stark naked, parading through the crowded streets to the very real astonishment of unsuspecting passers-by. To create Zé do Caixão, Marins cloaked himself from head to toe in the garments of evil; Finis Hominis shows him stark naked and open to the world.

During the early seventies, the most popular Brazilian films, and the ones least likely to suffer from problems with the censor, were softcore sex comedies. These were called *pornochanchada*, an ironic nod to the *chanchada* musicals of a more innocent age. Marins worked on a couple of sex movies in the early 1970s. Later he graduated to hardcore porn as censorship loosened in the mid-eighties. However, in 1974 something unexpected happened: he was invited to France to present his work at a festival of *film fantastique* in Paris.

As related in his celluloid autobiography *Demons and Wonders*, this event had huge personal significance for Marins. It showed that, in spite of his inability to make a new horror film in Brazil, he was at least finding recognition overseas. Perhaps this could provide the breakthrough he needed. At the festival he met mavericks like Jean Rollin, as well as international stars like Christopher Lee, whom Marins tried to sign up for one of his own films! The incident was reported in the Brazilian press and Marins returned home to find himself something of a celebrity. The resulting fame led to his most mainstream movie to date, *Exorcismo Negro* (*Black Exorcism*).

The film's posters and publicity made great play of the José Mojica Marins/Zé do Caixão connection and the film begins with Marins on-set shooting a scene for one of his horror anthologies, *A Estranha Hospedaria dos Prazeres*

***Left:** Two masters of horror: Marins with Christopher Lee at a Paris convention in 1974.* ***Below:** 'Bring on the dancing girls!'* Exorcismo Negro.

(Strange Hotel of Naked Pleasures). It's coming up to Christmas, and the famous film director decides to spend the holiday with the family of an old friend who lives up country. Here he's welcomed like a true star. As he works on the script for his next movie, strange things begin to happen. Furniture starts to move by itself, his friend's elderly father goes crazy and tries to kill Marins, a toy piano plays at night, and snakes and spiders crawl over the Christmas tree.

It transpires that the family's eldest daughter, Vilma, was the product of a pact with a witch. The girl's terrified mother is now trying to break the deal, in which she promised her daughter in marriage to the Son of Satan. The climax of the film has Marins taking on the Devil's disciple, who appears in the guise of Zé do Caixão.

"You're *my* creation! You can't be more powerful than

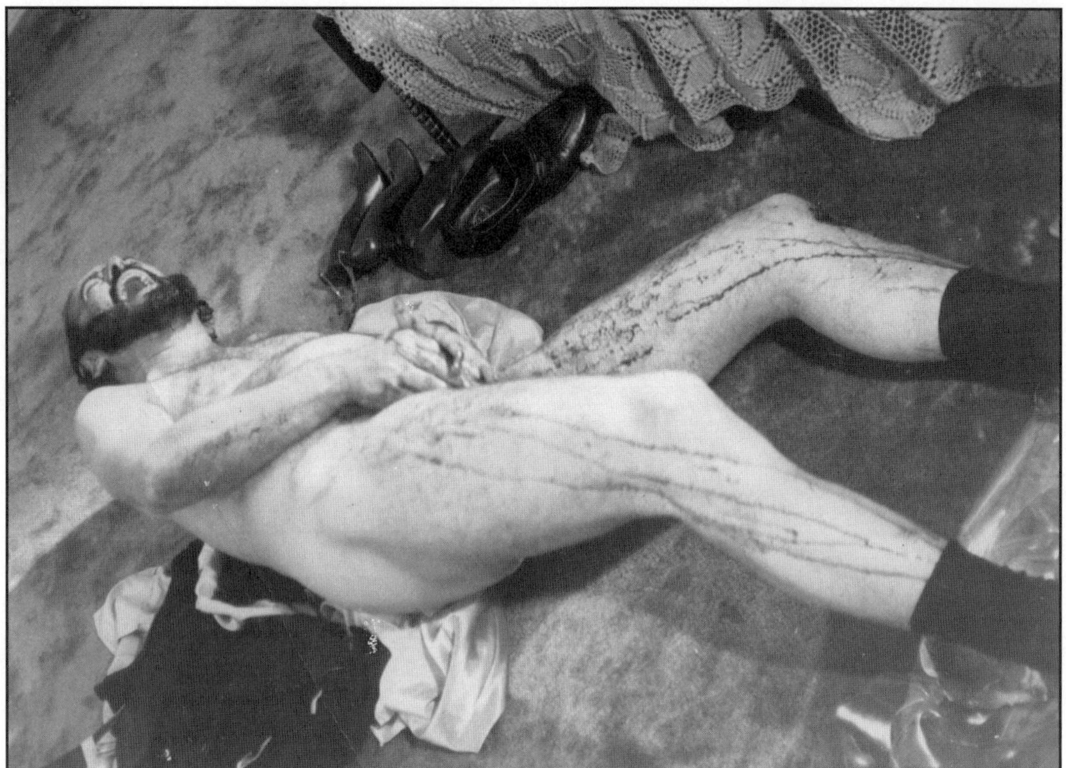

Right: *Rough justice for rapists in* Perversão.
Below: Inferno Carnal, *the story of a mad scientist's revenge, was one of Marins' most conventional films.*

me!" cries Marins.

The scenes showing the Devil's wedding orgy are, naturally, the highlight of the picture. It's like a Spanish inquisition gone mad. Fingers are cut off in gruesome close up, tongues are ripped out and hands lopped off with a giant axe. Hooded monks chant, and hairy, naked men leap about like demented monkeys while Zé does his now obligatory walk down a human staircase. Finally, in a shocking reversal of his earlier anti-clericalism, Marins brandishes a crucifix and calls on Christ to help him destroy the evil.

Exorcismo Negro, capitalising on the recent success of *The Exorcist*, was a big hit. Unfortunately, as he was only a hired hand on the project, Marins saw none of the film's profits. Frustrated at his inability to make the next Zé do Caixão picture, he decided to put together a sort of celluloid version of his greatest hits, just to keep the idea alive. *Delirios de Um Anormal* (*Hallucinations of a Deranged Mind*), released in 1977, is about a psychiatrist, Hamilton, who is having visions of Zé do Caixão. He becomes convinced that Zé has identified his wife as the elusive 'perfect woman' to give birth to his son. Hamilton's colleagues call in Marins who tries to persuade the man that Zé do Caixão doesn't exist. He even shows him a comedy script featuring Zé.

The story is a framing device to allow Marins to edit together a series of scenes taken from his earlier films. Most of these consist of the Hell sequence from *Esta Noite Encarnarei no Teu Cadáver* and the hallucinations from *Ritual dos Sadicos*. It was a kind of two-fingered gesture to the censor who had banned the latter film. Ironically, *Delirios de Um Anormal* itself was shown without any cuts.

Sadly, this cinematic scrapbook represents the last major appearance on screen of Zé do Caixão. Marins continued to use the character for his on-stage horror shows and in 1992 he appeared leading a samba school in the Rio carnival. Yet, to date, the new Zé do Caixão film still awaits a backer. Despite the relative success of some of his movies and the undoubted fame of Zé, Marins' example has not led to a huge upsurge in horror or fantasy films in Brazil. Of course, there have been some. Serious film-makers like Nelson Pereira dos Santos have experimented with the form. His *Quem é Beta?* (Who is Beta?) is a science fiction allegory set in some post-apocalyptic future. Another by-product of the *cinema novo* movement was the anarchic comedy *Macunaima*, which includes episodes of cannibalism, a magic amulet and a spring that turns a black Brazilian into a white man. Some

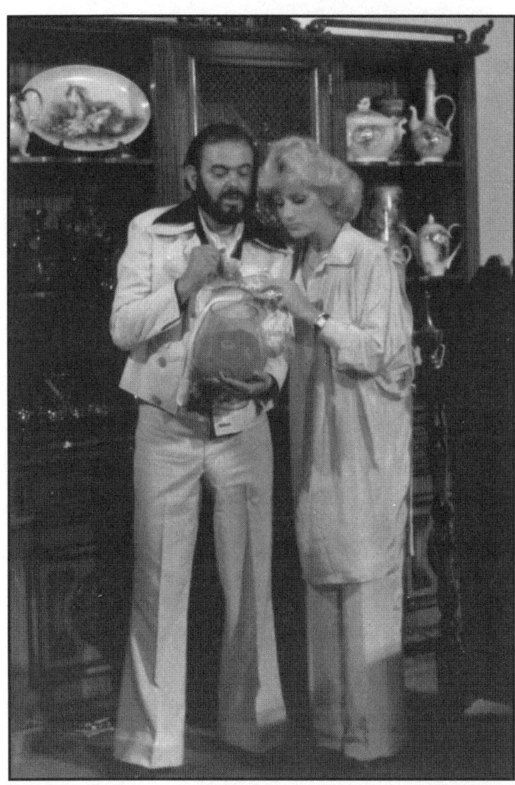

of Marins' former employees and associates have also released their own horror projects. The most successful has been Ivan 'The Terror' Cardoso. His films, *O Segredo da Múmia* (*The Secret of the Mummy*), *As Sete Vampiras* (*The Seven Vampires*) and *Escorpião Escarlate* (*The Scarlet Scorpion*), are in a long line of comedy horrors and parodies that Brazilians are especially fond of. Western hits like *The Exorcist* ('remade' as *O Jeca Contra o Capeta*) *Jaws*, (*Bacalhau*) and *King Kong* (*Costinha Contra o King Mong*) have all been remodelled as knockabout comedies with popular comedians. Recently there have been porno/gore/trash hybrids like *Atracção Satanica* (Satanic Attraction) and *Ritual de la Morte* (Death Ritual) from the sex film-maker Faudi Manzur. However, horror has failed to establish itself as a genre in Brazil.

Consequently, Marins' macabre side has had to find other outlets. Even when hired to make a hardcore porn film he finds it impossible not to go over the top. *24 Horas de Sexo Ardente* (24 Hours of Hot Sex) was made for a producer who had promised to finance a new Zé do Caixão film. Marins wanted to make a kind of anti-porn statement. "I chose the ugliest women in the country. I wanted to go overboard, I wrote in a scene where penises and vaginas talk to each other." He also included a sex scene with a dog. "The dog ended up being a better lover than many men... I thought people would be utterly grossed out by the porn genre. I myself was unable to have sex for six months after I made the movie." To his great surprise, the film was a big hit. Unfortunately, the promised Zé do Caixão film never materialised.

One of the few of Marins' non-Zé do Caixão films to be screened in Europe was another sex and violence shocker. The 1978 production *O Estupro* (The Rape), was shown that year at the Sitges festival in Spain under the new title of *Perversão* (*Perversion*). Here Marins plays a repulsive character called Vittorio Palestrina. This millionaire industrialist is what the original Zé do Caixão might have become if he'd won the lottery. Cruel and amoral, he takes great delight in teasing and tormenting his fair weather friends with his eccentric ways. Sometimes his eccentricities take a decidedly nasty turn. The film begins with Vittorio seducing a young, innocent girl. During the act, he bites off her nipple. Vittorio's power and prestige allow him to get off scot free at the subsequent trial. Like Zé, Vittorio seems to be searching for the perfect, amoral female companion. Meeting the beautiful Veronica, he thinks he has finally found her. His method of seduction is to show her the nipple preserved in a brandy glass.

However, he's in for a shock. Veronica plays hard to get and when she finally accedes to Vittorio's demands, she cuts off his testicles while he's making love to her. She then reveals that she is the sister of the woman he mutilated.

While films like *Perversão* are certainly shocking and provocative, they lack the commitment and sheer originality of the films featuring Zé do Caixão. Although Marins hotly denies that Zé is in any sense his *alter ego*, it remains a fact that the character seemed to bring out something special in Marins, both as actor and film-maker.

Most horror movies, including many of Marins', are little more than exercises in bad taste or cheap shocks. However, throughout the world there have been a select few who have used the form to express a personal vision. Mario Bava in Italy, Nobuo Nakagawa in Japan, Alexandro Jodorowsky in Mexico. And to this short list has to be added the name of José Mojica Marins. His films may be cheaply made, crudely edited and occasionally over-reaching, but through the best of them shines his unique vision. If horror is to have any lasting importance, it has to be as a vehicle for realising dreams and fantasies. And the cinematic dreams of José Mojica Marins are amongst the most powerful ever to reach the screen. ■

Grateful acknowledgement is made to Horacio Higuchi, from whose writings much of the biographical detail and many of the translations used in this chapter have been taken.

Above: *The nipple in the brandy glass scene from* Perversão.
Left: As Sete Vampiras *was directed by former Marins associate Ivan 'The Terror' Cardoso.*

LA
VENGANZA
DEL SEXO

PEL
MEX

con
GLORIA PRAT – RICARDO BAULEO ALDO BARBERO
JUSTIN MARTIN – SUSANA BELTRAN

EMILIO VIEYRA ORESTES TRUCCO

"Meat on Meat!"

Today, the best known Argentinian films tend to be the serious ones. Political dramas like *La historia oficial* (*The Official Version*), which won the Oscar for best foreign film in 1985, and art films like Maria Luisa Bemberg's *Miss Mary.* Yet at one time Argentina was a major producer of Spanish-language films, rivalling Mexico and Spain. From within this burgeoning industry came horror films, sex films and all the other staple genres of exploitation cinema.

The first horror film produced in Argentina was *Una luz en la ventana* (A Light in the Window), a story about the physical deformity called acromegaly, directed in 1942 by Manuel Romero. Today the film seems a little old-fashioned, but some scenes, particularly its terrifying climax, are still highly effective. It marked the screen début of Narcisco Ibañez Menta, widely regarded as the Boris Karloff of Argentinian cinema. Born in 1912 in Asturias, Spain, Ibañez Menta grew up in a family of actors who moved to Argentina while he was still a child. A few years later, during a short stay in the United States, he met Lon Chaney. Inspired by 'the man of a thousand faces', Ibañez Menta became totally absorbed in the world of costume and make-up. His transformation into the gruesome acromegalic of *Una luz en la ventana* is very convincing.

Argentinian cinema failed to fully exploit Ibañez Menta's taste for the sinister. However, television, at the end of the 1950s, took an extremely macabre turn that made good use of his talents. In some cases genuine autopsies were filmed using real corpses and special effects in a bold, gory style that never found its way to the big screen. When it was made as a television serial starring Ibañez Menta, Gaston Leroux's *The Phantom of the Opera* was a big hit. On the nights when the character was unmasked, the streets of Buenos Aires were practically empty — everyone was glued to their television sets to see the hideous face of Narcisco.

While making his bizarre television programmes, at the height of the small screen craze, Ibañez Menta starred in one his best films, *Obras maestras del terror,* an anthology drawn from the works of Edgar Allan Poe, directed by one of the most commercially successful of all Argentinian filmmakers, Enrique Carreras (not the Enrique Carreras who had a hand in founding Hammer, it should be pointed out). In the film, Ibañez Menta appears first as an old miser in 'The Tell-Tale Heart', then as a sadistic murderer in 'The Cask of Amontillado' and finally as the mesmerist in 'The Facts in the Case of M. Valdemar'. Inexplicably, when the film was dubbed into English and given its American première by Jack '*The Blob*' Harris (under the title *Master of Horror*), the longest and best episode — 'The Tell-Tale Heart' — was dropped. That episode featured the actor's son, Narcisco Ibañez Serrador, who had also served as director and scriptwriter on some of his father's best television work. In Spain some years later Ibañez Serrador directed two seminal horror films: *La residencia* (*The House That Screamed*) and *¿Quién puedo matar a un niño?* (*Who Can Kill a Child?* aka *Island of the Damned*). None of the films that Enrique Carreras made either before or since match up to *Obras maestras del terror.* In the opinion of many people involved in the production, Ibañez Serrador's work behind the camera with his father was an essential element in the film's success.

Ibañez Menta's last Argentinian film was a black comedy, *Los muchachos de antes no usaban arsénico* (Guys Never Used to Need Arsenic). During the 1970s he began to work increasingly in the Spanish cinema, often in horror films. His Spanish films include *La saga de los Dracula* (*The Dracula Saga*), directed in 1972 by the Argentinian León Klimovsky, who also worked with Narcisco in *Odio mi cuerpo* (*I Hate My Body*). After presenting horror films on Spanish television, Narcisco Ibañez Menta returned to the big screen in 1996

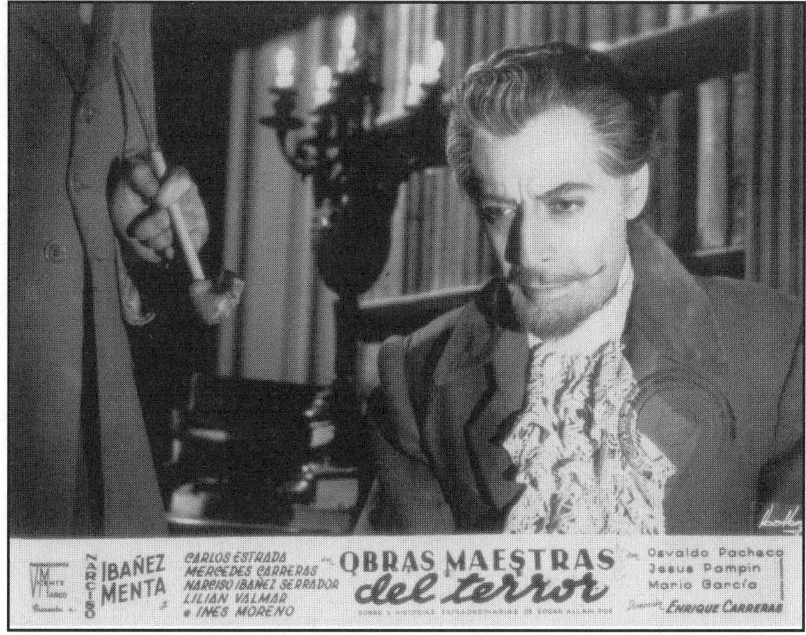

Opposite: La venganza del sexo *was released in America as* The Curious Dr. Humpp *(!).*

Above: *Narcisco Ibañez Menta in one of the few Argentinian films to be released abroad, under the title* Master of Horror.

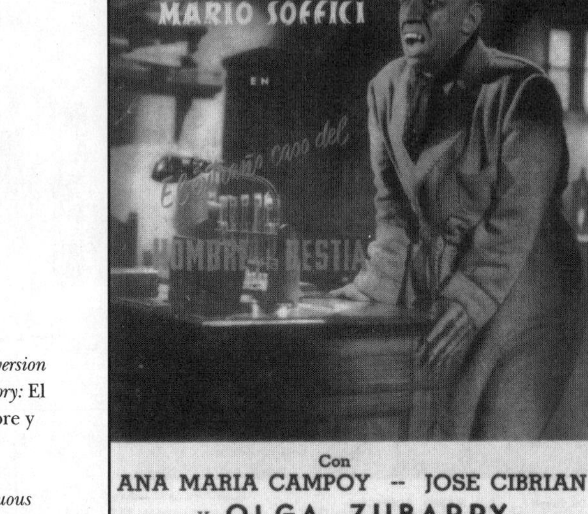

Right: *An Argentinian version of the Jekyll and Hyde story:* El estraño caso del hombre y la bestia.

Below right: *The voluptuous Isabel Sarli, Argentina's favourite sex symbol.*

with a role in the Spanish horror comedy *Solo se muere dos veces* (You Only Die Once), directed by the Ibarretxe Bros.

By the 1950s, the Argentinian film business was booming. To exploit the good times while they lasted, some talented directors began to add new themes and tones to the standard melodramas and comedies that were flooding the screens. Some of these films are now considered classics. *El estraño caso del hombre y la bestia* (The Strange Case of the Man and the Beast) was an Argentinian version of Jekyll and Hyde directed by and starring Mario Soffici. The film had some superb visual touches, particularly during a transformation that takes place in a train tunnel, and a brief but intense performance by Olga Zubarry.

This memorable star, a presence in many of the best Argentinian films, came up against another dangerous character in Román Viñoly Barreto's *El vampiro negro* (The Black Vampire), a remake of Fritz Lang's *M*, with Nathán Pinzón in the role that made Peter Lorre famous. Vinoly Barreto's version of the story is full of hallucinatory scenes, strange creatures and distorted images, greatly enhanced by the photography of Anibal Gonzalez Paz, one of the most imaginative lighting men in Argentinian cinema. Like Lorre, Nathán Pinzón became typecast in sinister roles, using a macabre laugh which became his trade mark when he introduced a series of horror films on television.

Another memorable Argentinian psychopath was featured in the poetic *Si muero ante de despertar* (If I Die Before I Wake), based on a story by William Irish and directed by the maverick Carlos Hugo Christenson. Christenson's film was an exploration of childhood terror through the figure of 'el hombre de la bolsa' (a kind of Argentinian bogey man), who is finally revealed as a mythical psychotic child abuser (thirty years before Freddy Krueger!).

One flavour entirely absent from Argentinian screens in the 1950s was eroticism. To fill this gap, director and producer Armando Bo took a former Miss Argentina under his wing and transformed her into Isabel Sarli — the country's first sex star. Although their films were censored to a point that was almost surreal, ignored by critics and roundly attacked by the country's middle classes, the Sarli-Bo duo changed Argentinian cinema forever. With her angelic face and devilish curves, Isabel was the sex symbol that the country had been crying out for.

An interesting aspect of Isabel Sarli's personality is how closely her real life matched the characters she portrayed on screen: 'pure women' who succumb before the desperate passions of men. From a deeply Catholic background, Sarli resisted doing nude scenes, even though Bo — who as well as being her director was also her lover — did all he could to get her to disrobe on screen. In sex scenes she insisted that he was the only person who could touch her and, if the scene involved another actor, inserts of Bo's hands had to be used.

At the beginning of Isabel Sarli's career her erotic scenes always appeared in a serious context, in films with a nominal message, such as *El trueno entre las hojas* (Thunder Among the Leaves) or *Sabaleros* (*Put Up or Shut Up*). However, from the beginning of the sixties, the films took a marked dive into sexploitation that in some ways puts them on a par with Russ Meyer's early sixties work in the States. Although Armando Bo made some picaresque comedies, dramas were where he excelled, creating incredible scenarios filled with violence, perversion and eroticism, matched by a formal originality of style worthy of the anti-cinema of Jean-Luc Godard. The hyperkitsch aesthetics were accentuated by the hallucinatory designs of Paco Jamandreu. This former designer for Eva Peron also worked with Mamie Van Doren when the sexy star made *Una Americana en Buenos Aires* (An American Girl in Buenos Aires) for George Cahan in 1961.

Most of Bo's films follow a similar pattern, and his work generally contains two main themes. One is that of the 'good woman' who, in spite of herself, stirs up a whirlpool of passion, sex and violence. The other deals with nymphomania — the woman's inability to curb her passions, which nearly always ends in tragedy. A variety of stock characters appear, such as rapist fathers, arrogant policemen, impotent husbands, invalids and tarts with hearts of gold.

Amongst the more representative of Bo's films are *La tentación desnuda* (*Woman and Temptation*), *Carne* (*Flesh*), *Fuego* (*Passionate Desires*), *Furia infernal* (Evil Fury), *Insaciable* (Insatiable) and *Una mariposa en la noche* (A Butterfly in the Night).

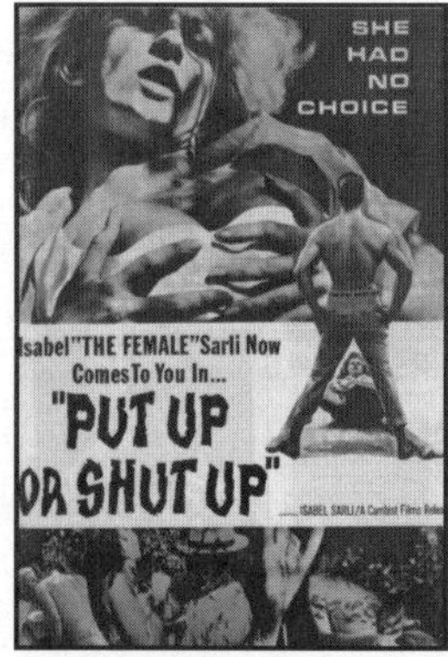

Carne is perhaps the best of all the Bo-Sarli creations, an absolute classic of the genre. The line "Meat on meat!" — delivered to the actress just before she's screwed on top of an animal carcass — is one of the most famous pieces of dialogue in Argentinian cinema. The film's leading man is played by Victor Bo. As Armando Bo's son, he had the tricky task of performing love scenes with his father's wife. A similar tension informs *Furia infernal*, a sort of Patagonian Western, which has Sarli kidnapped and abused by a rancher, who then gives his son a hard time for desiring the same woman. It's one of the most violent of all Armando Bo's films.

In 1969, Bo and Sarli went to Brazil to shoot two films that were very strong by Argentinian standards, *Extasis tropical* (*Tropical Ecstasy*; released in Brazil as *Tentaçao nuda*) and *Embrujada* (Dangerous Woman; Brazilian title: *Mulher pecado*). Both also starred Bo and were cut to shreds by the censor when shown in Argentina in 1976 and 1978 respectively.

During her period of stardom, Isabel Sarli acted in only two films not directed by Bo, Leopoldo Torre Nilsson's *Sententa veces siete* (Seventy Times Seven) and the South African production *The Virgin Goddess*, directed in 1975 by Dirk de Villiers, in which Bo co-starred. The latter was an adventure yarn, with Isabel playing a shipwreck survivor worshipped by an African tribe who take her for the white goddess of an ancient legend.

With the return of democracy to Argentina in the eighties, censorship was abolished. However, Isabel Sarli had abandoned cinema following the death of Bo in 1981 and was unable to capitalise on her name and fame. Finally, in 1996, she was invited by avant-garde film-maker Jorge Polaco to star in *La dama regresa* (The Lady is Back), a film with artistic pretensions which received mixed reviews in Argentina. Its best feature is unquestionably the presence of Sarli, playing a role similar to that of Mae West in *Sextette*.

Another Argentinian sex symbol who had a successful career abroad was the opulent, blonde-haired Libertad Leblanc. Her films don't have the kitsch appeal of those of Isabel Sarli, her everlasting rival — probably due to the lack of an auteur with the personality of Armando Bo behind the camera.

Libertad's greatest hits include *La flor del Irupe* (*Love Hunger*), Emilio Vieyra's enjoyable crime movie *Testigo para un crimen* (made for the American market where it was called *Violated Love*) and the crime thriller *Acosada* (*The Pink Pussy*). With Vieyra, the Argentinian sex bomb also filmed the drama *Maria M*, but both she and the producer disowned the film due to censorship problems. The original story dealt with a passionate relationship between a woman and a Catholic priest.

In Mexico, Libertad made *Fuego en la sangre* (Fire in the Blood), where she is dark-haired for a change, and *La cómplice* (The Accomplice), both for director René Cardona Jr. She also worked for Alfonso Corona Blake, a film-maker who specialised in the 'wrestling-horror' genre starring the likes of El Santo, 'the man in the silver mask'. In Corona Blake's *Mujeres de medianoche* (Midnight Women), Libertad has a double personality. As a critic explained at the time in the Argentinian newspaper *La nación*: 'On account of her schizophrenia, Pilar turns into Kitty who, besides being a prostitute, is also a drug trafficker, kills people, blackmails businessmen and their children and does many other reprehensible things.'

Libertad Leblanc's more lurid films include several Argentinian productions, among them *Cuando los hombres hablan de mujeres* (When Men Talk About Women) and Héctor Olivera's imaginative pop comedy *Psexoanálisis* (Sex-analysis). The latter features endless *double entendres*, psychedelic sets and a strange sixties party where Libertad is accompanied by a chimpanzee.

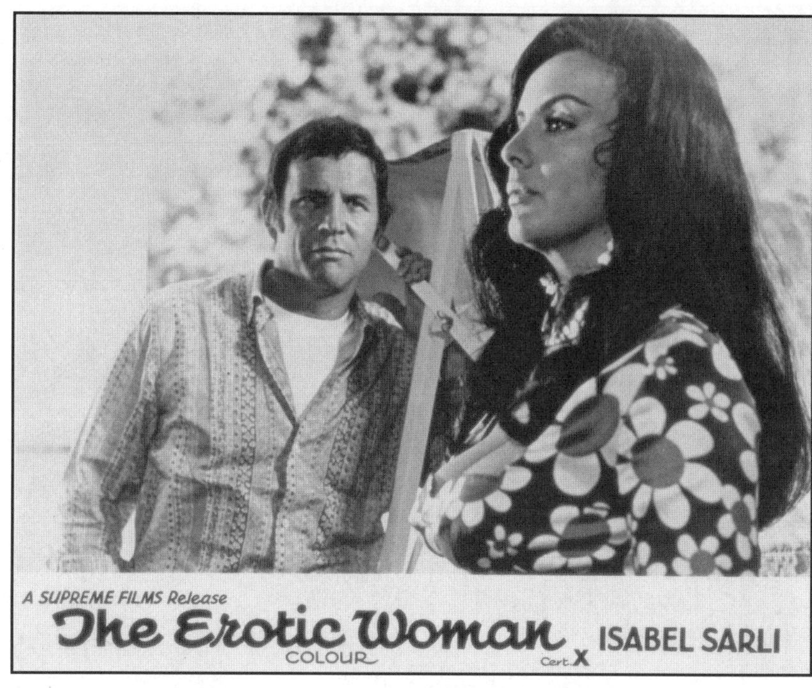

A SUPREME FILMS Release
The Erotic Woman
COLOUR
Cert. X
ISABEL SARLI

***Above:** Isabel wonders what's on his mind.*

***Below:** Film frames from Isabel's private collection.*

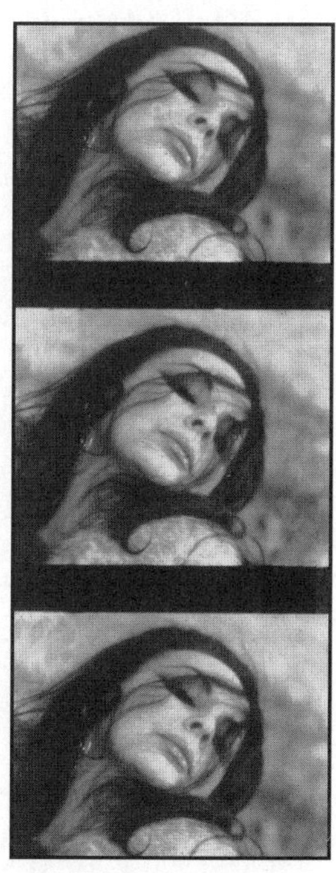

Nowadays, Héctor Olivera is one of the most prestigious of Argentinian directors, thanks to films with a strong political message like *La Patagonia rebelde* (Rebel Patagonia) and *No habrá más penas ni olvido* (*A Funny Dirty Little War*). But Olivera has made plenty of sexy exploiters too. Following in the psychedelic footsteps of *Psexoanálisis* he filmed *Psexoanalizados* (Sex Analysed), another erotic comedy, which was very daring for its time. The censor promptly slapped a ban on the film, which finally opened under the title *Los neuróticos* (The Neurotics). This time the film didn't feature Libertad Leblanc, but another Argentinian actress who specialised in strong roles, Marcela López Rey. In the seventies she worked with Alexandro Jodorowsky in *The Holy Mountain*.

Libertad Leblanc's most controversial films include two classics of Argentinian eroticism, both directed by Julio Porter — *La casa de madame Lulu* (The House of Madame Lulu) and *Deliciosamente amoral* (Deliciously Amoral). Her best known film today (probably because it's the only one available on video in Argentina) is *Furia en la isla* (Rage on the Island), a crime thriller set against a tropical background that mixes the innocent and the corrupt: in one scene a *louche* lesbian tries to take advantage of Libertad by kissing her breasts while she's feeling dizzy, for which outrage the film was savagely cut by the Argentinian censor of the time.

At the beginning of the sixties one Argentinian director was being mercilessly attacked by the country's film critics at the same time as he was achieving some of his best box office results. That film-maker was Emilio Vieyra who, despite the brickbats, has now become an idol for a new generation of fans. Today he's admired for being the only Argentinian director who dedicated a large part of his career to the production of horror, macabre and fantastic subjects.

There are two main reasons for the constant attacks Vieyra suffered. During the sixties, serious cinema succumbed to the dominance of *cinéma d'auteur* and art films. While these may have been strong in pretensions and political 'message', they so often lacked dramatic or aesthetic

Above left: *Libertad Leblanc makes a monkey out of her co-star in* Psexoanálisis.
Above right: Los neuróticos.

interest. In this context, Vieyra's exploitation films seemed cheap and vulgar. But that wasn't all. Apart from his lack of artistic pretensions and his obvious commercial motivation, Vieyra was guilty of an even greater sin. His first film as director, the crime movie *Detrás de la mentira* (Behind the Lie), was an anti-communist melodrama. The film appeared in 1962, during one of Argentina's rare periods of democratic government. He was heavily criticised for making it and lost the state subsidy that most producers received. *Detrás de la mentira* marked him out forever as a director who not only dealt in sordid or popular subjects, but was also 'politically incorrect'.

In a film culture as opposed to the fantastic and macabre as that of Argentina, Vieyra was probably the only man brave enough to release five consecutive films during the mid-sixties that all had strong supernatural or horrific elements. The films are: *Extraña invasión* (*Stay Tuned for Terror*), *Placer sangriento* (*Deadly Organ* aka *Feast of Flesh*), *La venganza del sexo* (*The Curious Dr. Humpp*), *La bestia desnuda* (The Naked Beast) and *Sangre de vírgenes* (Blood of Virgins).

Extraña invasión came about when an American-based producer asked Vieyra to think of an idea for a science fiction movie. The film was being shot in Argentina to save costs. With Richard Conte in the lead role, as a man who has to deal with an invasion of cathode rays emitted by a series of strange television broadcasts, Vieyra made a film very much in the style of American 1950s 'B' movies. Strangely, this American co-production was only ever screened in Argentina. The theme was certainly an original one, considering that metaphors about the dangerous power of television only really began to appear in the eighties — Cronenberg's *Videodrome* being the classic example.

The film has lots of intriguing ideas, including some interesting reflections on the addictive power of television. The massive withdrawal symptoms caused when the sets are switched off leads to violent chaos. In one scene, a character who isn't affected by the addiction rebukes one of the television junkies: "I don't understand what you're doing, always staring at these psychedelic patterns."

"So what," the addict replies. "It's a free country, isn't it?"

After his experiences with *Extraña invasión,* Vieyra became involved in a scheme to make low-budget films in Argentina aimed at the large Spanish-speaking populations of the big North American cities: "The American distributors who operated in the Latin areas required, above all, that the films should contain a healthy dose of sex. For my part, as I'd always been interested in film noir and macabre subjects, I felt it would be more interesting to put these erotic elements into a horror story."

This combination gave birth to *Placer sangriento,* filmed in ten days in 1965 on a beach in neighbouring Paraguay. Its cast includes two of the director's favourite actors, Ricardo Bauleo and Gloria Prat. The film is a psycho thriller about a mysterious serial killer who frequents all night pop circles, murdering his victims with a lethal dose of heroin. The subjects of drugs and psychedelia, very much of their time but still unusual for Argentinian cinema, are always present in Vieyra's films. In one particularly daring scene, the police use LSD to extract a confession from the only survivor of a heroin overdose administered by the killer.

One of the director's obsessions was that no one should be able to guess the identity of the murderer in his films. In *Placer sangriento* this idea was taken to its limits: "The script that I gave the actors didn't reveal who the killer was, so everybody played their roles without knowing whether they were criminals or not. For a while during the filming even I wasn't quite sure who the killer was going to be. I had various possible characters to choose from and didn't finally make up my mind until a few days before the shooting finished."

In 1966, again in less than two weeks, Vieyra filmed the incredible *La venganza del sexo,* one of the most original and imaginative of all Argentinian films. A spate of disappearances has the police beaten, and a journalist (Ricardo Bauleo) decides to mount his own investigation. Soon he comes up against a mad scientist, the satanic Dr Zoide (Aldo Barbero), who is being controlled by a brain kept in a jar. The doctor is conducting strange sexual experiments — he forces couples to have "sex at a distance" connected by cables to "suck the life force out of each other." The most remarkable thing about *La venganza del sexo* is that even with no precedents to fall back on (there is no sci-fi tradition in Argentinian cinema), lacking a big budget and not even being a fan of the genre, Vieyra managed to make a film that easily exceeds the wildest visions of the era's American 'B' movies. *La venganza del sexo* was shown in cinemas in Latin American areas in America and was also dubbed into English under the title *The Curious Dr. Humpp.*

In 1967 Emilio Vieyra turned out his most psychedelic

film, the thriller *La bestia desnuda*. The story is similar to *Placer sangriento*, with a masked psychopath killing strippers in a downtown theatre. At one point, all of the characters involved with the nude review attend a psychedelic party that they call "el happening!" The film is worth watching for this scene alone. The wild party includes gay and lesbian episodes, all kinds of weird characters and a startling climax featuring a guillotine. Vieyra himself appears as the party organiser.

Finally, again in 1967, Vieyra created a new genre when he made the first Argentinian vampire film, *Sangre de vírgenes*, starring Ricardo Bauleo, Susana Beltrán, Gloria Prat and Rolo Puente. There's lots of gore, presented in an up-front splatter style, as well as lengthy sex scenes of a type not previously seen in a locally produced film. The movie was banned for many years. It resurfaced briefly in 1974, during a short period of democratic rule, along with Bertolucci's *Last Tango in Paris*. A few months later they were both banned again. It was only in the 1980s that either film could be shown publicly in Argentina.

"It was producer Orestes Trucco's idea to make a vampire film," Vieyra recalls. "I remember that when I told my wife about it, she said I was completely nuts." A particularly bizarre detail of *Sangre de vírgenes* is that there are no traditional bats in the movie. Instead these are replaced with shots of flying seagulls tinted red on the film stock. That shows Vieyra's nerve. Lacking money for special effects and with no archive footage of vampires available, he was brave enough to risk ridicule rather than make a vampire film with no shots of flying creatures.

In the style of the great American showman William Castle, Trucco came up with an advertising gimmick to attract the crowds. In the theatres where *Sangre de vírgenes* was playing, the busty vampiress Susana Beltrán was hired to wander the aisles in her night-dress, flashing her blood-covered fangs...

By the end of the eighties, *Sangre de vírgenes* had became one of Argentina's biggest cult films. Remarkable, considering that it's not even officially available on video. In the nineties, Vieyra's five sex and horror movies were shown in one of Buenos Aires' foremost cultural centres, the ICI (Institute of Spanish American Co-operation), which is funded by the Spanish Government. However, these five titles were not Vieyra's most successful films. Musicals like *Gitano* (Gypsy), starring Sandro, the Argentinian Elvis, the kids' film *Los mochileros* (The Back Packers), the James Bond parody *La gran aventura* (The Great Adventure) and the comedy Western *Los irrompibles* (The Indestructables) were seen by several million people throughout Latin America.

Following the return of democratic rule in the eighties, Vieyra took advantage of the abolition of censorship to film much stronger material. *Sucedió en el internado* (the English release title *Perversion in a Girls' School* is self-explanatory) and *Correccional de mujeres* (Women's Prison), are both relentlessly sleazy with all the clichés of their respective genres. *Correccional de mujeres* was paid homage by a punk rock group of the time, Attaque 77, who used several clips from it in one of their videos.

Although no longer as prolific as he once was, Vieyra is still an active force. In 1996 he returned to the fray with the musical melodrama *Adiós Abuelo* (Goodbye Grandad). The film caused controversy with what was seen as its less than 'politically correct' view of the late seventies' military dictatorship in Argentina.

In Buenos Aires during the 1950s no one knew what cannabis was — cocaine was the drug of choice for tango musicians. And yet, in 1950 one of the country's biggest studios, Sono Film, produced the crime thriller *Marijuana*. The film was directed by former dentist León Klimovsky, who, twenty years later, would be making classic horror movies in Spain, like the Paul Naschy vehicles *The Werewolf vs the Vampire Woman* and *Dr. Jekyll and the Werewolf*. According to Alberto de Mendoza, one of the film's stars, "the producers got the idea from the outcry over Robert Mitchum being arrested in Hollywood for possessing marijuana." The film certainly lives up to its scandal sheet origins. After smoking joints, people dance strange tropical dances and see blurred visions. Soon these human scum are ready for the worst acts imaginable. Unlike the American exploitation classic *Reefer Madness*, the film actually has a well handled thriller plot, good film noir atmosphere and a slightly less laughable attitude towards the effects of marijuana on the young.

In 1968 the film was remade as *Humo de Marihuana* (Marijuana Smoke). The director Lucas Demare made good use of serious actresses like Marcela López Rey. She recalls: "At the time nobody was smoking dope in Argentina. It only really became popular in the seventies. The director made us smoke the joints in a very peculiar way, clutching them in both hands as though we were trying to hold on to the smoke." Inspired no doubt by the idea of opium dens, Demare had his characters tokeing away in dark little rooms, so full of smoke that in some scenes it was difficult to make out the faces of the actors.

Throughout the 1960s, anti-drug films became relatively common in Argentinian cinema. One of the funniest is 1962's *Los viciosos*, (*Debauched*) directed by Enrique Carreras who had earlier made the Poe anthology *Obras maestras del terror*. The movie was partly a crime thriller about the international cocaine trade and partly an exploitation version of Fellini's *La dolce vita*, which was hitting the headlines at the time. Carreras hired Graciela Borges, then the most popular actress in Argentina, and had her play the part of an innocent girl destroyed by drugs. First she becomes a stripper

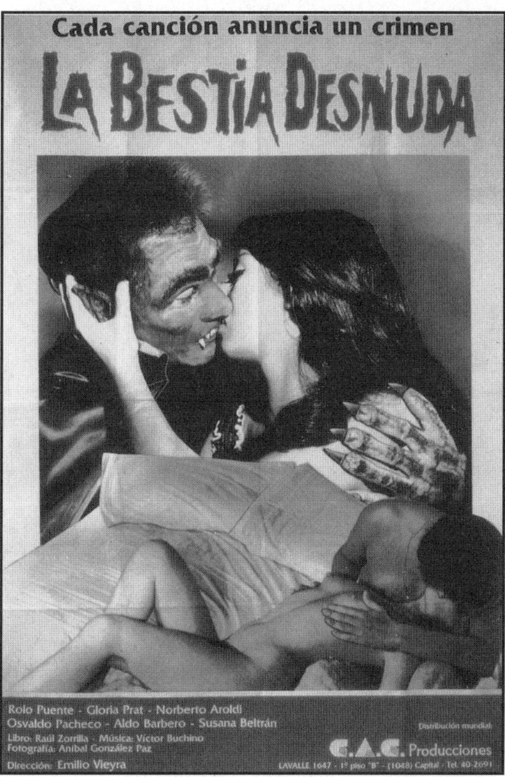

Left: La bestia desnuda *(The Naked Beast). The lurid titles of Emilio Vieyra's films drew enthusiastic audiences in the sixties.*

***Above:** More lurid fare from Emilio Vieyra.*
***Right:** Bug-eyed robot men from* La venganza del sexo.

and is then forced to prostitute herself in a filthy brothel. She ends up working for a syndicate of drug traffickers, getting kids hooked on dope. Finally the poor girl commits suicide when she discovers that her drug-dealing lover is in fact an undercover cop. *Los viciosos* features a topless scene starring a beautiful woman called Cocinelle. In reality, Cocinelle was a transsexual, well known at the time in the night-clubs of Buenos Aires, although the film makes no reference to the fact that this woman is no lady...

With nearly 100 films to his credit, the late Enrique Carreras (he died in 1995) was the most prolific Argentinian director. For the most part his work consists of dumb comedies full of gruesome pop songs. However, he also made some exploitation movies, which he described as "message" films. In this spirit, *Los viciosos* was followed in 1963 by *Los hipócritas* (The Hypocrites), in which Marcela López Rey is given a hard time for refusing to accept a drugged drink that the head of a white slave racket tries to give her. In the same year López Rey also starred in *Los evadidos* (The Runaways), a tough crime thriller about a prison break out, which is more realistic, although less fun, than the others.

In 1974, Carreras made his contribution to the women-in-prison genre with *Las procesadas* (The Accused). Such films have been produced in Argentina since the 1950s, with titles like *Deshonra* (Shame), directed by Daniel Tinayre in 1952. Of course, in those days the lesbian undercurrents were barely hinted at. Carreras included all the elements of the genre, emphasising the sleazy scenes, especially those detailing the humiliations suffered by poor Olga Zubarry. Unfortunately, *Las procesadas* suffers from a lack of imagination and is rather plodding. Carreras continued with his '*Trainspotting à la espagnol*' in *Los drogadictos* (The Drug Addicts) and the incredibly over-the-top *Las barras bravas,* a film about football hooligans (the *barras bravas* are a bunch of violent fans who cause mayhem during matches). After this film, full of surreal drug-taking episodes, Carreras abandoned the "message" film to make a rather insipid crime thriller called *Delito de corrupción* (Crime of Corruption).

Throughout the sixties and seventies, Argentinian producers made a lot of money with sexy comedies. Due to strict censorship, the erotic elements usually went no further than a shot of a girl in her undies. The protagonists were never allowed to actually have sex. Alberto Olmedo and Jorge Porcel, two popular stage and television comedians, made dozens of films like this, with titles such as *Los caballeros de la cama redonda* (Knights of Group Sex) and *Las mujeres son cosa de guapos* (Women Are Mighty Fine). Jorge Porcel (known as 'El Gordo' — the Fat Man) later became a top comic on Spanish-language television in the States. His fame led to his being hired by Brian De Palma to appear alongside Al Pacino in *Carlito's Way.* He gave up cinema when he became a born again Christian.

A uniquely Argentinian form of sexploitation was the *hotel alojamiento* film. The title refers to hotels hired for the hour by couples seeking a place to be alone. Such establishments were (and still are) an institution in the city of Buenos Aires. The genre was kicked off by the 1963 film *La cigarra no es un bicho* (*The Games Men Play*), which featured Narcisco Ibañez Menta, Olga Zubarry and a cast of top Argentinian stars. After the film's huge success, similar productions proliferated right into the eighties. The plots usually involved some basic twist, such as an outbreak of illness or the arrival of a gang of delinquents at the hotel, to stop the couples from doing what they came for.

The success of these movies gave rise to a wide range of sexy films some of them very low-budget. For example, Juan Antonio Serna's *Juegos de verano* (Summer Games), about a cosy group reunion in a summerhouse, was reissued and exported abroad in many different versions, ranging from

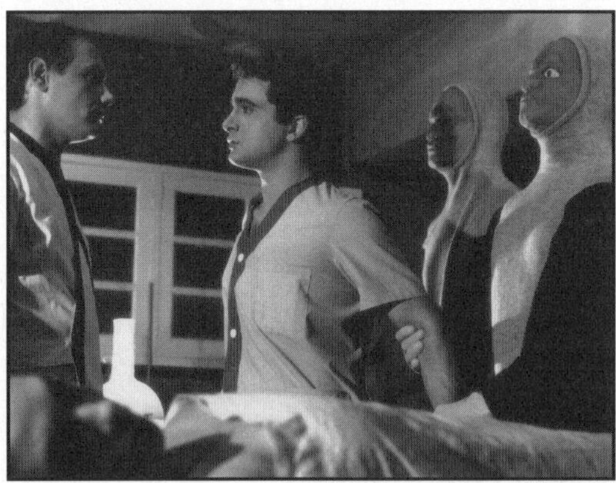

the very innocent to the decidedly hardcore. *Natasha*, directed by Ever Lobato, was a strange melodrama graced by the erotic charms of the beautiful Thelma Stefani, who, like the character she plays in the film, committed suicide some years later. A strong feature of *Natasha* is its bizarre musical numbers, many with a decidedly psychedelic flavour.

An entertaining women-in-prison movie directed by Anibal di Salvo, *Atrapadas* (Trapped), became one of the biggest box office hits of 1983. Using a script that reworked and improved on Enrique Carreras's *Las procesadas*, di Salvo filmed scenes of sex and violence that were unprecedented for the Argentinian cinema. In one scene, a bunch of vicious women humiliate the heroine Leonor Benedetto. Di Salvo persuaded one of the actresses to piss over their unfortunate victim without any special effects, in order to achieve a greater realism.

Unfortunately, unlike di Salvo, the producers of exploitation films following the return of democracy in the eighties didn't put so much effort into their work. There were a few successes, such as *Los gatos* (Cats), directed by Carlos F. Borcosque, and some amazing Z-grade movies. In Ricardo Suñez's study of 'forbidden relationships' *Relación prohibida*, a lesbian engages in long conversations with a picture of Sigmund Freud. However, by the end of the eighties, exploitation movies had begun to fade from view.

Today there are almost no films of this type made in Argentina. It's nearly impossible to produce anything without state support and the people who sit on the selection panels tend to favour art films or ones with a political message. Occasionally the Government puts money into a genre production and sometimes with reasonable results. One such case was the interesting 1988 horror film *Alguien te está mirando* (Someone is Hanging Around), directed by Gustavo Cova and Horacio Maldonado. A group of students undergo scientific experiments and begin to experience violent urges. Despite obvious budget limitations, the film caused quite a buzz. Some people were excited enough to talk about a rebirth of the Argentinian fantastic film. Well, we're still waiting... ■

By Diego Curubeto.

Above: *'Hey, let's be friends.'* Sucedió en el internado. ***Below:*** *'These movies make me sick!" Thelma Stefani in* Correccional de mujeres.

PROD. MIER Y BROOKS, S. A.
presentan a

ANA BERTHA LEPE

en

¡QUÉ LINDO CHA CHA CHA!

con
JOSE VENEGAS
FERNANDO CASANOVA
ANDRES SOLER

Director GILBERTO MARTINEZ SOLARES ★ Dist. por DISTRIBUIDORA INDEPENDIENTE, S. A.

Masked Men and Monsters

Mexico has a cinema whose character is like no other. Yet, outside Latin America and Spain, its films are virtually unknown and unheralded. Some will remember that Luis Buñuel made a few films in Mexico, others will be aware of the occasional arthouse hit from south of the border, like Alfonso Arau's *Como agua para chocolate* (*Like Water for Chocolate*) and Guillermo del Toro's *La invención de Cronos* (*Cronos*). And then there are the handful of 'cult' fantasy films like *El barón del terror* (*The Brainiac*) and *Santo vs. las mujeres vampiro* (*Samson vs. the Vampire Women*).

Those who know Mexican cinema only through the few productions available internationally are usually surprised to discover that a genuine industry flourished in Mexico for nearly six decades. Thousands of feature films were produced in all genres and styles. At one time Mexico had its own star system and dominated Spanish-language film production for many years. Some of these pictures closely resemble Hollywood productions — Westerns, musicals, dramas, comedies — with some peculiar twists and variations. But there are also genres and styles which are uniquely Mexican and reflect the nation's history, culture and personality.

Opposite: *The title translates as What a Beautiful Cha Cha Cha!*

Left: *Santo, the silver-masked wrestling hero, meets a Mexican mummy.*

Less than two years after the first moving pictures were exhibited there in 1895, Mexicans were making their own films. However, the widespread poverty and underdevelopment of the country hindered the growth of an indigenous film industry. In 1910 came the Revolution. The ensuing struggles and counter-struggles disrupted the social and economic fabric of the nation for more than a decade.

Hollywood fare dominated Mexican cinema screens in the 1920s and it was only with the arrival of talking pictures that production really started to take off. There were few trained cinema technicians and consequently it was willing volunteers — some with experience in Hollywood, others from the theatrical world — who helped create, virtually from scratch, what would soon become the dominant Spanish-language film industry.

The first sound feature film produced in Mexico, *Más fuerte que el deber* (Stronger Than Duty), was directed in 1930 by Raphael J. Sevilla. He had worked as a technical advisor at Warner Brothers in Hollywood and shot the film using 50,000 feet of raw stock that they'd given him. Only six features were made in Mexico in 1932, but in 1933 the industry grew considerably. Twenty-one films were produced — including the first sound genre film, *La Llorona* (The Crying Woman) — and by the end of the year three studios were in operation, regularly employing between 200 to 300 people. However, there was still no real Mexican film 'industry'. Few if any stable production companies existed. Most of them financed each new film with the profits from the previous one. The pictures made in these early years were largely melodramas, plus a few historical subjects, including films about the recent Revolution. What Mexican cinema really needed was an identity of its own.

Allá en el Rancho Grande (Down There on the Rancho Grande) was not the first *ranchera* film, but it helped define the genre and proved particularly palatable to Central and South American audiences. Its rural settings, colourful costumes, heavy emphasis on music, and themes of family and personal honour, loyalty and pride struck a deep chord. While *rancheras* may superficially resemble Westerns, the analogy is misleading. Rather, they are dramas (and later, comedies as well), set in the almost feudal society of rural Mexico with its own very particular rules and relationships.

It has been said that *Allá en el Rancho Grande* 'saved' the Mexican film industry by giving it a clear identity. While the popularity of *rancheras* would fluctuate over the years, the basic tenet holds true: Mexico could not compete on equal terms with Hollywood, so it had to provide films which were uniquely Mexican, and attractive to Latin audiences for that very reason.

During World War Two, Mexico's annual film production began a steady increase. Many of the best films of Mexico's finest directors — Juan Bustillo Oro, Fernando de

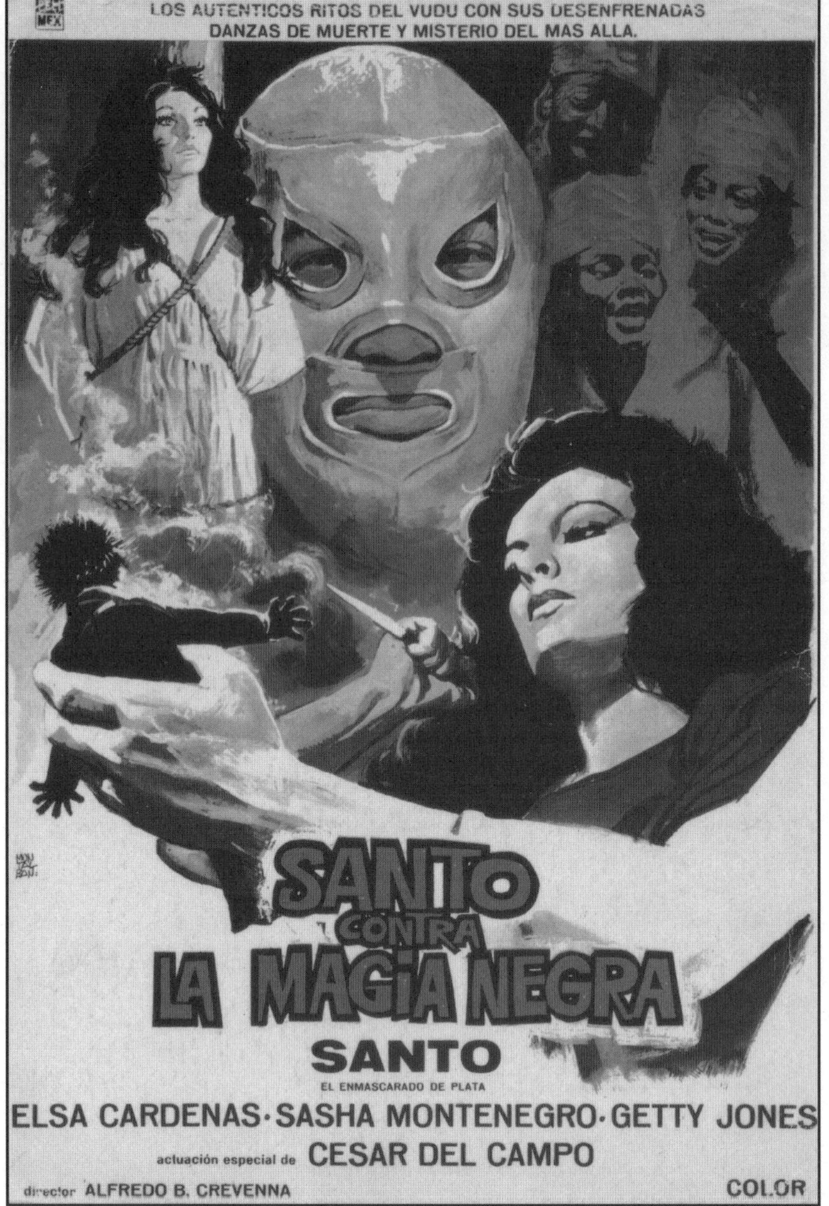

LOS AUTENTICOS RITOS DEL VUDU CON SUS DESENFRENADAS
DANZAS DE MUERTE Y MISTERIO DEL MAS ALLA.
SANTO
CONTRA
LA MAGIA NEGRA
SANTO
EL ENMASCARADO DE PLATA
ELSA CARDENAS · SASHA MONTENEGRO · GETTY JONES
actuación especial de CESAR DEL CAMPO
director ALFREDO B. CREVENNA
COLOR

***Above:** Santo takes on Devil-worshippers in this 1972 shocker.*

Fuentes, Emilio Fernández — date from the 1940s. The technical level of local productions equalled or surpassed much of world cinema. Films were made in a wide variety of genres and styles. One of the most interesting, if short-lived, was the *cabaretera* films of the late forties. In the archetypal *cabaretera*, an innocent female protagonist descends into the cabaret milieu of sleazy night-clubs, sensuous 'tropical' music and sinister gangsters.

Another highly popular genre in Mexico — and perhaps the one best known outside the country — is the *lucha libre*, or wrestling-hero film. These first appeared in the 1950s, but their roots go back much further. Professional wrestling was introduced into Mexico around 1933 by promoter Salvador Lutteroth, who imported the concept of masked wrestlers from the United States several years later. *Lucha libre* became an extremely popular spectator sport and the mythic aspects of the mask were developed and amplified. In some matches the loser was forced to unmask, a step which effectively ended his career (at least under that name), since his face and identity were now publicly known.

However, the simple existence of a group of professional wrestlers who wore masks did not directly lead to the development of the *lucha libre* film. There were other Mexican sports dramas — in the Hollywood tradition — about boxing, wrestling, soccer, and even bullfighting, but these were quite distinct from the *lucha libre* genre. In its purest form, the films feature a protagonist who is both a masked wrestler *and* a crime-fighting superhero. It's the combination of these two factors which makes the films unique. Playboy Bruce Wayne has to become Batman to fight crime, but El Santo is always El Santo. In his films, in his comic books and in his wrestling career his true identity and real appearance remain a closely guarded secret. Thus, the duality of most masked heroes (hero versus 'normal' person) does not exist in *lucha libre* films, where the hero's double life is split between his career as a professional wrestler and his crime-fighting duties. His personal life, if any, is also carried out while masked — Santo even sleeps in one!

1952 saw two seminal *lucha libre* films released: *Huracán Ramírez* and *El Enmascarado de Plata* (The Man in the Silver Mask). The former is not dissimilar to many sports films — a father disapproves of his son's career in the ring — but with a masked wrestler in the protagonist's role. However, Huracán does little or no crime-fighting, pausing only briefly in his domestic and professional struggles to thrash some hoods who have kidnapped his father. *El Enmascarado de Plata*, filmed as a twelve-chapter serial (but apparently never shown in Mexico in that format), was inspired by the comic book exploits of El Santo (The Saint), who had been a popular professional wrestler since the 1940s. Santo chose not to appear in the film himself and the hero's role was given to another pro grappler, El Medico Asesino (The Killer Doctor).

Other early films moving towards the pure form of the genre included four 1954 pictures starring La Sombra Vengadora (The Avenging Shadow). Once again, these were made in imitation of Hollywood serials, with a hero who is 'just' a superhero, not a pro wrestling superhero. La Sombra, who had no secret identity in the films, was played by athletic wrestler Fernando Osés. As actor, stuntman and scriptwriter, Osés was a ubiquitous fixture in *lucha libre* films for many years.

El Enmascarado de Plata and several of the Sombra films had some mild science fiction and fantastic aspects. However, it was the 1956 film *Ladrón de cadáveres* (Body Thief) that first combined strong fantasy elements with the *lucha libre* milieu. The story tells of a gorilla's brain transplanted into a wrestler's body with predictably dire results. In 1958, the real Santo made his début in two films shot in Cuba: *Santo contra hombres infernales* (Santo vs the Infernal Men) and *Santo contra cerebro del mal* (Santo vs the Evil Brain). Neither contain any arena wrestling scenes, and Santo himself has relatively little to do in either film.

The first film to contain all the elements of the genre was the 1961 production *Santo contra los zombies* (*Invasion of the Zombies*), directed by Benito Alazraki. The versatile Fernando Osés co-wrote the script. Here Santo is depicted as a working professional wrestler. Scenes of actual matches are included in the picture along with specially filmed bouts directly related to the plot. In one of these Santo takes on and destroys a zombie wrestler played by Fernando Osés. It is interesting to note that Santo had not always been the brave superhero his comic books and films made him out to be. For many years he was a *rudo* (bad guy wrestler), and only later did he change his ring personality to conform to his heroic image in the media.

The most important aspect of *Santo contra los zombies* is

that Santo is shown to be both a wrestler and a famous crime-fighter. He has his own laboratory, is consulted by the police, and so forth. He literally interrupts his crime-fighting to rush off to a scheduled wrestling bout, and vice versa. Setting the standard for the great majority of wrestling-hero films which followed, there are strong fantastic elements in the plot of *Santo contra los zombies,* in this case the titular automatons who are created by a mad scientist to carry out his nefarious orders. The film was certainly influenced by the new trend towards horror, which had begun to appear in Mexican cinema in the late fifties in the wake of films like *Ladrón de cadáveres* and *El vampiro* (*The Vampire*).

For the next few years, Santo had the wrestling-hero genre pretty much to himself, aside from the occasional Huracán Ramírez picture (still principally domestic sports dramas) and a few one-shots such as *El asesino invisible* (The Invisible Killer). In this film, the hero — future action star Jorge Rivero in his film début — tried to go one better than Santo by billing himself as 'El Enmascarado de Oro' (The Man in the Gold Mask). In 1962 came *Santo vs. las mujeres vampiro* (dubbed into English as *Samson vs. the Vampire Women*), a movie considered one of the classics of the wrestling-hero genre, which established El Santo as a major star of Spanish-language cinema.

Not since *Ladrón de cadáveres* and *El vampiro* had a Mexican fantasy film attracted such international attention. *Santo vs. las mujeres vampiro* has now become a well-known 'camp' or 'cult' classic, due not only to its *outré* combination of masked wrestler and slinky vampire women, but also because it is one of the more accessible of the *lucha libre* films (amazingly, only four of Santo's fifty-plus movies have been dubbed into English). Vampiresses Tundra and Zorina (Ofelia Montesco and Lorena Velázquez) and their henchmen (Fernando Osés, 'Lobo Negro' and 'Frankestein') want revenge on Santo. His ancestor had foiled their evil plans centuries earlier. Now they are trying to induct the innocent Diana (María Duval) as their new queen. Many struggles ensue. In one, Osés meets Santo in an arena wrestling match; Osés has his mask pulled off, revealing his werewolf-like face. He escapes by transforming into a bat. Eventually the evil vampires are vanquished and Santo, his job done, drives off in his shiny Jaguar convertible.

El Santo, whose real name was Rodolfo Guzmán Huerta, was already forty-seven years old when he made *Santo vs. las mujeres vampiro.* He soon became one of the top box-office draws in Latin America. Of course, he wasn't required to be much of an actor: his facial expressions were hidden by a mask and his dialogue was dubbed by someone else. Not all the early Santo features were fantasy-oriented, but Santo's best and most popular films were those which had strong fantastic elements. After *Santo vs. las mujeres vampiro* came *Profanadores de tumbas* (Grave Robbers), *Santo y Blue Demon vs. Drácula y el Hombre Lobo* (Santo and Blue Demon vs. Dracula and Wolfman), *Santo el Enmascarado de Plata vs. la invasión de los marcianos* (Santo the Man in the Silver Mask vs. the Martian Invasion) and *Las momias de Guanajuato* (The Mummies of Guanajuato). In these films, the silver-masked superman fought witches, werewolves, vampires (male and female), Frankenstein-type monsters, mummies, 'La Llorona', Martians, alien blobs, hordes of mad scientists, zombies, gangsters, robots, diabolical axe-wielding killers, scar-faced stranglers... you name it, Santo wrestled it.

Santo y Blue Demon vs. Drácula y el Hombre Lobo borrows plot fragments and motifs from a number of other films — including the gory vampire-resuscitation method used in Hammer's *Dracula Prince of Darkness* — but manages to combine them into a reasonably coherent, well-crafted whole. Santo has a steady girlfriend (the cute Nubia Marti) and comes up against the suave Aldo Monti as Dracula. They had previously met in 1968 in *El tesoro de Drácula* (The Treasure of Dracula), also released as *El vampiro y sexo* (Sex and the Vampire). In addition to a hunchback and Dracula's wolf-man sidekick (named 'Rufus Rex'), there are zombies, more vampires and a whole pack of werewolves. Blue Demon is a

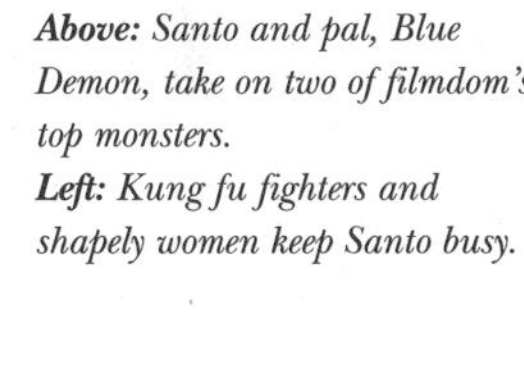

Above: *Santo and pal, Blue Demon, take on two of filmdom's top monsters.*
Left: *Kung fu fighters and shapely women keep Santo busy.*

sort of third wheel, although he does help Santo out during the final battle, when Dracula and his hirsute accomplices are tossed into a pit full of wooden stakes.

Ironically, many of the later, colour Santo films are less technically accomplished and look tackier than black-and-white efforts like *Santo vs. las mujeres vampiro.* Somehow the monsters always look like wrestlers wearing make-up — or worse. For example, 1971's *Asesinos de otros mundos* (Killers From Other Worlds) has a monster 'blob' from outer space impersonated by three men under a greasy tarpaulin. Aware of such shortcomings, the producers 'borrowed' footage from the Japanese film *Kaiju Daisenso* (*Monster Zero*) for the

Above: *Santo meets a sex-crazed vampire.*
Right: *Mummies, masked wrestlers, horror and sex — this one has it all!*

1969 outing *Santo contra Blue Demon en la Atlantida* (Santo vs. Blue Demon in Atlantis).

The cheapness of the films, the incoherence of some of their plots, the random borrowings — none of this seemed to matter. The silver-masked wrestler had become the idol of Latin America. In a nod to his widespread popularity, later films featured scenes shot in the United States, Colombia, Ecuador, Puerto Rico, Haiti and Spain.

There were other pretenders to El Santo's wrestling crown. 1964 saw the first appearance of the man who would become Santo's closest competitor, Blue Demon (real name Alejandro Muñoz), who was signed for a series of films by Luis Enrique Vergara. Santo, also under contract to Vergara at the time, made a cameo appearance in *Blue Demon vs. el poder satánico* (Blue Demon vs. the Satanic Power), but the two wrestlers were not officially teamed on screen until 1969. Eventually they made eight films together. For some reason, Blue Demon was never as popular as Santo. When fighting mad scientists, robots, aliens and other villains, 'Blue' (as his friends referred to him in the movies) just didn't project the same mythic aura as his silver-masked rival. The best Blue Demon films are the first two, *Blue Demon — el demonio azul* and *Blue Demon vs. el poder satánico,* both reasonably atmospheric horror pictures directed by Chano Urueta. Also of note is *La sombra del Murciélago* (The Shadow of the Bat), a version of *The Phantom of the Opera* transposed to the world of professional wrestling. The film features Fernando Osés as the scarred, pipe organ-playing, wrestling villain.

There were other wrestling heroes who made films, including Mil Máscaras and Superzán. There were even six pictures about wrestling women — Las Luchadoras. In fact these fighting femmes pre-dated all of the male heroes except El Santo. 1962's *Las luchadoras vs. el médico asesino* (*Doctor of Doom*) was the first adventure of Loreta (Lorena Velázquez) and the 'Golden Rubí' (Elisabeth Campbell). Later the girls would meet the Aztec Mummy, a cult of panther women, a killer robot and other horrors. The series had an obvious selling point — sexy women in tights versus monsters — and an equally obvious drawback: the real women wrestlers who handled the action scenes weren't exactly beauties, and the doubling was sometimes painfully obvious.

At the beginning of the seventies, producer Rogelio Agrasánchez began to assemble multi-hero casts (up to five masked wrestlers at a time) for films like *Los campeones justicieros* (The Champions of Justice) and *El castillo de las momias de Guanajuato* (The Castle of the Mummies of Guanajuato). However, audience tastes were changing, moving away from the adventures of masked wrestlers towards more violent, contemporary action pictures.

Santo continued to make movies even when *lucha libre* films were passé. After 1977's *Misterio en las Bermudas* (Mystery in the Bermuda Triangle; considered the official end of the genre), he went on to star in four more pictures. His last appearance was in a film starring his wrestling son, El Hijo del Santo (Son of Santo). He died in 1984, suffering a heart attack while appearing in a comedy sketch in a variety theatre.

In the late eighties and early nineties, a few sporadic attempts were made to revive the *lucha libre* genre (Mil Máscaras made a couple of comeback films, and masked wrestlers Octagón, Canek and Máscara Sagrada appeared in one or more films), but they were isolated examples. José Buil's *La leyenda de una máscara* (The Legend of a Mask) was an affectionate, retrospective look at the masked wrestler phenomenon. This was a 'quality' film which paid homage to the *lucha libre* films that even the Mexican intelligentsia remembered fondly. But the genre was effectively dead.

Even the relatively elaborate and financially successful *Santo — la leyenda del Enmascarado de Plata* (Santo: the Legend of the Man in the Silver Mask), starring El Hijo del Santo as himself and the former Huracán Ramírez, Daniel García, as El Santo, failed to spark a new wave of masked-hero films.

Why were the *lucha libre* films so successful? In part, their appeal can be attributed to the widespread popularity of professional wrestlers — their celebrity status converted into box-office clout — combined with entertaining action and outrageous fantasy plots. But, particularly for Latin American audiences, the presence in these films of 'real' heroes like El Santo and Blue Demon added a verisimilitude not present in movies featuring fictional characters such as Neutrón or La Sombra Vengadora (or Superman or Batman, for that matter). There was no need for a willing suspension of disbelief. El Santo *was* El Santo, not an actor playing a part, and many members of the audience would have seen him personally during the more than forty years he spent travelling around Latin America as a professional wrestler. Although Rodolfo Guzmán Huerta probably never encountered any vampires or Martians in real life, as an heroic icon, a symbol of strength and decency, he was virtually without peer for four decades. And while audiences knew the heroes of the *lucha libre* films weren't really out there fighting evil and injustice in the world... perhaps they wished they were.

If the *lucha libre* genre often contained strong fantasy elements, it is far from being the only genre to do so. The fantastic plays a strong part in much of Mexican cinema, reflecting cultural attitudes about life, death and the supernatural that exist in Mexican society. However, the industry produced very few serious fantasy films in its first two and a half decades of sound production. *La Llorona* (The Crying Woman) is a rare example of both an early Mexican fantasy film and one which was based on an indigenous legendary character. The Crying Woman is a ghost whose sad cries ("Ayyy, mis hijos!" — "Oh, my children!") announce her presence. Some sources describe her as the spirit of Doña Marina (also known as La Malinche), the Indian mistress of conquistador Hernán Cortés, whose son was taken from her to be raised as a Spaniard. Others maintain she is the ghost of a woman who murdered her own children and then went mad. The 1933 film contains versions of both these stories, told as flashbacks as part of the primary plot about a curse that threatens the life of the protagonist's young child. An odd combination of mystery, fantasy and costume drama, *La Llorona* did not immediately inspire imitators. Even so, 'The Crying Woman' would reappear in at least half a dozen films over the next four decades.

Other notable fantasy films of the 1930s include *El fantasma del convento* (The Ghost of the Convent), *El baúl macabro* (The Macabre Trunk), *El superloco* (The Super Madman), and *El signo de la muerte* (The Sign of Death). *El baúl macabro* stars Ramón Pereda as a mad doctor who kidnaps young women in an attempt to cure his paralysed wife. When his experiments fail, he dismembers his victims and disposes of their bodies. René Cardona, later a prolific director (he made *El enmascarado de plata* and many other genre films), is the hero. *El superloco* was even more *outré.* Carlos Villarías (who had substituted for Bela Lugosi in the Spanish-language version of *Dracula*) was cast as the sinister Dr Dyenis, who creates a monster and discovers the secret of eternal youth.

El signo de la muerte is a fairly close pastiche of contemporary Hollywood thrillers like *Doctor X.* Its crazed mystery villain turns out to be the curator of a museum who wants to resurrect Aztec civilisation by sacrificing a certain number of "chosen virgins." Competing newspaper reporters provide the hero and heroine and comic relief comes via the top-billed Cantinflas and Manuel Medel. The film also contains a few glimpses of nudity and gore which would certainly not have passed the Hollywood Production Code of the day.

The 1940s were less fruitful, although there were a fair number of fantasy comedies such as *Un día con el diablo* (One Day With the Devil), *El que murió de amor* (He Who Died of Love), and *Lo que va de ayer a hoy* (That Which Came From Yesterday to Today). These films were reminiscent of Hollywood pictures such as *Topper* and *I Married a Witch,* good-naturedly utilising fantasy elements to further their comedic and/or romantic plots. Other films with fantasy elements included *El ahijado de la muerte* (Death's Godson). This *ranchera* drama was directed by Hollywood expatriate Norman Foster and starred singing star Jorge Negrete as a man who

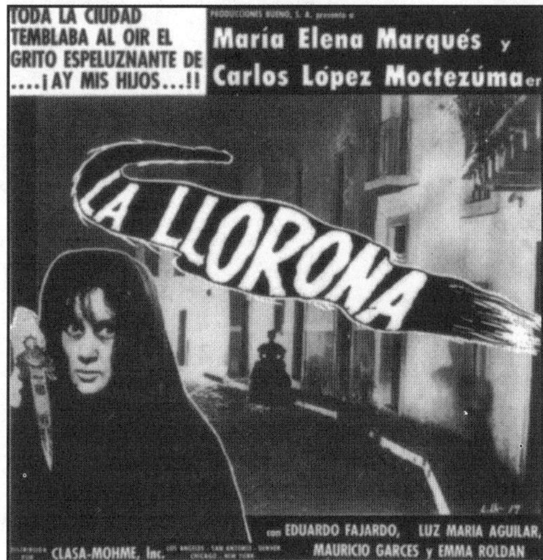

Left: The spooky 'Crying Woman' featured in several Mexican fantasy films. ***Below:*** *The suave Germàn Robles as* El Vampiro.

believes he is immortal because Death is his godmother.

Despite the predilection for the fantastic in the Mexican national character — after all, where else do you get an annual Day of the Dead with picnics in graveyards — it was not until the 1950s that horror really developed as a separate genre. There were several false starts before the right formula was discovered. In the early 1950s Chano Urueta made two films which borrowed themes from Hollywood horror pictures: *La bruja* (The Witch) and *El monstruo resucitado* (The Revived Monster). Although he had directed *El signo de la muerte* in 1939, Urueta had been mostly unable to express his macabre side on-screen. In *La bruja*, a deformed hag is converted into a beautiful woman. A scientist plans to use her as the instrument of revenge on unscrupulous industrialists who stole a valuable formula from him and killed his daughter. The film is reminiscent of the Bela Lugosi vehicle *The Devil Bat*, but its plot more closely resembles Hollywood melodramas such as *A Woman's Face*. Urueta sets the film in an unspecified European city and — in a sequence borrowed from Fritz Lang's *M* — there is a sinister 'Tribunal of the Night', where thieves, beggars and other criminal outcasts judge their peers. *El monstruo resucitado* has a similar mad scientist-seeks-revenge story, but with an odd twist: while the scientist is ugly (José María Linares Rivas made up to resemble Lon Chaney's Phantom of the Opera), his monster (Carlos Navarro) is handsome.

Urueta's two films had no immediate influence on the industry. He returned to prominence in the early sixties with two of the most outrageous Mexican horror films of all time: *El espejo de la bruja* (*The Witch's Mirror*) and *El barón del terror*. Meanwhile, the film which proved to be the seminal Mexican horror film was Fernando Mendez's *Ladrón de cadáveres* produced in 1956. The film borrows from *Frankenstein*, *House of Wax*, *King Kong* and *The Wolf Man* in its tale of a mad scientist (Carlos Riquelme) who transplants a gorilla's brain into a wrestler's body, creating a monster (played by Wolf Ruvinskis). Word of mouth was apparently so strong about this picture that — even before its official release — producer/actor Abel Salazar hired Fernando Méndez to direct another horror film, *El vampiro*.

While *Ladrón de cadáveres* was popular and influential, *El vampiro* marks the real beginning of the only true horror cycle in Mexican cinema. Salazar had been producing films for almost fifteen years, usually light comedies with himself in the leading role. By 1957 he was looking for something different. He drew his initial inspiration from Hollywood, recalling that Universal Pictures — "a company that was quite small compared to the others" — was a success in the thirties due to its "monster films... and those of Deanna Durbin. That was what sustained Universal. Therefore I decided to make a horror film and I chose *El vampiro*. I basically made *Dracula*... located on a Mexican hacienda." A mysterious foreigner named Duval (who happens to be a vampire) arrives in a rural sector of Mexico, intending to revive his brother (another vampire), who had been killed there 100 years earlier. Duval and his vampiric associate Eloísa are eventually destroyed, more through the efforts of an elderly woman than the actions of the putative hero (played by producer Salazar himself).

Salazar had originally signed veteran screen villain Carlos López Moctezuma for the title role of El vampiro, but changed his mind and hired Germán Robles, a Spanish *émigré* actor who had not yet appeared in a Mexican film. Robles played Count Duval with suave dignity, and was one of the earliest screen vampires to sport the now-regulation oversized fangs. *El vampiro* is a stylish and fairly traditional vampire film, benefiting from atmospheric photography by

Rosalío Solano and sets designed by noted artist Gunther Gerzso. The film has some glaring plot flaws and a clueless, ineffectual 'hero' but, on the whole, is still a respectable film and proved to be highly influential.

El vampiro was a critical and popular success, and Salazar immediately followed it with a sequel, *El ataúd del vampiro* (The Vampire's Coffin). Over the next four years his production company ABSA turned out a succession of horror pictures: *El hombre y el monstruo* (*The Man and the Monster*), *El mundo de los vampiros* (*The World of the Vampires*), *El espejo de la bruja*, *La cabeza viviente* (The Living Head), *La maldición de la Llorona* (The Curse of the Crying Woman) and *El barón del terror* (dubbed into English as *The Brainiac*).

With the exception of the routine *La cabeza viviente* and the delirious *El barón del terror*, Salazar's productions are serious, almost Gothic horror films. They are all well cast and, despite their low budgets, feature excellent photography and art direction. *El hombre y el monstruo*, directed by the underrated Rafael Baledón, is a Faustian werewolf film. Enrique Rambal plays a musician who sells his soul to the Devil in order to become the world's greatest pianist. As usual the Devil has a trick up his sleeve and Rambal turns into a hairy, murdering monster whenever he plays a particular tune. *El mundo de los vampiros* introduced a new vampire star, Argentinian actor Guillermo Murray, as Count Sergio Subotai. Its many camp scenes include vampiric henchmen with bat heads and Murray playing a pipe organ constructed out of bones.

Chano Urueta's *El espejo de la bruja* stylishly combined witchcraft with elements of Franju's *Yeux sans visage* (*Eyes Without a Face*) and included some audacious (if not always successful) optical effects, a Urueta trademark. *La cabeza viviente* has its moments — Urueta directed again — but it was one of the lesser ABSA productions, a mummy film without a real mummy. As though to apologise for this misfire, Urueta returned with his most famous film, *El barón del terror*. Although very cheap-looking (back projection is particularly abused), the film is nonetheless very bizarre and highly entertaining.

Salazar himself plays a wizard who, after being burned at the stake by the Inquisition, returns to earth on a comet and periodically becomes an ugly, brain-eating monster.

La maldición de la Llorona starred Abel Salazar and Rosita Arenas (soon to be his wife) as newlyweds menaced by a sort of witch-vampire (Rita Macedo) and her hunchback assistant. The latter role featured Carlos López Moctezuma, finally getting to appear in a Salazar film after losing the lead in *El vampiro*. Director Rafael Baledón turned in an excellent job in what was to be the last ABSA horror film.

In the 1960s, several packages of Mexican fantasy films were dubbed into English. Some were released theatrically, while others were sold directly to American television. Many were distributed under the aegis of promoter K. Gordon Murray; *The Man and the Monster* (*El hombre y el monstruo*), *Little Red Ridinghood* (*La caperucita rojo*) and *The World of the Vampires* (*El mundo de los vampiros*) are some of the more notable examples. These movies served for many years as the chief means by which non-Spanish speakers could see Mexican fantasy films. All the Abel Salazar films were dubbed, often with little or no cuts, and fairly faithful translations of the original dialogue.

Envious of Salazar's success, other Mexican producers were soon jumping onto the horror bandwagon. Calderón

Opposite top: *Ad mat for the influential* Ladrón de cadáveres.
Opposite bottom: *Mad doctor pits human robot against Mexican mummy.*

Above: *The amazing* El báron del terror *was dubbed into English as* The Brainiac.
Left: *Bad actors go bats in* El mundo de los vampiros.

contributed three 'Aztec Mummy' films, the América studios produced four serial features starring Germán Robles as vampiric mastermind Nostradamus, and Miguel Morayta directed a linked pair of vampire films — *El vampiro sangriento* (The Bloody Vampire) and *La invasión de los vampiros* (The Invasion of the Vampires). There was also a mini-boom in supernatural themes, with ghost/witchcraft films such as *Misterios de ultratumba* (*Black Pit of Dr M*), *Misterios de la magia negra* (Mysteries of Black Magic), *Espiritismo* (Spiritualism) and *El beso de ultratumba* (The Kiss From Beyond the Grave).

During this golden age of Mexican horror, almost every monster or fantasy plot exploited by Hollywood was resurrected and also given a Latin makeover. There were dinosaurs in a lost world, in *La isla de los dinosaurios* (The Island of the Dinosaurs); space operas, for example *El planeta de las mujeres invasoras* (The Planet of the Female Invaders); the Abominable Snowman in *El terrible gigante de las nieves* (The Terrible Giant of the Snow); voodoo and zombies in *Muñecos infernales* (Curse of the Doll People); Frankenstein-type monsters in *Orlak, el infierno de Frankestein* (Orlak, the Hell of Frankenstein); and Dr Jekyll and Mr Hyde in *Pacto diabólico* (Diabolical Pact; with John Carradine) and *El hombre y la bestia* (The Man and the Beast). The Invisible Man put in an appearance, in *El hombre que logró ser invisible* (*The New Invisible Man*); there were werewolves in *La casa del terror* (The House of Terror; with Lon Chaney Jr reprising his Universal role) and, of course, plenty of mummies (Aztec, not Egyptian) and vampires. At least four dozen Mexican movies from 1957 to date have featured vampires.

A partial exception to the general dearth of genre specialists in Mexican cinema is Fernando Méndez, director of *Ladrón de cadáveres*, *El vampiro*, *El ataúd del vampiro* and *Misterios de ultratumba*. The first two pictures are among the most famous and successful Mexican fantasy films of all time, but *Misterios de ultratumba* may well be Méndez's unsung classic. Méndez had learned his trade in Hollywood in the 1930s, working as a make-up artist on Dwain Esper's *Maniac* and *Marijuana, Weed With Roots in Hell*. In the early forties he began a journeyman career as scriptwriter and director in Mexico, turning out the usual mix of genres — comedies, *rancheras*, Westerns, dramas — mostly for producer Raúl de Anda. His films were competent but showed no particular distinction. It was in the horror field that he really found his forte.

Misterios de ultratumba tells the story of Dr Magali's pact with a colleague: whoever dies first will return to reveal what lies beyond the grave. Unfortunately, Magali's collaborator returns from the dead in a decidedly bad mood, and a sequence of events leads to Magali's arrest and subsequent execution for a murder he didn't commit. Magali does manage resurrection, albeit with his soul in the scarred body of his dead assistant (the real murderer) and only for a short period of time. *Misterios de ultratumba* is a very stylish film, even more atmospheric and brooding than *El vampiro*. Víctor Herrera's photography and Gunther Gerzso's sets were expertly done and Méndez managed to avoid most of the inconsistencies and flaws that hurt *El vampiro*. It seemed that Méndez had at last found his niche, just as his career was coming to an end. More than a decade would pass before another director with such a personal style and unique vision — Juan López Moctezuma — made his mark in Mexican fantasy cinema.

1957 to 1966 were the peak years for Mexican fantasy cinema, and in 1961 nearly one in five of all films produced were fantasy-oriented. Among the more notable films of 1966 — the last true year of the horror boom — were *El imperio de Drácula* (The Empire of Dracula), a colour vampire film heavily influenced by Hammer's Dracula series, *La endemoniada* (A Woman Possessed), a semi-remake of *Black Sunday* starring the frequently-nude Argentinian actress Libertad Leblanc, and *Autopsia de un fantasma* (Autopsy on a Ghost), an extremely strange but amusing fantasy-comedy featuring Basil Rathbone, John Carradine, Cameron Mitchell and an all-star cast of Mexican comedians.

Most of the Mexican fantasy films produced during this period were, at least critically, the equivalent of 'B' pictures in Hollywood, although the performers and technical personnel were often well-known and respected. There were few prestige genre efforts during these years. *Macario*, *Los cuervos estan de luto* (The Ravens Are in Mourning) and *Pedro Paramo* were the most prominent exceptions. As in many countries, horror movies were generally considered entertainment for less discerning tastes.

From 1967 to 1973, an average of eleven fantasy films were made each year, but these were increasingly split between fantasy-comedies (such as those starring Gaspar Henaine — 'Capulina') and the last surge of the *lucha libre* genre. By 1974, *lucha libre* films were virtually extinct and, on average, only three fantasy films per year were produced over the next decade.

One of the bright spots of the seventies was director Juan López Moctezuma. While working in radio and theatre, he had made the acquaintance of Alexandro Jodorowsky, a Chilean theatrical director resident in Mexico. López Moctezuma assisted Jodorowsky on his first two films, *Fando y Lis* (*Tar Babies*) and *El Topo*, and in 1971 made his own directorial début with *El mansión de la locura* (*Dr. Tarr's Torture Dungeon*). Loosely based on Edgar Allan Poe's story 'The System of Doctor Tarr and Professor Fether', the film did not receive the sort of cult reception afforded *El Topo*, although it was fairly well-regarded critically. Like most of López Moctezuma's films it was shot in English and Spanish versions, so it was therefore rather more widely distributed than the average Mexican film.

López Moctezuma, like Jodorowsky, never became part of the commercial film industry in Mexico (he was unable to get into the STPC director's union, which was notoriously restrictive), so his films were few and far between. *Mary, Mary, Bloody Mary* was a pseudo-vampire film starring model Cristina Ferrare (with John Carradine in a small role); *Alucarda, la hija de las tinieblas* (*Sisters of Satan*), was a stylish period picture about demonic possession; the thriller *Matar a un extraño* (*To Kill a Stranger*) featured Mexican singer and actress Angélica María, alongside English-speaking actors Donald Pleasance, Dean Stockwell and Aldo Ray. Several years before his death in December 1995, López Moctezuma made his final two (as yet unreleased) films: *El alimento del miedo* (The Food of Fear) and *Yo el vampiro* (I, The Vampire).

El mansión de la locura and *Alucarda, la hija de las tinieblas* are both very stylish, well-made films, reminiscent of Jodorowsky while at the same time retaining their own unique, Gothic flavour. López Moctezuma includes scenes of Hieronymous Bosch-like depravity, lust and anguish, set in decrepit, decaying, almost organic castles and mansions. His contemporary films are less intense, but they still have a perverse, brooding atmosphere all their own.

Mexican film-makers also tried their hand at comic book adaptations, the most elaborate of which was the two hour-plus *Kalimán, el hombre increíble* (Kalimán, the Incredible Man). Jeff Cooper stars as the mystic, turbaned superhero, an expert in the martial arts, who faces monsters, mummies and aliens. Director Alberto Mariscal undertook extensive location shooting in Egypt, was given a multinational cast, Panavision equipment, and a budget of 5,000,000 pesos to bring the adventures of Mexico's most popular comic book superhero to the big screen. The money invested in *Kalimán* was nearly four times the cost of a routine genre picture such as *Santo en la venganza de las mujeres vampiro* (produced the same year). Mariscal and Cooper returned for a sequel, *Kalimán en el siniestro mundo de Humanón* (Kalimán in the Sinister World of Humanón), but this second film was made on a much smaller scale and was less successful.

The Kalimán films may have been the most spectacular Mexican comic book adaptations, but a number of other characters made the transition during this period, including the Jungle Jim/Tarzan clone 'Chanoc' (eight films between 1966 and 1981) and the rural hero 'El Payo', played by Jorge Rivero in three well-regarded pictures made between 1971 and 1973: *El Payo, Los caciques* (The Overlords) and *La montaña del diablo* (The Devil's Mountain). The only Chanoc entry with strong genre elements was *Chanoc contra el tigre y el vampiro* (Chanoc vs. the Tiger and the Vampire), a shoddy but mildly diverting picture about a vampire who sets up shop near the coastal village where Chanoc lives. The El Payo films were far superior, both in production values and general execution. In a throwback to some 1940s films, the hero is occasionally assisted by Death, appearing as a beautiful woman (Irlanda Mora), as he faces greedy landowners, exploiters, vampires and ghosts. These films are excellent examples of the way the supernatural is treated in Mexican society and popular culture, with the fantastic elements blended matter-of-factly into the rural action plots.

Although not based on a comic book, the two films starring escape artist Zovek (Francisco Javier Chapa del Bosque) are similar in tone and style to the comic book adaptations, as well as containing elements from the *lucha libre* pictures. *El increíble profesor Zovek* (The Incredible Professor Zovek)

Opposite top: *Dracula comes to Mexico and puts the bite on some local lovelies.*

Left: *Mexican sci-fi: Ana Luisa Peluffo in* Conquistador de la luna.

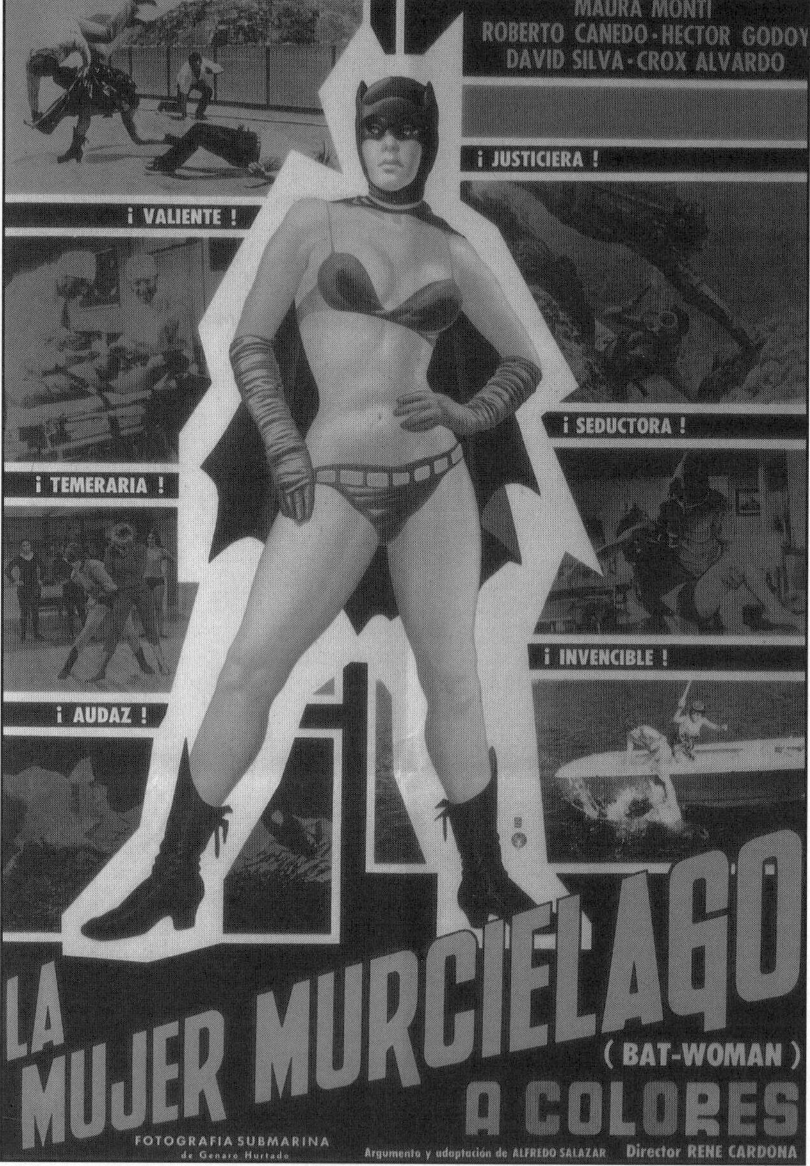

MAURA MONTI
ROBERTO CANEDO · HECTOR GODOY
DAVID SILVA · CROX ALVARDO
¡ JUSTICIERA !
¡ VALIENTE !
¡ SEDUCTORA !
¡ TEMERARIA !
¡ INVENCIBLE !
¡ AUDAZ !
LA MUJER MURCIELAGO
(BAT-WOMAN)
A COLORES
FOTOGRAFIA SUBMARINA
Argumento y adaptación de ALFREDO SALAZAR
Director RENE CARDONA

Above: *Batwoman — Bruce Wayne's* other *secret identity.*

Opposite top: *The horned Dr Satan and his army of sweater girls.*
Opposite bottom: *Mexican monster mayhem.*

presents the muscular performer as an escape artist and illusionist (which he was in real life), but also endows him with exceptional mental powers and expertise in the martial arts. He requires all of these abilities to defeat a mad scientist (José Gálvez, one of the pre-eminent villains of Mexican cinema from the late fifties through to the early seventies) who has a castle full of cannibal dwarves, deformed monster men and other unpleasant surprises. *Invasión de los muertos* (Invasion of the Dead) was inspired by *Night of the Living Dead.* A large black sphere from space mysteriously causes the dead to rise from their graves and attack the living. Unfortunately, Zovek was killed in an accident before the picture was finished and the producers were forced to pad the final product with new, mostly inferior, footage starring Blue Demon. Nonetheless, the two Zovek vehicles — both directed by René Cardona Sr — are among the more entertaining Mexican fantasy films of the early seventies.

Alfredo Salazar, the author of many earlier horror films, wrote and directed the bizarre *Una rata en la oscuridad* (A Rat in the Darkness), which featured a transvestite ghost (!) and large doses of full nudity in its tale of the supernatural problems suffered by two women (Ana Luisa Peluffo and Anais Melo) who move into an old house ("What a bargain!" — well, we know what that means).

La dinastía Drácula (The Dracula Dynasty) was a respectable, if cheaply made, period vampire film directed by veteran Alfredo B. Crevenna. It begins with the execution of a vampire by the Inquisition, and picks up in the late 1800s with the arrival of a witch (Erika Carlson) and "the Baron" (Roberto Nelson), a long-haired vampire in a small provincial town. They plot to take possession of a hacienda (called Los Sicamoros, in an homage to 1957's *El vampiro*), where the original vampire (who was the witch's lover) is entombed.

In contrast to the horror and fantasy genres, there have been very few serious science fiction films made in Mexico. One of the rare exceptions is *El año de la peste* (The Year of the Plague), which — until *La invención de Cronos* — was the only fantasy film to win Mexico's Ariel (the equivalent of the Oscar) for Best Picture. Its director Felipe Cazals also took the Best Director prize. Noted author Gabriel García Márquez and two other writers adapted Daniel Defoe's novel *A Journal of the Plague Year,* setting it in Mexico in the near future. A mysterious illness strikes the country, and the government, which first attempts to cover up the seriousness of the situation, is forced to take drastic measures to combat it. The rather vague script, ensemble acting (the picture lacks a clear-cut central hero or heroine) and oblique, inconclusive ending result in a film that is unusual and interesting but uncommercial. The low-budget and cheap production values also lessen the picture's impact. However, *El año de la peste* deserves credit for at least trying something different.

As the Mexican film industry began to shift its attention towards extremely cheap pictures intended primarily for video release, the number of non-comedy fantasy films increased, and some of them were reasonably well made. However, most of the films in this new wave of Mexican fantasy were close imitations of Hollywood horror films, slicker and less camp than pictures like *El barón del terror* and *Santo y Blue Demon vs. los monstruos.* Movies like *Cazador de demonios* (Demon Hunter; a good werewolf film) and *La noche de la bestia* (The Night of the Beast; whose subterranean menace seems to have been inspired by the worm monsters in *Dune,* which had been filmed in Mexico several years before) were entertaining, but lacked the outrageous aspects that made earlier Mexican fantasy movies such fun to watch. Ironically, two of the weaker points of the 'classic' Mexican horror films — make-up and special effects — actually improved during the eighties and nineties, even though the general technical quality of the films had declined steadily.

Less entertaining and even more slavishly imitative of Hollywood were films like *Cementario de terror* (Cemetery of Terror) and *Vacaciones de terror* (Vacations of Terror). Only the presence of Mexican performers differentiated these pictures from scores of low-budget horror movies made in the United States.

At the other end of the spectrum were quality films like *Los enviados del infierno* (The Envoys of Hell), *Hasta que la muerte nos separe* (Until Death Do Us Part) and *La invención de Cronos.* The first title was a spin-off from a popular supernatural-themed television series, *El Maleficio* (The Evil One). It starred Ernesto Alonso, who had featured in Buñuel's *Ensayo de un crimen* (*The Criminal Life of Archibaldo de la Cruz*) in 1955 and went on to become one of the most powerful television producers in Mexico. *El Maleficio* contained some fairly elaborate special effects in its tale of supernatural possession. Its female star, singer-actress Lucia Méndez, returned several years later in another fantasy-oriented telenovella, *El extraño retorno de Diana Salazar* (The Strange

Return of Diana Salazar).

Hasta que la muerte nos separe was a rare directorial effort by prolific screenwriter Ramón Obón. It featured a star of forties and fifties Mexican cinema, Rosita Quintana, along with genre veteran Hugo Stiglitz, the star of, among other films, *La noche de los mil gatos* (*Night of a Thousand Cats*). Made on a limited budget, but produced and directed with care, this period old dark house thriller (its alternate title was *La mansión del terror*) was a pleasant surprise that unfortunately attracted little attention.

La invención de Cronos was directed and written by Guillermo del Toro, a young horror movie fan who had worked in television and special effects but had never made a feature film before. The result was not only a splendid fantasy film (and one of the most expensive films of any type made in Mexico for many years), it was also a critical success, winning eight Ariel awards, including Best Picture and Best Direction. An antiques dealer (played by Argentine actor Federico Luppi) discovers a small device which bestows immortality on its owner, but exacts a horrific toll. Ron Perlman is the brutal gringo henchman of dying industrialist Claudio Brook, who is trying to steal the clockwork machine. Handsomely produced, with superb production design and photography, *La invención de Cronos* is a highly entertaining film, but one which actually has little Mexican flavour. In fact, Del Toro admits he was influenced more by Hammer and Universal horror films than by Mexican fantasy movies.

So-called 'video homes' — cheaply shot pictures intended only for video release — have accounted for the bulk of Mexican production over the past few years. They generally have few pretensions towards quality or significance and are made on minuscule budgets (often $75,000 or less) and rushed schedules (two weeks is the norm) for an undemanding audience. However, there are always exceptions to any generalisation. One odd but entertaining example is *Hades — vida después de la muerte* (Hades — Life After Death). Director Paco del Toro (no relation to Guillermo) makes commercial films with an evangelical Christian message. He's not afraid to portray sin (lust, drug use, greed) on-screen. To be sure, this is so he can later demonstrate the wages of sin — nonetheless, his films are usually far from dull. *Hades* tells of a dissolute young man killed in a car accident. Because he was not a good Christian (unlike his female passenger, who goes straight up to Heaven), the protagonist spends the film fleeing from several demons in surprisingly good make-up. Eventually he is caught and dragged off to a low-budget but still unpleasant-looking Hell.

Another director whose work bears watching is Sergio Goyri. Goyri, who also produces and acts in most of his own movies, has made a number of low-budget fantasy films. *Retén* (Roadblock) is a futuristic action tale starring Goyri as a policeman in charge of keeping mutants and other undesirables in their own sector of a large city. *El arma secreta* (The Secret Weapon) combines science fiction with comedy and crime-fighting: Goyri's father's brain is implanted in a Frankenstein-like monster (Agustín Bernal) by a mad scientist (comedian Rafael Inclán). Goyri's best film is probably the fantasy *El troño del infierno* (The Throne of Hell), in which he plays a mystical warrior charged with defeating a demon (Roberto Ballesteros), who changes into a werewolf-type monster (Agustín Bernal again) at the climax. The film includes levitation, demonic possession, telepathy, a blind wizard, a horribly burned corpse that comes back to life and other fantastic elements. The production values are adequate and the effects and make-up above average for a video release.

As Mexican cinema enters its second century, it is understandable that local film-makers and audiences might think that the glory days of their national film industry lie in the past. In the forties and fifties, annual production totals surpassed 100 films and Mexico's directors, actors and technicians were turning out world-class cinema. And horror fans may be forgiven for considering the period between 1957 and 1967 as the golden age of the fantastic film in Mexico, when El Santo, El Vampiro and the Aztec Mummy reigned supreme. These periods and the films they produced are certainly something to be proud of. But it would be wrong to dismiss all of the movies made in Mexico over the past three decades as cheap, crude, commercial efforts tailored for the lowest common denominator. Like all national cinemas, Mexican movies are a unique window into the society that produced them. The best Mexican fantasy films — *Santo vs. las mujeres vampiro, El barón del terror, Misterios de ultratumba* — have plenty to delight and thrill the genuine movie lover. Considered within their cultural context and — in some cases — on their artistic merits alone, there are plenty of Mexican films worth seeking out and, even today, film-makers and performers whose work is worth looking for. ■

By David Wilt

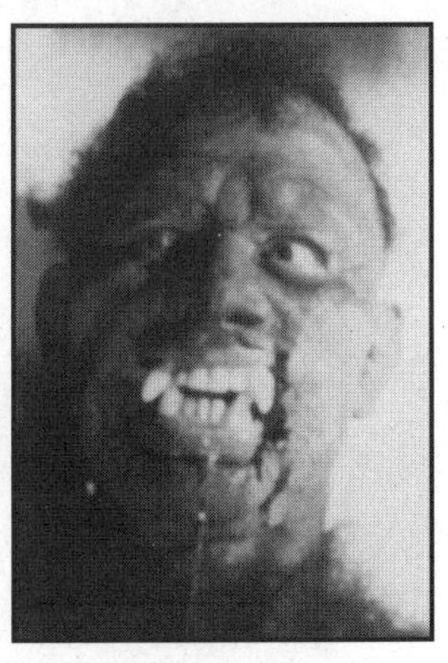

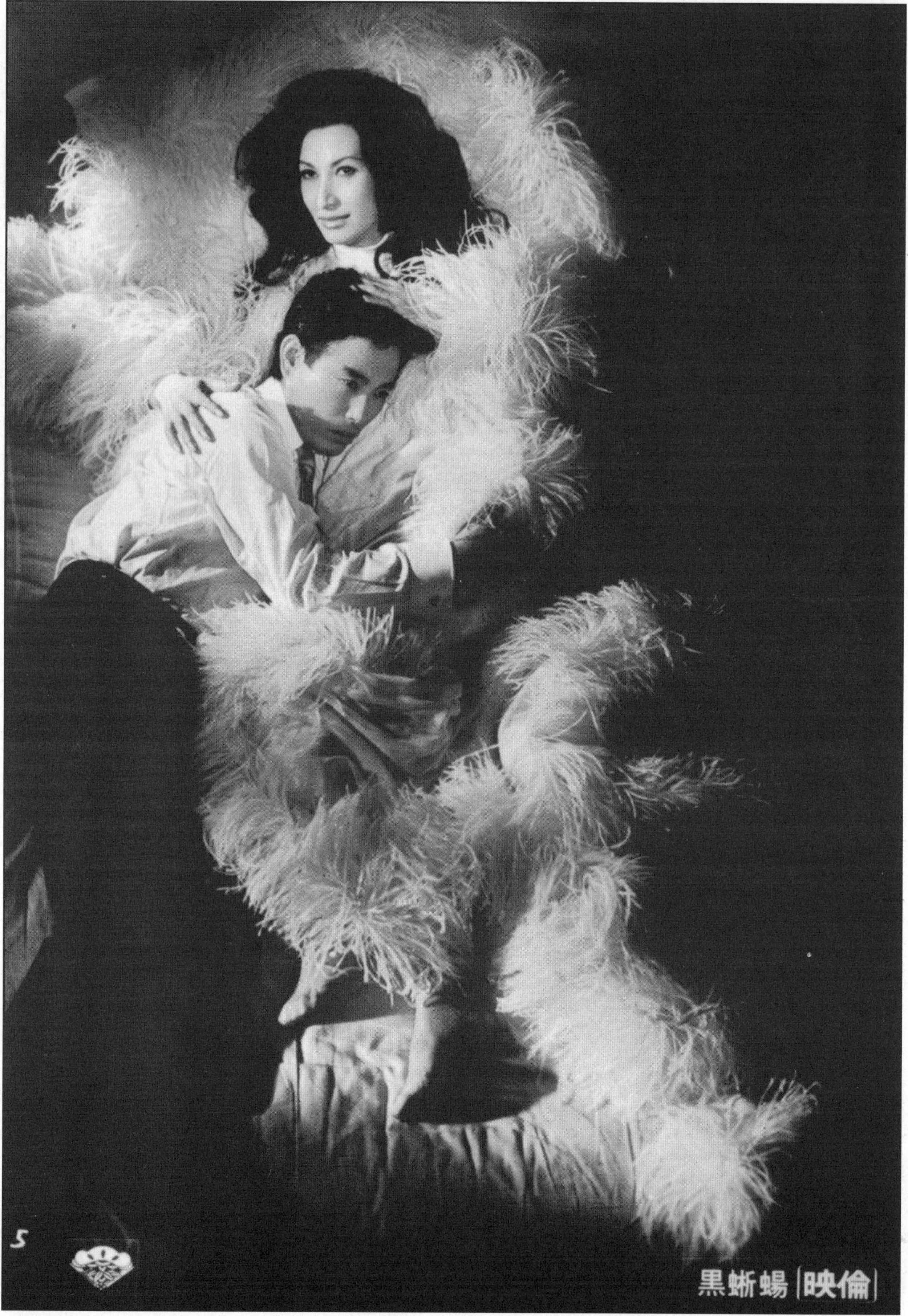
5
黒蜥蜴
映倫

JAPAN PART ONE

When the Kissing Had to Start

One problem with Japanese cinema is that there's so damn much of it. During the boom years of the late fifties, Japan was the biggest film factory in the world, even topping the prodigious output of India. In 1960, the five main Japanese studios turned out a total of 547 films, compared with Hollywood's 154. Inevitably, only a handful made it to the West, and the ones that did were an odd bunch indeed. This sad state of affairs has led to a weirdly warped view of the Japanese. Judged from the kinds of films we see in the West, they must be either stoic warriors with an unfathomable code of honour or sexual monsters with a bizarre schoolgirl fetish. Giant monster films, cut and dubbed to the point of near incoherence, rub shoulders with martial arts epics and immensely long and complex animation series. Violence, sex and creaky special effects — that just about sums up the Western viewer's attitude to Japanese cinema.

Initially, the range and breadth of this enormous industry seem daunting. Fortunately for us, the Japanese must have thought so too. From the beginning they made films to suit specific audience tastes: genre films that can be explored almost in isolation. Of course, Western cinema has these genres too but, as film critic Donald Richie points out, 'they do not think well of it and attempt to hide it. The Japanese do no such thing.'

The numerous genres of Japanese cinema can be divided into two main types: historical films, or *jidai-geki*, and contemporary films, or *gendai-geki*. In the 1950s, the big companies began to concentrate on particular genres. Toho made science fiction and comedy movies — it was from their Tokyo studios that the famous *Godzilla* series came. Daiei specialised in costume dramas and were renowned in the West for films like *Rashomon* and *Ugetsu Monogatari* — the sort of Japanese films that won prizes at international festivals. Nikkatsu was home to youth-oriented action films and, later, classy sex films in the studio's romantic pornographic (or 'roman porno') series of the seventies. Shochiku, once the spawning ground for radical film-makers like Nagisa Oshima, was kept alive by a series of sentimental comedies starring a loveable layabout called Tora San. The forty-eighth episode of the series was released in 1996.

Following the collapse of the studio system in the 1980s, the genre distinctions have practically vanished. Historical films, for example, are expensive to make and most now exist only as television serials. But, according to Donald Richie, the Japanese still retain a high regard for conventions and a relatively low regard for originality. There's nothing they like more than to see a well-known story reworked with fresh faces in familiar roles. The famous *Tale of the 47 Ronin* (commonly known as *Chusingura*) has been remade more than 220 times. There's even an erotic version — *Chusingura Hishou* (Secret Story of Chusingura) — and Kinji Fukusaku's 1994 film (*Yotsuya kaidan — Chusingura Gaiden*) combined this samurai tale with The Yotsuya Ghost Story.

Japanese cinema in its early days drew heavily on literary sources. Originally these were the *kabuki* plays that had grown out of theatres attached to the *mizu shobai* (floating world). These pleasure quarters were the source of much of the art and entertainment of the Edo period. In a rigidly feudal and regulated society they acted as a kind of safety valve, a place where rebels, outcasts and outsiders could find a safe haven. During the early nineteenth century, as the power of the shogun began to crumble, a decadent influence began to creep into *kabuki*. One of the masters of this strand was the playwright Nanboku Tsuraya. His most famous work is *Yotsuya Kaidan* (The Yotsuya Ghost Story). The play was first performed in 1825 and filmed as early as 1912. Now it's one of the classics of the Japanese horror repertoire, as familiar to a local audience as Dracula or the Frankenstein monster.

***Opposite:** A tender moment from* Black Lizard, *starring famed female impersonator Akihiro Maruyama.*

***Above:** Japanese superhero and monster films found a ready market in the West.*

***Left:** A tattooed, gun-toting lady boss — a familiar figure in Japanese popular cinema.*

***Right:** The mysteries of the universe revealed in* Warning From Space.
***Below:** The tattooed spider woman takes revenge on men.*

The decadent *kabuki* had its pictorial equivalent in artists like Kunisada Utagawa. His drawings for the traditional Chinese ghost story *Botan Doro* (The Peony Lantern) include one of its samurai hero making love to a skeleton. This image, or milder versions of it, has occurred in many Japanese films. The most famous (in the West) is probably the episode of *Kwaidan* called *Kurokami* (Black Hair). Kenji Mizoguchi's 1953 arthouse hit *Ugetsu Monogatari* also tells the story of a man seduced by a beautiful woman who turns out to be a ghost. The idea was even explored in a Nikkatsu softcore porn film from 1972 — *Seidan Botan Doro* (*Immortal Love*).

Today in tourist haunts like Nara Park one can buy key-rings that feature a heavily pregnant woman; turn her over and her womb contains a hideous skull. Sex and death, key components for horror movies, have long been associated in the Japanese psyche. Gaikotsu Miyatake wrote a book called *Jakumetsu-Irakuku* (*To Annihilate Oneself in the Experience of Pleasure*). He collected a long series of exclamations made by Japanese women during orgasm. All of them, he claimed, were in some way related to the idea of death.

Horror also carries with it an awareness of decay and physical degeneration. Ghosts in Japanese stories are often deformed in some way. This is not just to scare the audience, but to show the effects of the evil within and how it contaminates the body. A famous Japanese legend tells of how the goddess Izanami dies and is pursued into the underworld by her husband. He lights a candle and sees her corpse, crawling with maggots. In fury, she sends a swarm of hideous she-demons after him. The story neatly unites the themes of corruption, revenge and the deadly female into one convenient package.

The link between sex and death; repressed emotions seeking an outlet in devious cruelty and horror; the modern and the ancient side by side; these elements were central to the work of two twentieth century writers who would have an enormous influence on Japanese cinema through numerous adaptations: Junichiro Tanizaki and Edogawa Rampo. Of the two, Tanizaki is the best known in the West. His novel *Kagi* (*The Key*) was filmed in 1984 by Tinto Brass. The story of *Kagi* is ostensibly that of a middle-aged married couple who can no longer communicate with each other. They pour out their fantasies into diaries which each makes sure that the other is reading in secret. At least, that's the outward shape of the story. In fact, as a coda after the husband's death, it is revealed that the wife was using her diary to stoke the fire of her husband's rising sexual obsession as a way of destroying him.

Beginning with *Chijin no Ai* (A Fool's Love) in 1924, Tanizaki relentlessly explored the idea of the destructive and sexually rapacious woman. The object of the love is Naomi, a poor waitress, and the fool is Joji, the novel's middle-aged male protagonist. He is initially attracted to Naomi by her Western attributes (she reminds him of silent film star Mary Pickford). He adopts her and tries to turn her into his ideal woman. This combination of Pygmalion and Lulu soon turns the tables and ends up destroying her creator. In a climactic scene, Naomi gets on Joji's back and rides him like a horse. Soon he is forced to watch her enjoying an increasing stream of foreign lovers. *Chijin no Ai* has been filmed several times, the best version being Yasuzo Masumura's 1967 release with Michiyo Yasuda as the irresistible Naomi.

An even more chilling creation is Mitsuko in Tanizaki's 1928 novel *Manji*. With exquisite skill he describes the devious machinations of this bisexual rich girl and her need to possess and destroy a whole family. There's never any attempt to explain why she's doing it, which of course is what gives the novel its power. The first film version, directed by Masumura in 1964, was released in the West as *Passion*. Critics didn't know what to make of it: 'is it a kind of black comedy... or just another example of the new-style Japanese sensationalism (naked ladies embracing, strange goings-on with three in a bed)?' queried Britain's *Monthly Film Bulletin*. The 1983 remake, with its far more graphic sex scenes, would have had that reviewer's eyes popping out of his head.

Another dangerous woman is featured in Tanizaki's story *Shisei*, in which a famous tattooist drugs a woman and engraves a huge spider across her back. From being an innocent, she now becomes a predatory *femme fatale*, to whom all men are potential victims. Released in the West as *Spider Lady*, the 1966 film version of the story was again directed by Masumura. The script was written by Kaneto Shindo who wrote and directed two classic horror films about vengeful women — *Onibaba* and *Kuroneko*.

Edogawa Rampo is less well known in the West than Tanizaki, but his influence in Japan, particularly on the development of the horror film, has been just as strong. Born Taro Hirai in 1894, he took his pseudonym from the Japanese pronunciation of the name of his literary hero, Edgar Allan Poe. Before Rampo began publishing his own stories in 1922, the mystery or detective story was known in Japan only through translations of European and American originals. Rampo read them avidly. In creating his popular detective hero, Kogoro Akechi, he was strongly influenced by the likes of Conan Doyle and Maurice Leblanc. The flavour of his work, however, is unmistakably Japanese, marked in particular by the 1920s vogue for so-called *ero-guro-nansensu* (the erotic, the grotesque and the nonsensical). Rampo's tales are full of bizarre sexual fetishes, voyeurism and repressed sado-masochistic impulses.

An important story in the Rampo canon is *Inju*, published in 1928. This classic 'hell of mirrors' concerns a writer of detective stories who is contacted by one of his readers, a woman called Shizuko. She believes that the mysterious persecutor who is sending her threatening letters is another famous but elusive writer of crime stories, with whom she had a brief affair many years before. Nothing is what it seems and the writer finds himself plunging deeper and deeper into a mystery that is soon spinning out of control.

A key moment occurs when he first meets Shizuko. Tellingly, this takes place in a museum while he is gazing at a wooden statue of Kannon, the ancient Goddess of Mercy, who is closely associated with the erotic imagination. As Shizuko descends a staircase in front of him, he looks down and notices on her neck, disappearing below the collar of her kimono, a series of scars or scratches, like red weals on her flesh. With this revelation, for him her ethereal and formerly unattainable beauty becomes something real and tangible: 'All her elegance had now gone and there emanated from her a strange impression of obscenity that overpowered me.'

Later, in a cupboard in the woman's house, he finds a horse whip. "Was your husband fond of riding?" he asks innocently. When Shizuko blushes and tells him no, he suddenly realises what had caused the marks on her back. 'And wasn't I also, to my shame, gripped by that same mad passion?' he tremblingly confesses to the reader.

Many of Rampo's stories have been filmed. One of them, *Moju* (The Blind Beast), is an unsung classic of horror cinema. Claustrophobic, fascinating, obsessive and above all kinky — just like the best of Rampo's tales.

So famous was Rampo that, like Edgar Allan Poe with *The Man With a Cloak* and Dashiell Hammett with *Hammett*, he eventually became a character in a tricksy mystery film based around events taken from his own life. *Rampo* was loosely derived from the story *Inju*. Although not the 'total crap' that Tony Rayns described it, the film certainly misses as many targets as it hits. The problem is that it tries for so much: a history of Japanese popular cinema and Showa-era censorship, the influence of the Marquis de Sade, a biography of Rampo, as well as a reference-filled meditation on his fictional themes. There are numerous subplots, an animation sequence and even a black-and-white 'film within a film' featuring bondage, transvestism and rape. Perhaps some of the confusion arises from the fact that two versions of *Rampo* were released at the same time, one of them extensively reshot by its producer.

Tanizaki and Rampo both began writing during the Taisho era, Japan's brief Jazz Age of the 1920s. This was the period of the so-called *moga* (modern girl) and her male counterpart, the *mobo* (modern boy). Marxist ideas in politics and the Western look in fashion were essential badges for the trend-setters of the time. The apoplectic comments of dissenters and a rising tide of anti-Western feeling led inevitably to a backlash. The Showa-era censors began to come down hard on Western-influenced art, on leftist politics, on anything deemed un-Japanese. The command went out to film-makers to "banish insincere thoughts and words from the screen."

The militaristic, expansionist mood of the new Japan swept away most traces of the liberal, left of centre culture of the twenties and early thirties. The Japanese are great assimilators, and very soon artists and writers who had been enthusiastically espousing Western ideas were just as eagerly attacking them. Nor were we slow to retaliate. Following the attack on Pearl Harbour, anti-Japanese sentiments reached a peak of hysteria. Watching an American propaganda film like *Samurai* today, it's impossible to believe that such stereotypes were taken seriously. But they were. By the time the bomb fell on Hiroshima it was hard for anyone in the West to think of the Japanese as anything more than sadistic robots. Inscrutable, untrustworthy and totally incapable of individual thought.

After the Second World War the allied forces began a programme of enforced liberalisation and Westernisation. Many types of films were banned — including traditional samurai stories which were thought to promote militaristic values. Script approval and official support was given to films that pushed the theme of democratisation. An individualistic spirit was cultivated and the emancipation of women was brought once again onto the agenda. One of the by-products of this process was the first appearance of a kiss in Japanese cinema — in two films that appeared in almost the same week in 1946: *Aru Yo no Seppun* (A Certain Night's Kiss) and *Hatachi no Seishun* (A Young Girl of Twenty).

Sex education films also made a tentative appearance. As in the West, these were usually a cover for the exploitation of prurient interest. Nevertheless, they exerted a fascination for audiences and film-makers well into the sixties. Encouraged by the mood of openness promoted by the SCAP (Supreme Commander Allied Powers) forces and fired by their own commercial instincts, film companies began to tentatively explore the new freedoms. In the mid-fifties, ten years after that first celluloid kiss, modern youth in all its naked glory began to invade cinema screens across Japan. ■

Below: *Deadly Japanese mercenary in* Shogun Assassin.

Thinking Pink

The 1950s was a time of enormous change in Japan. Against a background of anti-American protests came a gradual rise in the standard of living. This was the start of an 'economic miracle' that lasted more than twenty years. From being a defeated Third World country, Japan was beginning the leap forward that ended with it being one of the richest nations on earth. For young people in the mid-fifties, this meant an increase in consumer goods, rock and roll music, motorbikes, movies and leisure.

Novelist Shintaro Ishihara began to write a series of stories about troubled teens. Taking their cue from the title of one them, *Taiyo no Kisetsu* (Season of the Sun; translated into English as *Season of Violence*), these were called sun tribe books, and their subjects were the loves, trials and tribulations of this new generation of hedonists. Many of Ishihara's stories were filmed and they in their turn influenced other films. So long as they had the word *taiyo* (sun) in their title they would be a hit. Often set by the sea and featuring moody boys on motorbikes and girls in bikinis, they had a superficial resemblance to American films like *Rebel Without a Cause*, but were much more sexually explicit. Kon Ichikawa's *Shokei no Heya* (*Punishment Room*), for example, told of a young student who drugs a girl in order to have sex with her. The newspapers were outraged, predicting a rash of copy-cat crimes.

The biggest hits of this sun tribe wave were *Taiyo no Kisetsu* and *Kurutta Kaijitsu* (*Crazed Fruit*). Based on Ishihara's novels, they also starred his younger brother, Yujiro. Aware of his popularity with both girls and boys, Nikkatsu promoted him, together with fellow heartthrobs Akira Kobayashi and Keiichiro Akagi, as their 'Diamond Line of Mighty Guys', building films around them and launching their Nikkatsu Action Series to feature them.

The sun tribe films were short-lived, but their legacy was a host of violent, sexy, youth-oriented exploitation movies with come-on titles like *Zekkai no Rajo* (*Naked Island*), *Nude Model Satsujin Jiken* (*Nude Model Murder Case*), *Nihiki no Mesuinu* (*Night Ladies*) and *Monroe no Yona Onna* (*A Girl Like Monroe*). Many of them were crime films or set in the glamorous but deadly world of the Shinjuku cabaret. *Osen Chitai* (*Yellow Zone*), for example, features a prostitution ring, a tough detective and the shapely Yoko Mihara as a girl who dances sensuously in front of masked foreigners in a sleazy club. The look of these films was heavily stylised, derived from American crime movies and post-war comic books. Lots of close-ups disguised the lack of production values, while odd camera angles kept viewers interested and glossed over the formulaic, clichéd plots. Filled with sneery tough

Opposite: *Tits and tentacles — a film genre unique to Japan.*

Left and far left: *Juvenile delinquents, Japanese style.*

guys in black leather and haughty temptresses in tight skirts, these films soon caught the mood of the public and the studios fell over themselves to fulfil an obvious need.

In 1946, the cinematic kiss had been a scandal. Ten years later, moviegoers were flocking to the new wave of Japanese nudies. Shintoho, who were in financial trouble, pushed the boat out (literally) with a series of girl diver films. *Onna Shinjuo no Fukushu* (Revenge of the Pearl Queen), starring the busty Michiko Maeda, was the first of a long line. There was precious little excuse for these films other than to show shapely females in skimpy swimming costumes. Some of the girl divers were shown topless and later films flirted with total nudity. Donald Richie reported that 'talent scouts were going about Japan looking for bigger bosoms to bare, a search quite necessary since in Japan large breasts are the exception rather than the rule'. Yoko Mihara certainly fitted the bill and in *Ama no Bakemono Yashiki* (*The Girl Divers From Spook Mansion*) she combined the girl diver film with the traditional ghost story.

The early sixties saw a drop in production. The industry began to sense the first of many crises. The days of big-scale classics like *Rashomon* and *The Seven Samurai*, so popular in the West, were over. To fill the gap came a host of small companies, turning out sex flicks, teenage nudie movies and violent crime films. With low budgets and even lower ambitions, these films were practically invisible to anyone who didn't look too hard — which the Government certainly weren't doing. Memories of pre-war censorship and post-war proscription were too strong to allow any sort of state intervention. The only apparent taboo was (and to an extent it still is) the showing of pubic hair. Japanese producers and directors became extremely skilled in using total nudity but disguising the offending portions behind arms of chairs, carefully placed legs or flower pots.

Then, in the mid-sixties, something happened that brought it all out into the open. Initially it may have been sparked off by the attention focused on Japan during the 1964 Olympics and International Expo. These two events marked the country's re-entry into the international community. To demonstrate their keenness, the Government began a huge clean up of the red light districts of Tokyo. They also started to look at what was being shown in cinemas. The first real shock came with an item called *Hakujitsumu* (*Daydream*), made by novice director Tetsuji Takechi, who had previously been involved in live cabaret shows and

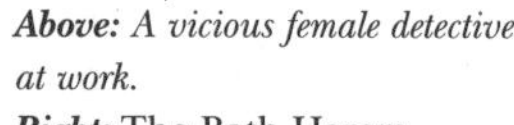
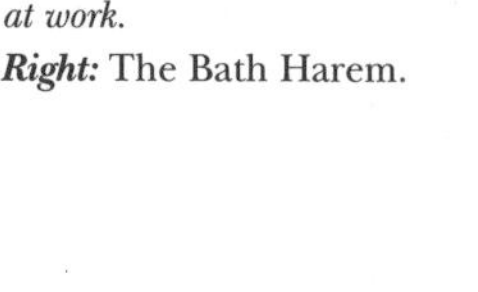

Above: *A vicious female detective at work.*
Right: The Bath Harem.

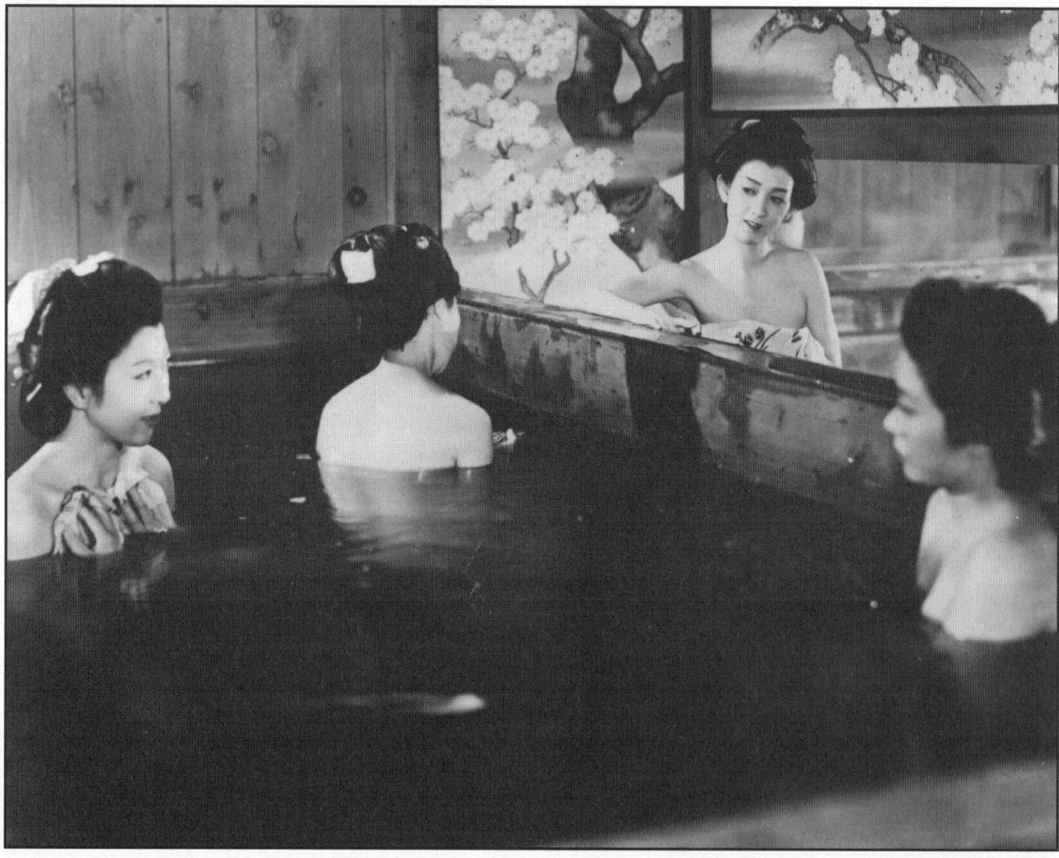

nude revues. *Hakujitsumu* was based on a story by prestigious novelist Junichiro Tanizaki. Consequently, it was being given a much wider distribution than the standard low-budget sexploiters that were filling the fleapit cinemas.

The story tells of a woman's visit to the dentist and of the sexual fantasies of a young male patient who imagines her being raped and otherwise abused while she's under anaesthetic. In one lengthy scene the boy watches helplessly through a large plate glass window while an older man strips the woman, binds her with ropes and suspends her from the ceiling. "Let's play electricity," her devious tormentor suggests. "You will experience a new thrill." He then unties her and wires her up to a transformer, sending jolts of electricity through her body as she flails helplessly in the throws of pleasure and pain. Perhaps the most disturbing aspect of the film is the almost religious intensity with which it presents its catalogue of torments. The face of the woman (brilliantly played by Kanako Michi), even in the midst of her worst agonies, has an expression of ecstatic beatitude, not unlike that of Renée Falconetti in Dreyer's *La Passion de Jeanne d'Arc*.

Hakujitsumu was immensely successful. It had been produced by an independent company (Daisan) from whom Shochiku had bought the distribution rights for seventeen million yen. The film took over 200 million yen in only two weeks. There were scores of complaints, even from the Japan Dental Association. The knives were out for Takechi. His next film was another adaptation from Tanizaki — *Kokeimu* (Dreams of the Red Chamber) — which the Government could hardly ban, although they did cut it by almost forty minutes. Then, in 1965, the shit really hit the fan with his third film, *Kuroi Yuki* (Black Snow), released this time by Nikkatsu Corporation.

The film relates the story of a young tearaway who murders a black GI. There are lots of sex scenes, marked by the fact that the boy can only get an erection when holding a loaded gun. In a shot repeated in countless later pink movies and porn films, a girl is shown running naked through the streets. Like the common nightmare of waking up in a crowd with no trousers on, this is an image that seems to haunt Japanese sex film-makers.

This time the authorities were ready. *Kuroi Yuki* was banned and Takechi was sued by the Tokyo police on a charge of public obscenity. The case became a *cause célèbre* and an important event in the history of the Japanese sex film when Takechi claimed political motivation. He described the film as an allegory of the rape of the Japanese people by the American occupation forces. Whether they believed Takechi's claims or not, many intellectuals rallied to his defence. Film-maker Nagisa Oshima made the most incisive comments. He pointed out that the pink film and eroduction had been born out of a crisis within the Japanese film industry: "To discriminate against one's own bastard offspring is surely the prototype of all prejudice."

Politics and pink movies gave each other a convenient mutual excuse. A film like *Kofun* (*Naked Pursuit*), for example, is really little more than an extended rape scene (probably the longest in cinema history outside the notorious *I Spit on Your Grave*). A young man in handcuffs chases a girl along a deserted beach. Every time he catches up with her, she loses more of her clothes until finally she's totally naked. The film is framed by an interrogation where it's revealed that the man is *zengakuren*, a member of the revolutionary students' group, and that he has killed a policeman. The girl, it turns out, is planning suicide, driven to the act by her parents' (and by implication Japan's) lack of moral purpose. The rape shocks the girl out of her death-wish and 'causes

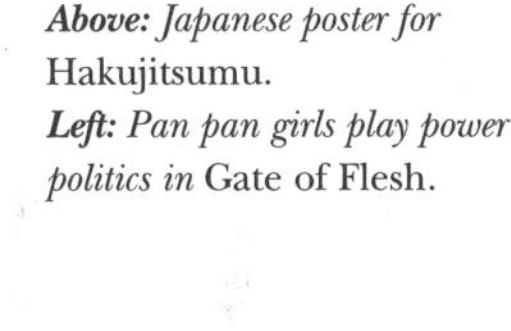

Above: *Japanese poster for* Hakujitsumu.
Left: *Pan pan girls play power politics in* Gate of Flesh.

***Above:** The gruesome climax of* Violated Angels.
***Below:** Naomi Tani gets the bird.*

her to re-evaluate her outlook as she recognises some of the passions of life' — according to the advertising blurb. Armed with this knowledge she marches off (naked) to confront her parents.

By 1969, more than half the total output of the Japanese movie industry was coming from outside the big five producers — and many of these independent films were so-called 'eroductions' or pink movies. Of the 495 films released that year, 240 were sex movies. This violent subculture began to develop its own star system. The innocent-looking Naomi Tani was tied up, whipped and generally abused in so many of these productions that she later complained that the shape of her body had become permanently altered by the demands of her work. The titles of her films, ranging from *Boyoku no shikibuton* (Colourful Bed of Violent Desire) in 1967 to *Zangyaku no onna gomon* (Cruelty of the Female Inquisition) in 1992, give some idea of the indignities visited on the body of Japan's diminutive bondage queen.

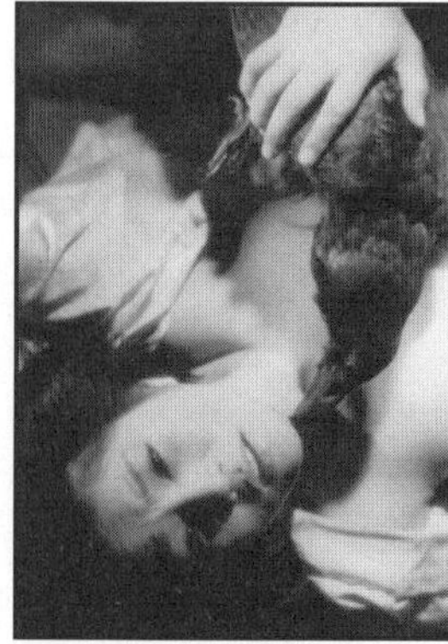

Of course, the majors hadn't been ignoring the siren call of sex — far from it. Nikkatsu, who had inaugurated the youth cycle back in the fifties with *Kurutta Kaijitsu* were also prolific makers of pink movies. In the same year of the Olympics that had seen the controversy over *Hakujitsumu*, one of Nikkatsu's most talented and wayward directors, Seijun Suzuki, made his own bid for notoriety with *Nikkutai no Mon* (*Gate of Flesh*).

The film is set in Tokyo in the immediate post-war years. Japan is a rubble-strewn wreck. Its people are demoralised, doing whatever they can to get by. The protagonists of the film are a bunch of *pan pan* girls — prostitutes who cater in particular to American servicemen. They operate from a bombed-out building in one of the most run down districts of town. A Japanese soldier on the run from the authorities hides out in their basement. The film shows the power struggles that ensue, with the women variously asserting their independence from him or trying to get him into bed.

Suzuki's film was one of the earliest examples of pink cinema to be distributed in Europe (it was shown in Belgium as *Barrière de chair*) and what most shocked the critics who saw it was its anti-Americanism and violence. In one scene, the girls all turn on O-Machi, a rather aloof woman who has broken one of their codes: she has allowed a man to make love to her for free. In a scene as shocking for its emotional as for its physical violence, she is stripped, tied up and viciously beaten by O-Sen, the girls' tough leader. Suzuki underlines the playground politics of the scene by having the plump O-Roku, the fool of the group, suddenly turn into a blazing harridan, picking up a razor to inflict even more damage on the hapless O-Machi.

Seijun Suzuki made his films firmly within the commercial mainstream. Much more underground but no less subversive were the films of Koji Wakamatsu. After many years as an assistant on films and television programmes, he directed his first feature in 1963, a very low-budget quickie called *Amai Wana* (Tender Trap). Two years later, in the same year that the scandal broke over *Kuroi Yuki*, Wakamatsu's eighteenth film, *Kabe no Naka no Himegoto* (*Secret Act Behind Walls*) was presented by a German distributor for screening at the Berlin Film Festival.

Wakamatsu's early films had been gangster movies and low-budget youth flicks. Inspired by the success of the pink movies, he had begun to include more sex in his films. *Kabe no Naka no Himegoto* was his most extreme yet. It featured masturbation, voyeurism and rape. The Japanese authorities reacted with fury when they discovered that the film was to be shown as a Japanese entry at Berlin. It had not been officially sanctioned for export and had not even been seen in Japan. Tokyo newspapers wrote about 'the shame of the Japanese cinema being exposed to the world.' Their ambassador made representations to the West Germans. The whole thing threatened to become a major diplomatic incident. Western critics suddenly began to sit up and take notice. The Japanese pink movie had come of age and Koji Wakamatsu was to become its most prominent exponent.

Like all his early films, *Kabe no Naka no Himegoto* was made on a very low budget and is marked by its extreme violence and apparently arbitrary political trappings (a poster of Stalin on the wall of an apartment, one of the spied-on lovers being an arms manufacturer). These early movies were all shot in black and white and had strange, oblique edits and jerky camera work. Commenting on this later, Wakamatsu was amused by the serious questions he was asked about his style. Very often, he explained, the idiosyncratic editing and odd camera angles were necessary to avoid showing pubic hair or full frontal nudity — which would have ensured that the film was banned. It's certainly true that his mainstream films, such as *Kimpeibei* (*The Concubines*), are much more traditional-looking.

The Berlin scandal did Wakamatsu no harm. After all, the film had been made very cheaply. With the publicity it was getting he was likely to make a heap of yen. Even better, he was now being fêted by the intellectual elite from whom he had always felt excluded. Buoyed with his success, he left Nikkatsu and set up his own production company. Already used to a fast working schedule, Wakamatsu now began to turn out films in one or two weeks for a budget of around $5,000. Many of them have only one set — usually a single room — and a small cast. He constructed his films around images and generally had either no script or only the rough sketch of one. To attract audiences, he thought up outrageous titles: *Taiji ga Mitsuryo Suru Toki* (*When the Embryo Hunts in Secret*), *Sex-Jack*, *Tenshi no Kokotsu* (Angelic Orgasm), and *Yuke, Yuke Nidome no Shojo* (Go, Go, Second Time Virgin). As he confided to French writer Romain Slocombe: "When they read the word 'virgin', people instantly imagine something sexy's going on and they rush to see the film." Even given this deception, few came out of Wakamatsu's films asking for their money back.

Perhaps his most notorious film, fairly widely distributed in the West at the time, is *Okasareta Byakui* (*Violated Angels*). Again it was made quickly, in only three days, using the cast from a more commercial film he was working on at the time. The initial inspiration was a case Wakamatsu read about in the newspapers, where a man in Chicago had murdered twelve nurses. What intrigued him was the fact that one of the nurses had survived. In Wakamatsu's story, this is because she understands the frustrations that are driving the killer. She embraces him and in some symbolic way becomes his mother. If this all sounds very sweet and innocent, bear in mind that the film begins with an extended lesbian sex session, includes a long scene of the killer stripping the skin from one of his victims, and ends with all but one of the women dead, their bodies arranged in a circle on the floor around the killer.

By the mid-sixties, more than half the movies in production were pink films of one sort or another. And it wasn't just the independents. Nikkatsu, Shochiku and Toei were all involved. Perhaps as a reaction to the political content of Wakamatsu's movies and potential censorship troubles, Daiei and Toei turned to *jidai-geki*, or historical films, creating a subgenre of ero retro. The model for this was Tetsuji Takechi, the man whose *Kuroi Yuki* had caused such a rumpus a few years before. In 1964 he had made erotic versions of the famous tales of Genji (*Genji monogatari*) and *Kokeimu*. Both were based on adaptations by Tanizaki. Wakamatsu also tried his hand at retro porn. His *Kimpeibai* was a colourful if occasionally confusing adaptation of the Chinese erotic classic *The Golden Lotus*. Elegantly shot, with many scenes of flogging and kinky lovemaking, the film is something of a departure for Wakamatsu from his usual contemporary themes. Yet the crazed antisocial bandit hero, driven mad by

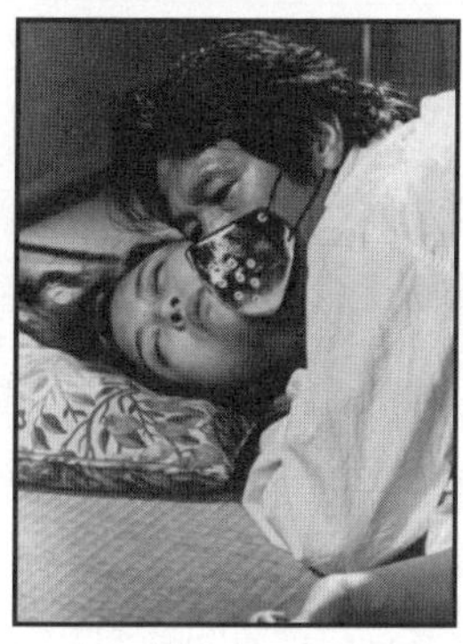

Above: *Wakamatsu's* A Pool Without Water.
Below: *Love behind the veil in* Notorious Concubines.

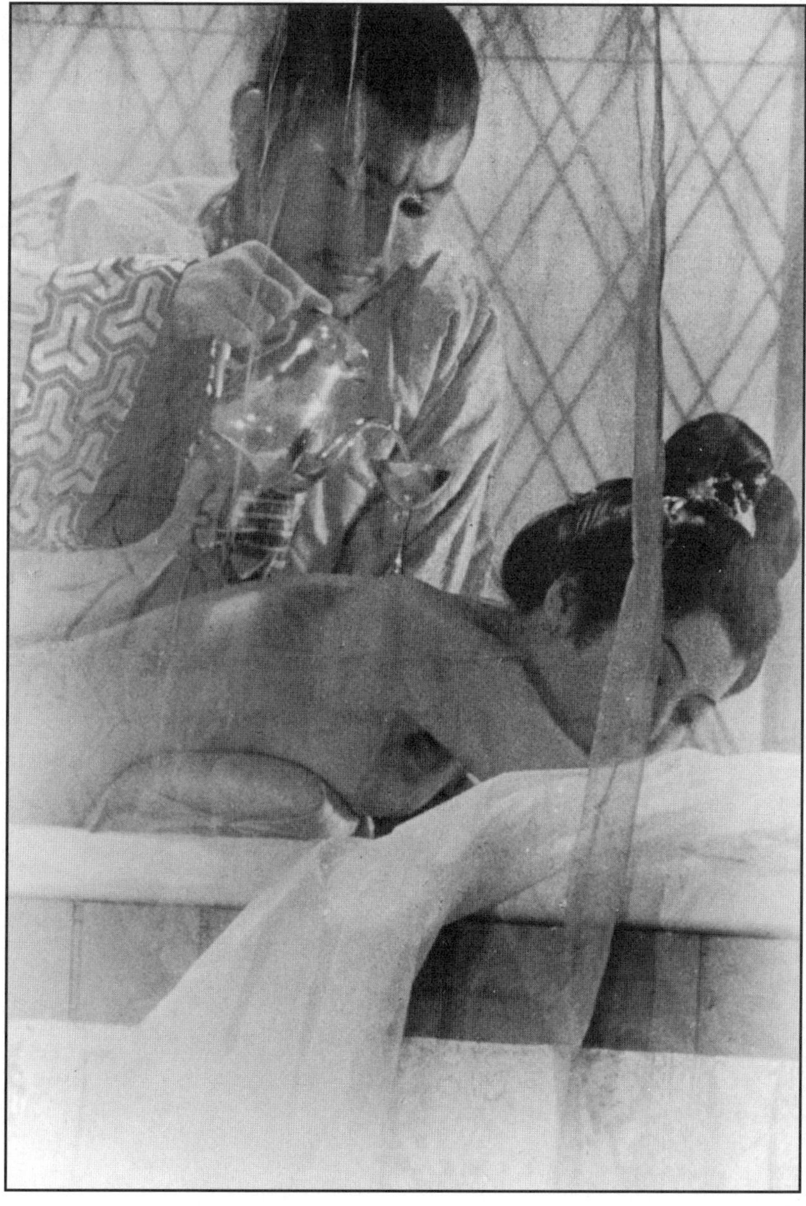

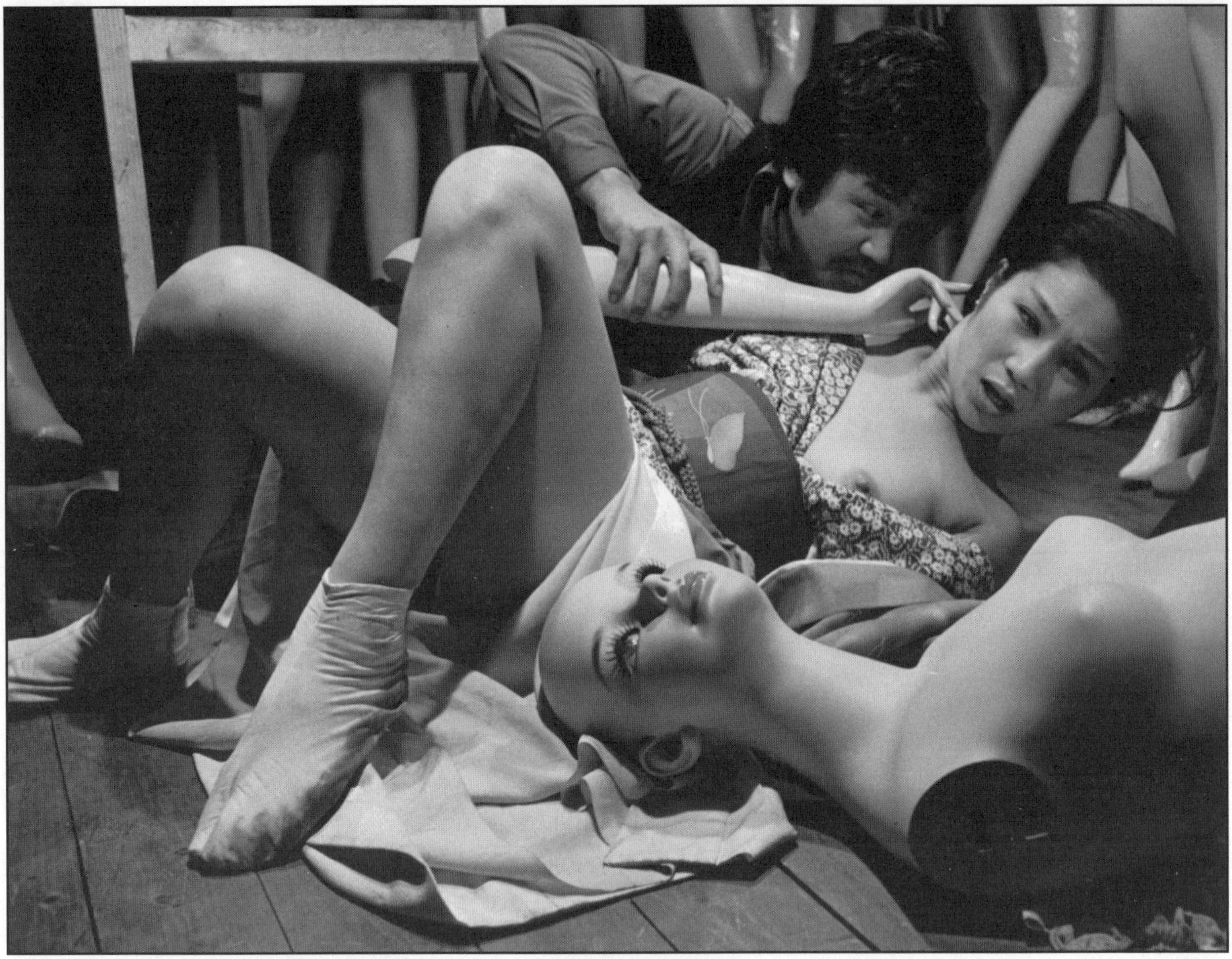

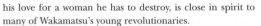

Above: *Japanese pink movies of the 1970s were notorious for their bizarre sex scenes.*

his love for a woman he has to destroy, is close in spirit to many of Wakamatsu's young revolutionaries.

In the mid-sixties, several companies began to make women's films — but not films for women, needless to say. These were films about women. Or, more accurately, about certain men's fantasies of them.

The Japanese have long been fascinated by the idea of communities of women. In its most innocent form there is the Takarazuka Opera Company, founded in 1914 by railway magnate Ichizo Kobayashi. Here, in their all-female paradise of pink buildings, anything up to fifty girls perform such works as *Berasaiyu no Bara* (*Lady Oscar*), about a beautiful girl disguised as a boy who becomes a hero of the French Revolution. Of course, there is no sex in Takarazuka performances. That need is amply catered for by stories about the shogun's harem. The title of a 1968 film, *Tokugawa Onna Keizu* (*The Shogun and 3000 Women*), is a rather fanciful inflation of the actual numbers involved. In his heyday the Tokugawa emperor Ieyasu kept a retinue of 600 females. Obviously not all of these were for sex, but a central core of up to twenty concubines were expressly employed to provide for the shogun's physical needs.

Many films and television series have exploited this subject. Two productions released in 1967 — *Ooku Maruhi Monogatari* (*The Shogun and his Mistresses*) and *Zoku Ooku Maruhi Monogatari* (*Women Around the Shogun*) — depict the petty intrigues, jealousies and sexual one-upmanship of the shogun's *ohoku* or harem. In this closed world there was a rigid division of labour, with important posts being jealously fought for. The 1971 production Castle Orgies, set during the reign of Ienari the eleventh shogun, tells of the *ojoro*, the woman whose job it was to regulate the shogun's visits to his concubines. While the shogun took his pleasure, the job of the *ojoro* was to wait in an adjacent room, listen to everything that was said, and note it down for future reference. She also had to keep track of the shogun's dalliances in case any children resulted from them. To ensure the legitimacy of such offspring, new additions to his harem were required to be virgins. In the 1976 film *Ooku Ukiyo-buro* (*The Concubine's Palace*), a love-sick samurai decides to rescue his girl from the harem by deflowering her before the emperor can have his wicked way with her.

As might be expected, the shogun's appetite often exceeded his ability to deliver. The communities of women, as shown in *Irogoyami: Ohoku Hiwa* (*Castle Orgies*) and many other shogun sex films, were often self-servicing, leading to the plethora of lesbian scenes that are another feature of these films. The *harigata*, or dildo, was perfected to a fine art, made of carved wood, ivory or leather (which could be soaked in warm water to achieve the right feel and consistency).

Nuns were another obvious source of fascination. The 1969 film, *Hiroku Onnadera* (*Secrets of a Woman's Temple*), tells the story of Oharu, who enters a convent to find out about her brother's murder. She uncovers a nest of intrigue, depravity and lesbian affairs. Behind it all is the evil mother superior, Shigetsuin, who entertains men in her chambers and then has them killed.

Norifumi Suzuki's 1974 film, *Sei Ju Gakuen* (Convent of the Sacred Beast), like *Hiroku Onnadera*, is a sort of nunsploitation version of Sam Fuller's *Shock Corridor*. In Suzuki's film, Maya submits herself to holy orders to find out what happened to her mother, a nun in the Sacred Heart Convent. The convent is a hot-bed of lesbianism, self-flagellation, secret torture and demonic desires. The villain of the piece is a wild and hairy monk who borrows his sartorial style from Rasputin and his bedroom manners from the Marquis de Sade. From time to time he comes to the convent to takes his pleasure with the nuns. It was he who seduced Maya's mother and caused her suicide when he learned she was pregnant.

Sei Ju Gakuen is extremely well filmed, with some astonishingly blasphemous scenes. In one eye-opening moment, a tortured nun is forced to urinate over an image of the crucified Christ. She tries to hold back, but eventually the flood gates open and steaming urine gushes over the sacred object. Heavenly choirs sing "Gloria... Gloria...!" as the tormented nun expires. A drop of blood falls from her mouth and mixes with the urine, turning the drowned Christ's image red.

Norifumi Suzuki was a prolific and occasionally inspired film-maker who wore many hats over his long career. However, it was the sexy stuff that really brought out the beast in Suzuki. His erotic ninja movie *Shinobi no Manji* (*The Secret of Fylfot*) started the ball rolling in 1968, but it was with *Sentensei Inpu* (*The Insatiable*) and *Shikijo Daimyo* (*The Erotomaniac Daimyo*), both made in 1971 with French sex star Sandra Julien and busty glamour girl Reiko Ike, that he really found his feet.

These are incredible productions and, by today's standards, totally reprehensible. *Shikijo Daimyo*, for instance, includes a sexy hara-kiri scene, of all things. The suicide disembowels herself to the strains of romantic 'dadadadada' music, while blood splatters across her ample bosom. The *Daimyo* (feudal lord) of the film's title is Taderatu, married to the shogun's daughter, but apparently not interested in the physical side of things. A local businessman attempts to spice up the *Daimyo*'s sex life by introducing a series of willing and able maidens into his harem. These include a busty black girl (very unusual for Japanese movies) and a red-haired French temptress who's delivered to him in a large box, wrapped up with ribbons like a birthday present. After a lesbian show between the black girl and Frenchie, the *Daimyo* is all stoked up and ready to go. In fact, he enjoys himself so much that he subsequently forbids any of his subjects to engage in sexual intercourse. He can't bear the thought of mere commoners enjoying such fun for free.

Suzuki's most notorious film, and probably his best, is the 1979 production *Dabide no Hoshi: Bishoujo-gari* (Star of David: Beauty Hunting). Like *Sei Ju Gakuen*, this is also based on a comic book. The gruesome and gripping story centres

Above: *French sex star Sandra Julien made two films in Japan. Here's* The Erotomaniac Daimyo *from 1971.*

Left: *Female ninjas on the rampage.*

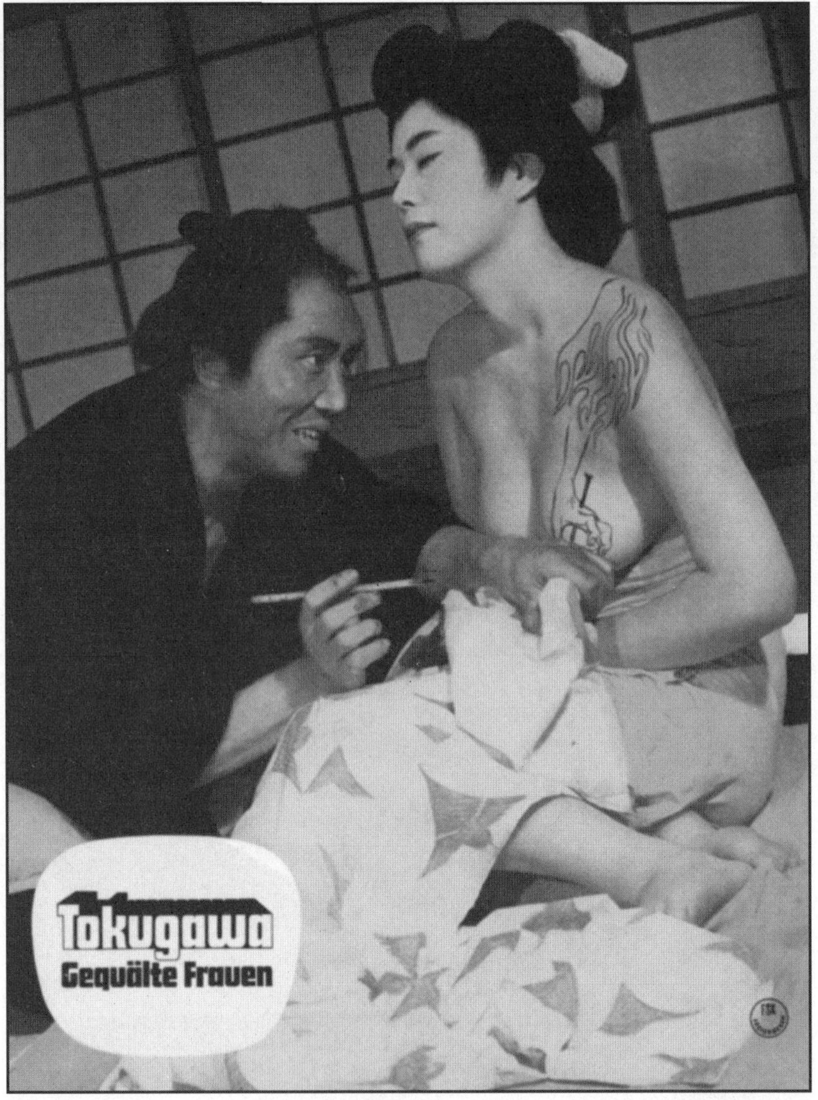

***Above and opposite:** German lobby cards from the 1968 film* The Joys of Torture.

on a young man, born as the result of a savage rape, who grows up obsessed with Nazi iconography and his absent father. He constructs a secret torture dungeon where he imprisons young women.

The depiction of torture as a form of entertainment has been around in Japanese art for many years. Novelist Oniriku Dan specialises in writing bondage-themed S&M novels. "Torture was used invariably and routinely for exacting confessions throughout Japanese history," he explains. "With such precedents, the association in the popular imagination has spawned patterns of sado-masochism quite different from Europe and the United States." Given the Japanese talent for ritualising just about anything, it's hardly surprising that different types of torture, not to say different types of ropes and knots, were used for different types of crime. Tokugawa period lawmen were required to be up to date on the etiquette of the torture chamber.

In the mid-sixties, Japanese studios began to turn out a cycle of films, mostly set in the Tokugawa period (1603-1867), that combined the prurient fascination with communities of women and the upfront depiction of scenes of torture, lacking even the slim justification of a political message that Wakamatsu and Takechi brought to their pink movies. Again, these films were immensely popular. If Oniriku Dan is right when he claims that "most Japanese men think that women are all masochists", then their success should hardly be a surprise.

Daiei was one of the first studios off the block with this new trend in entertainment. They were in financial trouble and were searching for anything to pull in the punters. *Hiroku Onna-ro* (*Secrets of a Women's Prison*), directed by Akira Inoue, was one of the most successful films of 1967. It's the story of a prostitute wrongly accused of murder and locked up in a brutal prison where her sister is one of the guards. The troubled studios went into overdrive and produced at least six sequels in rapid succession before finally shutting up shop in 1971.

Toei picked up the challenge with a series of films directed by the versatile and prolific Teruo Ishii. Ishii had formerly worked as a contract director for the aggressively commercial Shintoho company and later for Nikkatsu. For Toei, he turned out a group of eight films that mixed sex, violence and history into a very heady brew indeed. Most of the films were compendiums of three or four stories, with settings ranging from the early Tokugawa period to the mid-sixties. The first, and in many ways the best, of the bunch was 1968's *Tokugawa Onna Keibatsushi.* The film was released in the West as *Criminal Women* or *The Joys of Torture.*

The film begins with three short scenes showing the shocks to come: one woman is hung upside down and decapitated, another is burned alive and the last unfortunate is ripped apart by wild bulls. And this is even before the credits have finished. After that things settle down a little as the first story develops, featuring the illicit love between a brother and sister. A rich merchant covets the sister and tells the authorities of the couple's sins. Pretty soon the poor girl is tied up and bent double, while a couple of enthusiastic inquisitors take it in turns to give her a good birching. Confessing to her 'crime' of incest, she is crucified — upside-down! — and left to drown in the rising waves on a lonely beach.

The second story jumps straight into the action. This is set in a temple full of bald-headed Buddhist nuns. We witness the furtive coupling of a new nun and a young monk. The mother superior takes a shine to the monk and forces him to make love to her under a thundering waterfall. Then she decides to get rid of his girlfriend. The series of tortures that follow are pretty hard to watch. They include the girl being immersed in a barrel of water filled with small fish that swim up her privates. In an even worse scene, the jealous nun fills the girl's vagina with red hot chillies. It's a relief when the end comes and the poor thing is finally put out of her misery.

The third segment is even more devious. A famous tattooist is challenged by a sadistic torturer to create a design showing a face in the throes of real agony. The tattooist agrees to accompany the torturer during one of his sessions. At the climax of the act he stabs the torturer in the guts, twisting the knife until he gets exactly the right expression of agony. Now he has the model for his final masterpiece.

The tattoo theme is continued in Ishii's 1969 film, *Tokugawa Irezumi Shi — Seme Jigoku* (*Hell's Tattooers*), which has a complete story rather than segments. Set in the mid-nineteenth century, when Westerners were starting to make their influence felt in Japan, it tells of the rivalry between two brothers, both expert tattooists. They fall in love with the same girl and both, naturally, want to make their mark on her smooth, unblemished skin. Although much of the film takes place in a brothel, there's no straight sex. Here, the act of tattooing a woman replaces the notion of having sex with her. When the brothers discover a new girl, the first thing they look at is her back, to see if her skin is suitable for the application of their coloured needles. The climax of the film comes when a devious Westerner, Clayton (with red hair, like all 'foreign devils'), attempts to buy a bunch of tattooed prostitutes for the amusement of his friends. Although previously prepared to suffer any indignities, the girls find this too much and rebel. One of the brothers kidnaps Clayton's young daughter and tattoos her as an act of revenge. The ending is a real slice of sixties psychedelia, featuring nude girls covered with fluorescent tattoos dancing in the dark.

Throughout the 1960's, television had become an increasing attraction, drawing audiences away from the cinemas. Much of the original impetus for this stemmed from the 1964 Tokyo Olympics, when television set ownership rocketed following an extensive marketing campaign. The big studios' dabbling in sex and exploitation films were attempts to come up with something audiences couldn't find on the small screen. Their desire to regain centre stage were hampered, however, by the relentless rise of the independents. These low budget companies were able to make films that were much more daring, and more profitable, than the majors. The late 60's was a time of high creativity and experimentation in Japanese cinema. Film-makers as different as Susumu Hani, Yasuzo Masumura and Toshio Matsumoto were using the freedoms of the pink movie to deal with more serious subjects than 'just' sex.

Matsumoto's *Bara no Soretsu* (*Funeral Parade of Roses*) begins with what looks like a typically steamy sex session. Then, as the man dresses, we hear his girlfriend off camera talking to him and we realise that the lovers are both male. The film is a version of *Oedipus Rex* with most of the sexual roles reversed. Punctuated by moments of extreme violence, as well as speeded up comedy inserts, films within films, even interviews with the cast discussing their roles, it's the kind of crazy cocktail that could only have come from the late 60's. Peter, the actor who portrays Eddie — the girlfriend in the film's opening scenes — had a bizarre subsequent career, with roles in Kurosawa's classic *Ran* as well as the ultra-violent *Guinea Pig* series. In *Bara no Soretsu*, aged only seventeen, he made a stunning debut. The ending, where Eddie pokes out his eyes on discovering that his middle-aged gay lover is also his father, is horrifyingly brutal.

Just as devastating is Susumu Hani's *Hatsukoi Jigokuhen* (*Inferno of First Love* aka *Nanami*). The film begins in classic blue movie style. Shaky camerawork, almost burnt out black and white stock; a couple go to a hotel room to make love. The girl, Nanami, is a nude model and bar hostess, the boy, Shun, is too nervous to have sex with her and too embarrassed to explain why. From this first unconsummated encounter the film becomes an exploration of their separate worlds and an examination of Shun's impotence.

One time Shun comes searching for Nanami and finds her at work in a seedy basement studio. Some sweaty, pig-faced gangsters have set up an S&M sex show for a bunch of middle aged men. Unlike similar scenes in many eroductions this one has a real emotional kick to it. There are no tortured close ups of Shun's face, but we know exactly what effect it's having on him, seeing the girl he's unable to make love to tied-up, whipped and abused. The obviously fake play-acting of the scene only makes it more poignant. What a strange place is this world of adults, Shun must be thinking, where such pantomimes substitute for real relationships.

The scriptwriter of *Hatsukoi Jigokuhen*, Shuji Terayama, had a background in radical theatre and radio production. His first short film, *Emperor Tomato Ketchup*, caused quite a stir when it was shown at the London Film Festival in 1970.

***Top:** Nikkatsu Roman porno:* The True Story of Abe Sada. ***Above:** Toei sex movie from the early seventies.*

The film is a series of short episodes in which children act like adults and adults play increasingly violent children's games. It's all very theatrical and very late sixties. One extended episode, an orgy between some naked harpies and a pre-teenage boy, has decided pædophile overtones. The uncomfortable nature of this scene, mid way between innocent play and actual abuse, has given the film considerable notoriety over the years. The notion of children adrift in a world of adult sexuality also colours Terayama's first feature film, *Sho o Suteyo Machi e Deyo* (*Throw Away Your Books, Let's Go Into the Streets*), released in 1970. It's a kind of updating of some of the themes of *Hatsukoi Jigokuhen* but set in a much more violent world, where you have to fight hard to maintain any grip on tenderness and humanity.

Rock and roll, sex, drugs, the Vietnam war, these were the yardsticks by which Japanese youth measured out their distance from the past. Nikkatsu, the oldest of the big four film companies, decided to take advantage of this new explicitness. Sex was in the air. The popularity of TV programmes like the famous *11pm Show* and of books like *How to Sex* showed the way. Nikkatsu decided to scale down their operations and concentrate entirely on a series of low budget soft core movies. Their plan was to make the films in a couple of weeks each for the equivalent of $160,000, using more or less the same technical crew and interchangeable sets. Given the talents at their disposal it was hoped that the results would be a little bit more ambitious, a little bit classier than the majority of the anonymous pink films.

Their first batch of releases appeared in August 1971. The films — which included *Danchizuma: Hirusagari no Joji* (*From Three to Sex*) and *Hachigatsu no Nureta Suna* (*Wet Sand in August*) — were a big success and Nikkatsu were in business. Things went well until the following year when the police decided that two of the films — *Koi no Karyudo* (Love Hunter) and *Oi Nikki: Mesuneko no Nioi* (The Smell of the Wildcat) — were obscene. Nine people involved with the production of the films were taken to court. The trial eventually lasted for eight years. To the great embarrassment of all concerned, three of the defendants (Nikkatsu employees) were members of the censorship body, the EIRIN film commission.

The trial certainly didn't stop Nikkatsu. For the next twelve years they turned out a huge number of films, sometimes as many as seven a month. As usual in Japan, popular films led to series. Amongst many others, Nikkatsu had the *Pink Curtain* series, the *Zoom Up* series (based on the life of a glamour photographer) and the self-explanatory *Onna Kyoshi* (Female Teacher) series. In 1973, they introduced kinkier S&M themes with *Hirusagari no Joji: Koto Mandara* (Afternoon Affair: Kyoto Holy Tapestry). The director of this film, Masaru Konuma, together with its star, Naomi Tani, made several of the best in this subgenre, including *Hana to Hebi* (Serpent and Flower), based on a series of books by the popular writer of sex novels Oniriku Dan. Nikkatsu began to get a reputation as a studio that took risks and managed to attract some interesting young film-makers. There was always enough new blood and new ideas to keep them from getting stale.

Within the limits of budget and shooting schedule, several directors turned out noteworthy films in the roman porno style. Today, the reputation of the series survives largely through the work of two film-makers: Tanaka Noboru and Tatsumi Kumashiro.

Kumashiro's 1972 film *Ichijo Sayuri: Nureta Yokujo* (Wet Desire) was based around a real-life Osaka striptease artist, Sayuri Ichijo. Her main claim to fame was as one of the pioneers of the 'open stage' or *tokudashi* show. This involved the performer squatting on the edge of the stage and exposing her pubic area to the open gaze of the audience. To aid their enjoyment, magnifying glasses and small torches were passed out to the lucky few who had made it to a front row position. While her public may have welcomed this new explicitness, the authorities were appalled, and Sayuri was taken to court for obscenity. She defended herself with a forthright indignation that won her the respect and admiration of many artists on the radical fringes.

Nureta Yokujo is the story of Harumi, a young, ambitious stripteaser who wants to upstage Sayuri. Kumashiro makes

very explicit the difference between the two women: Harumi — ambitious, petulant and filled with self loathing; Sayuri — contented, demure and entirely at ease with her work. The high point of Sayuri's performance is a famous scene where she drips hot wax from a lighted candle over her breasts while masturbating herself to a climax. The audience, of mostly middle aged men, attest to the authenticity of the act by observing, at extreme close quarters (from about two inches) Sayuri's sopping wet vagina. Harumi's attempt to imitate the act is a dire failure. She secretes wads of milk-soaked tissue inside her. As she tries to force the liquid out, one of the wads shoots from her vagina like a bullet. The film's last, freeze frame, shot shows the astonished faces of the punters as the object flies past them like a floppy egg.

In most of his films Kumashiro deals with strong female characters, often strippers or prostitutes. The roman porno genre was structured around scenes of bare flesh and lengthy (but always softcore) lovemaking. He took advantage of these plot restrictions to concentrate on the women, making them the active centre of his story and not just objects for the camera's gaze.

Stories about prostitutes were a recognised and respected genre of Japanese art and literature. In the 1950s, Mizoguchi had specialised in them. His 1956 film, *Akasen Chitai* (*Street of Shame*), is a heartfelt cry of sympathy for these sad victims of circumstance. Inevitably, Kumashiro's 1974 release *Akasen Tamanoi: Nukeraremasu* (*Street of Joy*) has to be seen as a comment on the earlier film. It's set just after Mizoguchi's film, on New Year's Eve 1957, the day before the enactment of a law that abolished the licensed brothels. However, Kumashiro takes a very different stance from Mizoguchi. His film is more a bittersweet elegy to a time passed than a celebration of the liberation of women from their slavery.

The film takes place throughout one day in a pleasure house in Kofuku, Tokyo's red light district. Like the earlier *Ichijo Sayuri: Nureta Yokujo, Akasen Tamanoi: Nukeraremasu* is also a story of rivalry between two women. Waking up in the morning, Naoko receives her first client. Discovering that the older Shigeko had once serviced twenty-six clients in one day, she decides to set a new record. The idea becomes an obsession with her. At 11.30 that night, with only half an hour to go, Naoko scours the streets, frantically searching for her twenty-seventh client. "You look like a ghost," a man tells her, "with your wild hair and staring eyes."

As Naoko beds the man, breaking the record, Shigeko sets off on her bike to another brothel. 'And they say that Shigeko's cunt was as large as the ocean', the elegant inter-titles inform us. A sentimental song plays on the soundtrack and we see dawn rising over a lonely seascape.

Kumashiro's 1979 film *Akai Kami no Onna* (The Woman With Red Hair) was voted fourth-best film of the year by the prestigious *Kinema Jumpo* magazine. Again it's the story of a strong, sexually assertive woman. Set against a working class background, amongst construction workers and truckers, Kumashiro gives a very intimate portrait of the red-haired woman of the title. Two truckers meet her one day on the road, sheltering from the rain, and give her a lift. She moves

Above: *Top stripper Sayuri Ichijo confronts her rival.*
Left: *Poster for the controversial* Maruhi: Shikijo Mesu Ichiba.

Kumi Taguchi
in
EMMANUELLE
IN TOKYO X
An Intercontinental Release

Top: *The Japanese Emmanuelle, Kumi Taguchi.*
Above: Empire of the Senses.

in with one of them, Kozo, and pretty soon is subjecting him to a gruelling regime of sex, sex and more sex. One morning he wakes up and is startled to find that she's not in bed beside him. Throwing off the covers, he finds her under the sheets, asleep, with his penis in her mouth.

Kozo's friend becomes jealous of his relationship with the red-haired woman and demands the right to have sex with her. Eventually Kozo agrees and, one night when he's making love to the woman, he lets his friend take over. Kozo goes for a walk. He begins to have a desultory wank in a back alley, but then decides to go to a bar. A jolly but sluttish prostitute tells him not to worry, a stiff cock has no conscience. Then, while he's still sitting at the bar, she climbs on his lap and gives him a ride, after first lubricating his penis with her spit.

Kumashiro's films are very matter-of-fact and show a lusty engagement with the raw facts of life. Tanaka Noboru's roman pornos are much more studied and at times almost surreal in their intensity. "I make two kinds of film: those that are realistic and those that are completely artificial," he wrote. "And it's the second type that appeals to me more." In this vein, his most interesting film is 1976's *Stroller in the Attic,* based on stories by Edogawa Rampo. Although conceived as a sex movie, the film has such a weird atmosphere and is so loaded with macabre touches that it was marketed as an arty horror film and was very well received by critics and audiences at the time.

Noboru's most controversial movie, and maybe one of the very best of the Nikkatsu series, was the 1974 release *Maruhi: Shikijo Mesu Ichiba* (Confidential Report — Female Sex Market). The film was made as part of a series on the history of prostitution and it's interesting to compare this bleak drama with Kumashiro's story of happy hookers. *Akasen tamanoi: Nukeraremasu* ends with an image of the sea (a symbol of purity and motherhood); Noboru's movie ends with suicide and one of the most bizarre scenes of any roman porno.

The film is set in mid-seventies Osaka and deals with the lives of two women, a mother and daughter, who both ply their trade as prostitutes in run-down alleys that back onto the railway line. The look of the film is almost neo-realist, photographed in gritty black and white, with no shying away from the sordid facts of the girls' low down life. One of the background scenes shows a man whose job is to wash and dry condoms so they can be reused time after time. However, the construction of the film leads increasingly away from any realistic reading of its 'plot'. Noboru explained: "It's not necessary to explore 'reality' through an orderly narrative structure; in fact, I want to destroy orderly structures and then observe the lives of my characters."

The sex scenes in the film are as frequent and hot as in any of the more conventional roman pornos, but their context drains them of all eroticism. Nineteen year-old Tome and her mother live in a run-down hovel with Tome's imbecilic brother. He watches Tome servicing clients in the shack, grunting moronically as drool runs down his chin. In the sex scenes, the camera concentrates on the face of Tome. She always seems remote, as though drugged, her thoughts as far from pleasure as it's possible to be. The only times she shows any tenderness is when she encourages her brother to paw her breasts and slobber over her body. Finally, at the end of the film, she allows the cretin to make love to her. Far from liberating him, the experience pushes him over the edge and he hangs himself. The next scene shows Tome with one of her clients, a man with a bad smoker's cough. Pulling away from him, Tome lies down with her legs stuck up in the air. "Put your cigarette in here," she says, indicating her vagina. When the man demurs, she says, "But it's only a hole."

Nikkatsu roman porno represented the creative peak of the pink movie during the 1970s. But they were far from the only examples. Companies sprang up almost overnight to crank out sexy exploiters. The range was broad, from cheap comedies like *Games for Lonely Housewives* (sex shenanigans within a mah jong circle) to bigger-budget movies like *Deep Throat in Tokyo* (a rich businessman has a girl's clitoris surgically transplanted to her throat!)

What made the pink movie notorious outside Japan was not only the quantity of films, but the violence and abuse of women they portrayed. Donald Richie, for example, wrote a passionate dismissal of the genre, designed, presumably, to ensure that they would never be taken seriously. 'One rightly suspects that the eroductions are about something other than the joys of sexual union,' he wrote, claiming they were 'about the denigration of women.' The films of Giichi Nishihara must have been exactly the kind of things he was thinking of.

Nishihara made some of the sleaziest pink movies ever. He churned out his films quickly and cheaply and mostly for fly-by-night companies seeking only a sure-fire return on their investment. They certainly weren't looking for art. According to Thomas Weisser, one of the companies for whom Nishihara worked was a front for the Tokyo yakuza.

For such short movies — they usually clock in at less than an hour — Nishihara's films have surprisingly dense plots. His 1976 epic *Mou Ichido Yatte* (Please Rape Me Again) has a very complex time structure. The film concerns a young couple who go off on a fishing holiday. While the husband, Hideo, is at the river bank casting his rod, a passing fisherman takes a fancy to his wife, Mitsuyo, and forces her to have sex with him. Unable to make love to each other after the rape, the couple split up and Hideo remarries. In the street one day, Mitsuyo encounters the river-bank rapist and begins a brief affair with him. She pays the man to break into her ex-husband's flat, tie him up and force him to watch while he rapes his second wife. Then comes the twist. In a brief flashback, it's revealed that Hideo had actually hired the rapist to assault Mitsuyo in the first place. This would provide him with an excuse for divorcing her and marrying his girlfriend!

Rape as a form of revenge occurs again in what is undoubtedly Nishihara's sleaziest and queasiest film. The aptly titled *Gendai Ryoki Sei Hanzai* (Grotesque Perverted Slaughter) from 1976 begins like a pink film, but by the end is dripping red with gore. A couple are having an adulterous affair. The man promises that he will divorce his wife, but the girlfriend spies on them making love and realises he is fooling her. She pays a couple of toughs she meets in a bar to break in and rape the wife. Then she turns up to gloat. The two women fight and the wife overpowers the girlfriend and strangles her. Then she gets a vicious looking meat cleaver... *and slices off the girl's legs*!!! All shown in unwavering close-up as the blade snicks through the bloody flesh. As if that weren't enough, she also cuts off the poor girl's head. She hides the body parts under her mattress. The film concludes with the wife's manic laughter as she and her husband make love on the bed. "Can you smell something bad?" the husband asks.

By the beginning of the eighties, there wasn't really any place left to go. Just about everything had been tried. Softcore was pretty much a thing of the past. Nikkatsu had pioneered the making of hardcore films in the late seventies. The days of ensuring there was a convenient plant pot or bowl of fruit in the way were over. The only thing that kept the wrath of the censors at bay was an annoying piece of masking, usually done in the processing, that blocked out the genital area. There was a feeling that, following the censorship fiasco over Oshima's *Empire of the Senses* and with the rise of the home video market, a more open attitude might start to prevail and fully unmasked hardcore films would become legal. Veteran pink film-maker Tetsuji Takechi took advantage of this more liberal climate in two new versions of his 1964 film *Hakujitsumu.*

The 1981 remake follows the original fairly closely, with a boy and a girl in neighbouring chairs in a dentist's surgery. Under anaesthetic the boy begins to have fantasies about the girl and the rather reptilian dentist (played here by 'bad guy' actor Kei Sato). There appear to be two levels of fantasy going on. One is the boy's violent dreams of the older man dominating and abusing the girl; the other is the girl's much more gentle fantasy of consensual sex with the man. The two worlds of fantasy seem to meet when the girl wakes up in an anonymous hotel room. She sets off naked with the room key dangling from her hair for some reason. The dentist, now dressed like Dracula in a huge red and black cloak, pursues her. He tracks her to a huge, deserted department store. She tries to escape by running up a down escalator. He simply waits at the bottom until she's exhausted herself. The moving belt then delivers her to his waiting arms where he consummates his passion for her.

The ending, as in the 1964 film, takes place in a crowded shopping mall, where the boy stabs the woman. Naked and covered in blood, she runs through the mall.

"I killed her! I did it!" the boy announces to indifferent passers by.

Basically, the theme of both this and the earlier film is *amour fou* — crazy love that defies social conventions. This is made very explicit in the third and latest version of the story released in 1987.

This time the dentist is a glamorous older woman. With her victim safely anaesthetised, she gets down to some extended lesbian action. The girl wakes up in an anonymous hotel room and Takechi really begins to pile on the surrealism. The film becomes a strange fairy-tale, like a porno version of Hans Christian Anderson's *The Snow Queen.* The room door opens onto the fast lane of a massive superhighway. Through the window is a field of huge flowers and behind the wardrobe doors are the crashing waves of the sea.

Takechi has an undoubted eye for creating beautiful scenes. Later, after the girl has escaped by making a rope from her bed sheets, she gets onto a deserted train. The rapacious lesbian dentist reappears, dressed as a ticket inspector, and seduces the girl on a leather-covered banquette. The two women's naked bodies entwine, while through the window behind them we see the just-before-dawn suburbs speeding by. The scene is like a Paul Delvaux painting come to life.

The film ends in a torture chamber, where the evil lesbian tries to force a boy to have sex with her by threatening

Left: Schoolgirls on the rampage in seventies Japanese exploitation pic.

his girlfriend. In a ridiculous but oddly moving conclusion, the girl, hanging upside down in front of the boy, manages to get his penis into her mouth. As they consummate their love, the evil tormentress can only watch in horror, powerless to stop them. Eventually she bursts into flames and the whole room is destroyed in the conflagration.

"My love, now we are saved," murmurs the boy as the fire consumes them too.

By the mid-eighties the commercial justification for films like Takechi's and the glossy roman porno series was looking very shaky. Their intended audience of young single men or factory workers living in multi-occupation dormitories had drifted away. Cable television and rented videos were more suited to their type of one handed viewing. Films made cheaply on video, specifically for this market, began to appear. As they were never intended for cinema exhibition, these videos could explore darker and more deviant areas than even the lower-budgeted cinema films. In 1988, sales of video cassettes topped $2.4 billion against film sales of only $1.3 billion.

One of the most successful purveyors of video porn is former encyclopaedia salesman and sex magazine publisher Toru Muranishi. His Diamond Productions recently moved into satellite television with a two billion yen loan with which he hopes to conquer the whole South East Asian market. Muranishi was one of the pioneers of documentary porn, where apparent real-life events, including interviews, are combined with hardcore sex acts.

The female stars of Muranishi's videos are invariably young — eighteen to twenty-one — and are usually office girls, students or dancers looking to earn a few yen or hoping to move on to a career in straight movies. Several specialist agencies have sprung up to provide the talent for sex videos and they will each have up to 100 willing actresses on their books at any one time. Muranishi's preferred types are innocent-looking, typically Japanese girls but with, in his favourite phrase, "a lustful vagina." They are paid anything from $2,500 to $7,000 per session, depending on their skill and experience.

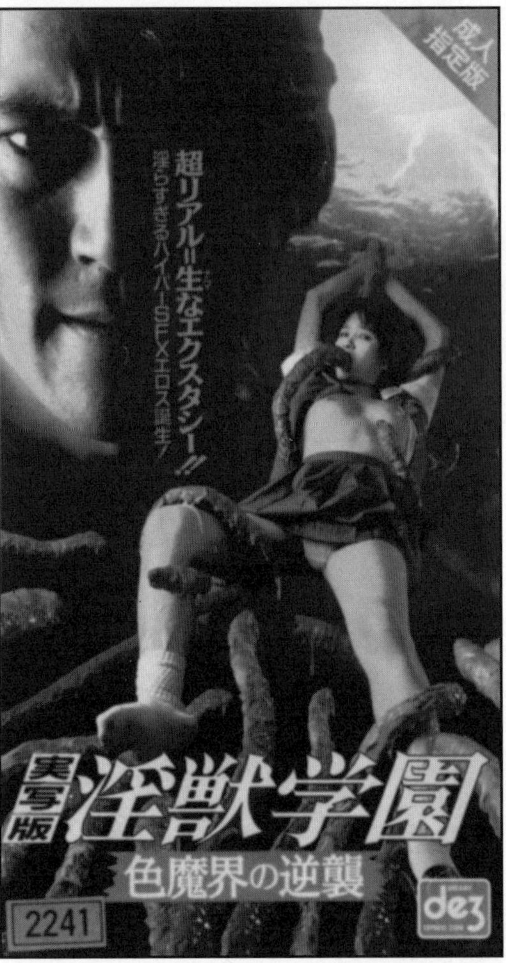

Above: *Young girls with white knickers. A popular fantasy image in Japanese porno.* ***Right:*** *More tits and tentacles in this 1996 video release.*

A typical Muranishi video involves a girl in some sort of uniform. These include schoolgirls, nurses and air hostesses. His top star, who hides her middle class family name under the pseudonym of Kaoru Kuroki, is a former art student who has since become a familiar face on television chat shows. Her main claim to fame is her abundant under-arm hair — an obvious substitute for the pubic hair denied to viewers by obscenity laws.

The new breed of sex video makers have inherited some of the subversive, situationist spirit of their sixties forebears. A video like the 1989 production *Meiwaku-Daibatsu* (Persistent Punishment) is very close in spirit to the confrontational street theatre of the late 1960s. Here the prying camera follows a girl who gives blow jobs to strangers — in the train, in the street, even, in one case, to a guy trying to commit suicide. The film looks terribly real — no faking here. As the hapless girl pumps away beneath the newspaper of one startled commuter in a tube carriage, the look on the faces of the other passengers is something to see. At one time, Japanese pink movie-makers used to pepper their films with shots of naked girls running through the deserted Sunday morning streets. Now it's blow jobs on busy rush hour trains.

The made-on-video revolution has effectively killed off the hardcore sex film. Since the collapse of the studio system, the focus of the Japanese exploitation industry has shifted to cheaper products made for smaller, specialist audiences. And, of course, you don't get an audience much more specialised than that for sex movies.

Intended for a similarly specialist audience are made-for-video animations like *Urotsukidoji* (also known in the West as *Legend of the Overfiend*), the first Japanese cartoon to include hardcore sex and extreme violence. The success of this series pioneered a new genre known as 'tits and tentacles', where gruesome monsters ravage innocent, sailor-suited schoolgirls in a post-apocalyptic, neo-Tokyo. The OAVs (original animation videos) led logically to live-action videos based on cartoon characters. One of the most notorious is the *Rapeman* series, based on a bestselling adult manga. So far this series has run to five episodes, each around an hour long. The plot, believe it or not, concerns a masked, leather-clad superhero who goes round righting wrongs using not his physical strength, but his penis. By day, he's a mild-mannered teacher in a girl's school, by night he's — Rapeman! If this sounds like an appalling concept, it has to be born in mind that a similar premise was behind the very successful 1970s film series *Hanzo the Blade*, which starred one of Japan's most popular actors, Shintaro Katsu. Katsu plays an eighteenth-century detective who uses his penis to interrogate women suspects. With a stone block and a huge hammer, he hardens his member until it's a deadly weapon.

Both the *Hanzo the Blade* series and the *Rapeman* films were based on popular comic books. One of the pioneers of this form of adult manga, Go Nagai, also turned his talents to the OAV sex movie. His 1991 animation *Kekko Kamen*

Far left: *Weird images abound in Japanese made for video films.*
Left: *The notorious* Rapeman.

(Kekko Mask) was so popular it led to a live-action series. *Kekko Kamen* — the name is a reference to the late-fifties television series *Gekko Kamen* (The Man in the Moonlight Mask) — is a female superhero who defends a bunch of Japanese schoolgirls from the likes of Gestapo Girl and Taro Schwarzenegger. The unusual thing about Kekko is that she performs her stunts naked, apart from her cape and mask. She uses her glowing vagina to attract men's gaze and then breaks their necks between her thighs — rather like a female version of Hanzo the Blade, when you come to think of it. In the live-action version, Kekko is played by Chris Aoki, Japan's Playmate of the Year in 1990. *Maboroshi Panti* (Legendary Panty Mask) has a similar theme. This time the setting is the wild West and the eponymous heroine wears a mask constructed out of a pair of girl's leather knickers.

Today the pink movie and sex video are such a part of Japanese life that it seems unlikely they will ever go back under the counter, where they existed in the early 1960s. Tatsumi Kumashiro and Tanaka Noboru have taken their place, along with Immamura and Seijun Suzuki, as film-makers whose work has to be taken seriously. Koji Wakamatsu now directs films for television and makes guest appearances in prestigious, big-budget movies like *Rampo.*

Even so, the sex movie is not an aspect of life that the Japanese are exactly proud of. The modern day equivalents of Wakamatsu — film-makers like Gaira and TKO Nakano — still work in a sort of underground ghetto, far from the bright lights of high-gloss publicity. In the incredible free market of today's Japan, they manage to make a living pursuing their fantasies because they are shared by enough of their contemporaries to make it commercially viable. Of course, many people in the West share these tastes and fantasies too, only we're not allowed to express them as openly as the Japanese. In Japan, the attitude is very much, let people do what they want as long as they don't make a fuss about it. Over here, the attitude is more, if people want to do something, let's make a fuss about it and stop them. Occasionally the two world views meet head on.

Recently, following a notorious murder case in Japan and the involvement of actor Charlie Sheen, the made-on-video *Guinea Pig* was briefly banned in America. This deliberately provocative series of gruesome shorts was apparently started by manga artist Hideshi Hino. While the films lack the sadistic refinement of his books, such as *Panorama of Hell,* they share the same love for stomach-churning scenes of carnage. In a similar mood of 'what will the neighbours think', Nikkatsu banned the export of their recent Roman XXX hardcore movies. They felt that it might be bad for business if the Americans saw what passed for 'entertainment' back home. One of the films, *Hako no Naka no Onna 2* (Captured for Sex), presents the delightful tale of a sex slave kept in a box. She escapes her tormentor and then goes back to him when she realises how much she misses the kiss of the whip... maybe Nikkatsu were right to be nervous.

Of course, these few examples of censorship are the exceptions that prove the rule. It's an interesting subject (and the province of a separate book) to chart the course whereby Japan moved from being one of the most regulated and controlled societies to being, in sexual matters at least, one of the freest. Suffice to say that this *laissez-faire* attitude has affected other areas of film-making, and none more notoriously than the horror movie. In the next section we look at how this genre has grown and developed over the last thirty or so years. It's a story that holds plenty of surprises. ■

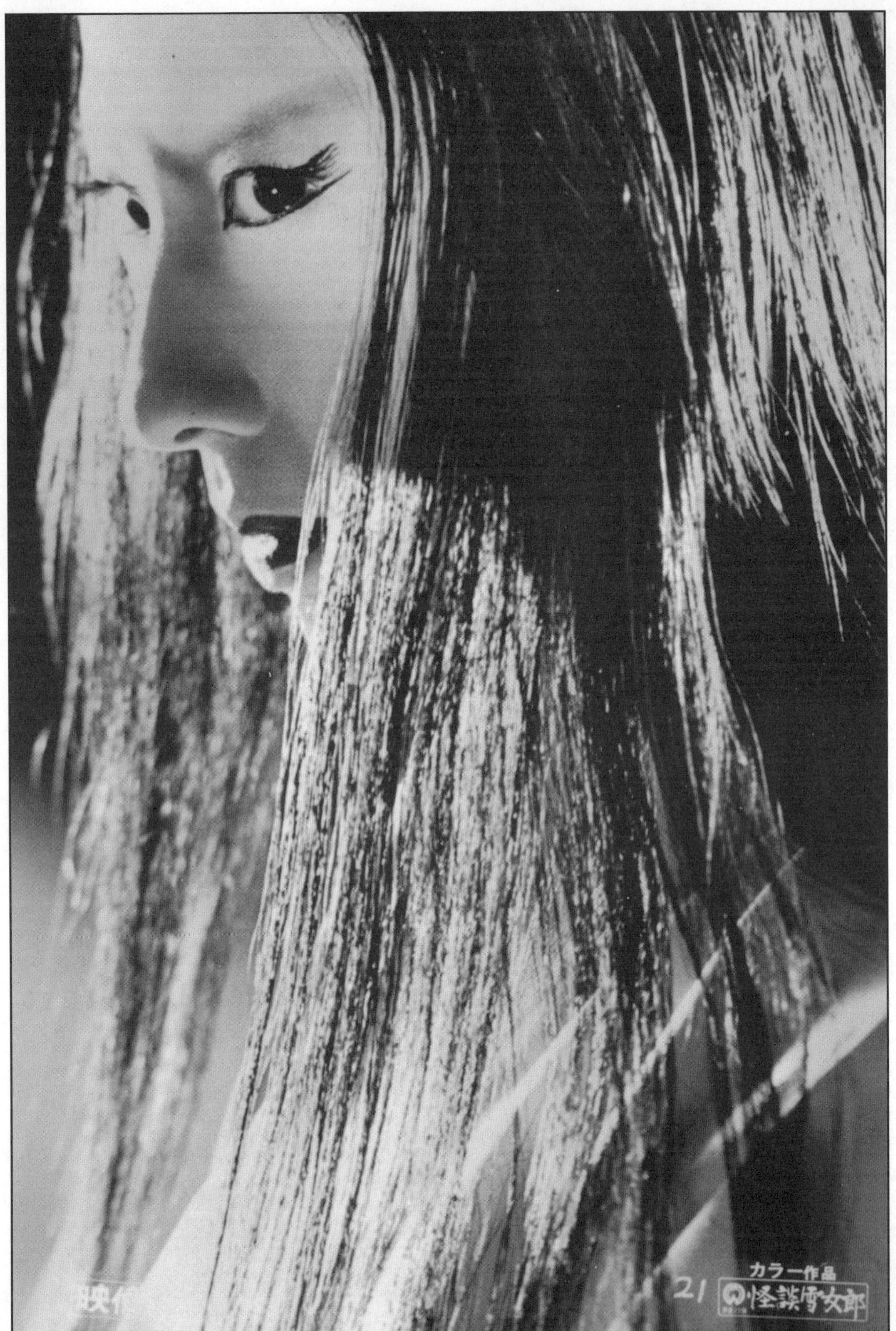
映作
21
カラー作品
怪談雪女郎

Bloodthirsty Eyes

Tales of lovelorn ghosts, vengeful cat spirits and murderous samurai were a staple of Japan's famous *kabuki* theatre. Inevitably these popular stories formed the basis of many early films. *Yotsuya Kaidan*, a tale of ghostly vengeance, has been filmed more than twenty times. Another perennial favourite is *Botandoro*, based on an ancient Chinese legend about a man who falls in love with a dead woman. This idea is common in Japanese films and literature, where ghosts are often very physical creatures, rather than the ectoplasmic wisps we get in the West.

In the 1920s, the Japanese horror film began to move away from its theatrical origins. Women appeared for the first time on screen. Previously, all female parts had been played by *onnagata*, or female impersonators. The more liberal climate of the times saw a Western influence creeping in. *Jasei no In* (Lasciviousness of the Viper), written by the prestigious Tanizaki, was directed by Kizaburo Kurihara, who had worked in Hollywood. Two Lon Chaney hits, *The Hunchback of Notre Dame* and *The Phantom of the Opera*, were also adapted for Japanese cinema. However, the best horror film of the decade was yet another version of *Yotsuya* — *Shinpan Yotsuya Kaidan* (New Ghost Story of Yotsuya), in1928.

After the Second World War, ghost stories soon regained their former popularity with a version of the *Yotsuya* story and a cat ghost film — *Nabeshima Kaibyo-den* (Ghost Cat of Nabeshima) — both released in 1949. These old-fashioned tales served as a welcome relief from present day horrors for Japanese cinemagoers. Moreover, they were probably the only traditional stories that the occupation forces would sanction. Samurai films and historical epics were seen as too fascistic and a possible call to arms. Stories of white-faced female demons seemed a lot less dangerous.

The first Japanese horror film distributed in the West was *Ugetsu Monogatari*, directed by Kenzi Mizoguchi. Its theme is man's seduction by a ghost, a common enough occurrence in commercial Japanese horror films, but this time played much less for cheap thrills and more for the sad poetry of the situation. Mizoguchi's film is set in the early part of the seventeenth century, a time of constant wars and intrigues between rival clans. It tells the story of two brothers who live in a primitive village. One of them is a hard-working potter, the other a layabout who dreams of becoming a noble samurai. The brothers and their wives travel to the city to sell their pots. They do good business, but the would-be samurai is seduced by the sight of a splendid suit of armour and steals the money to buy it before running off to become a hero, leaving his wife to fend for herself. The potter, meanwhile, is delivering some of his wares to an isolated manor house and falls under the spell of the beautiful widow who lives there. Completely forgetting his own wife and child, he moves into the mansion and becomes the mysterious woman's lover.

Opposite and above: *The white-faced female demons from* Kwaidan.

As might be expected, their dreams turn sour. The samurai finds the wife he abandoned entertaining troops in a brothel and the potter is horrified to discover that the beautiful woman with whom he is living is a ghost. A passing priest tells him he has death on his face and paints his body with Sanskrit symbols to ward off evil. His ghostly paramour senses their presence and they fight. The potter falls unconscious and when he awakens finds the manor house in ruins and the beautiful woman and her retainers all gone.

Ugetsu Monogatari was the first post-war masterpiece of Japanese horror cinema. It took the basic material of the traditional ghost story and turned it into a great humanistic and universal statement. Made less than ten years after Japan's humiliating defeat in war, the film, on one level, is an obvious comment on the vanity of dreams, showing how ambition distorts our vision and makes us blind. And yet it retains all the trappings of the tale of terror, including the Sanskrit writings on the body and the unnaturally beautiful, white-faced ghost woman. In common with many female ghosts in Japanese

Right: *Shigeru Amatsu in* The Ghost of Yotsuya.
Below right: *A vengeful cat demon in the 1969 film* Hiroku Kaibyo-den.

tales, she is both seductive and dangerous. The *femme fatale* may seem to be a European obsession, but the Japanese have taken it to new heights of emotional terror.

Ugetsu Monogatari was released in 1953. A positive torrent of ghost films followed. Toei, Daiei and Shintoho incorporated spectral cats, vengeful females and haunted swamps into their scenarios with a single-minded dedication to thrill and chill. All of these films were made for the domestic market, a fact underlined by their regular appearance in the months of July and August. This is the time of *O-Bon*, the festival of the dead. The purpose was two-fold: to put patrons in a suitably respectful frame of mind and to cool them down with a few well-placed shivers. By the end of the decade, the genre had pretty much run out of steam and 1959 was more or less the swan-song for the traditional spook story. As desperation set in, hybrids like *Ama no Bakemono Yashiki* (*Girl Divers From Spook Mansion*) appeared. This one combined the ghost story with another popular genre — films about topless pearl divers. In the same year, the star of *Ama no Bakemono Yashiki*, Yoko Mihara, appeared in a much more gruesome shocker, *Kyuju-kyuhonme no Kimusume* (*The Blood Sword of the 99th Virgin*). This terrifying tale of ancient ritual and savage bloodlust was a watershed for the Japanese horror film. It marked the end of the old-style spookiness and announced a new agenda of sex and sadism that would be relentlessly pursued throughout the sixties.

By the end of the fifties, ShinToho, one of the largest purveyors of ghost stories, was on its last legs. The company finally went bankrupt in 1960, but not before delivering up two of the best Japanese horror movies since *Ugetsu Monogatari*. While one was a version of a traditional tale, *Tokaido Yotsuya Kaidan* (*The Ghost of Yotsuya*), the other, *Jigoku* (*Hell*), was something else again.

Nobuo Nakagawa, the veteran writer and director of both films, had worked in all sorts of genres, from musicals to costume dramas. When he began working for ShinToho in the 1950s he inaugurated the series of horror films for which he's best remembered today. These include versions of the story of the Kasane Swamp, *Kaidan Kasane Gafuchi* (Ghost Story of Kasane Swamp) and cat ghost films like *Borei Kaibyo Yashiki* (*Black Cat Mansion*). More innovative were two films dealing with the vampire myth, *Kyuketsuga* (The Vampire Moth) and *Onna Kyuketsuki* (The Female Vampire). Of course, these

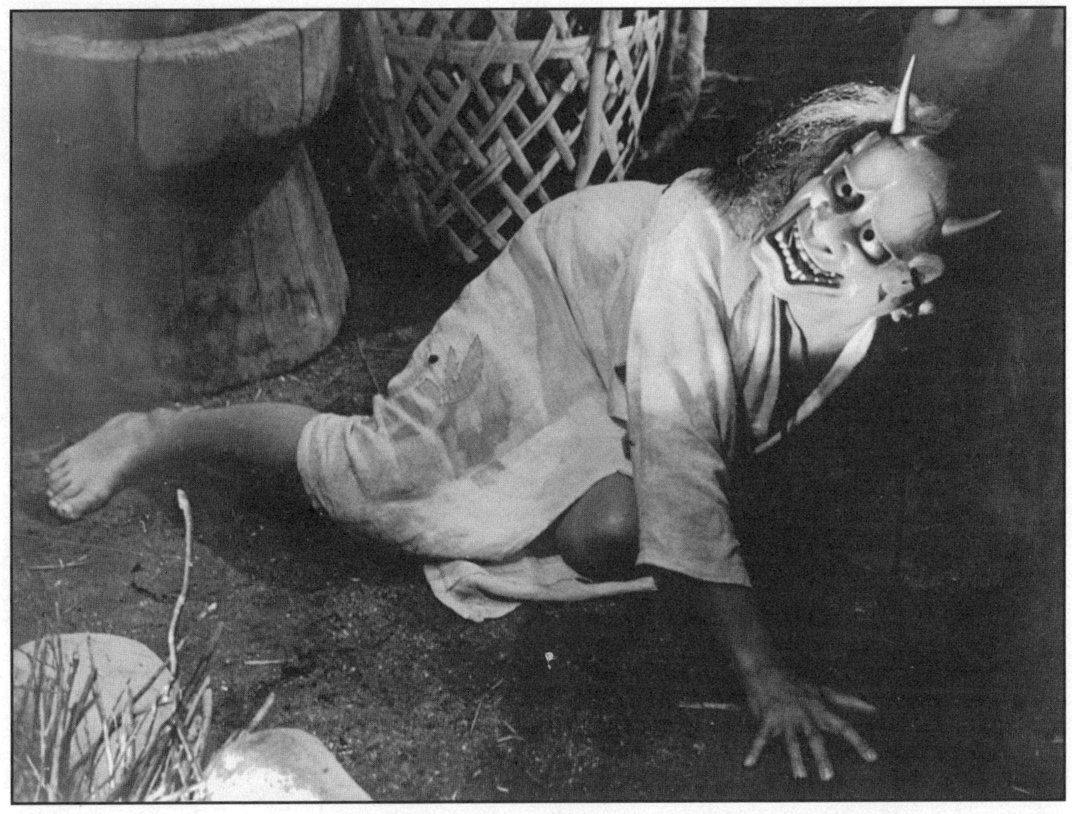

Left: *The devilish mask from* Onibaba.
Below: *The 1979 remake of* Inferno.

weren't straightforward bloodsuckers. The first was a spooky thriller about a serial killer and the second featured a 300 year-old descendent of Shiro Amakusa, a Christian rebel in seventeenth century Japan. This vampire is allergic to moonlight and in one scene turns a woman into a wax doll.

Nakagawa's *Tokaido Yotsuya Kaidan* (Ghost Story of Yotsuya at Tokaido) was one of three versions of this famous story that appeared in 1959. He makes explicit the theatrical origins of the tale by opening with a stage set, where a black-robed narrator gives a kind of prologue in verse of what is to come: "Why did her husband poison her? Why? Why?... No wonder her ghost wanders and haunts him day and night."

The film tells of Iemon, an embittered samurai who kills the father of his intended bride, Iwa. Egged on by an ambitious friend, the slimy Naosuke, he commits further murders until at last both get what they want. Very soon things start to turn sour. Living in genteel poverty in Edo (ancient Tokyo) with his wife and young child, Iemon soon plots to dump the poor woman to marry a rich man's daughter. The devious Naosuke works out a plan involving a fat, bald masseur who is in love with Iwa. Iemon gives the masseur permission to seduce his wife and at the same time slips a deadly poison into her drink.

In a horrifying scene, as the masseur attempts to seduce Iwa, the poison takes effect and she begins to turn hideously ugly and her hair starts to fall out. She cuts her throat with a knife just as Iemon turns up and kills the masseur for attempting to make love to his wife. Together with Naosuke, the samurai nails the two bodies one on each side of a wooden door and dumps them in a nearby swamp.

However, neither man is able to enjoy the fruits of their crime. The hideously scarred bodies of Iwa and the masseur keep appearing to them. Rising from the floor in a swirl of bloody water, and in one case, floating eerily from the ceiling, they drive the men mad. Iemon slashes out with his sword at the hideous apparitions, inadvertently killing both his new wife and father-in-law. Eventually he kills Naosuke too. In a bravura touch, as the body falls to the floor, the room suddenly fills with mist and the bloody water of the swamp bubbles up from the reed matting to swallow the corpse.

Although it's traditionally a story of vengeance, Nakagawa's version of *Yotsuya* is really about karma, about the flowering of the seeds of destruction that we plant through our evil acts and mistaken ambition. *Jigoku*, made the following year, takes this idea a stage further and shows us the actual Hell into which our misdeeds can plunge us.

The film begins with nails being hammered into a coffin. Then, behind the credit sequence with its bongo-crazy jazz score, Nakagawa shows us a parade of brazen showgirls baring their bodies. Sex is the signpost on this particular road to Hell and the film shows the seductive lures that lead to damnation.

The first hour deals with the story of two students, a mild-mannered good guy played by Shigeru Amachi and a lusty adventurer played by the marvellously demonic Yoichi Numata. They set off in a flashy American car looking for fun and inadvertently run over a drunk on a lonely country road. This accidental act is the beginning of their descent into Hell, as they progress through a series of lurid dives. In a fantastic night-club scene, with a saxophone sounding like it's being played at the bottom of a deep well, Amachi dances with a sluttish bar girl in a red dress. It transpires that she's the wife of the drunk they killed and she lures him to a rickety bridge over a ravine, planning to murder him. Unfortunately, it's the girl herself who falls to her death, soon followed by Amachi's friend.

In a cheerless drinking den where he's gone to dull the edge of his pain, the hapless Amachi tries to strangle the apparition of his dead friend. As the hands of the clock freeze, the guilt-ridden student tumbles over the edge of darkness and finds himself on the shores of a milky white lake that borders Hell.

For the next forty minutes or so, Nakagawa treats us to

Right: *Don't eat the giant mushrooms!* Matango — *fungus of terror.*
Below: *Lust leads to violence in* Onibaba.

one of the most complete pictures of damnation ever committed to film. In garish neon colours, lit by the dancing flames of the pits of torture, we see such sights as bodies crawling like maggots across a surreal desert, rows of corpses stretching out to infinity and skeletons locked in a dry embrace. One hideous image shows a living man being cut in two by a giant saw. A woman has her head pulled from her body and living corpses are shown skinless, their glistening organs still pulsing with life. Sudden flashes of naked showgirls dancing to smoochy jazz only underline the horror of it all. Lacking any will of their own, Nakagawa's characters stumble from one horrifying set piece to the next, condemned to relive for eternity the foolish actions that brought them to... Hell.

Throughout the 1960s the choice for Japanese horror film-makers was between making Western-influenced shockers for possible export or finding a way to revitalise traditional Japanese themes. While it's difficult to imagine a film like *Jigoku* being made anywhere but Japan, Hajime Sato's 1965 film *Kaidan Semushi Otoko* (*Ghost of the Hunchback*) is practically a carbon copy of the Italian gothics made by the likes of Mario Bava and Riccardo Freda. 1964's *Kwaidan*, although based on traditional Japanese stories, was aimed at the overseas market. The film was shown at Cannes in 1965 and was a great success. Also making a splash at Cannes that year was another Japanese tale of terror, *Onibaba*.

Directed by former script writer Kaneto Shindo, this medieval shocker is set in one of the most atmospheric locations imaginable — a huge swamp filled with acres of rustling reeds. Two women live there, a young wife and her mother-in-law. They survive by killing any wounded men who wander into the swamp and selling their armour to a lecherous merchant. The soldiers' bodies are stripped naked and thrown down a deep hole.

One day the older woman encounters a samurai wearing a horrifying mask. Its purpose, he tells her, is to cover his face which is so beautiful that anyone who sees it would instantly fall in love with him. Immediately she's fascinated. "Ever since I was born," she confesses, "I've never seen anything really beautiful."

The woman leads the man off through the reeds and, in the darkness, he tumbles down into the hole. She tries to remove his mask. She discovers that it had become fastened to his face and underneath it he is hideously scarred. Foolishly, she later puts on the mask herself to frighten her daughter-in-law from visiting a local farmer for whom she has the hots. Now the old woman in her turn is unable to remove the mask. Her daughter-in-law runs away from her in terror, believing her to be a real demon. As the masked woman tumbles blindly into the corpse-filled pit, her last words echo out: "I *am* a human being... I *am* a human being..."

Onibaba, like many memorable films of the sixties, was made by an independent production company. The big studios were too busy pursuing the commercial main chance to take risks with such material. Toho, for example, devoted most of their production energy to films featuring giant monsters stomping all over scale models of Tokyo. Fortunately their star director, Ishiro Honda, had shown himself to be master of a more subtle, atmospheric type of movie when given the chance. In 1963, Honda took a holiday from Godzilla to make the classic *Matango* (*Attack of the Mushroom People*).

The film begins with some marvellous model shots evoking the garish neon madhouse of early sixties Tokyo. The camera pulls back to reveal that we have been looking through the window of a real nuthatch. The narrator and inmate is Murai, the only survivor of a group of five well-heeled young Tokyoites who set sail in a friend's yacht looking for fun and adventure. In a flashback he tells their tale.

Out on the high seas they run into stormy weather. The group are confident they will be all right. The boat can't sink — after all, it cost forty million yen. In a touching scene, a young singer, Mami, tells them she will soon be sailing to Europe with Kosei, the yacht's millionaire owner. Then she mentions a string of cities — Paris, Rome, Vienna — all of which are resolutely landlocked.

Contrary to their predictions, the ship is wrecked and the group find themselves stranded on a rocky island. As they cross the ominous black sand beach in search of food and water, a thick mist descends. Following a trail to the far side of the island, they find a spooky sailing ship stranded in the mud, its black sails torn and rotting. Their first sight of this distant ship has an almost hallucinatory quality to it, like something out of a painting by the gloomy German romantic Caspar David Friedrich. *Matango* is full of such moments of visual poetry. It's worth bearing in mind that Eiji Tsubaraya, the film's special effects director, had also worked on the classic 1920s surrealist movie *Kurutta Ippeiji* (*A Page of Madness*).

The ship is deserted. Possibly it has been on the island for years. Everything in it is covered with slimy fungoid growths. Even odder is the fact that all mirrors appear to have been removed from its walls.

The group set up camp in the ship while they plan their escape. The island soon becomes their prison. There seems to be almost no food there — only the mushrooms, which the log on the deserted ship warns them not to eat. As the days pass, the social glue that binds the group begins to weaken. The ship's hand blames it on the two women, claiming that their presence is unsettling the men, filling their fevered brains with sexual fantasies. The brazen Mami delights in this role. "Everyone wants me," she asserts proudly, powdering her face. On the other hand, Murai's shy girlfriend is only confused by all the attention.

Then, one night, a strangely deformed man-like creature is seen on the ship. It seems that the sailor's claims might be true. Perhaps the men are being driven mad by lust and starting to see things that aren't there.

In fact, the island is peopled by these creatures, formerly the crew of the abandoned ship. They are — literally — mushroom heads. They ate the fungus and became addicted to it. It rewarded them with powerful psychedelic fantasies, while at the same time gradually taking over their bodies. That's why the mirrors had been removed from the walls, to save the men from being confronted with the results of their addiction.

The group begin to succumb to the seductive lure of the fungus. First is Yoshida, a bumptious writer, followed by Mami, the singer. They are both thrown off the ship. Adam and Eve banished from the garden of Eden. As Mami looks back, she sees the black bulk of the dead ship like a strange gothic vision on the far horizon. The very next shot shows the mushrooms rising like giant penises from the lush, damp undergrowth of the island's forest floor.

That night Mami appears on the ship again. A vision of chic loveliness, her blue eye make-up and red lipstick perfect, as though she had just left a Ginza beauty parlour. She seduces her millionaire boyfriend into following her and feeds him mushrooms. Soon only Murai and his timid girlfriend are left untouched. But the mushroom heads have laid a trap for them...

Matango is amazingly pessimistic for a film made in 1963 — the year before the Olympics and the Tokyo Expo that were the signs of Japan's re-entry into the international community. In many ways it's a complete rejection of much of the so-called progress that the country had made since the war. The story is bookended by two comments. One, near the beginning, is made by Yoshida, the detective story writer. After praising the little group of swingers around him, he avers that: "Tokyo is a great city and it's full of life. Everything in it is important." Later, right at the end of the film and with all his friends dead, Murai bitterly avers: "Tokyo's not very different from that island. People in cities are cruel, aren't they?" In the film's very last shot he reveals how he finally succumbed and ate the mushrooms to join his friends in oblivion. It was better to escape into the fantasies that the mushrooms gave than to live in the neon madhouse of modern Japan.

Along with Ishiro Honda's earlier *The H Man/The Human Vapour* movies, *Matango* is a film about bodily transformation. This is a common enough theme in Japanese cinema, but here given a very different treatment. The transformation in *Matango* is not into a ghost cat or a white-faced demoness, it's not affected for revenge or through karmic law. The mushrooms act as a catalyst for the people who eat them, freeing something that's already inside them — the closest parallel would be to the Jekyll and Hyde story. As the

Above: *A poetic approach to science fiction from Ishiro Honda.*
Below: *Tokyo swingers meet walking mushrooms in* Matango.

Right: *The Majin is attacked.*
Below: *The Majin attacks.*

crewman hinted, it's probably suppressed sexual desire that made them prime candidates for the change. In that sense, *Matango* is one of the first really modern Japanese horror films. Its theme of transformation from within would be relentlessly mined during the eighties and nineties.

From the same monster movie mould that had spawned *Matango* came Daiei studio's 1966 release, *Majin.* This was the start of a trilogy of movies set in the Tokugawa period that took the 'man in a rubber suit' idea and married it to more traditional Japanese stories. In the first film, a wicked landowner murders a benevolent feudal lord and takes over his territory. The murdered man's children, a boy and a girl, take to the hills. High up on the mountain top, wreathed in mists, they find a huge stone carving of the fearsome local god, the Majin. The years pass and the children grow up, while for the people in the valley things go from bad to worse under the harsh rule of the cruel usurper. Eventually he tracks down the kids, bringing with him a team of men who attempt to hack the Majin to bits. They subject it to all kinds of indignities, including hammering a giant steel spike into its forehead. Only at the sight of the girl's tears does the monster awaken. Then he takes his terrible revenge. The sky darkens and huge earthquakes destroy the landlord's estate. The Majin seeks out the man and skewers him on the spike that had been hammered into his forehead. Nothing seems able to stop the carnage. Then, just as his huge foot is poised ready to crush her, the Majin recognises the girl whose tears had awoken him. He passes a hand in front of his face and turns once more into stone. As the sky clears and the sun bursts through the gloom, the giant monster crumbles into dust.

The appearance of the Majin is a masterpiece of art direction. His blue, scowling face and heavy, lumbering gait are genuinely eerie and the sets have a suitably monumental look. The effect is to create a truly mythic atmosphere, something missing in all but the very first of the *Godzilla* movies.

In 1968, *Majin*'s director Kimiyoshi Yasuda and special effects maestro Yoshiyuki Kuroda delivered another horror extravaganza based around traditional Japanese stories. *Yokai Hyaku Monogatari* (One Hundred Ghost Stories) begins in fine style with a traveller passing through a spooky wood. Suddenly the sky darkens. He hears a rustling in the bushes and turns round to see a huge eye staring out at him. He runs. The eye follows and a giant, hairy beast grabs him by the head.

This dramatic opening is a tale told by an old man — a village storyteller. His skills are later put to good use when a ruthless landowner sets up camp in the local shrine, much to the disgust of the villagers. The storyteller is summoned, and he entertains the unwelcome newcomers with an uncanny tale about two fishermen who ignore an old man's warning not to fish in a certain spot. Their catch has a weird effect. The fisherman's wife finds she can't wash its blood off her hands. To her husband's horror, she then grows a great long neck which she wraps around his body, crushing him, like a giant python with a human head.

Gradually the stories begin to come true. Creatures resembling those on the painted screens brought in to accompany the storyteller begin to make appearances in the real world. The first to manifest itself is an umbrella ghost. This bizarre, one-legged creature has a long tongue with which it licks the face of the landowner's simple-minded son. Other creatures are less loveable. An army of faceless men and a giant laughing head materialise and drive the landowner's retainers mad. Other creatures resemble masks from old *Noh* plays, along with fire-snorting demons, a pumpkin-headed goblin, white-faced ghost women and lanky-limbed demons with huge stomachs. When the evil landowner kills himself by falling onto his sword, a jubilant procession of the hundred monsters moves off into the night, gradually getting fainter until they fade into the distant horizon.

The film was a big success and the same team returned with a sequel: *Yokai Daisenso* (*Great Monster War*). Again, this has a very dramatic opening. Two graverobbers break into an ancient Babylonian tomb, inadvertently setting free the monster, Daimon, who is imprisoned there. Daimon, looking a little like the Majin but with feathered wings and a giant beak, is a creature of terrifying powers who brings storms and destruction in its wake. It flies off across the vast oceans and eventually ends up in eighteenth-century Japan, where it takes over the body of a local magistrate. From being a wise and kindly man, he turns into a vampiric tyrant who uses his position to suck the blood of his subjects.

A local *kappa*, or water spirit (which looks like Donald Duck with a flat head), is able to see through Daimon's disguise and realises that the magistrate has become possessed. The water spirit summons up his friends, the hundred monsters from the previous film, to do battle with the invader and defend Japan. Essentially this is a version of Toho monster spectaculars like *Kaiju Soshingeki* (*Destroy All Monsters*), but this time with creatures drawn from the vast body of Japanese mythology. The whole thing ends in a knock-down, drag-out monster war, with our old friends the rubber-necked woman and the white-faced demoness also putting in appearances.

Throughout the sixties and seventies the familiar ghost stories continued to appear, now pepped up with healthy doses of sex and more liberal amounts of gore than Nakagawa or Shozo Makino might have been allowed. Kaneto Shindo, whose *Onibaba* had been heavily promoted in the West on account of its allegedly daring scenes*, returned to horror in 1968 with the atmospheric *Kuroneko* (The Black Cat), another version of the old cat ghost story. A young wife and her mother-in-law are raped and murdered by a bunch of renegade warriors in seventeenth-century Japan. Animated by a cat spirit, they return to seek revenge. Setting up house in the middle of a dark and lonely forest, they seduce any passing samurai and suck their blood. The twist in the tale comes when the local warlord sends his hero to put an end to the monsters. The brave samurai turns out to be the young cat-woman's former husband.

As the involvement of Shindo, and later Oshima and Hani shows, horror and fantasy in Japanese cinema were not just the province of cheapjack exploiters. Respected actors and directors were often found working in the area. Throughout the sixties and seventies several new wave film-makers dabbled in horror. One of the more unexpected examples came from Susumu Hani. His *Inferno of First Love* had been quite a hit in the West and it was probably the success of arty horror films like *Kwaidan* and *Onibaba* that led Hani to make *Aido* (Slave of Love), which was released in 1969. The film is another version of the traditional tale about a man who falls in love with a dead woman. In Hani's film, the young man, Shusei, meets a woman during the festival of *O-Bon*. She leads him to a splendid palace by a lake where lives the lovely Aido, with whom he enjoys a series of erotic encounters. Later, determined to solve the mystery, he finds a golden coffin hidden in the waters of the lake. It contains the body of Aido, who tells him she is "the spirit of sensuality — the slave of love."

In literature, fantasy was seen as a perfectly legitimate way of exploring serious issues. Acclaimed writers like Kobo Abe — *Tanin no Kao* (*The Face of Another*) — and Kawabata — *Nemureru Bijo* (*House of the Sleeping Virgins*) — were as well known for fantastic and macabre stories as for their more naturalistic work. There were also many writers, like Ryonosuke Akutagawa and Kyoka Izumi, who specialised in the macabre. Both writers' work has been used as the basis for films. *Jigokuhen* (Hell Screen) from Akutagawa and *Yashagaike* (*Demon Pond*) from Izumi are both stand out productions.

One of the most consistently popular writers of horror fiction in Japan was Edogawa Rampo. His work had first been brought to the screen as early as 1927. However, it was during the post-war period that the studios really began to take an interest in his stories. With traditional samurai dramas banned by the allied forces, there was a need for contemporary but equally popular stories to turn into films. *Palette Knife no Satsujin* (The Palette Knife Murder) was released in 1946 by Daiei, and Shochiku and Toei followed suit with *Yurei To* (Ghost Pagoda) and *Kaijin Nijumenso* (Phantom With Twenty Faces) the following year. These, like most of the Rampo adaptations that appeared in the 1950s, were based on his detective stories, many of which feature his *alter ego*, Kogoro

Top: One Hundred Ghost Stories. *On the left, the umbrella monster.*
Above: Great Monster War.

* *'... an amalgam of sexual indulgence, sadism and violence', wrote the* International Film Guide. *In a similar mood,* Continental Film Review *saw the film as 'ostensibly a commercial chore, heavily erotic and sadistic... makes Bergman's* The Silence *look very innocuous by comparison.'*

***Right:** Sculptor and model in* Moju.
Below: The Stroller in the Attic.

Akechi, the Japanese Sherlock Holmes. However, Rampo had also written many bizarre and disturbing tales of terror. In the more liberal climate of the 1960s it was possible to bring some of these to the screen for the first time.

Voyeurism, the killing power of the look, and the dangerous, solipsistic world of the obsessive creator are constant themes in Rampo's stories. The 1969 film *Moju* (The Blind Beast), directed by Yasuzo Masumura, takes these ideas about as far as they can go. The protagonist is a blind sculptor obsessed by the body of a young model that he knows only through touch. He kidnaps the girl and imprisons her in a large room. To her horror she discovers that the walls of the room are covered in huge casts of body parts: eyes, legs, noses, arms. The rest of the space is taken up with two huge rubber statues of female bodies. The girl attempts to escape and she and the blind man play a bizarre game of tag, chasing each other over the mountainous limbs of the giant rubber statues. Eventually the girl agrees to let the man make a model of her, which he does by caressing her body and memorising the shape of her limbs before transferring his impressions to clay.

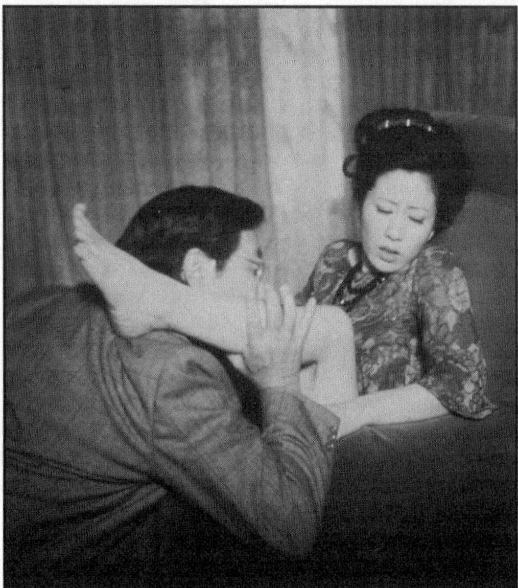

Alone in the darkened room, with no light and no food, the pair become deranged. Time seems to lose all meaning and the outside world ceases to exist. They begin to indulge in erotic games that get more intense and more violent. It starts with the girl biting the man's body. It ends when he fetches a butchers' knife and a hammer, and chops off her arms and legs. Curled up into a foetal position, the man waits for the darkness to swallow him. The only touch of light in the room is the glint of a tear in the dead girl's eye.

In the same year as *Moju*, a more traditional horror film was made from another of Rampo's stories, *Kyofu Kikei Ningen. The Horror of Malformed Men*, as it was called in English, is another in the long list of horror films set on an island. Like *The Island of Dr Moreau* and *Terror is a Man*, this tells of a mad scientist who uses his surgical skill to create a race of monsters. The motive is provided by the surgeon's fear of his own ugliness. He wants to create a world peopled by creatures more physically deformed than he is. Teruo Ishii, who directed the film, is better known for his series of torture films made for Toei, such as *Tokugawa Onna Keibatsushi* (Joys of Torture). In *Kyofu Kikei Ningen* he presents a convincing portrait of a twisted hell made by modern science, with vistas of the blindfolded monstrosities rampaging across a bleak landscape, being ridden like animals and raging behind the bars of their cages.

The pessimism and sense of isolation manifested in films like *Moju* and *Kyofu Kikei Ningen* became more pronounced as Japan's economic miracle began to turn sour in the seventies. This was a time of reflection and in some ways a rejection of the rampant economic growth of the previous decade. The oil crisis of 1973 sounded a particularly ominous note in a country like Japan, where so much of the wealth depended on imported raw materials. The uncertain mood of the times is strongly reflected in the 1976 film *Yaneura no Sanposha* (*The Stroller in the Attic*), directed by Tanaka Noboru based around several stories and themes of Edogawa Rampo.

Here we meet the perfect couple: a voyeur (male) and an exhibitionist (female). The man watches the woman kill someone. She is now in his power. To level the playing field he also kills someone. Then, together, they murder a third time.

The story is set in a boarding house in 1920s Tokyo. The voyeur is a rich, idle young man who has made holes in convenient places in the attic of the house so that he can spy on the various lodgers. In one of the rooms, he observes the activities of a prostitute and her clients. The woman, who knows she is being watched, is really a middle class housewife indulging her own fantasies in her work. She forces her clients to abase themselves before her, dressed as clowns. She strangles one man between her thighs while he is performing oral sex on her.

Yaneura no Sanposha includes a version of one of Rampo's most bizarre tales, *The Human Chair*. This is about a man who hides inside a piece of furniture he has built and becomes obsessed with the erotic experience of having beautiful women sit on him. In *Yaneura no Sanposha* it is the prostitute's chauffeur who inhabits the chair. After satisfying his desire, the woman pours alcohol into the upholstery and sets fire to it.

The film has a unique, spellbinding atmosphere, with long periods of almost total silence and a stately pace that draws us into the voyeur's strange world. When, for instance, he decides to kill a man whose snores are annoying him, the voyeur crawls to a spot in the attic above the man's bed and allows small amounts of poison to drip down into the sleeper's open mouth. Watching this scene you find yourself almost holding your breath, hoping that the man won't wake up and catch the voyeur.

The film ends with the famous earthquake that flattened Tokyo in 1923 — coincidentally also the year that Rampo found his first success as a writer. The voyeur and the prostitute have persuaded a lesbian artist who lives in the boarding house to decorate their bodies with strange, rootlike patterns. As they begin a violent sex game that ends with the painter's death, the house starts to shake and the mighty roar of the earthquake drowns out their screams. Tokyo is destroyed, and with it the strange house of perversity and all the secrets it contained. The film's final shot shows a woman standing on top of the devastation and pumping water up through a well. As she gaily sings, the water turns to blood.

The most bizarre Rampo adaptation was not a horror film but a version of one of his popular detective stories. *Kurotokage* (*Black Lizard*), which was filmed in 1968, was based on a version of a Rampo story adapted for the stage by

Above: Black Lizard.
Below: *The blind sculptor 'sees' through touch in* Moju.

Above: Lake of Dracula.
Below: *Outer space vampires in* Goke — Bodysnatcher from Hell.

Yukio Mishima, who plays a small role in the film. The Black Lizard of the title is a famous female jewel thief. But precious stones aren't the only thing she collects. She also gathers bodies to add to her macabre assortment of human statues. Detective Akechi is called in to find the kidnapped daughter of a jewel merchant. Needless to say, the tough detective soon falls for the dangerous charms of the slinky woman in black. The story itself sounds exotic enough, but what really tips it over the edge is the fact that the lovely Lizard is played by a man — famed female impersonator Akihiro Maruyama. The film was successful enough to spawn a sequel, *Kurobara no Yakata* (Black Rose). Here Maruyama plays a mysterious *femme fatale*, loved by both a night-club owner and his son.

During the late sixties, the boundaries between genres had begun to blur. Samurai films often used horror elements. Both the *Baby Cart* and *Son of the Black Mass* series made forays into horror territory. The hero of the latter was a master swordsman born of the rape of a Japanese nun by a foreign adventurer. Flashbacks throughout the series show this gruesome scene, each time becoming more satanic, with suggestions of torture by black-robed monks quaffing from blood-filled goblets.

Science fiction films had also begun to flirt with horror. One of the most interesting of these hybrids was the 1968 film *Kyuketsuki Gokemidoro* (*Goke — Bodysnatcher From Hell*). The director of the film was the underrated Hajime Sato, who had earlier made the gothic horror *Ghost of the Hunchback. Goke*, like Honda's *Matango*, is an incredibly pessimistic film. It opens with an airliner flying through an ominous, blood-red sky. Birds seem to be committing suicide as they hurl themselves against the plane's windows. Inside the cabin, things are no better. The motley group of passengers, including a corrupt politician, an arms manufacturer, a Vietnam war widow, a suspected terrorist and a hired assassin, are rapidly falling out with each other as they debate the state of contemporary morality. Suddenly, the plane is buzzed by a huge flaming light in the sky and crashes to the ground out of control. The hired assassin escapes and is drawn towards the glowing object, which turns out to be a vehicle from space. Its inhabitants are slime-like vampire creatures from the planet Gokemidoro. They possess the man's body by splitting open his forehead and crawling inside his skull. They then use him to suck the blood of his fellow passengers.

The vampires eventually explain why they chose to invade Earth. "The time has come. Mankind is on the verge of destruction. It is your own fault that we have chosen you as our first victims. You have already turned your world into a monstrous battlefield." At several points in the film Sato cuts to documentary stills of wars, riots and social insurrection, coloured in sickly yellows and lurid reds. This kind of technique, also used in contemporary films by Wakamatsu and Oshima, is to say the least unusual in a commercial horror exploiter.

The film's vampires are a long way from the fanged monsters of Hammer. In fact, traditional vampires are comparatively rare in Japanese movies. Nobuo Nakagawa's 1959 film *Onna Kyuketsuki* was one of the first films to feature vampires of a sort, but it wasn't until 1970 that Western-style bloodsuckers made an appearance. The 1970 film *Chi o Suu Ningyo* (*The Vampire Doll*) was the first of a trilogy that transplanted the Western vampire into a Japanese setting. All three films were produced by Toho and directed by Michio Yamamoto. *Chi o Suu Me* (literally Bloodthirsty Eyes, released in the West as *Lake of Dracula*) followed in 1971 and *Chi o Suu Bara* (*The Evil of Dracula*) a few years later in 1975.

The first film is the most Japanese of the three. It uses the traditional idea of a man falling in love with a dead woman, only this time she turns out to be a vampire. A flashback shows the girl's mother selling her daughter's soul to the devil to gain eternal life. The second film, *Chi o Suu Me*, makes explicit reference to the Dracula myth, showing how descendants of the king vampire had fled to Japan to escape

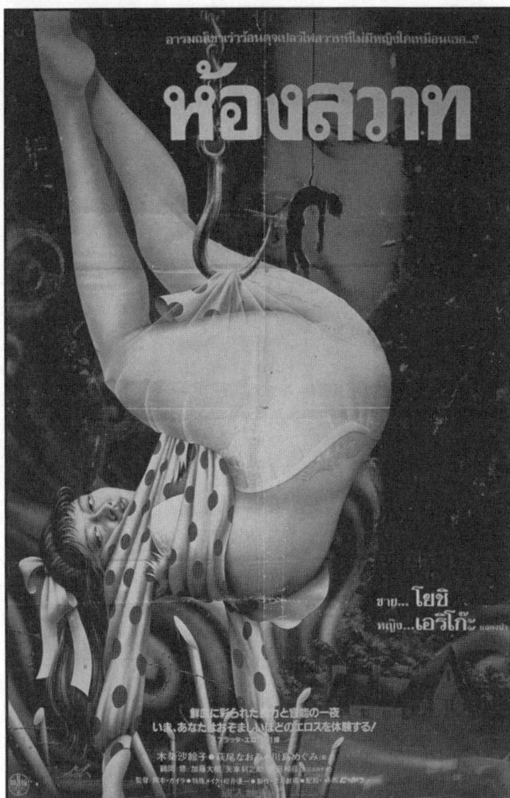

extinction. The final film, *Chi o Suu Bara*, makes even more obvious the notion of vampirism as a curse brought to Japan by foreigners. A flashback tells of a shipwrecked sailor (with red hair, like most 'foreign devils' in Japanese films) being tortured for his Christian beliefs. He renounces God and is set loose to wander in the desert. Close to death, he drinks his own blood to survive and is soon draining the life fluid of young Japanese girls.

The Toho films never really lived up to their expectations. They appeared at just the time when the classic vampire film was losing its appeal in the world market. Lesbian vampires, black vampires and gay vampires all made valiant attempts to keep the myth afloat, but by the end of the seventies it had pretty much ceased to be of interest to the public, in Japan as in the rest of the world. In fact, it wasn't until many years later, in 1991, that theatre director Takeshi Kawamura came up with a really original Japanese revision of the myth.

Kami Tsukitai (My Soul is Slashed) concerns a young woman, Mohara, who becomes obsessed with vampires after the death of her father. She discovers that the Romanian dictator Ceausescu had been experimenting with Dracula's blood before his overthrow and contrives to have a packet of the plasma delivered to the hospital where she works. Unfortunately, the blood is used in a failed operation to save the life of the disgraced boss of a drug company. Mohara attends the funeral and collars the man's daughter, Saeko. "I'm sorry to ask you this," she says, "but are you a virgin?" If she is, Mohara advises her to drip some of her blood on to her father's ashes and he will come back to life.

In a spirit of 'Why not?', the man's daughter does as Mohara suggests. However, it takes a year for her father to put in a reappearance, by which time the world has moved on. His job has gone to someone else, the circumstances surrounding his death have destroyed his reputation and his wife is about to remarry. Mohora and Saeko then have to face the problem of what to do with him... and how to keep him supplied with fresh blood.

An American film would probably use such a plot for a series of comedy episodes. While not avoiding humour, *Kami Tsukitai* concentrates more on the emotional complexities of the situation. Saeko in particular is confused. Her father is a much nicer person dead than he was when alive.

The notion of the absent father, which is one of the themes of *Kami Tsukitai*, had been a common subject for Japanese cinema from the seventies onwards. This was inevitable in a culture where dedication to work and the company ethos had become national obsessions. It was not unusual for commuters to be up at dawn and not return home until well after their children had gone to bed. In the sixties, with the economic miracle still growing, maybe this was not seen as a problem. Then came the seventies, a time of reflection and increasing pessimism. It must have seemed pertinent to pose the question as to whether the salaryman's dedication to his job was not an empty pursuit. In manga comics like *Dame Oyayi* (No Good Dad), as well as in many films, the role of the father came under heavy attack. Inevitably, seventies horror movies reflected this concern.

One of the most savage indictments of the father came in the 1979 film *Dabide no Hoshi: Bishoujo-gari* (Star of David: Beauty Hunting). This gruesome sex/horror hybrid, based on a manga series, was directed by the prolific and versatile Nori Suzuki. The film opens to the gentle sound of Beethoven's 'Moonlight Sonata'. Torrential rain washes over the wrought iron gates of an isolated country mansion. An escaped convict breaks into the building. He viciously rapes the lady of the house, while forcing her bound and gagged husband to watch. So begins the descent into Hell.

The wife becomes pregnant and gives birth to a son. Her rich husband, who was impotent, now becomes a sadistic monster. He begins to act like the evil rapist. He accuses his wife of having enjoyed the crime. He ties her up, whips her and takes photographs of her in bondage, which he pastes into his diary. In one scene, witnessed by their young son through the keyhole, he has sex with a prostitute while his trussed-up wife is forced to watch. Naturally enough, the son grows up a bit strange. Following the death of his father, he

***Left:** 'The demon of male sexuality', as typified by this Thai poster for an eighties Japanese sex 'n' horror movie.* ***Below:** 'Banned everywhere except here' proclaims German ad mat for* Star of David.

inherits great wealth. Although outwardly normal, and an eligible young bachelor, in the cellar of his mansion he has constructed a well-appointed torture dungeon, through which he paces wearing a hideous metal demon mask. Over the course of the next hour or so he captures and abuses a series of hapless females while innocently wooing his virginal fiancée.

After the first abduction, Suzuki cuts from the man whipping a prostitute in his dungeon to scenes of him playing tennis with his prim girlfriend and canoodling with her in a flowery garden. The notion of sentimentality as the flipside of sadism is neatly presented during a scene showing the man's birthday celebrations. Suzuki contrasts a girl playing a sugary mazurka on the piano with a horrifying scene in the dungeon where the man disembowels a chained prostitute. Then, with her blood splattering all over him, he has sex with her dying body. Upstairs, one of his party guests, unable to control her emotions, sobs uncontrollably at the schmaltzy music.

The young sadist's next victim is a schoolgirl whom he spots on television, extolling the virtues of the Japanese education system. He kidnaps her and forces her to masturbate in front of a video playback of her television broadcast.

Below: House.

Then he sets his sights on a haughty female pop star. He captures both the singer and her starstruck assistant and imprisons them in cages in his dungeon. At first he is content to merely torment them by showing them newspaper reports of the fruitless police search. Then he becomes more devious. The pop singer is chained like a dog and made to eat out of a bowl on the floor, while her assistant is pampered and treated to splendid banquets. Eventually the girl is given a whip and encouraged to beat her former mistress.

This is a prelude to the bleakest scene in the whole picture. The two women trick the man into dropping his guard, allowing the singer's assistant to escape. She runs naked out of the house and through the large iron gates. Seeing a passing stranger, she cries out and throws herself into his arms, sobbing with relief. A relief that is short-lived. For the stranger turns out to be the vicious rapist from the beginning of the film, the young man's real father. He had spotted a story about his son's inheritance in a newspaper and has decided to claim a share in this unexpected good fortune. He drags the naked girl back to the house. Now reunited, father and son attempt to outmatch each other in depravity. Suffice it to say that their first act involves an Alsatian dog... For the benefit of faint-hearted readers, I'll leave the rest up to the imagination.

The film's shattering climax comes when the young man is reunited with his former fiancée, from whom he had become estranged. He invites her home to meet his father. The two men take turns in abusing the girl. The peak of her humiliation occurs when she is forced to urinate on the floor in front of them. The man dons the metal demon mask and watches as his father begins to have sex with his fiancée. Suddenly we see a line of tears trickling down his cheek from under the mask. He drops a noose over his father's head and strangles him. He releases the girl and they embrace. A locket from around the man's neck falls onto the floor. It opens to reveal a tiny photo of his mother trussed up in bondage. Onto the locket drops his fiancée's crucifix.

He leads her upstairs and they make love for the first time. The man drops off to sleep. When he wakes, the girl has gone and there is a letter for him. A suicide note. Rushing downstairs, he finds she has hung herself in the torture dungeon.

Dabide no Hoshi is not an easy film to watch. It's an impossible film to enjoy. Today, in the wake of Britain's Fred West case and other real-life atrocities, it's hard to conceive of a similarly well-made text book for sadists being produced anywhere in the world. Yet the film exists. Its superior cinematic qualities, the exceptionally powerful acting, in particular from famous 'heavy' Bunta Sugawara as the rapist father, only make it more disturbing. Watching it recalls Mishima Yukio's description of reading Kawabata's *House of the Sleeping Virgins.* The experience, he says, is like being in a submarine in which people are trapped and the air is gradually disappearing. "While in the grip of this story, the reader sweats and grows dizzy, and knows with the greatest immediacy the terror of lust urged on by the approach of death."

It's the demon of male sexuality that's conjured up by *Dabide no Hoshi.* The 1977 film *Ie* (*House*) looks, in an equally stylised but far less gruesome way, at aspects of female sexual identity. One of the themes of *Dabide no Hoshi* is the absence of the father; the starting point for *Ie* is the consequent role this gives to the mother. The father in *Ie* is almost literally absent, appearing in the film for only a few seconds. Mothers in Japanese families traditionally play a much bigger role in raising and educating children than their hus-

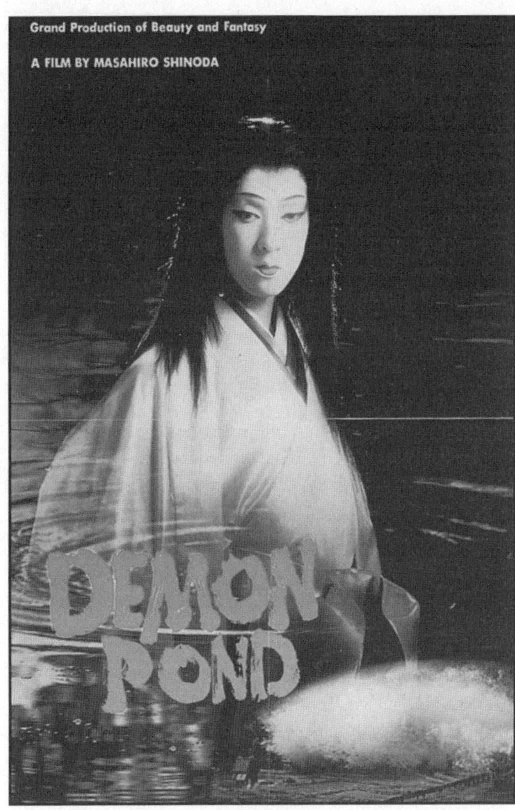

bands. Sometimes this has been taken to gruesome extremes. The 1985 film *Ma no Toki* (Time of Wickedness) is about a mother who consoles her son sexually when he has problems with his school exams. The story was apparently based on several true cases taken from contemporary newspaper reports.

Grand Production of Beauty and Fantasy
A FILM BY MASAHIRO SHINODA
DEMON POND

Given the huge importance of the mother in children's lives, *Ie* begins with one of the biggest sins a father can commit — remarrying and introducing a substitute mother into the household. An adolescent girl, Oshare, has been quite happy living with her widowed father, surrounded by pale memories of her dead mother. She is quite unable to accept the presence of the new wife, who is shown as a sophisticated, sexual creature — all flowing silk scarves and perfect make-up. The girl retreats into fantasies about her dead parent, and sets off to the country with her school friends to spend summer in her aunt's house. The woman lives alone. Grey-haired and confined to a wheelchair, she has turned into a classic, fairy-tale witch, complete with a cat familiar.

The tension in the film is between the dry, sexual graveyard that the aunt inhabits and the nascent sexuality of Oshare and her friends. The fairy-tale spirit of the film is underlined by the names of the girls (Fairy, Fantasy, Melody, etc) as well as by the unreal décor of the house, filled with strange clocks and sinister toys. In the course of one terrifying night, the house shows its evil nature and begins, literally, to consume the girls. Oshare is the only survivor. The ending of the film shows her welcoming her stepmother to the house, into which she, presumably, will also be absorbed.

Ie was the first feature directed by Nobuhiko Obayashi. He had begun his professional career as a maker of promotional films. Indeed, one of the criticisms of *Ie* was that its visual style made it look like a series of glossy adverts. Obayashi explained his intentions as an attempt to represent reality through the use of fantasy: "To go beyond the body and try to find out what is in the heart". Obayashi had a particular interest in the world of adolescents, children on the verge of adulthood. Several of his subsequent films, such as *Ijintachi Tono Natsu* (*The Discarnates*) and *Hyoryu Kyoshitsu* (Drifting Classroom), use science fiction and fantasy techniques to explore the ways we approach the responsibilities of growing older.

Obayashi has now moved away from fantasy into more conventional drama, which is a shame, as *Ie* is an astonishing creation, one of the most original horror films of the 1970s. Shot in a deliberately unrealistic style, an ornate combination of romantic kitsch and girl's magazine clichés, the film treads a fine line between humour and grotesque horror. For example, the scene where one of the girls plays a sloppy romantic theme on the piano, accompanied by a dancing skeleton, is intercut with another girl sitting at her dresser applying an obviously phallic lipstick. Her reflection in the mirror turns into a fanged vampire. Then the mirror catches fire and the girl herself breaks up into tiny shards of glowing flame.

The notion of the house as the ultimate womb symbol, as well as ideas of family and the role of women, are also explored in *Sweet Home*, a stunning production from 1988. The film was produced by and featured Juzo Itami, famous in the West for *Tampopo* and the *Marusa no Onna* (*Taxing Woman*) series. *Sweet Home* is a long way from the rib-nudging satire of those films. Its initial inspiration was the Steven Spielberg production *Poltergeist*. However, whereas Spielberg sets his story around a typical nuclear family group, *Sweet Home* introduces a much more problematic bunch of characters and tests to the limit the idea of what constitutes a family.

A film unit visits the country mansion of a famous artist. The house has been abandoned for more than thirty years and there are rumours that it is haunted. The team plan to film the restoration of a famous mural that is reputed to decorate its walls. The unit consists of a widowed producer and his teenage daughter, Emi, along with a female production manager, Aki. She is unmarried and childless, and Emi is desperately trying to get her paired off with her father. A cameraman and a female art restorer complete the team.

Inside the house they find the famous mural, but while restoring it they also discover more paintings, apparently depicting a tragic event involving fire and the death of a

Above left: Demon Pond. ***Below:*** *The demon mother from* Kuroneko.

PIONEER
愛という名の凶器が いま、振り降ろされる。
ちぎれた愛の殺人
佐野 史郎 横山 めぐみ
監督/池田 敏春 脚本/石井 隆

Above: *Shiro Sano in* Evil Dead Trap 3.

baby. It transpires that the artist's wife accidentally burned her own child alive and went mad. The house is now haunted by her desolate presence as she roams restlessly in the darkness, looking for her lost child. One by one the team are killed in a variety of gruesome ways, and eventually Emi is kidnapped by the ghost and taken into her world of shadows. In the film's finale, Aki has somehow to match her wits against the desperate ghost of the mad woman. She puts on a dress that belonged to Emi's mother and takes the dead baby that was found buried in the grounds. She goes back into the house and confronts the evil mother, who has now mutated into a genuinely terrifying monster, towering over the frail Aki in her borrowed dress and howling with rage.

Sweet Home is a real shocker, with moments of searing terror that could cause sleepless nights if watched alone. The special effects are by Dick Smith (of *The Exorcist* fame), who does a sterling job in translating some traditional Japanese spook styles into modern and believable terms. The film also has moments of strange beauty. The ending, where Aki pacifies the monster by returning its dead baby, is genuinely moving and cathartic, mixing both emotional and physical horror.

The final conflict between Aki, the childless woman, and the distraught ghost mother is the heart of the film. The implication is that it will be impossible for a childless woman to understand the desperate longings of a mother for her dead baby. Aki is seen as having married her career and thereby sacrificed her true nature as a woman. Ian Buruma quotes a Japanese magazine describing the feminine ideal as 'women full of maternal love.' One of the traditional roles of the mother was to live her own ambitions through her sons and husband. The central role given to Aki in *Sweet Home,* and the fact that she wins the battle, reflect the very real changes that women have undergone in Japan since the war. As Susan J. Napier outlines in her book on Japanese fantasy literature, women in the stories of Kyoka Izumi were seen in the twenties and thirties as conduits towards an older, more secure past. By the late 1960s the relationship with that past had become more problematic, as had the role of women.

In films, we see this in the confusion surrounding female characters in productions like Wakamatsu's *Okasareta Byakui* (*Violated Angels*). Here the male protagonist tortures and kills a group of nurses before subsiding into the arms of the only survivor. She sings him to sleep with a tender lullaby. Then the film, which has previously been in black and white, cuts to a colour image of the sea — a commonly used symbol for both motherhood and purity. The next shot, again in colour, shows the man curled up next to the woman in a sort of foetal position, while all around them are the bloodied bodies of his victims. The notion of motherhood (womanhood) is of someone who can accept and somehow 'fix' the tormented souls of men.

The torture films of Teruo Ishii reflect the other side of this equation. Here the victims are women who refuse to accept their natural roles and must therefore be punished. The 'criminal women' of his Tokugawa movies are nearly always sexual rebels, tortured for breaking the rigid codes of the age. One the other hand, this torture can also be seen as a sort of tempering in the furnace, a way of showing women's innate superiority over men. Through their suffering, women transcend their mundane existence and become symbols of purity and healing. Perhaps the high point of this strand is the almost religious suffering of the female victim in Takechi's 1964 film *Daydream.*

Actress Sachiko Hidari commented that "if you want to say something about Japan, you have to focus on women." The films of Mizoguchi and Shindo are often described as 'feminist'. The term is used very differently from the way it is in the West. In Japan it means movies about women or which revolve around women's roles. From the late 1970s, particularly in a series of films based on the work of Takashii Ishii, women became our guides into a real nightmare underbelly of modern Japanese life. At a stretch, these could also be called 'feminist' horror films.

Ishii began his career as a comic book artist in the early 1970s, before making the move into films. His major breakthrough was the series *Tenshi no Harawata* (Entrails of an

Angel), serialised in *Young Comic* magazine. In 1977, the film rights to this violent and sexually explicit series were bought by the ever-hip Nikkatsu company. They turned some of their best directors loose on it. Chusei Sone and Tanaka Noboru had both been schooled in the roman porno production line and brought their exceptional visual skills to bear on the material.

The first two films were directed by Sone. 1978's *Jokousei* (High School Coed) and *Akai Kyoshitsu* (Red Classroom) the following year both concern rape in a high school setting, the second taking the form of an investigation into a too-real film of a rape. The third film in the series, *Nami*, was directed by Tanaka Noboru and here begins the notion of a woman's eye view into Hell that would run through the rest of the series (seven to date). Nami is a reporter for a women's magazine who embarks on an investigation into the activities of a serial rapist.

As might be expected from an artist who had worked in the controversial field of adult manga, Ishii's scripts deal with the sometimes dark side of modern Japan: alienation of city life, pink movies, and sexualised violence. This preoccupation reaches a particularly disturbing peak in 1988's *Akai Senko* (Red Lightning), the fifth film in the series and Ishii's début as a director. In this film, Nami (a name shared by most of Ishii's heroines) is a designer working on a magazine. She is asked to be a stills photographer on a pink movie shoot. The movie's violent rape scene disturbs her so much that the film's writer, Muraki, has to take over. The film has awoken memories from Nami's past, of her own rape when she was a young girl.

She begins a bout of heavy drinking that ends with her waking up in a sordid love hotel with the body of a dead man beside her. The film's most uncomfortable scene occurs when Nami watches videotapes taken from a camera she found in the room. The tapes show her, still unconscious from drink, being abused and raped by the now dead stranger, a man she dimly recalls having picked her up in a bar. With the help of the pink movie writer, she begins to recreate the events of that night, determined to establish whether or not she actually killed the man.

One of the directors of the *Tenshi no Harawata* series was Toshiharu Ikeda, who in 1984 also made Ningyo Densetsu (Mermaid Story), based on another Ishii comic book. Four years later Ishii and Ikeda collaborated again on the first film of a trilogy that has produced some of the most disturbing images of modern Japanese horror. *Shiryo no Wana* (known in the West as *Evil Dead Trap*), like several modern Japanese horror films, bears the unmistakable influence of David Cronenberg. Here the starting point is Cronenberg's 1982 masterpiece *Videodrome*. Ikeda's film begins with a late night television hostess (again called Nami) being sent a snuff movie tape, apparently showing her own torture and death. With three female colleagues and a male director she sets off to find the location where the video was shot. Rather ominously, some very obvious clues have been left. The team end up in an abandoned government research station. Ignoring the warnings of a black-clad stranger, they set off to explore the place. One by one they are bumped off in exceptionally grisly and devious ways until only Nami survives.

We've seen this sort of thing before, except that here it's presented in a genuinely creepy and chilling fashion. This is not a film to watch alone. Maybe it's not a film to watch at all. As Nami asks at one point: "What's the fun in killing people?"

The influences on the film are obvious — Cronenberg has already been mentioned — but the insistent, keyboard-led score gives another name away: the presence of Dario Argento. On the other hand, *Shiryo no Wana* delivers the goods in a way that no Argento film since *Deep Red* has managed. Like *Deep Red*, Ishii's film also explores the notion of childhood evil reasserting itself in the present. However, the notion of vengeance being enacted on the mother (of whom Nami is the chosen symbol) is pretty much a Japanese one.

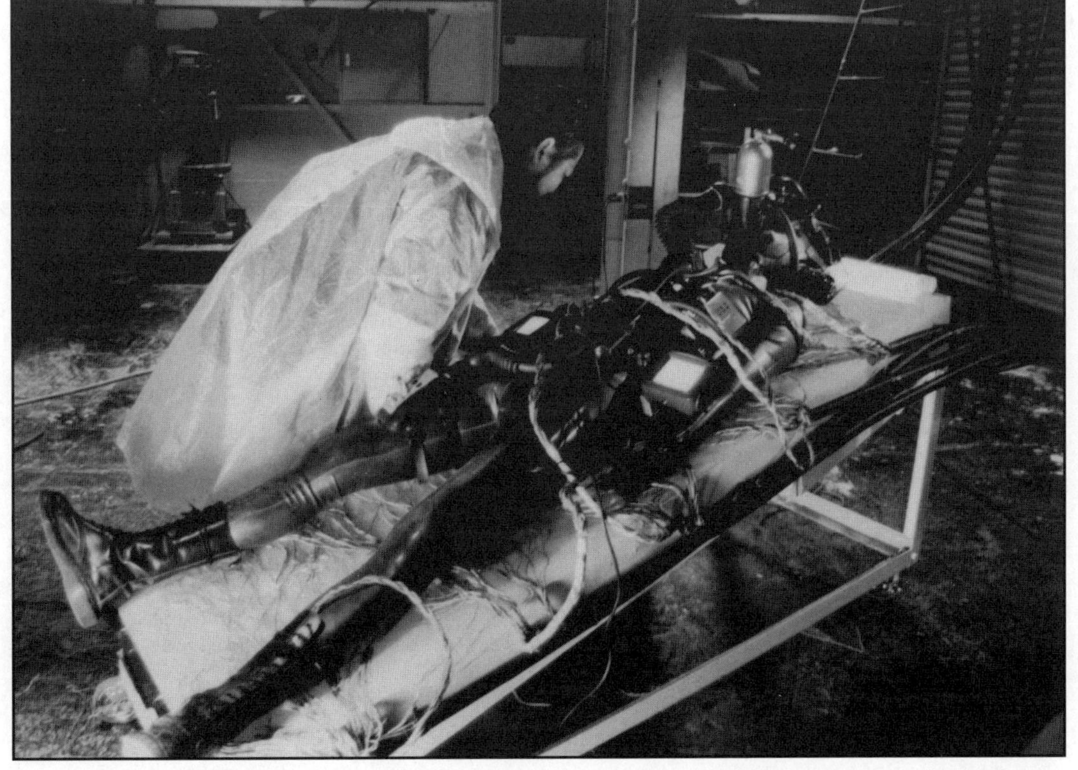

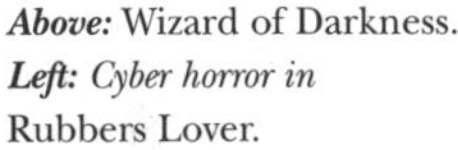

Above: Wizard of Darkness.
Left: *Cyber horror in* Rubbers Lover.

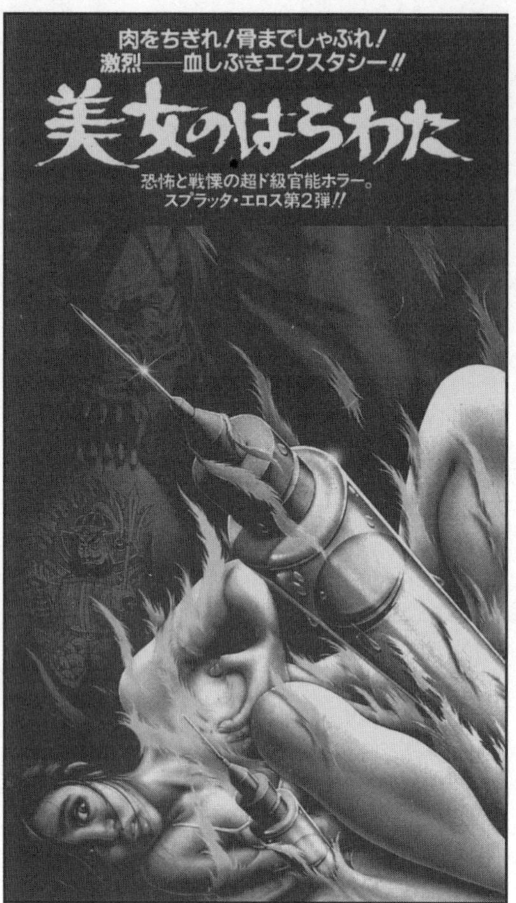

肉をちぎれ!骨までしゃぶれ!
激烈——血しぶきエクスタシー!!
美女のはらわた
恐怖と戦慄の超ド級官能ホラー。
スプラッタ・エロス第2弾!!

***Right:** She's got the needle!*
Guts of a Virgin.

Up to this point, the story has been deceptively straightforward. Most viewers will soon latch onto the fact that the black-garbed young man is also the killer. But then, just when you think it's all over — it's not. In its final scene the film leaps once more into Cronenberg 'body horror' territory when the guy gives birth to his evil twin brother. We see the gruesome mess literally erupt from the man's body.

This notion of transformation from within was mentioned earlier in connection with *Matango.* It's a staple of Japanese fantasy, as all those stories about fox spirits and ghost cats testify. It's also somewhere at the root of the famous Transformer robots. In Shinya Tsukamoto's *Tetsuo: The Iron Man,* the theme seems to be struggling to say something profound about contemporary Japan. *Shiryo no Wana* and its follow-up, *Hideki,* also appear to be located firmly in the middle of a debate about the relationship between the technological world we live in and our own bodies. The difference lies in the films' use of the transformation. Whereas *Tetsuo* follows the gradual progression of the protagonist's change into the 'iron man' of the title, in *Shiryo no Wana* and *Hideki* the birth from within comes towards the end of the film as a sort of *deus ex machina.* When the plot can develop no further along organic lines, it takes a nodal jump into a new dimension. It's this leap into the unknown, a layering of terror upon terror, that makes the films so disturbing. Their endings seem essentially arbitrary. The birth signals a new beginning. But a beginning of what...?

As literary critic Susan J. Napier writes: 'The notion of the self as mutable or monstrous suggests an enormous degree of insecurity lurking just below the surface of Japan's military and economic successes.' She was describing the writers of pre-war fantasy novels. In the post-war period this sense of confusion became even greater, especially for men. Their defeat in war and the occupation of the country put the very essence of their maleness into doubt. In this context it's important to note that it's the men in the *Shiryo no Wana* films who 'give birth', just as it's the childless woman who has to defeat the mother monster in *Sweet Home.* The ending of the latter film shows that Emi's father has been hiding in a womb-like cupboard to escape the monster. He emerges holding some kind of a talisman that could almost be a baby's dummy.

Besides these 'feminist' films, the other main strand of recent Japanese horror is the high school movie. The form may have been borrowed from American hits like *Carrie,* but dramas set in schools have a much deeper resonance in Japan than in the West. For us, school is largely a place of transition, somewhere to acquire the bits of paper that might later get you a job. The Japanese see school as the most important training ground for future good citizens. Even Japanese school uniforms reflect the military, disciplined nature of the institution. The boys wear tunics modelled on turn of the century German styles and girls wear sailor suits.

In the 1950s, the sun tribe books and films of Ishihara began to show a version of youth culture that questioned the effectiveness of the values being inculcated in Japanese schools. A huge question mark about their role as a repository of wisdom was also posed in Seijun Suzuki's 1966 film *Kenka Eriji* (*Elegy to Violence*). The film traces the rise of 1930s militancy amongst the ranks of frustrated schoolboys, where rigid discipline and martial games are used to combat and control rebellious sexual urges.

In later films, a sacrilegious sense of disorder and moral anarchy began to invade the very soul of the sacred institution. Go Nagai's 1968 manga *Harenchi Gakuen* (Shameless School) was one of the first notorious steps in this direction. In Nagai's school, sex, nudity and antisocial behaviour are the order of the day. Live-action films like the *Be Bop High School* series and *Boryoku Kyoshitsu* (Violent Classroom) were further chinks in the armour of this most sacred of Japanese institutions.

In the early eighties, reality caught up with fiction and there were serious problems within the Japanese education system. Discipline began to break down and there were reports of children being killed by teachers clamping down on hooliganism. One boy was kicked to death for taking a hairdryer on a school trip. In this context, the high school horror film began to make a lot of sense. It depicted school as a battleground, a place where the rules and codes of the outside world have been abandoned or distorted. All that the kids have to fall back on is their own sense of honour and justice. They have to fight their battles alone, adults are either powerless or actively evil.

Eko Eko Azaraku (*Wizard of Darkness*) is a typical example of the genre. A new girl, the mysterious Missa, discovers that the school is the centre of a five-pointed series of strange killings — a bloody pentagram. She sets about unravelling the mystery. Her friend Misato shows her a locked room where a woman teacher killed herself and then lets her into the school's big secret — maths teacher Miss Shirai 'likes girls' and is having a lesbian affair with one of the pupils. The male teachers are equally strange. One of them is a leering lecher who insists on personally checking that the girls are wearing knickers as they enter the school gates.

Kept late for a maths test by the lustful Miss Shirai, a group of the pupils find themselves unable to leave. All doors lead back to the same room and the windows are locked. One by one they are killed as a chalk number on the blackboard goes from thirteen down to zero. Eventually the culprit is revealed — it was Missa's innocent little friend, Misato. She needed thirteen sacrifices to summon the angel Lucifer. Following a series of incantations he duly turns up, towering over the school, suspiciously Caucasian in appearance. Of course, Missa, although apparently dead, saves the day, and Misato learns that she who plays with fire often ends up getting burnt — at least in this sort of film.

Essentially, *Eko Eko Azaraku* is an old-fashioned piece of hokum. A high school horror story with all the elements familiar from American productions like *Evilspeak* and *A Nightmare on Elm Street*, with a plot borrowed from Buñuel's *The Exterminating Angel*. Of course, being a Japanese film, *Eko Eko Azaraku* has its fair share of softcore lesbian gropings and gratuitous gore — blood hosing from the necks of decapitated schoolgirls and so on.

Much more ambitious was the 1991 production *Yokai Hanta — Hiruko* (Hiroku — Demon Hunter). This was director Shinya Tsukamoto's follow up to *Tetsuo 2: Bodyhammer* — itself a reworking of his experimental first feature, *Tetsuo: The Iron Man*. Many critics were dumbfounded that Tsukamoto had chosen to make what was seen as a straight teen horror film for his first big-budget outing.

On closer inspection, *Yokai Hanta — Hiruko* is anything but straight. It's a deeply Japanese film. The basic jumping-off point may have been the Indiana Jones series — the hero of *Hiruko* is a maverick archaeologist — but the driving forces of the plot are the typically Japanese concerns with duty and tradition. A school has been built over one of the gates of Hell. The guardianship of the gate is handed down via some mysterious rite of passage. The only way to combat the demons that the gate can unleash is to recite the ancient Japanese creation myth of the brother and sister gods Izanagi and Izanami.

Hiruko begins with the mysterious disappearance of a Professor Yabe and one of his female students, Reiko, during the long hot summer vacation. The professor's son and two of his friends go searching for him in the rambling grounds of the school. A former associate of the professor's, the maverick archaeologist Hieda, also turns up. Hieda has been sacked from his academic job because of his obsession with monsters. He brings with him a huge host of high-tech monster hunting paraphernalia — all of which turns out to be useless. The key to the mystery lies in ancient stones and sacred texts.

As they search through the deserted school building, the three boys encounter the old school caretaker, who seems to have gone mad. He chases them off with a vicious machete and cuts the phone lines to the outside world. Two of the boys are killed in gruesome ways — one of them is beheaded — and they seem to see the vanished Reiko. She has turned into a seductive ghost with strange blue skin and bright red lips. Even more bizarre are the physical changes being undergone by Professor Yabe's son. Huge, steaming boils start to grow on his back. When Hieda peels off the bandages, he discovers beneath them the faces of the boy's dead friends.

The caretaker tells of an event that happened sixty years before, when there was a terrible fire in the school. He saw a figure, the young Yabe's grandfather, standing in the flames wearing a strange horned crown on his head and yelling incantations. Later, after the fire was quelled, it was discovered that none of the burned corpses had heads.

The mystery of the vanished heads is revealed when Yabe junior follows his father's trail through the gate into Hell. Beyond, he finds a world inhabited by strange monsters with human heads and bodies like giant spiders. Hideous flying things, vegetal growths with snapping jaws and crawling beasties chase Yabe and Hieda back through the gates. Eventually, the boy realises his duty, puts on the ancient crown and steps back into Hell to repulse the invasion. The film ends with Yabe assuming the role of caretaker to guard the gateway to the underworld. The implication being that this is a role he will then pass onto his son as it was passed on to him.

Shinya Tsukamoto began his career as an amateur film-maker with 8mm shorts, but he always had his sights set on much more ambitious goals. In contrast, there still exists a healthy number of semi-underground film-makers in Japan, often working straight onto video, who have no real ambitions to move into the mainstream. Their work is often gruesomely violent and sexy, and is in a direct line from the violent eroductions of the sixties and the adult manga of the seventies and eighties.

Among the most notorious products of this video underground are the *Guinea Pig* films. This series of short exercises in bad taste makes explicit the connection between manga and video horror, in that several of its episodes were directed by artist Hideshi Hino. His books, such as *Panorama of Hell*, are a catalogue of confrontational scenes of violence and mayhem. Episode three, *Flowers of Flesh and Blood*, is fairly typical, both for the series and for Hino. In this forty-minute workout, a man in a samurai suit kidnaps a girl, straps her to a table and dissects her. The whole thing is a kind of *reductio ad absurdum* of films like Teruo Ishii's *Tokugawa Onna Keibatsushi* or Banmei Takahashi's *Tortures of Japan*. Both those films had reasonable production values and some

Above: The Guinea Pig.
Left: Exorsister!

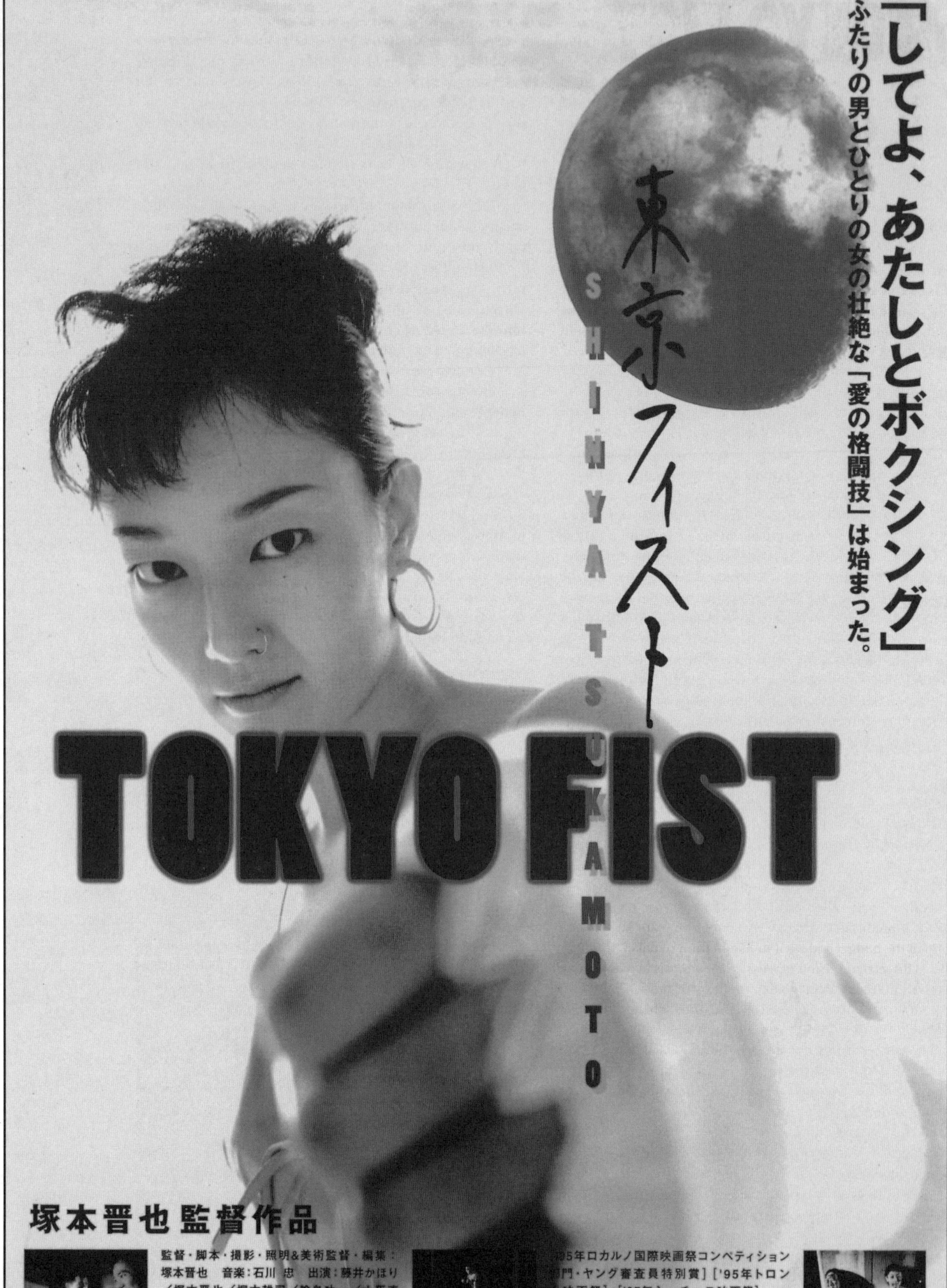
「してよ、あたしとボクシング」
ふたりの男とひとりの女の壮絶な「愛の格闘技」は始まった。
東京フィスト
SHINYA TSUKAMOTO
TOKYO FIST
塚本晋也監督作品
監督・脚本・撮影・照明&美術監督・編集：
塚本晋也　音楽：石川 忠　出演：藤井かほり
／塚本晋也／塚本耕司／輪島功一／六平直
政／竹中直人（'95年／35ミリ／カラー87分）
製作・配給：海獣シアター　©海獣シアター
95年ロカルノ国際映画祭コンペティション
門・ヤング審査員特別賞］［'95年トロン
映画祭］［'95年シッチェス映画祭］
'95年バンクーバー国際映画祭］［'95年東
京国際ファンタスティック映画祭］ 正式出品

attempt to place their violence in a historico-political context. Hino strips away all extraneous material and concentrates only on the gruesome carnage. Although little more than a slice of Grand Guignol, the film was seen by some in the West as the final statement on Japanese depravity and a genuine 'snuff movie'. While the effects may be good, considering the low budget, they're not that good. Thank God!

Takao Nakano is another prolific producer of made-for-video releases. Like many other video companies, his Raizoh operation is composed of a small group of like-minded friends who share the same enthusiasms and have managed to find a way to turn their hobby into a business. Nakano's first claim to fame was as a promoter of female sumo wrestling, or *joshi-puro.* When he began to make films, he mixed this bizarre form of entertainment with his love for the science fiction, 'B' thrillers and girl gang movies that he had consumed avidly as a teenager. Add to this a fair amount of sex, and you have a unique combination of *The Avengers, Monty Python* and *Deep Throat.*

With the *Exorsister* series, Nakano moved closer to straight horror. Or more accurately, into the 'tits and tentacles' subgenre unique to Japan. Loosely based on the *Urotsukidoji* animated series, *Exorsister* tells of the invasion of Earth by a hideous tentacled monster that emerges through a computer screen. The monster is obviously a man in a rubber suit and there's no attempt made to disguise it; his spotty face is clearly seen peeking out from under his rubber horns. The films feature endless scenes where girls are stripped and groped by the hideous man-thing. His tentacles are vacuum cleaner hoses manipulated by offscreen wires.

Nakano has now started to get some recognition in Europe. Several of his videos have been released in France and he has made appearances at the Freak Zone festival of trash cinema in Lille. Unlikely to find such an easy market are the rather less loveable productions of Kazuo Komizu, a former Koji Wakamatsu collaborator who often works under the pseudonym of Gaira.

His early productions were cheaply made video sex films. With his 1985 featurette, *Shojo no Harawata* (Guts of a Virgin), he made a more ambitious attempt to combine the yakuza and the horror genres. This is the story of a bunch of sleazy mobsters in an empty warehouse, who indulge in a bit of rape and drug abuse to pass the time. Injections of a peculiar chemical cause one of their victims to mutate. She turns into a monster with an enormous, animal-headed penis, which is then used to exact a predictable revenge. A couple of years later, Gaira upped the budget and went to 35mm for a remake.

This second version of *Shojo no Harawata* is in a direct line of descent from Italian 'golden age' horror movies like *Bloody Pit of Horror* and *Bay of Blood.* These are films where a group of kids go to a deserted house somewhere, have sex, and are then threatened by a hideous monster and killed in a variety of imaginative ways. Gaira's film uses some of the ideas and effects from his made-on-video cheapie, including some frighteningly realistic 'flesh rippling' effects. The bigger budget and better production values make it marginally less offensive. Even so, it's not a film to show your girlfriend on a first date.

The story begins with a group of photographers and sexy models during a photo shoot somewhere in the country. This is classic pink movie territory and we see the usual faked orgasms and white panty shots. Driving back to the city, the team get lost in a thick fog and take refuge for the night in an empty country house. A huge man-thing rises from the forest floor like some primeval earth spirit and comes to get them. He quickly dispatches the men and then turns his attention to the women. The carnage has driven one of the girls crazy, and the monster finds her masturbating with her boyfriend's severed arm. She gives the muddy giant an enthusiastic blow job, which concludes with him coming in great sticky waves all over her. Then he puts his hand inside her and pulls out her entrails. There's more, but this is the kind of film you should really see for yourself. As with much of this new Japanese 'transgressive' cinema, descriptions make it sound far more shocking than it actually is.

In the frenetic, underground spirit of films like *Tetsuo* came Shozin Fukui's 1992 production *964 Pinnochio.* A shady organisation has found a way to make humanoid robots. These unfortunate creatures are then sold to rich widows as sex androids. The film opens with a long orgy involving one of these oversexed widows, her girlfriend dressed in a nurse's uniform, and the overwhelmed android, Pinnochio. Unable to come up to scratch, the android is thrown out into the street, where it's rescued by a homeless girl. She teaches it to speak and to regain its memory. Meanwhile, the organisation is searching for Pinnochio. They know that he is virtually indestructible. And that once he remembers who he is he will come looking for revenge...

Eighties and nineties Japanese horror films bear the unmistakable mark of Western influence in a way that their fifties and sixties predecessors rarely did. Films like *Shiryo no Wana, Tetsuo* and *Tenshi no Harawata* draw heavily from Argento and Cronenberg. The unique thing is that in Japan these Western models are absorbed and 'Japanised' so that they can be used to express uniquely national concerns, becoming much more than the sum of their influences in the process. This ability to absorb and adapt is something that the Japanese have long been famed for. Whether it's Western pop music (Pizzicato Five), eighteenth century art (*cloisonné*) or deep fried cooking (*tempura*), the Japanese have an ability to go right to the essence of whatever they are adapting, give it a little twist and come out with something unique. *The Silence of the Lambs* gave rise to a large number of 'female doctor versus psycho' flicks. Lately *The X-Files* has begun to make tracks through Japanese cinema. A couple of recent films by former 'bad boy' Sogo Ishii show the influence of both of these Western hits. His 1995 movie *August in the Water* concludes with a degree of optimism that perhaps points to a sort of resolution of some of the issues raised by recent horror movies.

Ishii began his career as maker of Super 8 shorts. His breakthrough film was the violent biker movie *Crazy Thunder Road* in 1980, consolidated by the success of *Gyakufunsha Kazoku* (Crazy Family) in 1984. Then, for almost ten years, he concentrated on music videos and shorts. The climax of this period was the 1993 television movie *Tokyo Blood,* four short films about city life. *Street Noise* is an almost archetypal summation of new Japanese horror. A salaryman goes mad and runs through the darkening streets of an impersonal, high-tech Tokyo, getting faster and faster as the film fades away. With *Ana* (*The Hole*) and *Heart of Stone,* Ishii moved further into metaphysics. *Ana* features the examination in a mental hospital of a construction worker who has gone crazy. He has become convinced that one of the thousands of holes he has dug in the city's concrete holds the key to his sanity.

This kind of loopy logic underpins Ishii's return to feature films, 1994's *Angel Dust.* Someone is murdering young women. Every Monday night at 6.00pm, whistling a snatch of the 'New World Symphony', the killer injects a lethal dose of poison into them. The killings begin on crowded commuter trains and then move in an apparently random direction through the suburbs. A team of investigators is called in, including a woman expert in psychological profiling. The

***Opposite:** Japanese women fight back!* Tokyo Fist.

investigation begins to centre around a deprogramming clinic run, it transpires, by the woman's former lover.

The picture of modern Japan presented by *Angel Dust* is one familiar from recent headlines — anonymous commuter crowds, dehumanised high-rise living, killer cults abroad in the big city. The film begins inside Mount Fuji and the image of Fuji drifts through the film like some half-heard leitmotif. Recent reports shocked the Japanese when they read of the state of Fuji. A soft drinks machine now occupies its summit and more than 330lb of litter have to be carted away every week, while numerous tourist toilets flush directly on to the mountainside. The Japanese Alpine Club issued a statement saying: 'Mt Fuji is a symbol of the Japanese soul. The deterioration of its environment is a reflection of how that soul has been polluted.' A similar feeling runs through *Angel Dust,* although it would take more than just a few rubbish bins to sort out the problems the film raises.

Ishii's *Mizu no Naka no Hachigatsu* (*August in the Water*) is a high school story about the relationship between two kids, a boy called Mao and his girlfriend Izumi, a champion diver. The film has a nicely apocalyptic beginning, with images of water and much talk of an impending drought. Two boys lie on a roof in the blazing heat, waiting eagerly for the coming water festival. Will it be banned because of the drought? One boy's father tells him not to worry: "Festivals and brothels always survive."

The excavation of an ancient shrine up in the hills has unearthed what is described as a stone computer. Lots of vaguely mystical ideas are thrown into the pot. Astrology. Telepathy. Water is described as being like an exorcism. The earth is becoming parched. People are falling sick in the streets with the stone disease that turns their insides to rock.

At Mount Miko, the location of the ancient shrine, two meteorites have fallen very close together. A petrograph taken of the shrine reveals strange symbols, including what looks like a representation of someone diving. There is a prediction that on the twenty-third of the month there will be a disaster. This is the day of the diving festival in which Izumi is to compete.

Standing on the board about to dive, she gets the feeling that the water is becoming hard. She has a vision of it turning to stone that leads to a terrible accident. When she comes out of hospital she is different, prone to falling into trances in school, doodling strange symbols on her books and staring at the distant Mount Miko.

The film contrasts the dry, barren cityscapes, where people are dying of the stone disease, with the distant mountain and its ancient shrine. The bridge between these two comes through Izumi's sacrifice. She walks into the waters of a lake, drowning herself but breaking the curse. The pent-up energy that has hovered over every scene is suddenly released in the form of showers of rain. To emphasise the epic sweep of the film, the story is revealed to be the memories of Mao as a very old man. The ending shows him lying on the stone shrine. A vision of a still young Izumi appears before him. She holds out her hands and they embrace.

Mizu no Naka no Hachigatsu is an enigmatic film, but an optimistic one. Just as images of Mount Fuji dominated *Angel Dust,* so echoes of ancient Japan underpin the imagery of the later film. A key scene comes when Izumi cuts her finger on a rusty old pump from which water has long since ceased to flow. She holds her finger under the spout and a single drop of water falls onto it. Suddenly we see floods of water gushing out of the pump over her cut finger.

As mentioned earlier, women in the pre-war fantasies of writers like Kyoka Izumi and Tanizaki were seen as conduits to the past. They showed the way towards an ancient and truer wisdom, where Japanese values had primacy over the newly imported Western ideas. In the sixties and seventies, a kind of despairing hopelessness was visited on the bodies of women in horror films and eroductions. Now, having passed through the furnace, it seems that women have survived to show the way back to those same ancient truths.

It might appear strange to assert the power of women in films where they are so often depicted being abused and killed. However, in the solipsistic worlds of *Moju, Okasareta Byakui* and *Dabide no Hoshi* the man's gaze falls only on woman. She is the absolute reality in these films, the object *and* the subject. Like small boys taking apart a new toy, Japanese horror film-makers have shown us woman abused, tortured, dismembered and, finally, eaten. Now, they seem to be showing us woman putting herself back together again.

Even an apparently male-centred film like Tsukamoto's *Tokyo Fist* seems to hold out hope through the spiritual progress of its sole female character. This over-the-top tale of bloodlust, body mutilation and boxing shows its two male characters destroying themselves over a woman, Hizuru. She also goes through changes, mutilating her body with tattoos and piercing herself with steel pins and nipple rings, transforming herself into a vengeful demon of ancient mythology. Finally, the two men pummel themselves into monstrous mutations, blood spurting wildly from their open wounds. This is followed by a powerful image of Hizuru, her tattoos gone, the spikes and rings removed from her flesh. With her hair loose, staring beatifically into the camera, she presents the archetypal face of the spiritually whole Japanese woman. *Tokyo Fist* makes several references to *Metropolis,* specifically to the robot Maria who betrays the hero of Lang's epic. Only through letting women explore their fantasies and discover their real selves, the film seems to be saying, is there hope for a Japan lost in an architectural nightmare of high-rise buildings and empty consumerism, in thrall to the false goddess of the West.

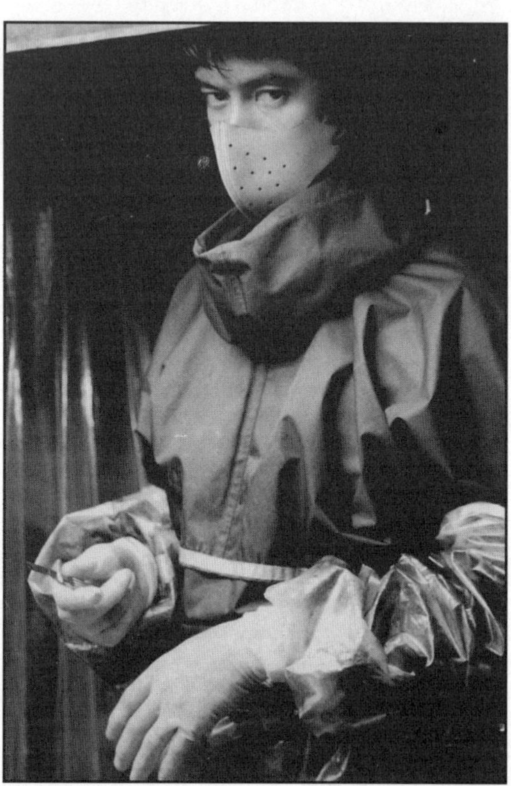

Above: *More underground cyber cinema:* Death Powder.
Right: *The sinister Saeki, organ thief.*

But let's not conclude with the impression that all modern Japanese horror films present such a positive message. In 1996 the terrifying *Organ* was released. The film was written and directed by a woman, Kei Fujiwara, and largely performed by members of her Organ Vital theatre troupe. However, the presence of a female hand on the tiller shouldn't lead to the conclusion that we're heading for something warm and cuddly. All the elements mentioned from previous films are present: the notion of the family as the source of moral values; ideas of bodily transformation; a journey of discovery into the underbelly of the city. In *Organ*, however, any optimistic messages are reversed. The transformation is just the sad fantasy of a sick mind; technology is present only by its total absence; woman is not a conduit to good but the architect of evil; and the journey turns out to be a dead end. There are no heroes. Everything is sad, sordid and ugly.

There are essentially two strands to the narrative. The film begins with a police investigation. "Tokyo, 1996," the voice-over of Detective Numata tells us. "The smell of death attracts the sellers of human organs..."

In a grimy shed known as The Slaughterhouse, a team of organ sellers, led by the one-eyed harridan Yoko (played by director Fujiwara), is dismembering a body. This time they've found a live one. An undercover policeman — Detective Numata's brother — who has infiltrated the gang, is too horrified to keep silent. "He's still alive... put it back!" he cries as the team's surgeon removes the man's liver. The gang abandon their gruesome lab and take the cop with them. The traumatised Numata then begins a relentless search for his missing sibling that leads to a terrifying climax.

The other strand of the story concerns Yoko's brother, Saeki. He's an apparently mild-mannered biology technician at a girls' high school. However, as we soon discover, behind the door of his lab lurks a terrible secret. In a giant vivarium he has the limbless torso of the captured cop. It's kept alive by strange drugs and fed on the blood of schoolgirls, whom Saeki also uses for weird sexual practices.

As Numata tracks down his brother, so too the yakuza gang who are behind the organ racket are attempting to eliminate Yoko and Saeki. They have become too wild, too extreme and out of control. When these two plot strands meet, at the end of the film, the result is a bloodbath of epic proportions; hideous, laughable and at times unwatchable.

As the film progresses from one incredibly grim set piece to the next, we learn the story of Saeki and Yoko. A flashback to their early childhood shows their mother attacking Saeki and trying to bite off his penis as revenge for his father's womanising. When Yoko attempts to stop her, the mother lashes out at the girl, blinding her in one eye. Saeki survives the attack, but is permanently maimed. His liver needs constant replacement — hence the pair's involvement in the organ racket — and the drugs he takes to stay alive seem to be turning him into some sort of pus-filled vegetable.

Everyone and everything in *Organ* is mean, sleazy and covered in slime and gore. On one level the film is a deliberate slap in the face to any notion of good taste. The cops are cripples who drive round in a battered old mini. One of them rapes Numata's wife on a stained mattress. After the act, she rolls back the mattress and urinates onto a pile of newspapers underneath it. Even the school mistress who uncovers Saeki's secret is a sexual deviant. Knowing he is in her power, she begins to seduce him. Stripping off his shirt, she finds the suppurating wound over his liver. Instead of being horrified, she is fascinated and cuts at it with a knife. Then she demands he make love to her. At the moment of orgasm, brown liquid spews from Saeki's mouth.

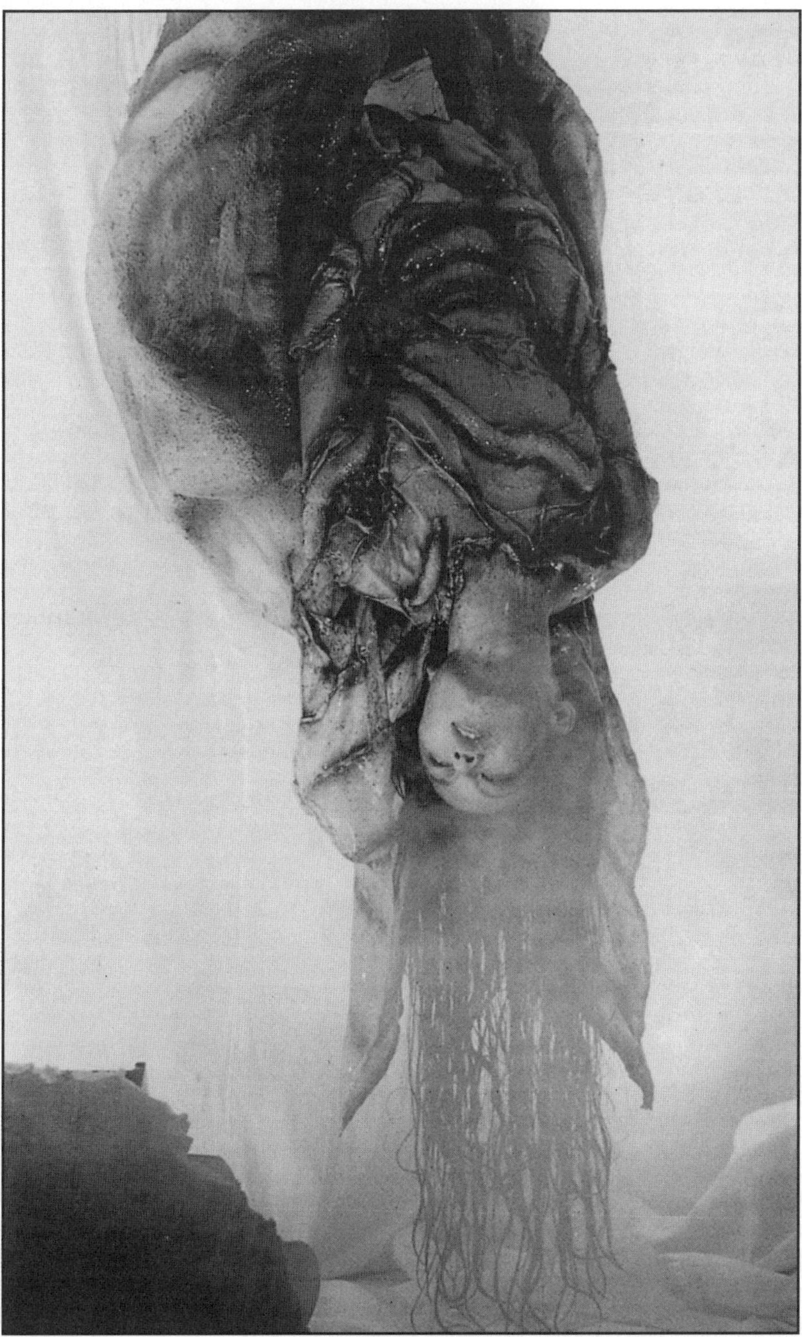

***Above:** Strange rebirth from* Organ.

Yes indeed, *Organ* is not a film to see on a full stomach. Its fetid atmosphere of abnormality should have you running for the exit. And yet you keep watching, fascinated. For all its mean-spirited nastiness, *Organ* is a perfect example of the power of the contemporary Japanese horror film to revolt, shock and intrigue all at the same time.

The film's mood of relentless pessimism is carried on even past the end titles. After the credits have rolled and the audience are shuffling out of the cinema, a final coda reveals Saeki, alive and well, working as a country doctor. He chats happily with a young mother and her baby, greedily accepting the gift of food they bring him. Then behind him, in the corner of the surgery, we see a door slightly ajar. Through it seeps the sickly green light of the vivarium. The experiment continues... ■

Top Tens

Listing is a dangerous activity. So much depends on the mood of the moment and the vagaries of memory. As technology advances apace, we can only hope that at some time in the future every film ever made will be available to everyone at the press of a button. Until then, the following lists are ample evidence of the wide range of tastes and flavours that inform the term 'fantastic'.

Tim Lucas
Critic, publisher and author, Tim is the driving force behind *Video Watchdog*, 'the perfectionist's guide to Fantastic Video'. For more than twenty years he has been instrumental in bringing a serious and informed perspective to bear on the study of the horror film and fantastic cinema. His typically eclectic list is presented in alphabetical order:

Black Magic 2 (HK; 1975)
Black Pit of Dr M (Mex; 1958)
The Criminal Life of Archibaldo de la Cruz (Mex; 1955)
The Exterminating Angel (Mex; 1962)
Jigoku (Jap; 1960)
Kwaidan (Jap; 1964)
Moju (Jap; 1969)
Onibaba (Jap; 1964)
Santa Sangre (Mex; 1989)
Vij (Rus; 1967)

Pete Tombs
The following films are chosen for the sheer viewing pleasure they've given me. Each country featured has undoubtedly produced films of greater 'significance', but these are all, in the own way, unique. In alphabetical order:

The Boxer's Omen (HK; 1983)
The Brainiac (Mex;1961)
Jigoku (Jap; 1960)
The Killing of Satan (Phil; 1974)
Moju (Jap; 1969)
Raat (Ind; 1991)
Ritual dos Sadicos (Braz; 1969)
The Stroller in the Attic (Jap; 1976)
Sweet Home (Jap; 1988)
Witch With Flying Head (HK; 1977)

Damon Foster
With wit, humour and his own very personal style, Damon Foster has been chronicling the furthest reaches of Asian cinema for almost two decades. His magazine *Oriental Cinema* was one of the first fan based publications to feature films from the Philippines, India and Korea, along with the more expected coverage of Hong Kong and Japan. His typically iconoclastic list is presented in no particular order.

Destroy all Monsters (Jap; 1968)
The most monsters ever brought together in a Godzilla movie! A classic!
The 7th Curse (HK; 1987)
Horror, monsters, martial arts and other fun stuff.
Three Fantastic Supermen (It; 1967)
Brad Harris, Tony Kendall and Nick Jordan in an action packed superhero caper with gorgeous women and martial arts.
Kamen Rider vs Shocker (Jap; 1971)
Theatrical featurette or mini-movie based on the *Kamen Rider* TV series. This thirty-two minute adventure is bursting with karate action as our cybernetic, bug-eyed hero tackles a variety of monsters.
Love on Delivery (HK; 1994)
A Hong Kong comedy which isn't really horror, sci fi or fantasy, but it spoofs everything from Terminator to Ultraman.
Los Momias de Guanajuato (Mex; 1970)
Though, like all Mexican movies, it's talky and boring at times, the climactic scenes of masked wrestlers battling mummies make up for it.
Invaders from Space (Jap; 1959)
Shintoho's classic superhero, Starman, thwarts an attack from the Salamander Man of Planet Kulamon. Budgetary limitations don't hamper this black and white Japanese masterpiece.
Mr Vampire (HK; 1985)
The classic prototype for Hong Kong vampire films. Horror, comedy, fantasy and a little kung fu highlight this influential movie.
Terror Beneath the Sea (Japan; 1966)
Effective Japanese sci fi chiller, with Sonny Chiba abducted and taken to an underwater laboratory. Monsters, action and slick music add more fun to this Toei movie.
Inframan (HK; 1975)
An imitation of Japanese TV shows like *Inazuman* and *Ultraman Leo.* Ripoff or not, *Inframan* is a masterpiece of colour, martial arts, special effects and superhero thrills! Big fun!!!!

Craig Ledbetter
The man behind the magazine and video label European Trash Cinema gives us a glimpse of his current faves.

Seytan (Tur; 1975)
A Turkish rip-off of *The Exorcist*, with Islamic symbols replacing the Christian iconography.
Ghost of the Hunchback (Jap; 1965)
If Mario Bava or Antonio Margheriti had gone to Japan in the sixties and made a Gothic horror film, I am convinced it would have looked just like this
Mystics in Bali (Indo; 1981).
My first experience with Asian horror, involving a flying head with spinal cord attached that goes round pulling babies from the wombs of pregnant women... Of course, it's also my only experience!
Hiroku (Japan; 1991)
I was not all that enamoured with the director's *Tetsuo* series, but this old-fashioned horror film, complete with creepy-looking spider creatures more than made up for those over hyped spectacles.
Black Pit of Dr M (Mex; 1958)
The only film from Mexico's golden age of horror that I can honestly say holds up to the terror test today. Another testament to the power of black and white photography when it comes to inducing chills.
Bunman (The Untold Story) (HK; 1992)
I can usually take or leave Hong Kong horror films, but Anthony Wong's character is a slice of dementia rarely seen on any country's screens.
Moju (Japan; 1969)
A horror film that would certainly discourage tourism to the far East.
Onibaba (Japan; 1964)
An obvious choice. The slow moving, wind blown reeds in the country night air still hypnotise.
Man Behind the Sun (HK; 1987)
Proof that real life horrors always out-do fake ones.
Seeding of a Ghost (HK; 1983).
A Hong Kong horror film that just missed catching a ride on the New Wave of films from that tiny island; which is probably why I like it. Goes out of its way to disgust.

Tom Weisser
Author, publisher and all round expert on Asian cinema, Tom presents his 'guilty pleasures'. "Right now, I'd rather rewatch any one of these movies than see anything else. So, I guess that makes them my favourites." In alphabetical order.

All Night Long series (Japan; 1992-96)
Maybe it's cheating to pick a series, but any one of these three mean-spirited films would qualify as a favourite. No movie has ever disturbed me the way this trilogy does.
Beauty Evil Rose (HK; 1994)
It's a sexy thriller featuring every possible gratuitous element in the exploitation genre — from nudity to witchcraft, torture to monsters. Plus a girls 'n' guns finale.
Diva in the Netherworld (Japan; 1980)
A famous classical singer (played by Yoko Kurita) must pay for her earthly success when she becomes lost in Hell. The highly kitsch and very gaudy art design adds to the fun. Director Nahamine also made the equally enjoyable *Legendary Panty Mask.*
Evil Dead Trap (Japan; 1988)
Toshiharu Ikeda is quite simply the best genre director in Japan. His films are a delight and his camerawork is unsurpassed.
Female Neo Ninjas (Japan; 1991)
In the vast world of exploitation there are very few movies so anxious, so willing, to simply do their job: entertain the audience. Director Masahiro Kasai understands his assignment well. He is not making *Rashomon* here. This is, after all, a goddamn movie about three cute ninja girls fighting crime and UFOs in contemporary Tokyo.
Rubbers Lover (Japan; 1996)
The images are as fascinating and revolutionary as anything David Lynch did in *Eraserhead.* But Shozin Fukui's mania for bodily fluids, exploding arteries and rupturing eyeballs is exorbitant to the point of gluttonous.
Supercoming (Japan; 1995)
Hiroaki Tada has created an irreverent religious parody, sprinkled with fantastic and horrific overtones. He's added some very chic black humour and delivered the whole project as a musical.
Swallowtail Butterfly (Japan; 1996)
A parable about anarchy and violence in Yentown, an imaginary city in the near future where people live a chaotic, dizzy existence. This three hour masterpiece is a crowning achievement for director Shunji Iwai and his incredible cinematographer Noboru Shinoda.
Weather Girl (Japan; 1995)
Based on an animated series about a girl who flashes her panties during the evening newscast and becomes the Weather Queen, but soon finds herself in a battle with an evil witch who wants the weather show for herself. Originally available only on video, it received a theatrical release and became one of the biggest films of the year (ranking twenty-six on Kinema Jumpo's forty best movies of 1996)
Who Can Kill a Child? (Spain; 1975)
Filmed in Spain by Argentinian director Narcisco Ibañez Serrador. A *tour de force.* There's something especially horrifying about a group of kids with murder on the brain.

And now the million dollar question: "How the hell can I see these movies?" The answer is, it really depends where you live. Many of the Indian films covered, for example, will be available from Indian video stores. Of course, that's no help if you don't have one in your town. The only real answer is mail order. The two companies mentioned below can supply a wide range of the films mentioned in this book. Be aware that tapes supplied in the States are usually NTSC standard and may not play at all on many British or European video machines. Contact the individual companies for more information.

Video Search of Miami	Something Weird Video
PO Box 16-1919	PO Box 33664
Miami FL 33116	Seattle WA 98133
USA	USA
Tel: (305) 279 9773	Tel: (206) 361 3759
Free catalogue available	Catalogue available

Both of the above accept payment by credit card.

Index of film titles